MCAT
BIOLOGY AND BIOCHEMISTRY

Strategy and Practice

NextStep
TEST PREP | nextsteptestprep.com

Printed in the United States of America

Third Printing, 2017

ISBN 978-1-944935-02-3

Next Step Pre-Med, LLC
4256 N Ravenswood Ave
Suite 303
Chicago, IL 60613

www.nextstepmcat.com

ABOUT THE AUTHORS

Bryan Schnedeker is Next Step Test Prep's Vice President for MCAT Tutoring and Content. He manages all of our MCAT and LSAT instructors nationally and counsels hundreds of students when they begin our tutoring process. He has over a decade of MCAT and LSAT teaching and tutoring experience (starting at one of the big prep course companies before joining our team). He has attended medical school and law school himself and has scored a 44 on the old MCAT, a 525 on the new MCAT, and a 180 on the LSAT. Bryan has worked with thousands of MCAT students over the years and specializes in helping students looking to achieve elite scores.

Anthony Lafond is Next Step's MCAT Content Director and an Elite MCAT Tutor. He has been teaching and tutoring MCAT students for nearly 12 years. He earned his MD and PhD degrees from UMDNJ - New Jersey Medical School with a focus on rehabilitative medicine. Dr. Lafond believes that both rehabilitative medicine and MCAT education hinge on the same core principle: crafting an approach that puts the unique needs of the individual foremost.

To find out about MCAT tutoring directly with Anthony or Bryan visit our website:

http://nextsteptestprep.com/mcat

Updates may be found here: http://nextsteptestprep.com/mcat-materials-change-log/

If you have any feedback for us about this book, please contact us at mcat@nextsteptestprep.com

Version: 2017-01-01

FREE ONLINE MCAT DIAGNOSTIC and

FULL-LENGTH EXAM

Want to see how you would do on the MCAT and understand where you need to focus your prep?

TAKE OUR FREE MCAT DIAGNOSTIC EXAM

Timed simulations of all 4 sections of the MCAT

Comprehensive reporting on your performance

Continue your practice with a free Full Length Exam

These two exams are provided free of charge to students who purchased our book

To access your free exam, visit:

http://nextsteptestprep.com/mcat-diagnostic/

TABLE OF CONTENTS

Introduction

Hello and welcome to Next Step's workbook for the new Biological and Biochemical Foundations of Living Systems Section of the MCAT. Since that name is quite the mouthful, we're just going to keep it simple for this book and call it "the Bio/Biochem section".

The book you're holding contains all of the information and practice that you need to start mastering this challenging new part of the MCAT. We'd like to start by giving you a brief overview of the Bio/Biochem section here in the Introduction.

The new Bio/Biochem section will consist of 59 questions which you'll have 95 minutes to answer. Those 59 questions will be presented in a mix of independent questions and questions associated with a reading passage (much like the old MCAT). The section includes 10 passages with a total of 44 questions and 15 stand-alone questions. We've followed these exact specifications for the practice sections in this book.

Each section of 59 questions will have roughly 25% of its questions testing the biochemical principles of living systems, 65% will test the biological principles that underlie the interactions in living systems, 5% will test the chemical concepts guiding biological reactions and 5% will focus on the organic chemistry principles within cell-based systems. Within those broad categories, the AAMC estimates that the 59 questions will break down as:

55%: The structures, mechanisms and metabolic pathways of biological molecules. These include proteins, carbohydrates, and nucleic acids

20%: The specialized functions and processes of cell division, cell differentiation and the life cycles of uni-cellular and multi-cellular organisms.

25%: The structure, function and homeostatic maintenance of human physiological systems. This will include the nervous, endocrine and organ systems.

The key to mastering this section involves taking a step-by-step approach, starting with reinforcing foundational content, then putting that content into an overall context, and practicing on MCAT-style questions. The key to great scores is practice, practice, practice!

Everyone here at Next Step would like to wish you the best of luck with your studies!

Thank you,

Bryan Schnedeker
Co-founder
Next Step Pre-Med, LLC

How to Use This Book

This workbook consists of five sections:

Chapter I is an outline of all of the content areas that will be covered in the new Bio/Biochem Section, arranged by content area and topic. This outline is provided primarily as a reference tool. If you want to double-check if a particular topic will be on the Bio/Biochem Section, come back to check this outline.

Appendix B is the self-study outline. Here, we have taken the outline from Section I and expanded the first several points. This is where you will lay down the foundation for your great score by doing the real work of learning new scientific content. Next Step's strategy and practice book is **not** a textbook. For your science content preparation, avoid using college textbooks unless necessary because they will contain **much** more scientific detail than is required by the new exam. To learn the proper content, you will need to purchase MCAT review books such as Next Step's Content Review series.

In Appendix B we model for you how to develop your own notes on these topics. Self-analysis and self study will be a key component to your success in medical school. By building up your own self-study outline, you will learn the material far better than simply skimming through some pre-written outline. This will ensure MCAT success as well as medical school success. If you wish to develop your own self-study outline, simply create a Word document and expand the entire outline from Chapter 1, following the template we've demonstrated for a few pages in Appendix B.

To use the Self Study version of the outline, fill in the space labeled "CL" with your confidence level (1, 2, 3, 4) on that topic. We suggest a simple self-assessment such as:

4 = total confidence. I could take the MCAT today and questions on this topic would be fine.
3 = strong confidence. I'd like to just refresh quickly, but I'd feel good seeing this topic on my MCAT.
2 = weak confidence. I've heard of it but can't explain it and I'd be nervous on this topic on my MCAT.
1 = no confidence. Is this English? I've never even heard of this before.

Once you've gone through and done a rigorous self-assessment, then use the large blank spaces under each topic to fill in your own definition or description of that topic for each topic you labeled 3 and 4. Once you've finished that, briefly investigate those topics using outside resources (an ideal resource here is simply Wikipedia – it's free, easy to understand, and the intro paragraphs of each article are a good level of knowledge appropriate for the exam.) For those topics you already feel comfortable with, a quick review of Next Step's content review book and should be more than enough. Remember that the Bio/Biochem section's level of detail is introductory level. If your descriptions of a topic were accurate, great. If you left things out or got things wrong, then highlight that topic. It's easy to learn new information, but harder to un-learn wrong information. So stuff you thought you knew (but you were wrong) will be a priority in your studies.

After you're done with your strengths, move to the topics you're not sure on. For those, simply go through your outside content (Next Step review books, Khan Academy, Wikipedia, etc.) and fill in a short description of each topic and sub-topic. If it looks like there's too much info to sum up in a few sentences, create a separate study sheet for your notes. Keep your work organized, as this will enable you to alter and build on these sheets in the future.

Once that's all done, give yourself a big pat on the back – that's the first major step in the process. As we said, the act of building up your own notes and supplementing with MCAT review books will lead to much more learning than simply whizzing through a pre-written outline.

Appendix C is a glossary of every key term you will be expected to know for the Bio/Biochem Section. With the same goal of turning this workbook into an active tool for learning (rather than something passive), we've arranged the glossary as a series of study sheets.

To use them, simply fold over the right-hand side of the page to cover the definitions. Then quiz yourself on the words on the right and check yourself.

It's important when learning these terms to avoid simply plowing through the terms in the same order over and over. You'll end up learning the terms in the context of the study sheet, rather than really learning each idea. We recommend that you use the following pattern:

1)   Go through the words in order, twice.
2)   Go through the odd-numbered pages, then the even numbered pages, and then repeat.
3)   Quiz yourself on the first word on each page, then the second word on each page, and so on.
4)   Finally, go through the whole glossary backwards, twice.

This dynamic style of information learning will reinforce the content much more effectively than rote memorization. By breaking up the order in which you review the words, you help your brain focus on learning each individual term rather than subconsciously memorizing the pattern in which the words are printed on the page.

Chapter 2 presents several practice passages and independent questions and discusses some simple strategies for organizing the information they present. Work through this section **after completing the self-study outline** in Appendix B and **after learning the terms** in the glossary in Appendix C.

Chapter 3 consists of four full, 95 minute, timed sections. Complete each of these sections in order, under *timed* conditions. You do yourself no favors by "cheating" and not holding yourself to time. It takes a lot of practice to get used to the tight time constraints on the test, and these sections are your first chance to practice.

When going through the passages, we discuss the use of a highlighter pen (the revised MCAT will still retain the on-screen highlighting function). For these timed sections, a valuable way to review is to go back into the passages with a different color of highlight after you've reviewed your work. If there are any questions you got wrong because you didn't highlight something important in the passage, then highlight after the fact with the new color.

As before, your emphasis is on active learning. This highlighting strategy lets you come back and review your work a couple of days later with a clear visual representation of how you should have been highlighting the first time through.

If you ever find yourself stuck and would like to ask questions or offer feedback contact us at mcat@nextsteptestprep. com, and visit www.NextStepTestPrep.com if you'd like to arrange for tutoring.

Outline of the Bio/Biochem Section

The AAMC has organized the MCAT content around general concepts that cut across disciplinary boundaries. To make the material more manageable for you, we have sorted the content into the MCAT sciences: biology, biochemistry, and organic chemistry. You will see certain topics listed more than once under multiple sciences. For example, amino acids are listed in both the biochemistry and biology sections. When a topic can be covered under multiple sciences, you may get questions that ask about that topic as it's normally taught in a biochemistry class, or as it's normally taught in a biology class.

PART I: BIOLOGY

1. Proteins
   A. Structure
      a) Protein Structure
         i. Primary
         ii. Secondary
         iii. Tertiary
         iv. Quaternary
         v. Protein Stability

   B. Protein Function
      a) Immune System
      b) Motor

   C. Enzymes
      a) Catalysts: Reduction of Activation Energy, Cofactors, Coenzymes
      b) Classification
      c) Substrate interactions
         i. Active Site
         ii. Induced Fit
      d) Vitamins
      e) Effects on Enzyme Activity
         i. pH
         ii. Temperature

   D. Enzyme Control
      a) Kinetics
         i. Michaelis-Menten
         ii. Cooperativity
      b) Feedback
      c) Inhibition
         i. Competitive
         ii. Non-competitive

      d) Regulation
         i. Allosteric enzymes
         ii. Zymogens
         iii. Covalently-modified enzymes

2. Molecular Genetics
   A. Nucleic Acids
      a) Structure, Function
      b) Nucleotides, Nucleosides: Sugar-Phosphate Backbone, Purines, Pyrimidines
      c) Watson-Crick Model: Double-Helix, Base-Pair Specificity
      d) Transmission of genetic information
      e) Denaturation, Reannealing, Hybridization

   B. DNA Replication and Repair
      a) Replication Mechanism
         i. Semi-Conservative
         ii. Enzymes
         iii. Replication Origin
      b) Replicating the ends of DNA
      c) Repair during replication
         i. Mutation Repair

   C. Genetic Code
      a) Triplets
         i. Codon-Anticodon
         ii. Degeneracy
         iii. Wobble Pairing
         iv. Missense Mutations
         v. Nonsense Mutations
         vi. Initiation
         vii. Termination

b) Transcription
    i. tRNA, mRNA, rRNA, snRNPs, snRNAs
    ii. introns, exons
c) Translation
    i. mRNA, tRNA, rRNA
    ii. ribosomes, initiation, termination co-factors
    iii. post-translational processing

D. Chromosomes
a) Repetitive DNA
b) Supercoiling
c) Heterochromatin
d) Euchromatin
e) Telomeres
f) Centromeres

E. Gene Expression
a) Prokaryotes: Operons, Jacob-Monod Model, Repression, Positive Control
b) Eukaryotes
    i. transcriptional regulation, DNA binding proteins, transcription factors
    ii. gene amplification, duplication
    iii. post-transcriptional control, introns, exons
    iv. cancer
    v. regulation of chromatic structure: methylation
    vi. non-coding RNAs

F. Biotechnology
a) Cloning
b) Restriction Enzymes
c) cDNA
d) Hybridization
e) PCR
f) Blotting
g) Electrophoresis
h) Stem Cells
    i. Applications
    ii. Ethics

3. Classical Genetics
A. Mendelian Genetics
a) Phenotype
b) Genotype
c) Gene
d) Locus
e) Allele
f) Zygosity
g) Wild-type
h) Recessive
i) Dominant
j) Co-dominant
k) Incomplete Dominance
l) Leakage
m) Penetrance
n) Expressivity
o) Hybridization
p) Gene Pool

B. Meiosis and Variability
a) Significance
    i. Differences with Mitosis
b) Gene Segregation
    i. Independent Assortment
    ii. Linkage
    iii. Recombination
c) Sex-Linkage
    i. Y Chromosome
    ii. Sex Determination
d) Extranuclear Inheritance
e) Mutation
    i. Types
    ii. Effects
    iii. Errors of Metabolism
    iv. Mutagens
    v. Carcinogens
f) Genetic Drift
g) Crossing-over

C. Analysis
a) Hardy-Weinberg
b) Test Cross
c) Crossover Frequency
d) Biometry

D. Evolution
   a) Natural Selection: Fitness, Differential Reproduction, Group Selection
   b) Speciation: Polymorphism, Adaptation, Inbreeding, Outbreeding, Bottlenecks
   c) Time as gradual random changes in genome

4. Metabolism
   A. Glycolysis
      a) Aerobic: Substrates and Products
      b) Anaerobic: Fermentation
      c) Net Results

   B. Regulation of Pathways

   C. Krebs Cycle: Reactions, Substrates, Products, Regulation

   D. Metabolism of Fat and Protein
      a) Fats: Digestion, Transport
      b) Fatty Acids: Oxidation, Saturated Fats, Unsaturated Fats
      c) Proteins: Metabolism
      d) Anabolism: Synthesis of Lipids and Polysaccharides

   E. Oxidative Phosphorylation
      a) Electron Transport Chain: Substrates, Products, Function
      b) NADH, NADPH, Flavoproteins, Cytochromes
      c) ATP Synthase, Chemiosmosis
      d) Net Results
      e) Regulation

5. Cell Biology
   A. Plasma Membrane
      a) Composition: Phospholipids, Steroids, Waxes, Proteins
         i. Receptors
      b) Solute transport
         i. Osmosis
         ii. Passive
         iii. Active
         iv. Na/K Pump
         v. Ion Channels
      c) Membrane Potential
      d) Exocytosis, Endocytosis
      e) Gap Junctions
      f) Tight Junctions
      g) Desmosomes

   B. Membrane-Bound Organelles
      a) Nucleus: Genetic Information, Nucleolus, Nuclear Envelope, Pores
      b) Mitochondria: Function, Membranes, Replication
      c) Lysosomes: Function
      d) ER: Rough vs. Smooth, Double Membrane, Biosynthesis
      e) Golgi: Structure and Function
      f) Peroxisomes: Function

   C. Cytoskeleton
      a) Microfilaments
      b) Microtubules
      c) Intermediate Filaments
      d) Cilia
      e) Flagella
      f) Centrioles
      g) Microtubule Organizing Centers

   D. Epithelial and Connective Cells

6. Microbiology
   A. Cell Theory
      a) History
      b) Development
      c) Impact

   B. Prokaryotes
      a) Archaea, Bacteria, Bacilli, Spirilli, Cocci
      b) Lack of Eukaryotic Features
      c) Cell Wall, Flagella
      d) Fission, Exponential Growth
      e) Quick Adaptation, Antibiotic Resistance
      f) Types: Aerobic, Anaerobic, Parasitic, Symbiotic
      g) Chemotaxis
      h) Genetics: Plasmids, Transformation, Conjugation, Transposons

C. Viruses
  a) Structure, Size, Lack of Organelles
  b) Bacteriophages
  c) Genome: DNA, RNA
  d) Life Cycle: Intracellular Reproduction, Attachment, Replication, Release
  e) Transduction
  f) Retroviruses
  g) Prions, Viroids

7. Cell Division, Cell Development, Reproduction, Embryology
  A. Mitosis
    a) Phases
    b) Structures
    c) Growth Arrest
    d) Control and Loss of Control

  B. Reproduction
    a) Gametogenesis, Meiosis
    b) Ovum, Sperm: Formation, Morphology, Contribution to Zygote
    c) Sequence: Fertilization to Birth

  C. Embryogenesis
    a) Stages
      i. Fertilization
      ii. Cleavage
      iii. Blastula
      iv. Gastrula
      v. Cell Movements
      vi. Neurulation
    b) Germ Layers: Endoderm, Mesoderm, Ectoderm
    c) Neural Crest
    d) Environmental Effects

  D. Cell Development
    a) Specialization: Determination, Differentiation, Tissue Types, Cell communication
    b) Cell Migration
    c) Stem Cells
    d) Gene Regulation
    e) Apoptosis
    f) Regeneration, Senescence, Aging

8. Nervous and Endocrine Systems
  A. Nerve Cell
    a) Structures: Soma, Dendrites, Axon, Myelin, Nodes of Ranvier
    b) Synapse: Structure, Neurotransmitters
    c) Resting Potential, Action Potential
    d) Excitatory, Inhibitory Fibers, Summation, Firing Frequency
    e) Glia, Neuroglia

  B. Nervous System
    a) Function, Organization
    b) Efferent, Afferent
    c) Sympathetic, Parasympathetic
    d) Reflexes: Reflex Arc, Spinal Cord, Supraspinal Circuits
    e) Endocrine System Integration

  C. Endocrine System
    a) Function, Major Glands, Major Hormones
    b) Mechanism of Hormone Action
    c) Transport of Hormones and Second Messengers

9. Physiology
  A. Respiratory System
    a) Function
    b) Thermoregulation
    c) pH control

  B. Circulatory System
    a) Structures, Functions, Regulation
    b) Heart: Chambers
    c) Systolic, Diastolic Pressure
    d) Pulmonary, System Circulations
    e) Arteries, Veins, Capillaries
    f) Blood Composition: Plasma, Cells, Chemicals
    g) Clotting
    h) Gas Transport: Oxygen, Carbon Dioxide, Hemoglobin, Hematocrit
      i. Lymphatic System
      ii. Structures
      iii. Functions

C. Immune System
    a) Innate: Macrophages, Phagocytes
    b) Adaptive: T cells, B cells
    c) Tissues: Marrow, Spleen, Thymus, Lymph Nodes
    d) Antigens, Antibodies: Ag Presentation, Ag-Ab Recognition, Structure of Ab
    e) Autoimmune Diseases
    f) Major Histocompatibility Complex

D. Digestive System
    a) Ingestion, Peristalsis
    b) Organs: Stomach, Liver, Gall Bladder, Pancreas, Small Intestine, Large Intestine
    c) Control: Muscular, Endocrine, Nervous

E. Excretory System
    a) Homeostasis: bp, osmoregulation, acid balance, nitrogenous waste
    b) Kidney: Cortex, Medulla
    c) Nephron: Glomerulus, Bowman's Capsule, Tubules, Loop of Henle, Collecting Duct
        i. filtration, counter-current multiplier, secretion, reabsorption, concentration
    d) Storage: ureter, bladder, urethra

F. Reproductive System
    a) Gonads
    b) Genitals
    c) Sexual Development
    d) Menstrual Cycle
    e) Pregnancy
    f) Lactation

G. Muscle System
    a) Function: Mobility, Circulatory Assistance, Thermoregulation, Shivering
    b) Smooth, Striated, Cardiac
    c) Muscle Structure: T-tubule, Contractile Apparatus, Sarcoplasmic Reticulum, Contractile Velocity
    d) Cardiac Muscle: Regulation
    e) Oxygen Debt
    f) Control: Motor Neurons, Neuromuscular Junction, Motor End Plates, Sympathetic and Parasympathetic, Voluntary, Involuntary
    g) Sarcomeres
    h) Troponin, Tropomyosin

H. Skeletal System
    a) Function: Support, Protection, Calcium Storage
    b) Bone Types, Joint Types
    c) Composition of Bone Matrix and Cells
    d) Cartilage, Ligaments, Tendons
    e) Endocrine Regulation

I. Skin System
    a) Structure
        i. Impermeability to Water
    b) Function
        i. Homeostasis
        ii. Osmoregulation
        iii. Thermoregulation
    c) Hormonal Control

PART II: BIOCHEMISTRY

1. Proteins
    A. Amino Acids
        a) Configuration
            i. Dipolar ions
        b) Side Chain
            i. Acidic
            ii. Basic
            iii. Hydrophobic
            iv. Hydrophilic

    B. Structure
        a) Protein Structure
            i. Primary
            ii. Secondary
            iii. Tertiary
            iv. Quaternary

   b) Protein Stability
       i.   Folding
       ii. Denaturing
       iii. Hydrophobic interactions
       iv. Solvation
       v.   Entropy

 C. Enzymes
   a) Catalysts
       i.   Reduction of Activation Energy
   b) Classification
   c) Interactions
       i.   Active site
       ii. Allosteric site

 D. Enzyme Control
   a) Kinetics
       i.   Michaelis-Menten
       ii. Cooperativity
   b) Feedback
       i.   Positive
       ii. Negative
   c) Inhibition
   d) Zymogens

2. Molecular Genetics
 A. Nucleic Acids
   a) Structure, Function
       i.   Sugar-Phosphate Backbone,
       ii. Purines
       iii. Pyrimidines
   b) Nucleotides
   c) Nucleosides
   d) Watson-Crick Model: Double-Helix, Base-Pair Specificity
   e) Denaturation, Reannealing, Hybridization

3. Metabolism
 A. Bioenergetics
   a) Thermodynamics/Bioenergetics
       i. ΔG
       ii. K_{eq}
       iii. Concentrations
       iv. Spontaneity
   b) Phosphoryl Groups
       i.   ATP Hydrolysis
       ii. Group Transfers
   c) Redox: Half-Reactions, Soluble Electron Carriers, Flavoproteins

 B. Carbohydrates
   a) Classification
   b) Configuration
   c) Hydrolysis of Glycosides
   d) Monomers
   e) Polymers

 C. Glycolysis and Gluconeogenesis
   a) Aerobic: Substrates and Products
   b) Anaerobic: Fermentation
   c) Net Results
   d) Gluconeogenesis
       i.   Pentose Phosphate Pathway

 D. Regulation of Pathways
   a) Regulation of Glycolysis and Gluconeogenesis
   b) Glycogen Regulation
   c) Metabolic Regulation

 E. Krebs Cycle:
   a) Acetyl CoA Production
   b) Reactions
   c) Substrates
   d) Products
   e) Regulation

 F. Metabolism of Fat and Protein
   a) Fats
       i.   Digestion
       ii. Transport
   b) Fatty Acids
       i.   Oxidation
       ii. Saturated Fats
       iii. Unsaturated Fats
       iv. Ketone Bodies

 G. Oxidative Phosphorylation
   a) Electron Transport Chain
       i.   Substrates
       ii. Products
       iii. Function
   b) NADH
   c) NADPH
   d) Flavoproteins
   e) Cytochromes
   f) ATP Synthase
   g) Chemiosmosis
   h) Net Results

      i)   Regulation

      j)   Mitochondria

             i.   Apoptosis

             ii.   Oxidative Stress

H. Hormonal Regulation

      a)   High Level Integration

      b)   Tissue Specific Metabolism

      c)   Obesity

4.   Cell Biology

   A. Plasma Membrane

      a)   Composition: Phospholipids, Steroids, Waxes, Proteins

             i.   Receptors

      b)   Solute transport

             i.   Osmosis

             ii.   Na/K Pump

             iii.   Solute Channels

      c)   Membrane Potential

      d)   Exocytosis

      e)   Endocytosis

PART III: ORGANIC CHEMISTRY

1. Proteins
    A. Amino Acids
    - a) Stereo Configuration
    - b) Dipolar ions
    - c) Acidic side chains
    - d) Basic side chains
    - e) Hydrophobic side chains
    - f) Hydrophilic side chains

    B. Structure
    - a) Protein Stability
        - i. Folding
        - ii. Denaturing
        - iii. Hydrophobic interactions
    - b) Separation Techniques
        - i. Isoelectric Point
        - ii. Electrophoresis

2. Metabolism
    A. Carbohydrates
    - a) Classification
    - b) Configuration
        - i. Isomerism
        - ii. Hydrolysis of Glycosides
        - iii. Glycoside links
        - iv. Mutarotation

3. Cell Biology
    A. Plasma Membrane
    - a) Phospholipids
    - b) Permeability
    - c) Steroids
    - d) Proteins

4. Nervous and Endocrine Systems
    A. Lipid Structure
    - a) Steroids
    - b) Terpenes
    - a) Terpenoids

5. Separations and Purifications
    A. Extraction
    B. Distillation
    C. Chromatography

6. Lipids: Storage, Triacyl Glycerols, Saponification, Phospholipids, Phosphatids, Sphingolipids, Waxes, Fat-Soluble Vitamins, Steroids, Prostaglandins

7. Carbonyl Compounds
    A. Nomenclature and Physical Properties of Aldehydes and Ketones
    B. Nucleophilic Addition to Carbonyl Carbon: Acetal, Ketal, Imine, Enamine, Hydrides, Cyanohydrin
    C. Oxidation of Aldehydes
    D. Enolates: Tautomerism, Aldol Condensation, Retro-Aldol, Kinetic and Thermodynamic Enolate
    E. Steric Hindrance of Carbonyl Bond
    F. Acidity of α hydrogens, Carbanions

8. Alcohols
    A. Nomenclature, Physical Properties
    B. Reactions: Oxidation, S_N1, S_N2, Protection, Mesylates, Tosylates

9. Carboxylic Acids
    A. Nomenclature, Physical Properties
    B. Reactions: Amides, Lactam, Esters, Lactones, Anhydrides, Reduction, Decarboxylation, Nucleophilic Acyl Substitution

10. Carboxylic Acid Derivatives
    A. Nomenclature, Physical Properties
    B. Reactions: Nucleophilic Substitution, Transesterification, Amide Hydrolysis
    C. Reactivity, Steric Effects, Electronic Effects, Strain, β lactams

11. Cyclic Molecules: Phenols, Hydroquinones, Ubiquinones, 2e⁻ Redox Centers, Aromatic Heterocycles

CHAPTER 2
Passage and Question Strategies

Independent Discrete Questions

The Bio/Biochem section can be difficult for many students. These sciences may be more familiar to many pre-meds than the physical science content but there's also so much material to learn. The difficulty of the test is in how it tests the material, not necessarily what material it tests. However, a focused strategy can help you score more points through understanding the material on a fundamental level, as opposed to superficial memorizing.

As we mentioned in the Introduction, each Bio/Biochem Section will consist of 15 independent questions and 44 passage-based questions. Time is tight on the MCAT and you'll want to make sure you make the most of each minute.

To that end, you must make sure you're moving at a good clip - about 8 minutes per passage and 1 minute per question on the discrete questions. They're typically arranged in clumps of three to four questions and will say something like "These questions are **NOT** based on a passage." at the top of the screen. The section will always end with a set of discretes and you don't want to miss out on them!

To start, we'll look at a few examples of these sorts of independent questions.

1. A patient with a tumor in his hypothalamus experiences a significant increase in vasopressin secretion from his posterior pituitary. Which of the following would be the most direct consequence of this disorder?

   A. Increased water concentration in the urine
   B. Increased total urine volume
   C. Decreased sodium ion concentration in plasma
   D. Increased secretion of thyroxine

This is an example of a relatively straightforward biology question. When reading through these independent questions, start by asking yourself, *"Exactly what is the question asking me for?"*. A classic sort of trap answer will be something that's the "right answer to the wrong question" - that is, it will be related to the topic of the question and will be a true fact, but not *exactly* answer the question.

Here, the question is asking us what the function of vasopressin is, though in a roundabout way. Once you've read the question and answer choices, and you know *exactly* what the question is asking for, ask yourself, *"What information is provided?"*. You've got to be careful not to make any unwarranted assumptions. The MCAT is a picky test and will expect you to pay attention to the exact information provided: We're told that the patient in question has a tumor that leads to overexpression of vasopressin and asks you for a likely consequence of the increased hormone level.

Next, ask yourself, ***"What outside information do I need?"***. The independent questions especially will draw heavily on outside knowledge. Here, you need to be familiar with the physiological function of vasopressin. Vasopressin, also known as antidiuretic hormone, is a peptide hormone found in humans and other mammals. Its two primary functions are to retain water in the body and to constrict blood vessels. Vasopressin regulates the body's osmolarity by acting to increase water reabsorption in the collecting ducts of the nephron. This results in more concentrated urine and more water present in the plasma. The increase in water in the plasma would decrease the concentration of sodium ions in the body.

Finally, ***evaluate the choices, either by prediction or process of elimination***. In "prediction" you simply skim quickly through the choices looking for what you already know the answer will say. That's often the case when you have a good content background in an area. If you're not exactly sure what they're looking for, don't delay – start eliminating choices.

Remember, ***answer every question, even if you're not sure!***

In this question, the answer is (**C**). Decreased sodium ion concentration in plasma. By its regulation of plasma osmolarity, the excess vasopressin in this patient will cause the patient to develop more concentrated urine and more water present in the plasma. The increase in water in the plasma would decrease the concentration of sodium ions in the body.

A: This is the opposite of vasopressin's effect. A greater degree of water reabsorption would lower the levels of water in the urine, thus decreasing the concentration of water in the fluid excreted.

B: This is the opposite of the effects of vasopressin. Greater water retention by the kidney would serve to lower total urine volume, not increase it. This could be result of a tumor that lowers vasopressin release, which is why it is important to be sure of exactly what the question is asking.

D: This answer is another MCAT favorite, the one that comes out of left field, but may seem plausible if you're unsure of your content. Vasopressin is a hormone that exerts homeostatic regulation via its effects on the kidney, which is not directly involved in the actions of the thyroid, which maintains homeostasis of the body via temperature control. The thyroid controls metabolism through the effects of the thyroid hormone, thyroxine, which acts to raise metabolic activity in the body. Thus vasopressin is not directly linked to metabolic rate, which thyroxine controls.

Now try another similar question:

2. Which of the following is an example of disruptive selection?

   A. Females of a species choose to mate with males of the species based on the size and color of the males' tail feathers, with females preferentially mating with males that have larger and more colorful plumage.
   B. An insect is preyed upon by several different species of bird that rely on vision for hunting, such that the birds are more easily able to see, catch, and eat the larger insects.
   C. A type of trout competes with another fish species for food and in such competition, trout that are significantly larger than average are able to intimidate the other fish species away and trout that are significantly smaller than average are able to access food by stealth without confrontation.
   D. In a certain species of crocodile, females that are smaller than average are subject to predation by snakes and females that are larger than average are subject to hunting by humans.

Exactly what is the question asking me for?

A situation that provides a clear example of the concept of disruptive selection.

What information is provided?

You have been given the name of the genetic concept to which you must match the answer, disruptive selection.

What outside knowledge do I need?

The MCAT will expect you to be familiar with the various theories and concepts in the biological sciences and to recognize them when shown an unfamiliar scenario.

Choice C is correct. Disruptive selection is a form of natural selection pressure in which members of a species gain an advantage by not being of the average type. Here, choice C gives us an example where especially large and especially small fish have a competitive advantage. This "disrupts" the population by leading to smaller and smaller fish and also larger and larger fish. Eventually these two types of fish may develop into entirely separate species.

A: This is an example of sexual selection, a mode of natural selection in which some individuals out-reproduce other member of a population because they are better at securing mates.

B: This is an example of directional selection, with smaller insects being favored. Directional selection is a mode of natural selection in which the environmental conditions favor an extreme phenotype over other phenotypes, causing the allele frequency to shift over time in the direction of the extreme phenotype.

D: This is an example of stabilizing selection. Stabilizing selection is a type of natural selection that favors the average individuals in a population. This process selects against the extreme phenotypes and instead favors the majority of the population that is well adapted to the environment, with average member of the species being favored.

Now that we've carefully examined a couple of questions, complete the questions on the next page to practice this process. The explanations follow.

3.   When exposed to milk contaminated with strontium, children's bodies will incorporate the strontium into their bones. The strontium tends to locate primarily in growing long bones. If examined, where would strontium most likely be found?

    A. Along the outer edges of the ala of the hips
    B. Near the sutures in skull bones
    C. Evenly distributed along the tibias
    D. The epiphyseal plates of the femurs

4.   At the end of an organic chemistry reaction a student is left with the end product in a 100 mL aqueous solution. She attempts to do an extraction using 25 mL of acetone. Which of the following correctly characterizes the results she will see?

    A. The extraction will work given acetone's relative solubility in water.
    B. The extraction will work with acetone or any other organic solvent since organic molecules are insoluble in water.
    C. The student should instead perform a distillation, as distillation is the only method that can separate an organic solute from an aqueous solvent.
    D. The extraction will be unsuccessful since acetone is miscible in water.

5.   Following a stroke, a patient loses certain motor functions leaving him unable to write with a pen. After months of rehabilitation he slowly regains this ability. This demonstrates:

    A. the regrowth of damaged tissues.
    B. neural plasticity.
    C. central nervous system functions being taken over by the peripheral nervous system.
    D. the substitution of regrown glial cell function for neuronal cell function.

6.   A soldier is exposed to a nerve gas which, when inhaled, binds irreversibly and non-competitively to acetylcholinesterase. The soldier is mostly likely to die from:

    A. tetanic contraction of the diaphragm.
    B. hypovolemic shock.
    C. gangrene.
    D. stroke.

Independent Question Explanations

3. When exposed to milk contaminated with strontium, children's bodies will incorporate the strontium into their bones. The strontium tends to locate primarily in growing long bones. If examined, where would strontium most likely be found?

    A. Along the outer edges of the ala of the hips
    B. Near the sutures in skull bones
    C. Evenly distributed along the tibias
    D. **The epiphyseal plates of the femurs**

The question states that strontium localizes to the growing portion of long bones, and long bones grow along their epiphyseal plates. There are four bone shapes in the human skeleton: long bones, short bones, flat bones, and irregular bones. Long bones have a tubular shaft and articular surface at each end (e.g. the bones of the arms and legs). Short bones have a tubular shaft and articular surfaces at each end but are much smaller compared to the long bones. The short bones include all of the small bones in the hands, the feet, and the clavicle. Flat bones are thin and have broad surfaces. The flat bones include the scapula, the ribs, and the sternum. Irregular bones are irregular in size and shape. They include the bones in the vertebral column, the carpal bones in the hands, tarsal bones in the feet, and the patella. The hips and the skull are flat bones, not long bones, so you may eliminate choices A and B. The question states that strontium localizes to the growing portion of long bones, and long bones grow along their epiphyseal plates. Thus choice D is correct.

A: The ilium is the uppermost and largest bone of the pelvis, and is a flat bone.
B: The skull and cranial bones are flat bones, not long bones.
C: Very tempting, because it does mention a long bone, the tibia, also known as the shin bone. However, the longitudinal growth of long bones is a result of ossification at the epiphyseal plate.

4. At the end of an organic chemistry reaction a student is left with the end product in a 100 mL aqueous solution. She attempts to do an extraction using 25 mL of acetone. Which of the following correctly characterizes the results she will see?

    A. The extraction will work given acetone's relative solubility in water.
    B. The extraction will work with acetone or any other organic solvent since organic molecules are insoluble in water.
    C. The student should instead perform a distillation, as distillation is the only method that can separate an organic solute from an aqueous solvent.
    D. **The extraction will be unsuccessful since acetone is miscible in water.**

To carry out an extraction, the two liquids mixed must not be soluble in each other. They will separate out forming two layers in the test tube, and the solutes within them will spontaneously sort to the layer in which they are more soluble. Acetone, as a very polar molecule, readily dissolves in water. Thus it's impossible to do a water-acetone extraction and choice D is the correct answer.

A: This is the exact opposite of the right answer, as described above.
B: Many organic molecules are soluble in water, including acetone and many alcohols.
C: There are many methods by which solutes can be separated from their solvent, not just distillation.

5. Following a stroke, a patient loses certain motor functions leaving him unable to write with a pen. After months of rehabilitation he slowly regains this ability. This demonstrates:

    A. the regrowth of damaged tissues.
    B. <u>**neural plasticity.**</u>
    C. central nervous system functions being taken over by the peripheral nervous system.
    D. the substitution of regrown glial cell function for neuronal cell function.

    Although parts of the brain are specialized for certain functions, when the brain is damaged some of that function can return through neural plasticity. The brain uses a new part to carry out the old function.

    A: The central nervous system does not regrow neurons.
    C: The peripheral nervous system functions to transport signals to and from the CNS and does not carry out complicated tasks like writing with a pen.
    D: The glia (e.g. Schwann cells and oligodendrocytes) are supporting cells and do not carry out nerve function themselves.

6. A soldier is exposed to a nerve gas which, when inhaled, binds irreversibly and non-competitively to acetylcholinesterase. The soldier is mostly likely to die from:

    A. <u>**tetanic contraction of the diaphragm.**</u>
    B. hypovolemic shock.
    C. gangrene.
    D. stroke.

    Acetylcholinesterase is the enzyme in the neuromuscular junction that breaks down acetylcholine. This breakdown is necessary for a nerve to stop stimulating a muscle to contract – the enzyme allows the muscle to relax. If this poison gets to the diaphragm, it would not be allowed to relax, preventing the victim from exhaling. This would asphyxiate the person.

    B, D: Shock and stroke relate to problems with the circulatory system, rather than the neuromuscular system.
    C: Nothing in the question stem suggests the soldier would have infected tissue subject to gangrene, a potentially life-threatening condition that arises when a considerable mass of body tissue dies.

Bio/Biochem Science Passages

The science passages on the MCAT will be anywhere from 250 – 550 words, and will often come with one or more diagrams. The types of information they present can be broadly categorized as informational or experimental. There are a number of different approaches possible here, but in this book we will opt for a relatively simple one: use the on-screen highlighter.

Some folks may like to go slowly and use the scratch paper provided to take notes, and others prefer to skim very quickly through the passage to get to the questions as quickly as possible. For some students those might work. But at least at first, we suggest you start with our "middle of the road" approach: don't skip right to the questions, don't bother taking notes on the scratch paper. Instead, read briskly – a little faster than you're normally comfortable with – and highlight important ideas as they come up.

When you come to experimental information, slow down and focus on one question: *what did they measure?* The MCAT loves to test your understanding of a passage by focusing on exactly what the experiment measured.

So what should you highlight?

There are four general categories of things worth highlighting: **key terms, opinions, contrasts, cause and effect relationships.**

Keep in mind, we're using these category names very loosely. What matters is that you've spotted a key idea, not what name you give it. Having said that, here's what to watch for:

Key terms:	These are things like proper nouns, technical terms, numbers, dates, etc. They're the words that you're going to want to be able to find again quickly if a question asks about them.
Opinions:	Most importantly, the author's. Opinions can be a view expressed by a particular scientist, or a view espoused by a school of thought. The main thing to watch for here is the emphasis words like should, ought, must, better, worse, etc. These are rare, but not absent in the science passages.
Contrast:	Just what it says. Watch for conflicting views, old vs. new, traditional vs. radical and so on. In science passages contrasts typically show up as opposite functions or effects (e.g. glucagon vs. insulin).
Cause and effect:	We're going to use the phrase "cause and effect" to refer to any logical connection, association, correlation, or literal cause-and-effect relationship presented in the passages. Any time the passages offers us a "because this, therefore that" relationship, we'll call it "cause and effect". To be clear, we don't mean these are always literal, scientific causes. Rather, we're using this phrase in a loose, rhetorical way.
Figures:	When you are presented with a figure/table/graph on the MCAT, is it important to approach it as you do the text. Focus on identifying the main purpose to the figure. For example, what relationship, findings, results, or data does it present? What kind of information is it (numbers, graphs, a schematic). Once you have identified what type of information it presents and what implications it could have on the type of questions asked, move on. You do not need to decipher the entire graphic now; if it is important, the questions will ask about it and we can earn points.

While using this book, have a yellow highlighter marker handy. Highlight in the book just like you would want to on the real exam. When you review the explanations afterwards, you'll see that we break down the material a couple of ways.

First, we use **bold and underline** text to show you the words and phrases you should have highlighted. Then, underneath each paragraph, we use **bold text** to describe why you should highlight those terms. The material is analyzed using the four categories above.

If you're the type of test-taker who likes to take notes on the scratch paper, then our **bold text** notes under the paragraph can serve as an example of the sorts of ideas worth noting in some form of short hand. Recall that on test day, time is a factor so when note taking, shorthand and abbreviations are an ideal way to convey full sentences worth of information without needing to write in complete sentences.

Another valuable strategy for the MCAT is to prioritize your quicker, easier points while saving tougher passages for later. Thus, it is in your best interest to practice all relevant topics on the exam. This will allow you to identify areas of strength and areas of weakness. Once identified, weaker areas can be attacked with diligent practice.

Passage Format

In addition to using content, you can also utilize the type of passage and the category of figures presented to prioritize passages. The images will also allow you to quickly identify the passage content.

Before jumping into a passage, take a few seconds to **scan the passage** for any figures, graphs, and equations. Next try to **identify the topic of the passage**. This will allow you ask yourself several important questions before you begin reading.

1) *"How comfortable am I with the presented topic?"*

2) *"How well do I recognize the ideas presented in the figures?"*

3) *"Is the format of the passage one with which I am comfortable?"*

The MCAT will present Bio/Biochem science passages in three different formats.

1) Information-based passages

These passages will be dense on information about a topic, and may present equations or figures related to that topic. However, they will not be centered around a research principle or experimental procedure.

2) Experiment-based passages

These passages will be built around a specific experimental procedure. The hallmark of an experimental passage is that there are unknowns which are measured. If the passage describes things like "a yellow precipitate formed" without telling you what that precipitate is, that's an experiment passage. The goal here will be to identify the goals, results and implications of the experiments performed. A solid understanding of what and why the experimenters carried out tasks is much more important to your reading than the exact details of the procedure.

3) Research-based passages

These passages are a hybrid of the other two passage formats. They will present a core concept of Bio/Biochem (typically with a medical slant) but they will do so in the context of a research project. The research passages released so far are broader in their scientific focus than the experiment-based passages. This also allows the MCAT to introduce questions that specifically test you on the design and execution of medically-related research. Unlike experiment-based passages, these research-based passages don't typically have unknowns in the passage itself. The passage text will simply tell you everything about a certain research project.

Question Format

Once you have completed the passage reading, it is on to the **questions**, which is **where all the points are!** Just like the passages, each question the exam presents is looking to test your ability to complete a task. The four question types are:

Task 1, Recall: 35% or about 20-21 questions.

Task 2, Problem Solving: 45% or about 26-27 questions.

Task 3, Research Design: 10% or about 5-6 questions.

Task 4, Data-Based and Statistical Reasoning: 10% or about 5-6 questions.

Task 1: Recall of Scientific Concepts

A big part of your success both in medical school and on the MCAT is demonstrating a solid understanding of scientific concepts and principles. The exam will test your ability to recall key formulas and concepts and your ability to identify the relationship between closely-related concepts.

Task 1 Example Question

7. A patient undergoes a radiation treatment that destroys all of his bone marrow. Which of the following would be expected to remain at normal levels despite this treatment?
    A. Erythrocytes
    B. Platelets
    C. Monocytes
    D. None of the above

This is a task 1 question because it simply requires you to recall the function of the bone marrow. The bone marrow is responsible for making red blood cells, choice A, as well as the cells involved in immune response, choice C, and in blood clotting, choice B. Thus destruction of the bone marrow would not allow any of these cell types to remain at normal levels and choice D is the correct answer.

Task 2: Problem Solving within Scientific Concepts

The MCAT is not just about recall. The exam tests a student's critical reasoning about scientific concepts, theories, and applications. Solving these questions will involve analyzing and assessing scientific explanations and predictions across chemistry and physics. You will see plenty of these questions in this book but take a look at the sample question below.

Task 2 Example Question

8. A woman who is a carrier for a sex-linked recessive trait marries a man whose father was affected by that trait. If they have a daughter, what is the probability that the daughter will be a carrier for the trait and the probability that she will have the trait, respectively?
    A. 0, 0
    B. ½, 0
    C. ½, ½
    D. 1, ½

This is a task 2 question, and you must use knowledge from classical genetics to solve this problem. In addition to recalling the concept of sex-linked recessive traits, this is a task 2 question because it requires you to apply the scientific principle of the genetic crosses to determine the genotypes of hypothetical offspring. Building the Punnett square, a diagram that is used to predict an outcome of a particular cross or breeding experiment, will allow you to arrive at the conclusion that any generation 1 daughters cannot express the disease. The genotypes of the parents are X^cX and XY. The father does not have the trait. Sex-linked traits cannot be passed from father to son since fathers only pass the Y chromosome to sons. So the fact that the grandfather had the trait is irrelevant. We're explicitly told that the mother is a carrier so we know her genotype is X^cX.

	X	Y
X	XX	XY
X^c	X^cX	X^cY

Doing a cross we see that ½ the daughters will be genotype X^cX and ½ will be XX. So the odds of being a carrier are ½ and the odds of having the trait are 0. Thus choice B is correct.

Task 3: Research Design

The new MCAT is looking to identify well-rounded future physicians. It will ask you to display a clear understanding of crucial components of scientific research. These questions will test your scientific inquiry skills by showing that you can actually design can carry out the "business" of science. You will be tested on your mastery of important components of scientific methodology.

To answer these questions correctly you will need to understand the methods that social, natural, and behavioral scientists execute research designed to test and expand the boundaries of science. These questions may seek to test your ability to recognize the ethical guidelines scientists must follow to ensure the rights of research subjects, the integrity of their work, and the interests of research sponsors.

Task 3 Example Question

9. The electrophoresis gel used in protein analysis contains SDS, a 12 member hydrocarbon chain attached to a sulfate group. Multiple SDS molecules will bind to the uncovered hydrophobic regions of denatured proteins. The use of SDS in electrophoresis works by allowing separation of proteins solely based on which property?
    A. Quaternary structure
    B. Tertiary structure
    C. Water solubility
    D. Molecular weight

This is a task 3 question and requires knowledge of proteins structure as well as analytical lab techniques. To answer this question you must understand the design of a protein electrophoresis experiment and the role that the gel plays in that experiment. The question states that the proteins being analyzed are denatured, which means they have lost any tertiary or quaternary structure the protein once had. This eliminates choices A and B. You need to also recall that during electrophoresis, all of the denatured proteins are coated by this SDS molecule, meaning they are all relatively equal in their solubility in water. Thus, you can determine that in SDS-gel electrophoresis, the proteins will be separated only by molecular weight. As a result of this work, choice D is correct.

Task 4 Data-Based and Statistical Reasoning

The last task for the new MCAT is really not that new. Interpreting figures, tables, graphs and equations has always been a necessary skill in reading passages efficiently. With these six questions (on average), the test will make this task more formal. To succeed you must train yourself to be able to deduce patterns in data presented in graphs tables and figures. It will also ask you to draw conclusions based on the scientific data given in a passage or question.

Task 4 Example Question

10. Nitric oxide has been shown to be an important molecule that can affect blood pressure by initiating vasodilation. Nitric oxide can also react with elemental oxygen in the gas phase to form nitrogen dioxide, which has a toxic effect on the body. The following data was collected concerning three blood tests run on a patient in the ER.

Test	[NO] (mol/L)	[O_2] (mol/L)	[NO_2] (mol/L)
1	5.3×10^{-6}	1.1×10^{-2}	8.2×10^{-3}
2	4.7×10^{-3}	1.1×10^{-2}	1.5×10^{-4}
3	2.6×10^{-2}	1.1×10^{-2}	1.1×10^{-5}

During which test is arterial radius expected to be the largest?

    A. Test 1
    B. Test 2
    C. Test 3
    D. All tests would give the same measurement result

This is a task 4 question because to answer it, you must consult the table of experimental data as well as understand the role of NO in the circulatory system. In humans, NO is a signaling molecule involved that is a powerful vasodilator with a short half-life of a few seconds in the blood. Thus, the greatest concentration of NO would cause the largest increase in blood vessel dilation, which is the expansion or widening of blood vessels. Examining the data you can see that test 3 showed the highest levels of NO in the blood. Thus, choice C is correct.

Use the four passages on the following pages as a way to practice your highlighting technique and your problem solving ability. You want to get comfortable with the different question types on the exam. For now, don't worry about time. Speed will come with practice.

THIS PAGE LEFT

INTENTIONALLY BLANK

Passage 1 (Questions 11-15)

A DNA polymerase is an enzyme that catalyzes the formation of a strand of nucleotides based on a DNA template. During the S phase of the cell cycle, two copies of DNA polymerase act on the existing genetic material to create two new copies. The process of DNA replication however, requires much more than the presence of DNA polymerase. The many enzymes involved and their function are outlined in figure 1.

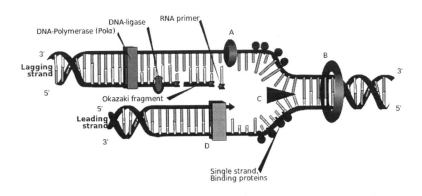

Figure 1 A schematic of DNA replication with all of the enzymes involved

The function of DNA polymerase is simply to read a single strand of DNA and add the correct nucleotide to complement the template. DNA polymerase can only add new nucleotides to the 3' end of the strand being synthesized. DNA polymerases make about one mistake per billion nucleotides added. Most DNA polymerases have the built in ability to recognize and correct these mistakes when they occur. When mistakes occur, the offending base is cleaved out of the strand by enzymes and DNA polymerase will add the correct base. After this, DNA ligase connects the loose ends.

DNA ligase catalyzes the joining together of two DNA strands by forming a phosphodiester bond between the two strands. DNA ligase first binds an AMP molecule to a lysine residue in its structure. This AMP is attacked by the 5' phosphate group between the nucleotides, transferring the AMP to the phosphate group. The addition of the AMP to the 5' phosphate makes the phosphorous atom more susceptible to attack by the 3' OH group of the next nucleotide. The attack results in the release of AMP and H_2O and the formation of a phosphodiester bond.

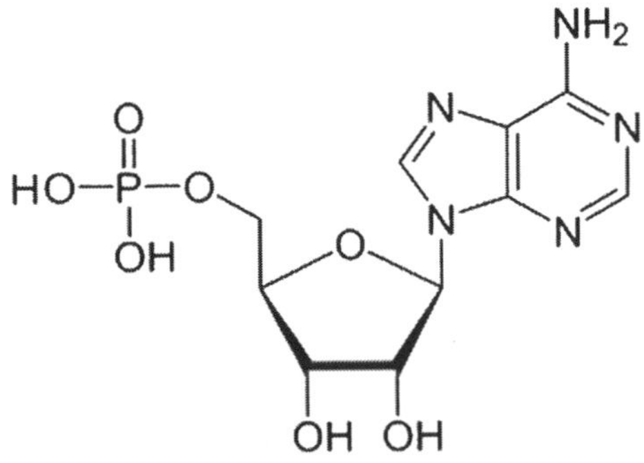

Figure 2 AMP

11. If there are 6 billion base pairs in a diploid cell, how many errors will occur on average during DNA replication in that cell?

    A. 3
    B. 6
    C. 9
    D. 12

12. If the following DNA strand is being opened and replicated from right to left, which strand will be the lagging strand?

$$5' \text{ AGTCTCCGGATTAACGATGC } 3'$$
$$| | | | | | | | | | | | | | | | | | | |$$
$$3' \text{ TCAGAGGCCTAATTGCTACG } 5'$$

    A. The top strand will be the lagging strand because DNA polymerase will be adding nucleotides in the 3' direction from left to right on the top strand.
    B. The top strand will be the lagging strand because DNA polymerase will be adding nucleotides in the 3' direction from right to left on the top strand.
    C. The bottom strand will be the lagging strand because DNA polymerase will be adding nucleotides in the 3' direction from left to right on the bottom strand.
    D. The bottom strand will be the lagging strand because DNA polymerase will be adding nucleotides in the 3' direction from right to left on the bottom strand.

13. Which of the following represents the bond formation between adjacent nucleotides being joined by DNA ligase?

14. Which of the following labeled enzymes on figure 1 is primase?

    A. A
    B. B
    C. C
    D. D

15. Which of the following best describes the effect of addition of AMP to a phosphate group?

    A. AMP is electron donating and contributes to the phosphate's nucleophilic affinity.
    B. AMP is electron donating and contributes to the phosphorus atom's electrophilic nature.
    C. AMP is electron withdrawing.
    D. AMP is electron donating and contributes to the phosphorus atom's electronegativity.

Passage 1 Explanation

A **DNA polymerase** is an enzyme that catalyzes the formation of a strand of nucleotides based on a DNA **template.** During the **S phase** of the cell cycle, two copies of DNA polymerase act on the existing genetic material to create two new copies. The process of **DNA replication** however, requires much more than the presence of DNA polymerase. The many enzymes involved and their function are outlined in figure 1.

Key Terms: DNA polymerase, template, S phase, DNA replication.

Cause and effect: This first paragraph tells us that DNA polymerase is the enzyme that creates new DNA from an existing template. We are told a little about how this process occurs.

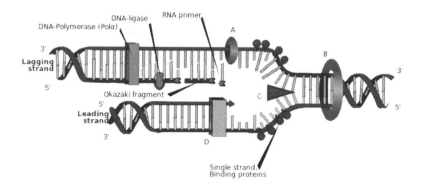

Figure 1 A schematic of DNA replication with all of the enzymes involved

Figure 1 shows the enzymes involved in DNA replication and where their action takes place.

The function of DNA polymerase is simply to read a single strand of DNA and add the correct nucleotide to complement the template. DNA polymerase can only add new nucleotides to the **3' end** of the strand being synthesized. DNA polymerases make about **one mistake per billion** nucleotides added. Most DNA polymerases have the built in ability to recognize and correct these mistakes when they occur. When mistakes occur, the offending base is cleaved out of the strand by enzymes and DNA polymerase will add the correct base. After this, **DNA ligase** connects the loose ends.

Key Terms: 3' end, one mistake per billion nucleotides, DNA ligase.

Cause and effect: We are told a little more about the function of DNA polymerase and how nucleotides are added. We are told that mistakes do occur and that DNA ligase is involved in connecting a break in a strand of DNA that might occur during nucleotide repair.

DNA ligase catalyzes the joining together of two DNA strands by forming a **phosphodiester bond** between the two strands. DNA ligase first binds an **AMP molecule** to a **lysine** residue in its structure. This AMP is attacked by the **5' phosphate group** between the nucleotides, transferring the AMP to the phosphate group. The addition of the AMP to the 5' phosphate makes the phosphorous atom more **susceptible to attack** by the **3' OH** group of the next nucleotide. The attack results in the release of AMP and H_2O and the formation of a phosphodiester bond.

Key Terms: phosphodiester bond, AMP molecule, lysine, 5' phosphate group, 3' OH.

Cause and effect: We are told about the function of DNA ligase and how it brings about the ligation of two adjacent nucleotides. It uses an AMP intermediate to catalyze the 3' OH attack of the adjacent 5' phosphate group.

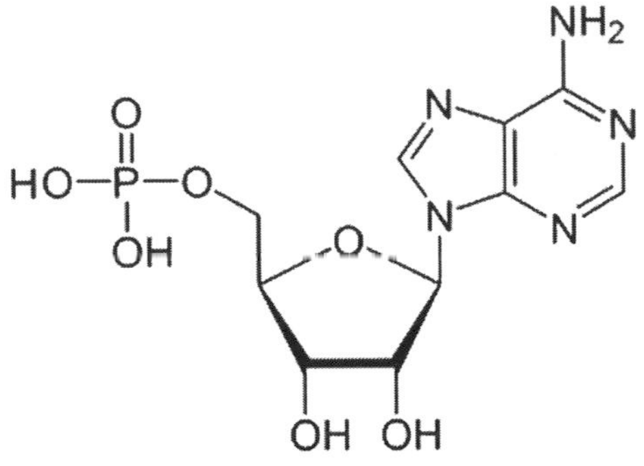

Figure 2 AMP

Figure 2 shows the structure of AMP, which is used in the mechanism of DNA ligase.

11. If there are 6 billion base pairs in a diploid cell, how many errors will occur on average during DNA replication in that cell?
    A. 3
    B. 6
    C. 9
    D. **12**

Answer: **D**. The passage states that 1 mistake will occur per billion nucleotides added on average. If the genome has 6 billion base pairs and we are making a copy of it, then we will need to add 12 billion bases. Thus choice D is correct.

12. If the following DNA strand is being opened and replicated from right to left, which strand will be the lagging strand?

```
5' AGTCTCCGGATTAACGATGC 3'
   I I I I I I I I I I I I I I I I I I I I
3' TCAGAGGCCTAATTGCTACG 5'
```

    A. The top strand will be the lagging strand because DNA polymerase will be adding nucleotides in the 3' direction from left to right on the top strand.
    B. The top strand will be the lagging strand because DNA polymerase will be adding nucleotides in the 3' direction from right to left on the top strand.
    C. **The bottom strand will be the lagging strand because DNA polymerase will be adding nucleotides in the 3' direction from left to right on the bottom strand.**
    D. The bottom strand will be the lagging strand because DNA polymerase will be adding nucleotides in the 3' direction from right to left on the bottom strand.

Answer: **C**. This question asks us to consider the fact that DNA polymerase must add nucleotides on the 3' side of the strand being synthesized. This means that it will synthesize in the direction of the 5' end of the template strand. Thus, if the DNA is opening at the right, the bottom strand will be the lagging strand where Okazaki fragments are formed. Thus choice C is correct.

13. Which of the following represents the bond formation between adjacent nucleotides being joined by DNA ligase?

Answer: **D**. This question asks us to interpret what is stated in the last paragraph. The paragraph states that the 3' OH group of one nucleotide attacks the 5' phosphorus of the next. Since we are dealing with DNA, the 2 carbon should not have an OH group attached. Thus choice D is correct.

A, C: The phosphate does not attack a carbon.
B: This is an RNA molecule attacking the phosphate.

14. Which of the following labeled enzymes on figure 1 is primase?

    A. **A**
    B. B
    C. C
    D. D

Answer: **A**. This question requires outside knowledge. DNA primase adds an RNA primer to which DNA polymerase can begin working. Thus choice A is correct.

B: This is topoisomerase, which helps prevent DNA supercoiling during transcription and duplication.
C: This is helicase, which unwinds the DNA during transcription and duplication.
D: This is DNA polymerase, which assembles the nucleotides needed during DNA duplication.

15. Which of the following best describes the effect of addition of AMP to a phosphate group?

    A. AMP is electron donating and contributes to the phosphate's nucleophilic affinity.
    B. AMP is electron donating and contributes to the phosphorus atom's electrophilic nature.
    C. **AMP is electron withdrawing.**
    D. AMP is electron donating and contributes to the phosphorus atom's electronegativity.

Answer: **C.** This question asks us to interpret what is stated in the last paragraph. The paragraph states that the addition of AMP to the 5' phosphate group makes it susceptible to attack by OH which is a nucleophile. This means that the phosphate group becomes less electron rich. This can only occur if AMP is withdrawing electron density from the 5' phosphate group. Thus choice C is correct.

A, B, and D: AMP cannot be adding electron density to the phosphate group because it is being attacked by a nucleophile.

Passage 2 (Questions 16-20)

Secretin is secreted by the small intestine in response to lowered pH. Secretin is a linear peptide hormone.

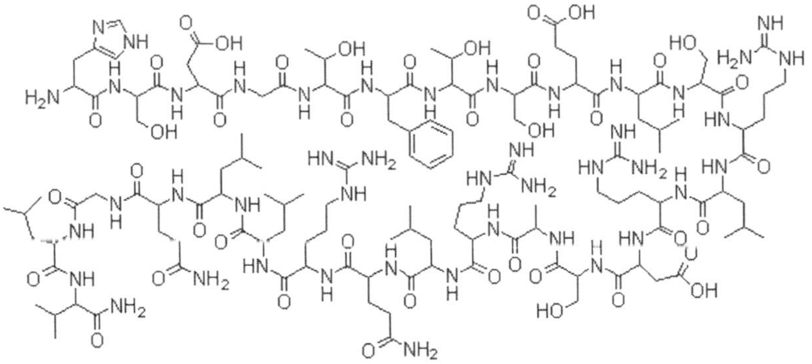

Figure 1 The structure of secretin

Cholecystokinin is an enzyme whose action is enhanced by the presence of secretin. Cholecystokinin is secreted from the duodenum when fat reaches the small intestine. Cholecystokinin stimulates contraction of the gallbladder and stimulates the pancreas to secrete enzymes to aid in digestion. The following enzymes are released by the pancreas:

Table 1 Some enzymes in pancreatic juice and their function

Enzyme	Function
Lipase	Break down fats
Nuclease	Break phosphodiester bonds
Trypsinogen → trypsin	Break down proteins
Chymotrypsinogen → chymotrypsin	Break down proteins
Amylase	Break down starches
Procarboxypeptidase → carboxypeptidase	Break down peptides

Trypsinogen, chymotrypsinogen and procarboxypeptidase are zymogens, inactive forms of enzymes. They are activated by trypsin, which is itself the active form of the zymogen trypsinogen. Trypsinogen can be formed into trypsin by the enzyme enterokinase, which is released from the cells of the duodenum.

Amylase, nuclease, and lipase are able to directly catalyze the metabolism of certain molecules. Amylase functions to break down starch, a polymer of glucose molecules.

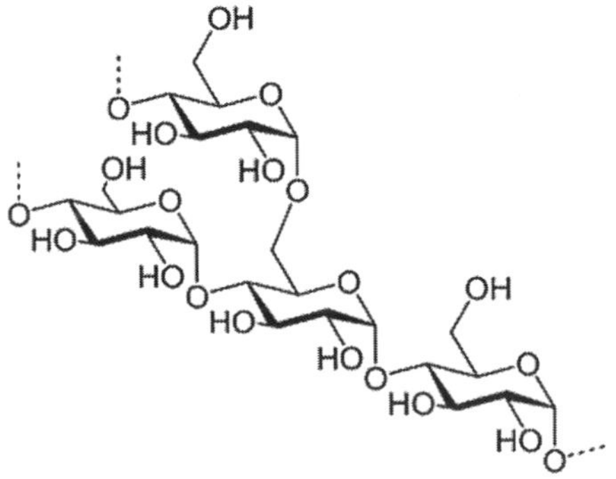

Figure 2 A starch molecule

Amylase breaks down starches into maltose subunits. Maltose is a disaccharide composed of two glucose units joined in an α(1-4) glycosidic linkage.

16. How does the small intestine know to release secretin only after a meal?
    A. The increase in hydrogen ions from the breakdown of peptides and carbohydrates lowers the pH in the small intestine.
    B. The release of hydrochloric acid in the stomach lowers the pH in the small intestine.
    C. Acetic acid, a byproduct of carbohydrate digestion, lowers the pH in the small intestine.
    D. The release of bile acids lowers the pH in the small intestine.

17. Which of the following, if absent, would lead to the biggest decrease in our ability to digest proteins?
    A. Chymotrypsinogen
    B. Chymotrypsin
    C. Carboxypeptidase
    D. Enterokinase

18. Which of the following enzymes catalyzes the reaction below?

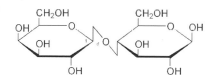

    A. Sucrase
    B. Lactase
    C. Maltase
    D. Lipase

19. Which of the following is the structure of maltose?
    A.

    C.

    B.

    D.

20. Which of the following is true concerning secretin?

    A. Secretin is unique because the carboxyl-terminal amino acid is an amide.
    B. Secretin is unique because it contains equal amounts of basic and acidic side groups.
    C. Secretin is unique because the amine-terminal residue contains a basic side group.
    D. Secretin is unique because the carboxyl-terminal residue is hydrophobic.

Passage 2 Explanation

Secretin is secreted by the small intestine in response to lowered pH. Secretin is a linear **peptide hormone**.

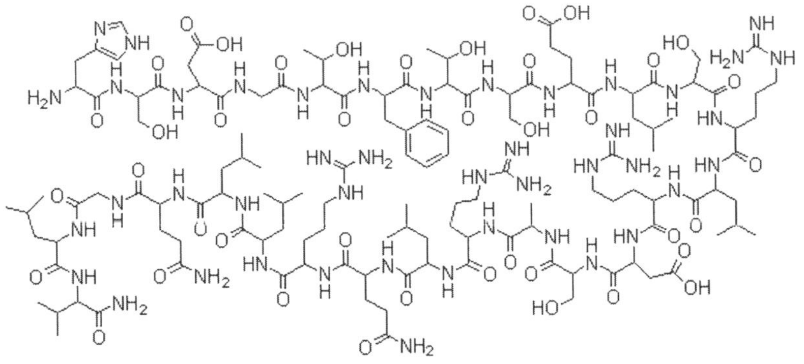

Figure 1 The structure of secretin

Figure 1 Shows the amino acid sequence of secretin

Cholecystokinin is an enzyme whose action is enhanced by the presence of secretin. Cholecystokinin is secreted from the **duodenum** when fat reaches the small intestine. Cholecystokinin stimulates contraction of the **gallbladder** and stimulates the **pancreas** to secrete enzymes to aid in digestion. The following enzymes are released by the pancreas:

Key Terms: secretin, peptide hormone, cholecystokinin, duodenum, gallbladder, pancreas.

Cause and Effect: secretin enhances the action of cholecystokinin. Cholecystokinin causes contraction of the gallbladder. Cholecystokinin causes secretion of pancreatic enzymes.

Enzyme	Function
Lipase	Break down fats
Nuclease	Break phosphodiester bonds
Trypsinogen → trypsin	Break down proteins
Chymotrypsinogen → chymotrypsin	Break down proteins
Amylase	Break down starches
Procarboxypeptidase → carboxypeptidase	Break down peptides

Trypsinogen, chymotrypsinogen and procarboxypeptidase are **zymogens**, inactive forms of enzymes. They are activated by **trypsin**, which is itself the active form of the zymogen trypsinogen. Trypsinogen can be formed into trypsin by the enzyme **enterokinase**, which is released from the cells of the duodenum.

Key Terms: trypsinogen, chymotrypsinogen, procarboxypeptidase, zymogens, trypsin, enterokinase.

Cause and Effect: enterokinase catalyzes the formation of trypsin from trypsinogen. Trypsin catalyzes the activation of all other zymogens in pancreatic juice.

Amylase, nuclease, and lipase are able to directly catalyze the metabolism of certain molecules. Amylase functions to break down **starch**, a polymer of glucose molecules,

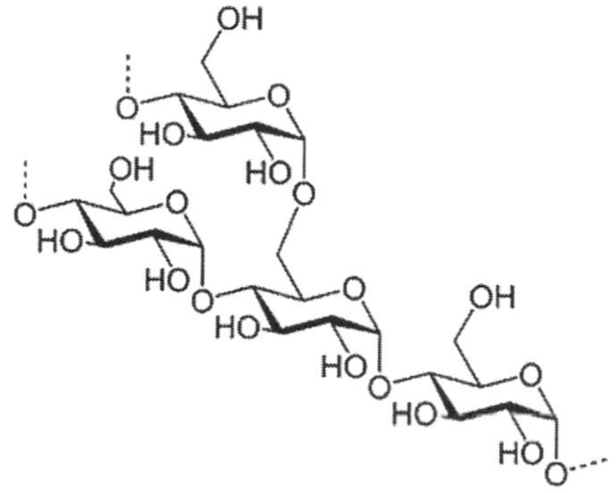

Figure 2 A starch molecule

Amylase breaks down starches into **maltose** subunits. Maltose is a disaccharide composed of two glucose units joined in an **α(1-4) glycosidic linkage**.

Key Terms: amylase, nuclease, lipase, starch, maltose, α(1-4) glycosidic linkage.

Cause and effect: The last section tells us about amylase and its function. We learn what a maltose disaccharide looks like.

16. How does the small intestine know to release secretin only after a meal?
    A. The increase in hydrogen ions from the breakdown of peptides and carbohydrates lowers the pH in the small intestine.
    B. **The release of hydrochloric acid in the stomach lowers the pH in the small intestine.**
    C. Acetic acid, a byproduct of carbohydrate digestion, lowers the pH in the small intestine.
    D. The release of bile acids lowers the pH in the small intestine.

Answer: **B** - This question asks us to consider why the pH of the small intestine will decrease after a meal. The reason is that the stomach releases hydrochloric acid so that the chyme entering the small intestine is acidic. Thus choice B is correct.

A: The breakdown of macronutrients doesn't lower the pH.
C: Acetic acid is not a byproduct of carbohydrate digestion.
D: The release of bile acids would lower the pH but secretin is one of the first things secreted and promotes the secretion of bile acids.

17. Which of the following, if absent, would lead to the biggest decrease in our ability to digest proteins?
    A. Chymotrypsinogen
    B. Chymotrypsin
    C. Carboxypeptidase
    D. **Enterokinase**

Answer: **D** - Remember that enterokinase activates trypsin which activates all the other zymogens that break down proteins. Thus choice D is correct.

18. Which of the following enzymes catalyzes the reaction below?
    A. **Sucrase**
    B. Lactase
    C. Maltase
    D. Lipase

Answer: **A** - Remember that a glucose linked to a fructose is a sucrose molecule. It makes sense that sucrase is the enzyme that catalyzes this reaction. Thus choice A is correct.

B: Lactase catalyzes the breakdown of lactose into glucose and galactose.
C: Maltase catalyzes the breakdown of maltose into two glucose molecules.
D: Lipase catalyzes the breakdown of fats.

19. Which of the following is the structure of maltose?

Answer: **D** - The passage states that maltose consists of two glucose molecules with an α(1-4) glycosidic linkage. Thus choice D is correct.

A: This is a beta linkage.
B: This is a beta linkage between galactose and glucose.
C: This contains a fructose.

20. Which of the following is true concerning secretin?

    A. <u>**Secretin is unique because the carboxyl-terminal amino acid is an amide.**</u>
    B. Secretin is unique because it contains equal amounts of basic and acidic side groups.
    C. Secretin is unique because the amine-terminal residue contains a basic side group.
    D. Secretin is unique because the carboxyl-terminal residue is hydrophobic.

Answer: **A** - This question requires us to consider Figure 1. Normally, the carboxyl terminal amino acid ends in a carboxylic acid. Secretin ends in an amide (which is a carbonyl group attached to a nitrogen group). Thus choice A is correct.

B: This is not true of secretin.
C, D: This is not unique to secretin.

Passage 3 (Questions 21-25)

Muscle contraction is a complicated process with many steps. It all begins with an action potential that is transmitted along a motor neuron towards muscle tissue. Efferent somatic neurons use the neurotransmitter acetylcholine:

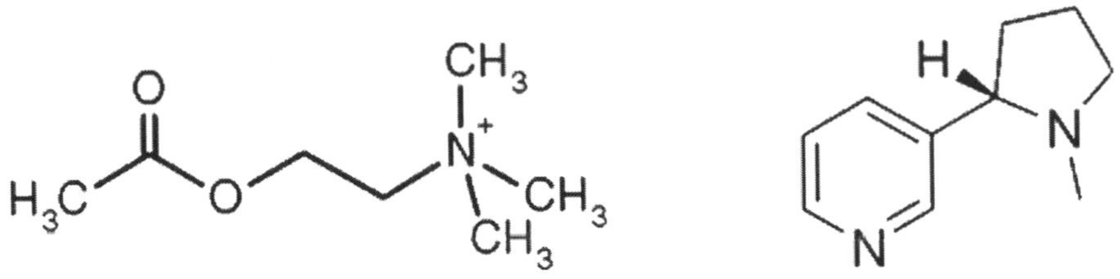

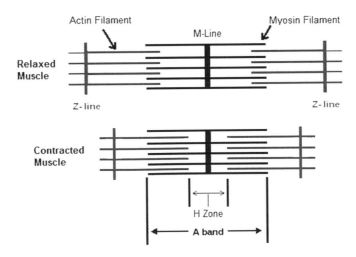

Figure 1 Acetylcholine (left) and nicotine (right)

When the action potential reaches a muscle cell, acetylcholine is released and binds a nicotinic acetylcholine receptor on the neuromuscular junction. Nicotinic receptors are so named because they also bind nicotine. When this receptor is activated, it causes depolarization of the sarcomere and an electrochemical signal is transduced along the muscle fiber, depolarizing all the sarcomeres in the fiber. When a sarcomere is depolarized, calcium channels in the cell's membrane open, which in turn opens the calcium channels of the sarcoplasmic reticulum and calcium rushes into the cytoplasm of the muscle cells.

The actual contraction of muscle occurs as a result of calcium binding troponin C, a compound found on thin actin filaments. The binding of calcium to troponin C causes tropomyosin, which normally blocks binding sites on the thin filaments, to move. The binding sites are exposed and thick filament myosin heads can interact with thin filaments, pulling them toward the M line.

Figure 2 The filaments in a sarcomere and how they move when the sarcomere contracts

Myosin can freely bind the thin filaments. Myosin at this stage is also bound to an ADP and inorganic phosphate group, which when released, cause the stroke and pull inward toward the M line. When ATP binds myosin, myosin releases the thin filaments and the ATP is hydrolyzed, allowing the myosin to revert to its original state, ready to bind another binding site on the actin fibers. Each stroke moves the thin filaments about 10 nm closer to the M-line.

21. Which of the following shortens during the contraction of two adjacent sarcomeres?
    I. Length of H zone
    II. Distance between Z lines
    III. Length of the I band

    A. I only
    B. I and II only
    C. II and III only
    D. I, II, and III

22. Which of the following would result in paralysis of skeletal muscle?
    A. A peptide hormone that agonistically binds nicotinic acetylcholine receptors
    B. A peptide hormone that antagonistically binds muscarinic receptors
    C. A peptide hormone that antagonistically binds nicotinic acetylcholine receptors
    D. A peptide hormone that agonistically binds muscarinic receptors

23. How many sets of power strokes in myosin filaments are required to shorten a sarcomere by 80 nm?
    A. 4
    B. 8
    C. 16
    D. It depends on the length of the sarcomere.

24. Given the need for a tertiary or quaternary nitrogen for nicotinic receptor binding, which of the following is LEAST likely to be able to bind a nicotinic receptor?

    A.

    B.

    C.

    D.

25. Which of the following must be present in abundance for skeletal muscle contraction to begin?
    I. Calcium
    II. ADP
    III. ATP

    A. III only
    B. I and II only
    C. I and III only
    D. II and III only

Passage 3 Explanation

Muscle contraction is a complicated process with many steps. It all begins with an action potential that is transmitted along a motor neuron towards muscle tissue. **Efferent somatic neurons** use the neurotransmitter **acetylcholine**.

Key Terms: muscle contraction, efferent somatic neurons, acetylcholine.

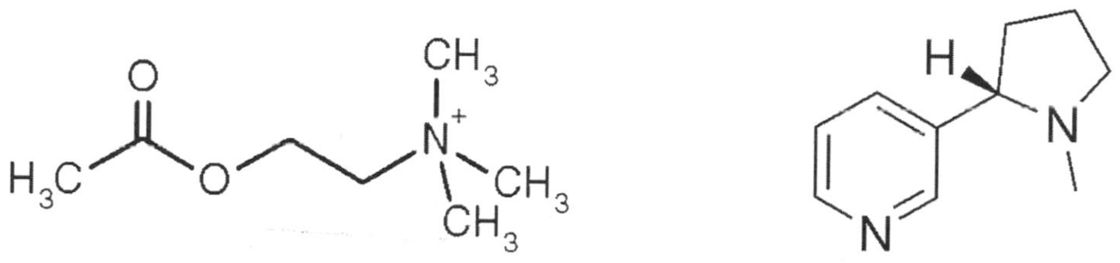

Figure 1 Acetylcholine (left) and nicotine (right)

Figure 1 shows the structures of acetylcholine and nicotine, which bind nicotinic acetylcholine receptors

When the action potential reaches a muscle cell, acetylcholine is released and binds a **nicotinic acetylcholine receptor** on the neuromuscular junction. Nicotinic receptors are so named because they also bind **nicotine**. When this receptor is activated, it causes depolarization of the sarcomere and an electrochemical signal is transduced along the muscle fiber, depolarizing all the sarcomeres in the fiber. When a sarcomere is depolarized, **calcium channels** in the cell's membrane open, which in turn opens the calcium channels of the **sarcoplasmic reticulum** and calcium rushes into the cytoplasm of the muscle cells.

Key Terms: nicotinic acetylcholine receptor, nicotine, calcium channels, sarcoplasmic reticulum.

Cause and Effect: the binding of acetylcholine opens voltage gated channels, which opens calcium voltage gated channels in the sarcoplasmic reticulum; this increases the calcium ion concentration of the cell dramatically.

The actual contraction of muscle occurs as a result of calcium binding **troponin C**, a compound found on **thin actin filaments**. The binding of calcium to troponin C causes **tropomyosin**, which normally blocks binding sites on the thin filaments, to move. The binding sites are exposed and thick filament **myosin** heads can interact with thin filaments, pulling them toward the **M line**.

Key Terms: troponin C, thin actin filaments, tropomyosin, myosin, M-line.

Cause and Effect: calcium binding troponin C causes tropomyosin to move, which allows for myosin head to bind actin filaments.

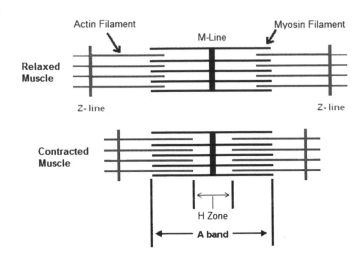

Figure 2 The filaments in a sarcomere and how they move when the sarcomere contracts

Figure 2 shows how a sarcomere changes after contraction.

Myosin can freely bind the thin filaments. Myosin at this stage is also bound to an **ADP and inorganic phosphate** group, which when released, cause the stroke and pull inward toward the M line. When **ATP** binds myosin, myosin releases the thin filaments and the ATP is hydrolyzed, allowing the myosin to revert to its original state, ready to bind another binding site on the actin fibers. Each stroke moves the thin filaments about **10 nm** closer to the M-line.

Key Terms: ADP, inorganic phosphate, ATP, 10 nm.

Cause and Effect: When ADP and P$_i$ are removed from myosin, the power stroke occurs. When ATP binds myosin, it releases the thin filaments.

21. Which of the following shortens during the contraction of two adjacent sarcomeres?
     I. Length of H zone
     II. Distance between Z lines
     III. Length of the I band

    A. I only
    B. I and II only
    C. II and III only
    D. <u>I, II, and III</u>

Answer: **D** - Remember that the Z-lines are being brought closer together and that the actin filaments are being brought closer together. Because there is more overlap between actin and myosin, both the H zone and the I band shorten, since those are places where the filaments don't overlap..

22. Which of the following would result in paralysis of skeletal muscle?
    A. A peptide hormone that agonistically binds nicotinic acetylcholine receptors
    B. A peptide hormone that antagonistically binds muscarinic receptors
    C. <u>A peptide hormone that antagonistically binds nicotinic acetylcholine receptors</u>
    D. A peptide hormone that agonistically binds muscarinic receptors

Answer: **C** - Paralysis of skeletal muscle will occur if the function of nicotinic acetylcholine receptors is interrupted. An antagonist is a molecule that interrupts the normal function of another enzyme or receptor. Thus choice C is correct.

23. How many sets of power strokes in myosin filaments are required to shorten a sarcomere by 80 nm?
    A. <u>4</u>
    B. 8
    C. 16
    D. It depends on the length of the sarcomere.

Answer: **A** - The passage states that each actin filament is moved 10 nm per power stroke. Since there are actin filaments on both sides of the Z line in figure 2, we require only a 40 nm movement on either side. Thus choice A is correct.

24. Given the need for a tertiary or quaternary nitrogen for nicotinic receptor binding, which of the following is LEAST likely to be able to bind a nicotinic receptor?

Answer: **C** - We are given two examples of molecules that bind nicotinic receptors in figure 1. Choice C is unlike either example and does not have a tertiary or quaternary amine. Thus choice C is the best answer.

A: This molecule has a tertiary amine group just like nicotine
B: This molecule has a quaternary ammonium ion just like acetylcholine.
D: This molecule has a tertiary amine group just like nicotine

25. Which of the following must be present in abundance for skeletal muscle contraction to begin?
    I. Calcium
    II. ADP
    III. ATP

    A. III only
    B. I and II only
    C. **I and III**
    D. II, and III

Answer: **C** - The passage states (and you should know from outside knowledge) that muscles need Ca^{2+} ions to contract. Once calcium binds to troponin, it causes a conformational shift in the tropomyosin protein. This shift exposes myosin binding sites on actin, which allows the actin-myosin cross links to form, which causes the filaments to slide over each other, causing contraction. Additionally, we need ATP to remove myosin from actin filaments. Thus choice C is correct.

A, B, D: ADP is the product of ATP hydrolysis and is not the energy source required for the muscle power stroke. We do not need ADP because ATP is hydrolyzed to ADP and P_i after binding myosin.

THIS PAGE LEFT

INTENTIONALLY BLANK

Passage 4 (Questions 26-30)

Erythropoiesis is the process by which new red blood cells are created in the body. Typical red blood cells will circulate for about 120 days, after which time they undergo apoptosis.

The process begins with the secretion of the hormone erythropoietin from the kidney. The kidney contains chemoreceptors that react to a drop in O_2 partial pressure in circulating blood. In response to a hypoxic environment, kidney cells produce erythropoietin.

Once erythropoietin is produced and secreted it targets cells in bone marrow to direct the formation of erythrocyte precursors from hematopoietic stem cells. A hematopoietic stem cell is a cell isolated from the blood or bone marrow that can renew itself, can differentiate to a variety of specialized cells, can mobilize out of the bone marrow into circulating blood, and can undergo programmed cell death. Once the cell reaches the stage of reticulocyte, it has only to increase production of hemoglobin to become an erythrocyte. The percent of reticulocytes in circulation is a good indicator of the level of new erythrocytes creation. Normally reticulocytes form around 1% of all red blood cells.

Red blood cell count needs to be carefully regulated so that complications do not arise from having too few or too many red blood cells in circulation at a given time. The fact that erythropoietin binds red blood cells while in circulation means that even in large amounts, erythropoietin will not act unless there is a significant reduction in erythrocyte count. Hepcidin is a peptide hormone that inhibits iron release from macrophages in bone marrow, making it impossible to form the heme group necessary for erythrocyte function. Increased levels of hepcidin therefore coincide with decreased hematocrit. Hepcidin also acts as an inhibitor of ferroportin, which transports iron from the gut into the body.

26. If a person donates blood on January 1, on which day are they most likely to have elevated amounts of erythropoietin in circulation?
    A. February 6
    B. March 4
    C. May 2
    D. July 1

27. Under which of the following categories does blood fall?
    A. Heart tissue
    B. Lymph tissue
    C. Kidney tissue
    D. Connective tissue

28. Which of the following might result from living at high elevation?
    A. Clogged arteries
    B. Greater plasma volume
    C. Reduced hematocrit
    D. Decreased hepcidin production

29. Which of the following would lead to reticulocyte count of 0.4%?
    A. Increased ferroportin activity
    B. Decreased hepcidin activity
    C. An increase in blood temperature
    D. An increase in blood pH

30. If each erythrocyte contains 2.8×10^8 hemoglobin molecules and there are 2.5×10^{13} erythrocytes in circulation, how many grams of iron are in circulation?
    A. 0.7 grams
    B. 2.6 grams
    C. 7 grams
    D. 10.4 grams

Passage 4 Explanations

Erythropoiesis is the process by which new **red blood cells** are created in the body. Typical red blood cells will circulate for about **120 days**, after which time they undergo **apoptosis**.

Key Terms: Erythropoiesis, red blood cells, 120 days, apoptosis

Cause and effect: We are told what erythropoiesis is and how long erythrocytes live in circulation.

The process begins with the secretion of the hormone **erythropoietin** from the **kidney**. The kidney contains **chemoreceptors** that react to a drop in O_2 **partial pressure** in circulating blood. In response to a **hypoxic** environment, kidney cells produce erythropoietin.

Key Terms: erythropoietin, kidney, chemoreceptors, O_2 partial pressure, hypoxic.

Cause and Effect: decreased O_2 partial pressure leads to erythropoietin secretion.

Once erythropoietin is produced and secreted it targets cells in **bone marrow** to direct the formation of **erythrocyte** precursors from **hematopoietic stem cells**. A hematopoietic stem cell is a cell isolated from the blood or bone marrow that can renew itself, can differentiate to a variety of specialized cells, can mobilize out of the bone marrow into circulating blood, and can undergo programmed cell death. Once the cell reaches the stage of **reticulocyte**, it has only to increase production of hemoglobin to become an erythrocyte. The percent of reticulocytes in circulation is a good indicator of the level of new erythrocyte creation. Normally reticulocytes form around **1%** of all red blood cells.

Key Terms: bone marrow, erythrocyte precursors, hematopoietic stem cells, reticulocyte, 1%.

Cause and effect: We are told in this paragraph that erythropoietin targets stem cells in bone marrow to direct the formation of erythrocytes. Reticulocytes are precursors of erythrocytes and are about 1% of all red blood cells in circulation. The number of reticulocytes in circulation indicates the level at which erythropoiesis has been taking place.

Red blood cell count needs to be carefully regulated so that complications do not arise from having too few or too many red blood cells in circulation at a given time. The fact that erythropoietin binds red blood cells while in circulation means that even in large amounts, erythropoietin will not act unless there is a significant reduction in erythrocyte count. **Hepcidin** is a peptide hormone that inhibits iron release from **macrophages** in bone marrow, making it impossible to form the **heme** group necessary for erythrocyte function. Increased levels of hepcidin therefore coincide with decreased hematocrit. Hepcidin also acts as an inhibitor of **ferroportin**, which transports iron from the gut into the body.

Key Terms: hepcidin, macrophages, heme, ferroportin.

Cause and Effect: hepcidin inhibits erythropoiesis, ferroportin allows it to take place.

26. If a person donates blood on January 1, on which day are they most likely to have elevated amounts of erythropoietin in circulation?
    A. February 6
    B. March 4
    C. **May 2**
    D. July 1

Answer: **C** - The passages states that erythrocytes live for about 4 months. If you donated blood on January 1, you would have an immediate increase in erythropoietin to create red blood cells and make up for your loss. However, the influx of red blood cells will all die at about the same time, 4 months from January 1. If this is true, those cells would die around May 2 and we would need an influx of erythropoietin. Choice C is the best answer.

27. Under which of the following categories docs blood fall?
    A. Heart tissue
    B. Lymph tissue
    C. Kidney tissue
    D. **Connective tissue**

Answer: **D** - Blood is connective tissue. Thus choice D is correct.

28. Which of the following might result from living at high elevation?
    A. **Clogged arteries**
    B. Greater plasma volume
    C. Reduced hematocrit
    D. Decreased hepcidin production

Answer: **A** - At a high elevation, oxygen is at a lower partial pressure, making it less readily available to enter the body. This means that the kidney will be signaled to release more erythropoietin, resulting in more red blood cells. Red blood cells are the heaviest and thickest part of blood. An increased hematocrit can lead to more viscous blood and arteries that are more easily clogged. Thus choice A is correct.

B: There is no reason to think that plasma volume will increase if red blood cell count increases.
C: There will be an increased hematocrit.
D: Hepcidin is an antagonist of erythropoiesis, thus we can expect higher levels of hepcidin if red blood cell count becomes abnormally high.

29. Which of the following would lead to reticulocyte count of 0.4%?
    A. Increased ferroportin activity
    B. Decreased hepcidin activity
    C. An increase in blood temperature
    D. **An increase in blood pH**

Answer: **D** - Remember that an increase in blood pH results in a greater binding affinity of hemoglobin for oxygen. This means that the kidney will sense higher levels of oxygen in the blood and release less erythropoietin, resulting in a lower reticulocyte count. Thus choice D is correct.

A: Increased ferroportin activity will lend itself to the creation of more reticulocytes.

B: Decreased hepcidin activity will allow for increased creation of reticulocytes.

C: An increase in blood temperature shifts the hemoglobin binding curve to the right, meaning that there will be less oxygen in the blood at the kidneys and they will release erythropoietin, resulting in a higher reticulocyte count.

30. If each erythrocyte contains 2.8×10^8 hemoglobin molecules and there are 2.5×10^{13} erythrocytes in circulation, how many grams of iron are in circulation?

    A. 0.7 grams
    B. <u>**2.6 grams**</u>
    C. 7 grams
    D. 10.4 grams

Answer: **B** - First we multiply 2.8×10^8 by 2.5×10^{13} to get 7×10^{21} hemoglobin molecules in circulation, each one contains four heme groups with one iron ion per heme. This means we have $7 \times 4 \times 10^{21} = 2.8 \times 10^{22}$ Fe atoms. Divide by Avogadro's number. We can approximate $2.8/6.022 = .5$ so we get 0.5×10^{-1} mol Fe. Multiply this by 56 grams/mole to get 2.8 grams of Fe. This is closest to choice B, which is the correct answer.

TIMED
SECTION 1
59 Questions, 95 Minutes

(Use the tear-out answer sheet provided in Appendix D)

Passage I (Questions 1-5)

Alzheimer's disease (AD) is a common form of progressive dementia observed in both familial and non-familial forms. To evaluate the potential involvement of dysfunctional intracellular Ca^{2+} mobilization on AD-associated cognitive deficits, Ca^{2+} signaling was measured as fluorescence from human skin fibroblasts taken from healthy age-matched (AC) and healthy young (YC) donors, and from individuals with Alzheimer's disease (AD), where all cell lines were loaded with the calcium indicator fura-2. Fibroblasts were either untreated, treated with bombesin, an agent that upon binding its G-coupled protein receptor activates phospholipase C (PLC) to generate inositol 1,4,5-trisphosphate (IP_3) (which triggers release of calcium into the cytoplasm), or treated with Ca^{2+} channel blockers—agents that disrupt the movement of Ca^{2+} through calcium channels. Measurements were made under the extracellular Ca^{2+} conditions indicated, along with the results of the experiments, in Figures 1 and 2.

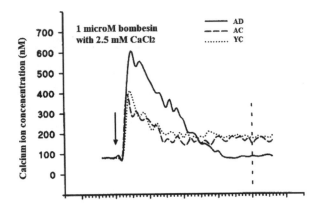

Figure 1 Ca^{2+} response induced by 1 microM bombesin (Note: arrow indicates the time of bombesin application).

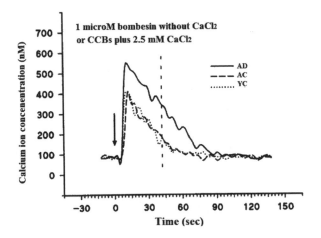

Figure 2 Ca^{2+} response induced by 1 microM bombesin without $CaCl_2$ present, and, when performed independently, Ca^{2+} response induced by 1 microM bombesin when 2.5 mM $CaCl_2$ and divalent blockers of calcium channels (CCB) were present in the media (Note: the Ca^{2+} response by cells under both treatment conditions was identical).

Further treatment of the cell lines with thapisgargin, an inhibitor of the Ca^{2+}-ATPase in the endoplasmic reticulum (ER) which acts to concentrate Ca^{2+} within the ER, elicited the same Ca^{2+} signals from AD, AC and YC cell lines.

1. Under several treatment conditions shown in Figures 1 and 2, tested fibroblasts displayed a sustained phase of constant Ca^{2+} signaling above baseline levels. Which of the following statements describing this sustained signaling is NOT supported by passage information?
    A. The sustained phase elicited by bombesin from AC and YC were eliminated by the removal of extracellular Ca^{2+}.
    B. Divalent cation Ca^{2+} channel blockers eliminated the sustained phase signals in all control cells.
    C. The sustained phases of fibroblast Ca^{2+} signaling do not depend on intracellularly stored calcium.
    D. The Ca^{2+} signal of AD fibroblasts showed no sustained phase.

2. The researchers concluded that AD-specific differences in initial bombesin-induced Ca^{2+} signaling in skin fibroblasts are due to dysfunction of an intracellular component of the PLC-IP$_3$ system. What additional findings would most *weaken* this conclusion?
    A. The thapisgargin-induced Ca^{2+} signal does not depend on extracellular Ca^{2+}.
    B. Bradykinin, another activator of PLC, elicited larger Ca^{2+} signals in AD than in YC cells.
    C. Radioligand binding revealed a greater number of bombesin binding sites in AD fibroblasts.
    D. Thapisgargin mobilized Ca^{2+} without a corresponding increase in inositol phosphates.

3. Which of the following steps in bombesin-induced Ca^{2+} signaling transduction depends on the availability of a high-energy bond?
    I.   Binding of bombesin to its receptor
    II. G-protein activation
    III. Ca^{2+} reuptake into the ER
    IV. Protein kinase C kinase activity

    A. I and III only
    B. II and III only
    C. II, III, and IV only
    D. I, II, III, and IV

4. The researchers wish to relate AD-associated cognitive deficits to the AD-specific alterations of Ca^{2+} shown in the passage. What additional finding would best support this connection?
    A. Both familial and non-familial AD skin fibroblasts display AD-specific alterations.
    B. AD-specific differences in Ca^{2+} signaling have systemic expression in AD cells.
    C. Ca^{2+} signaling in AD-neurons increases with greater extracellular calcium concentration.
    D. AD-specific alterations are restricted to AD skin tissue fibroblasts.

5. Cleavage of phosphatidylinositol 4,5-bisphosphate (PIP2) by PLC results in:
    A. retention of diacylglycerol (DAG) within the membrane and diffusion of IP$_3$ within the cell.
    B. retention of IP$_3$ within the membrane and diffusion of diacylglycerol (DAG) within the cell.
    C. retention of diacylglycerol (DAG) and IP$_3$ within the membrane.
    D. diffusion of diacylglycerol (DAG) and IP$_3$ within the cell.

Passage II (Questions 6-10)

The heart is a muscular organ responsible for pumping nutrient- and oxygen-rich blood to every part of the body. The human heart consists of four chambers, two atria and two ventricles, separated by valves. The pulmonary vein and artery directly connect the heart to the lungs, where blood is oxygenated prior to exiting the heart through the aorta. Heart rate is highly susceptible to changes in hormone levels. One example of this is epinephrine, which when secreted with activation of the sympathetic nervous system, can dramatically increase heart rate. The heart also secretes its own hormone called atrial natriuretic peptide (ANP). ANP is secreted by atrial myocytes in response to high blood pressure, causing vasodilation and loss of sodium from the blood. This leads to reduction in blood volume and thus reduction in systemic blood pressure.

There are two substantial differences between the fetal heart and the adult heart. In fetal circulation, there is an opening between the left and right atria known as the foramen ovale that allows a portion of the blood to go directly from the right atrium to the left atrium, thereby bypassing pulmonary circulation. The blood that does not enter the left atrium is pumped into the right ventricle before entering the pulmonary artery. Fetuses also have a special connection between the pulmonary artery and aorta called the ductus arteriosus, which allows the blood that does not pass through the foramen ovale to still bypass the lungs. When a baby is born, changes in pulmonary pressure cause the foramen ovale and the ductus arteriosus to close. In rare cases, the foramen ovale does not completely close when the child is born, and a hole remains between the two atria into adulthood. This is called an atrial septal defect.

In a physiology lab at a local hospital, a researcher discovers two important action potential recordings collected the prior week that were accidentally put in the trash. In the experiment, electrode recordings were taken in two separate muscle tissues in a single healthy patient. In an effort to avoid an uncomfortable discussion with the principle investigator, the researcher tries to match the recordings to the appropriate muscle tissue.

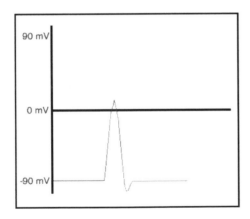

Action Potential Recording A

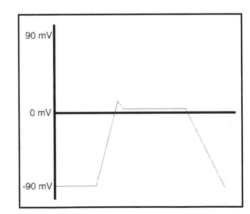

Action Potential Recording B

6. Upon entering the heart through the vena cava, blood travels through numerous tissues before it exits the heart. Which of the following represents the path that blood travels from the time it enters the adult heart to the time it enters systemic circulation?
   A. Right Atrium → Mitral Valve → Pulmonary Vein → Left Ventricle → Aorta
   B. Left Atrium → Tricuspid Valve → Pulmonary Artery → Right Atrium → Aorta
   C. Right Atrium → Tricuspid Valve → Pulmonary Artery → Pulmonary Vein → Left Ventricle
   D. Right Ventricle → Mitral Valve → Aorta → Tricuspid Valve → Pulmonary Vein

7. The researcher in the passage believes **Recording A** is from cardiac muscle and **Recording B** is from skeletal muscle. Is this correct?
   A. Yes – cardiac muscle action potentials have no refractory period whereas skeletal muscle action potentials have both an absolute and a relative refractory period.
   B. No – skeletal muscle action potentials have a larger depolarization than cardiac muscle action potentials, so **Recording A** is actually skeletal muscle and **Recording B** is cardiac muscle.
   C. Yes – **Recording B** is likely from a skeletal muscle that is being flexed, which is why there is a depolarized plateau seen in the recording.
   D. No – cardiac muscle has an influx of Ca^{2+} ions that balances out the outflux of K^+ ions leading to a plateau in the action potential, so **Recording A** is actually skeletal muscle and **Record B** is cardiac muscle.

8. Which of the following hormone levels would produce effects that would counteract high levels of ANP?
   I. High levels of angiotensin I
   II. Low levels of angiotensinogen
   III. High levels of aldosterone

   A. III only
   B. I and II only
   C. I and III only
   D. I, II, and III

9. An individual born with an atrial septal defect might have which of the following symptoms?
   A. Difficulties regulating body temperature
   B. ANP deficiency
   C. Hyperactivity
   D. Shortness of breath when exercising

10. The mean arterial pressure (MAP) is used to describe the average blood pressure during a single cardiac cycle in a part of the circulatory system. Where in the body is the MAP the highest?
    A. Inferior Vena Cava
    B. Right Ventricle
    C. Aorta
    D. Arterioles

Passage III (Questions 11-15)

Pancreatic ductal adenocarcinoma (PDAC) is a lethal cancer with extremely poor prognosis. The role of miRNAs in other cancers have been elucidated, but due to high tissue heterogeneity of PDAC, studies have not revealed any particular pattern of miRNA dysregulation.

MiRNAs are small non-coding RNA molecules that direct post-transcriptional regulation of gene expression. Typically, miRNAs are produced either from their own transcriptional units or derived from the introns of coding genes. Both undergo different avenues of processing to produce a miRNA/miRNA* duplex. Only one strand is incorporated into the RNA-induced silencing complex (RISC), which interacts with the mRNA, while the other strand is degraded. For partially complementary miRNAs to recognize their targets, only nucleotides 2 through 8 in the 'seed region' have to be perfectly complementary, located in the 3' untranslated region (UTR). As a result of binding, the mRNA is silenced by translational repression or deadenylation. When there is perfect complementarity, the mRNA is silenced by endonucleolytic cleavage and degradation.

The epithelial-mesenchymal transition (EMT), in which cells lose their polarity and adhesion, is the initial step in tumor metastasis. Epithelial cells are highly ordered and display polarity by adhering to one another via tight junctions, while mesenchymal cells differ in shape and display the capacity for migration. Studies have demonstrated that the miR-200 family, a group of functionally related miRNAs, inhibits EMT by negatively regulating transcription factors ZEB1 and ZEB2. Studies have also shown that the tumor suppressor protein E-cadherin regulates EMT through its role in cell adhesion and maintenance of cell polarity. Experiments were conducted to assess whether miR-200 family expression correlates with the epithelial phenotype in PDAC cell lines, and the results are below:

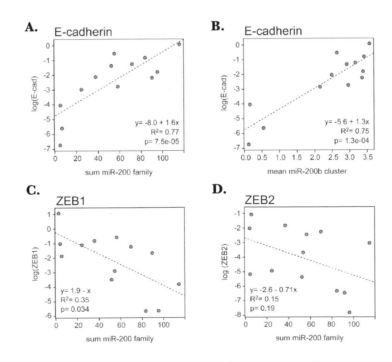

Figure 1 miR-200 family expression vs. log-transformed E-cadherin, ZEB1, and ZEB2 levels

In prostate cancer cell lines, miR-34a was found to be downregulated and suspected to have a role similar to E-cadherin. A vector was used to reintroduce expression of miR-34a into PDAC lines in order to elucidate its role, and some of the experimental data is shown below.

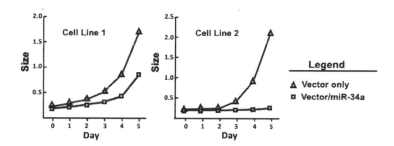

Figure 2 Growth rates of retrovirally-infected PDAC lines

11. Anti-miRs are oligonucleotide analogs have been used therapeutically to correct any defective miRNA-mRNA interaction that contributes causally to a disease. Based on the information given in the passage, which anti-miR would be most effective at silencing the miRNA for the following mRNA transcript?

    5'-...CUAGAGUCCCCGGCGCGCCUUUCUGCUGCUGU...-3'

    A. 5'-UGCUGCUGA-3'
    B. 5'-ACAGCAGCA-3'
    C. 5'-UCCCCGAUG-3'
    D. 5'-CGCGCCGGGG-3'

12. The 70 nucleotide hairpin structure of pre-miRNA is an example of secondary structure for nucleic acids. Which of the following structures would be similarly classified?
    A. DNA-RNA hybrid
    B. α-helix in transmembrane receptors
    C. tRNA cloverleaf
    D. disulfide bond in IgG

13. There are certain elements on a plasmid vector that are essential for ensuring expression of a particular miRNA in the transfected cell. Which of the following is NOT an essential component?
    A. Bacterial origin of replication
    B. Reporter gene
    C. Restriction enzyme sites
    D. Host transcription initiating sequence

14. Based on the growth rate charts of the retrovirally infected PDAC cell lines, what of the following statements best describes the role of miR-34a?
    A. miR-34a expression promotes extensive cell death and necrosis.
    B. miR-34a is less effective at promoting cell death in Cell Line 1.
    C. miR-34a exhibits potent antitumorigenic or anti-tumor forming properties in PDAC cell lines.
    D. miR-34a is strongly downregulated in a majority of the PDAC cell lines.

15. As defined by the passage, what is necessary for the maintenance of the "epithelial" phenotype?
    A. Low levels of miR-34a
    B. High levels of ZEB-1 and ZEB-2
    C. High levels of E-cadherin
    D. Low levels of miR-200

Discrete Set 1 (Questions 16-18)

These questions are **NOT** related to a passage.

16. During diastole:
    A. the ventricles contract and pump blood into the aorta and pulmonary artery.
    B. the vena cava contracts and pumps blood into the right atrium.
    C. the aorta smooth muscle stretches as it is filled with blood from the left ventricle.
    D. the ventricles relax and fill with blood from the atria.

17. When comparing the evolutionary similarity of two organisms, biologists determine that the closest evolutionary relationship between them is reflected by the fact that they are in the same order. Two species that are even more closely related would be placed in the same:
    A. sub-kingdom.
    B. phylum.
    C. family.
    D. class.

18. Which of the following places the components listed in the correct order, following the flow of fluid from the blood plasma to the urine?
    A. Glomerulus; distal convoluted tubule; ureter; collecting duct
    B. Renal artery; proximal convoluted tubule; ascending loop of Henle; descending loop of Henle; ureter
    C. Renal artery; glomerulus; descending loop of Henle; bladder; ureter
    D. Glomerulus; descending loop of Henle; ascending loop of Henle; bladder

THIS PAGE LEFT

INTENTIONALLY BLANK

Passage IV (Questions 19-22)

Parathyroid hormone (PTH) is secreted by cells of the parathyroid glands. It acts to increase the concentration of calcium in the blood, whereas calcitonin acts to decrease calcium concentration. PTH promotes bone resorption by indirectly stimulating osteoclasts, the cells responsible for resorbing bone tissue. Osteoclasts lack PTH receptors, but PTH does bind osteoblasts—cells responsible for bone synthesis. Binding stimulates osteoblasts to increase their expression of RANKL and inhibits their expression of OPG. Binding of RANK to RANKL stimulates osteoclast differentiation. OPG binds to RANKL and blocks it from interacting with RANK. Additionally, PTH acts on the kidneys, where it enhances active reabsorption of Ca^{2+} and Mg^{2+}, while decreasing reabsorption of phosphate. PTH further acts on the kidneys to increase their production of the active metabolite of Vitamin D, calcitriol, which increases the absorption of Ca^{2+} by the intestines.

A physician examining a 55 year old female patient complaining of abdominal pain suspected a dysfunction of calcium regulation. Laboratory analysis revealed a total serum calcium of 12.3 (normal 8.4-10.2), a serum phosphorous of 2.4 (normal 2.7-4.5), and elevated PTH. In order to make a diagnosis, the physician took the laboratory values into consideration along with the following information regarding PTH dysfunction:

Primary hyperparathyroidism can develop as a result of autonomous oversecretion of PTH by the parathyroid gland.

Secondary hyperparathyroidism is characterized by an appropriately elevated PTH response to low blood Ca^{2+} concentration.

Pseudohypoparathyroidism is a condition associated with resistance of cells to PTH.

An inappropriately low level of PTH in the blood due to decreased parathyroid gland function is known as hypoparathyroidism.

19. Secondary hyperparathyroidism is likely to be caused by all of the following EXCEPT:
    A. chronic kidney disease.
    B. decreased dietary calcium intake.
    C. elevated blood phosphate levels.
    D. a PTH secreting tumor.

20. Sarcoidosis, a disease involving the formation of nodules containing inflammatory cells, can lead to increased formation of calcitriol. Of the following, what is the most likely physiological effect of this disease?
    A. Decreased bone density
    B. Hypoparathyroidism
    C. Elevated urinary calcium
    D. Less intestinal calcium absorption

21. What would result from the total surgical removal of the parathyroid gland?
    A. Enhanced bone mineralization
    B. Increased cardiac contractility
    C. Neurological complications
    D. Kidney failure

22. The following findings in a symptomatic patient are most consistent with what disorder of calcium metabolism? (Note: measurements of serum Ca^{2+}, phosphates and calcitriol concentrations and in urinary phosphorus excretion after administration of biosynthetic PTH were unchanged).

    Serum [PTH]:   High
    Serum [Calcitriol]: Low
    Serum [Ca^{2+}]:   Low
    Serum [Phosphate]: High

    A. Primary hyperparathyroidism
    B. Secondary hyperparathyroidism
    C. Hypoparathyroidism
    D. Pseudohypoparathyroidism

Passage V (Questions 23-26)

Entry of enveloped viruses into cells can occur by membrane fusion or by endocytosis. Viral envelope proteins attach to receptors on the surface of target cells at neutral pH, triggering fusion with the host cell, uncoating and emptying of the viral contents into the cell. In endocytosis, viral particles are endocytosed by host cell endosomes. Following entry into the host cell, viral particles can be released from the endosomes in a pH-dependent mechanism, most likely because of conformational changes in envelope protein receptors caused by the action of host cell pH-dependent proteases during endosomal acidification.

Particles of human immunodeficiency virus (HIV)—an enveloped virus—produced in the presence of the viral factor Nef are more infectious than particles produced in the absence of this protein. The mechanism underlying this effect is poorly understood. In order to study Nef-mediated infectivity enhancement, HIV particles were engineered to contain envelope protein receptors from CXCR4-dependent (X4) HIV (an uncommon, receptor specific form of HIV which requires the cell surface protein CD4 for viral entry), amphotropic murine leukemia virus (ampho), or the vesicular stomatitis virus (VSV). The infectivity of these engineered particles, as well as that of a HIV particle containing the most common envelope protein, CCR5 (R5), were measured in the presence or absence of Nef. Results are given in Figure 1.

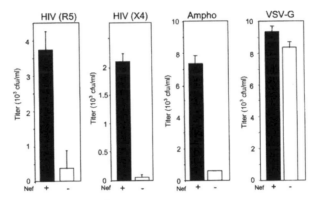

Figure 1 Effect of Nef on infectivity with hybrid viral particles containing various envelope proteins (Note: increased titer count correlates directly with increased viral infectivity; error bars indicate standard deviation).

To test the hypothesis that Nef-mediated rate enhancement is specific to envelope protein fusion at neutral pH, the scientists produced Nef+ and Nef− HIV hybrids with Ebola virus glycoprotein (Ebola-GP), which has recently been shown to facilitate fusion through a low-pH-dependent mechanism. The infectivity of these particles, as well as three previously synthesized hybrids, was tested in the presence or absence of bafilomycin A1, an agent that prevents the acidification of endosomes by blocking the function of the vacuolar H^+ ATPase. Results are shown in Figure 2.

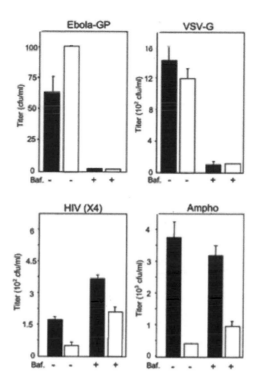

Figure 2 Effect of Nef and bafilomycin A1 (Baf.) on infectivity with hybrid viral particles containing various envelope proteins (Note: Black bars indicate Nef+ hybrid, white bars indicate Nef- hybrids; increased titer count correlates directly with increased viral infectivity; error bars indicate standard deviation).

23. Given passage information, target cell pH-dependent proteases required for viral release from endosomes have which of the following effects, if any, on the Ebo-GP envelope proteins of HIV particles in acidified endosomes?
    A. Reduced enzyme activity
    B. Protein dimer synthesis
    C. Formation of smaller protein fragments
    D. No effect

24. The trials shown in Figure 2 that were conducted in the in the presence of bafilomycin A1 confirm that:
    A. all particles tested are able to enter the cell through a neutral-pH mechanism.
    B. particles containing Ebola-Gp and VSV-G envelope proteins enter the cell in a pH-independent mechanism.
    C. particles containing HIV X4 and ampho envelope proteins enter through a low-pH dependent mechanism.
    D. particles containing Ebola-Gp and VSV-G envelope proteins enter through a low-pH dependent mechanism.

25. It is proposed that in some instances CXCR4-dependent HIV particles initially enter the cell through an endocytic route as mentioned in the passage. Is this consistent with the results shown in Figure 2 relating bafilomycin A1 treatment's effect on Nef+ particles containing HIV X4 envelope protein?
    A. No, an increase in endosomal pH due to bafilomycin A1 would decrease the likelihood of infection due to endocytosed HIV particles.
    B. No, the fraction HIV X4-containing particles that enter cells by the endocytic route fail to survive subsequent endosomal acidification.
    C. No, Nef+ particles containing HIV X4 envelope proteins display approximately equal infectivities with or without bafilomycin A1 treatment.
    D. Yes, treatment with bafilomycin A1 would prevent acidification and therefore could cause this usually nonproductive route of entry to become productive.

26. Which of the following results, together with data in Figure 2 that indicates the loss of Nef infectivity enhancement function in HIV-Ebola-GP hybrids, most strengthens the hypothesis that fusion at the cell surface is required for Nef enhancement of infectivity?
    A. In HIV particles bearing both X4 and VSV-G envelope proteins, no Nef infectivity enhancement was seen in cells lacking CD4.
    B. HIV particles containing only VSV-G envelope proteins showed the same Nef infectivity enhancement toward cells expressing CD4 as HIV particles bearing X4 and VSV-G envelope proteins.
    C. In HIV particles bearing both Ebola-GP and VSV-G, envelope proteins, greater Nef infectivity enhancement was seen in cells lacking CD4.
    D. HIV particles containing only Ebola-GP envelope proteins showed the same Nef infectivity enhancement toward cells expressing CD4 as HIV particles bearing both Ebola-V and VSV-G envelope proteins.

Discrete Set 2 (Questions 27-30)

These questions are **NOT** related to a passage.

27. When calcium ions are released from the sarcoplasmic reticulum:
    A. the muscle is able to repolarize after a fiber twitches.
    B. the acetylcholine in the neuromuscular junction is able to be reabsorbed by the presynaptic membrane.
    C. the myosin heads are able to disconnect from the actin filaments.
    D. they bind to troponin allowing the actin filament to bind to myosin.

28. Angiogenesis inhibitors can serve as an effective treatment for stopping or slowing the growth of tumors because:
    A. in the absence of a steady blood supply, the telomeres in the tumor cells will shorten, causing the tumor cells to stop dividing after approximately 50 rounds of division.
    B. lack of adequate vascularization triggers apoptosis in any cell.
    C. cells or tissues that can only receive nutrients by diffusion through surrounding tissues are size limited.
    D. the tumor growth factors that stimulate tumor development must be delivered via the circulatory system.

29. Which of the following is the structure of pyruvate?

    A.

    B.

    C.

    D.

30. Which of the following is NOT a bond that directly helps determine secondary and tertiary structure of a protein?
    A. Hydrogen bonds
    B. Peptide bonds
    C. Electrostatic bonds
    D. Disulfide bonds

Passage VI (Questions 31-34)

Mesenchymal stem cells (MSCs), which express the marker proteins CD109 and CD90, are stromal cells that, upon terminal differentiation, yield the cells of connective tissue. Scientists considering the influence of transcription factors on MSC lineage commitment studied the effects of a pool of four transcription factors thought to be involved in MSC differentiation. They noticed that fourteen days after injection of mouse MSCs with a pool of the four factors, the number of CD109-positive cells declined.

Fibroblast growth factor 2 (Fgf2) has previously been shown to reversibly inhibit differentiation of primary mouse MSCs, but the intracellular signaling pathways that maintain cells in an undifferentiated state remain largely unexplored. To further study the effects of transcription factors on MSC differentiation, mouse MSCs were cultured for seven days in complete culture media (CCM) supplemented with 20 ng/ml Fgf2. This treatment was shown to alter expression of genes for the four transcription factor pool versus levels of expression in untreated cells, as shown in Figure 1.

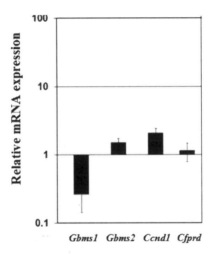

Figure 1 Relative levels of transcription factor expression by Fgf2-treated mouse MSC cell lines. Basal transcription rates in non-treated mouse MSC cell lines are assumed to be 1 (Note: errors bars correspond to standard deviation.)

In subsequent experiments, scientists attempted to determine the influence of those four transcription factors in the differentiation of MSC, by removing one of four transcription factors from the four-factor pool, and observing the presence of cells testing positive for bone gamma-carboxyglutamic acid protein (Bglap), a connective-tissue specific non-collagenous bone protein, or osteonectin, a component of basement membranes, after fourteen days. Results are shown in Figure 2.

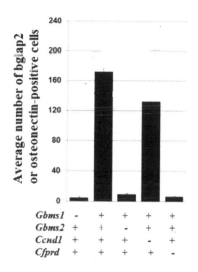

Figure 2 Average number of bglap2- or osteonectin-positive MSC cells present under the indicated transcription factor condition (Note: + indicates the presence of the gene for the given transcription factor and − indicates the corresponding gene's absence. Error bars correspond to standard deviation.)

31. Fgf2 is most likely to inhibit MSC differentiation through its modulation of the expression of what transcription factor?
    A. *Gbms1*
    B. *Gbms2*
    C. *Ccnd1*
    D. *Cfprd*

32. Based upon the results presented in the passage, which of the following factors least strongly influenced commitment of mesenchymal stem cells to the connective-tissue lineage in vitro?
    A. *Gbms1*
    B. *Gbms2*
    C. *Ccnd1*
    D. *Cfprd*

33. What is the most likely reason that the scientists chose to measure bglap2 levels in assessing the influence of transcription factors on the maintenance of MSCs in the undifferentiated state?
    A. bglap2 is expressed in all cells of mesenchymal origin.
    B. bglap2 is expressed by both connective tissue and mesenchymal stem cells.
    C. bglap2 induces differentiation of MSCs.
    D. bglap2 is expressed by cells with connective tissue-like phenotypes.

34. In terms of their gene activation potential, MSCs are best described as what type of progenitor cell?
    A. Unipotent
    B. Multipotent
    C. Pluripotent
    D. Totipotent

Passage VII (Questions 35-39)

Huntington's disease (HD) is an inherited neurodegenerative disease caused by progressive neuronal loss in the striatum region of the brain. The Huntingtin gene (HTT), which is located on the short arm of chromosome 4 and which codes for the cytoplasmic protein Huntingtin (Htt), contains a sequence of three DNA bases—cytosine-adenine-guanine (CAG)—repeated multiple times. This repeating sequence is known as a trinucleotide repeat. CAG codes for the amino acid glutamine, and the trinucleotide repeat results in the production of a chain of glutamine known as a polyglutamine (polyQ) tract. The length of CAG repeat varies between individuals and, depending upon the repeat length, dynamic mutation may increase its length between generations. When the length of this repeated section reaches a certain threshold, it produces an altered form of the protein, called mutant Huntingtin protein (mHtt), which is toxic to cells of the striatum.

Geneticists studying the inheritance pattern of HD found that it is rare for HD to be caused by a new mutation and noticed that the length of the repeated sequence influenced the age of onset and progression and severity of symptoms experienced by affected individuals and their affected offspring. The geneticists' findings are summarized in Table 1.

Table 1 Classification of the trinucleotide repeat on an HTT allele and resulting Huntington disease status (Note: probability of affected offspring in the case of one parent with a single expanded HTT allele containing the indicated repeat count and another parent with a repeat count < 26 on either HTT allele.)

Repeat Count	Disease status	Age of onset	Probability of affected offspring
< 26	Will not be affected	N/A	None
27-35	Will not be affected	N/A	Elevated, but much less than 50%
36-39	May be affected	After 40	50%
40+	Will be affected	Between 25-39; earlier with increased repeat count	50%

A pedigree showing the inheritance pattern of Huntington's disease in one affected family studied by the geneticists in shown in Figure 1.

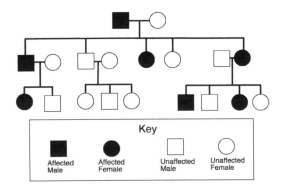

Figure 1 Familial inheritance pattern

35. The pedigree in Figure 1 indicates that Huntington's disease displays what pattern of inheritance?
    A. Autosomal recessive
    B. Autosomal dominant
    C. Sex-linked recessive
    D. Sex-linked dominant

36. Given results of the geneticist's work, what is the maximum number of possible glutamine residues in the polyQ region of *Htt* in an individual displaying a normal phenotype?
    A. 25
    B. 35
    C. 39
    D. 40

37. The geneticists concluded that the symptoms of HD generally become more severe and were diagnosed at an earlier age in affected offspring than in their affected parents. Is there a potential biological explanation for this phenomenon?
    A. No, the observation is due to heightened awareness of disease symptoms within affected families.
    B. No, regions of trinucleotide expansion, located on an autosome, occurs only in somatic cells.
    C. Yes, mutant mHtt protein is synthesized by individuals containing CAG repeats.
    D. Yes, dynamic mutation results in expanded trinucleotides associated with a more severe disease phenotype.

38. What is the probability that both of the children of an affected father with two copies of the HTT allele, containing more than 40 CAG repeats, and a mother with fewer than 26 CAG repeats, will express the mHtt protein?
    A. 25%
    B. 50%
    C. 75%
    D. 100%

39. The observation that not all individuals containing between 36-39 CAG repeats display clinical symptoms of Huntington's disease can be explained in terms of what property of the disease's inheritance pattern?
    A. Incomplete penetrance
    B. Variable expressivity
    C. Pleiotropy
    D. Genetic anticipation

Passage VIII (Questions 40-43)

Though the two conditions are characterized by similar symptoms, Diabetes Mellitus (DM) and Diabetes Insipidus (DI) have distinct and unrelated causes. In both DM and DI, patients experience polyuria (excessive urination). It is important for physicians to differentiate between DM and DI in order to properly treat their patients.

DM is caused by the impaired action of insulin in the body. People with type 1 DM produce insufficient quantities of insulin or sometimes no insulin at all. This is thought to be the result of the immune system attacking insulin-secreting cells. In type 2 DM, the body develops a gradual reduction in sensitivity to insulin, resulting in little or no response to the insulin the body produces. Type 2 DM is associated with obesity and increases the risk of many other health problems, including cardiovascular disease and nerve damage. Elevated levels of blood glucose in DM can exceed the capacity of the kidneys to reabsorb the substance.

DI is caused by the impaired action of antidiuretic hormone (ADH) on the kidneys. In central DI, the body does not produce sufficient ADH. Nephrogenic DI is characterized by normal serum ADH levels with an impaired ability of the kidney to respond to the action of ADH. Both types of DI can be hereditary in nature or caused by other factors.

A 15-year-old male with polyuria and polydipsia (excessive thirst) presents to his pediatrician. The doctor runs a series of blood and urine tests. In addition to the tests in Table 1 below, the physician performs a test to measure the patient's response to exogenous insulin, the results of which are normal.

Table 1 Results of the patient's laboratory tests. All reference ranges are for an adolescent male.

Value	Result	Normal Range
Fasting Serum Glucose	328 mg/dL	70-110 mg/dL
Serum ADH	3.6 pcg/mL	1-5 pcg/mL
Urine Glucose	Positive	Negative
Urine Osmolality	1127 mOsm/kg	50-1200 mOsm/kg

40. Nephrogenic DI is most plausibly caused by damage to ADH receptors in:
    A. the glomerulus.
    B. the pituitary gland.
    C. the collecting duct.
    D. the hypothalamus.

41. The patient's expected result serum insulin levels are:
    A. below normal.
    B. normal.
    C. above normal.
    D. The answer cannot be determined without more information.

42. Which of the following symptoms would be seen in DM but NOT in DI?
    I Excessive hunger (polyphagia)
    II Ketoacidosis from abnormally high fatty acid metabolism
    III Excessive thirst (polydipsia)

    A. I only
    B. I and II only
    C. II and III only
    D. I, II, and III

43. In a healthy person, ADH is most likely to be secreted when:
    A. blood pressure is high; blood osmolality is low.
    B. blood pressure is high; blood osmolality is high.
    C. blood pressure is low; blood osmolality is low.
    D. blood pressure is low; blood osmolality is high.

Discrete Set 3 (Questions 44-47)

These questions are **NOT** related to a passage.

44. Which of the following is NOT directly involved as a product or reactant in the conversion of pyruvate to acetyl CoA?
    A. CO_2
    B. NADH
    C. H^+
    D. ATP

45. Which of the following is a peptide hormone?
    A. T_4
    B. Leukotrienes
    C. Testosterone
    D. ACTH

46. If baldness is an X-linked recessive disorder, which of the following could NOT also have been a carrier of the gene or genes resulting in a man's baldness?
    A. The bald male's mother
    B. The bald male's maternal grandmother
    C. The bald male's paternal grandfather
    D. The bald male's maternal grandfather

47. The heart, femur and bicep most likely arise from which of the following primary germ layers?
    A. Endoderm
    B. Mesoderm
    C. Ectoderm
    D. Morula

THIS PAGE LEFT

INTENTIONALLY BLANK

Passage IX (Questions 48-51)

Pseudomonas aeruginosa is one of the most common Gram-negative pathogens accounting for over 10% of all infections. With its increasing prevalence, multidrug-resistant strains are becoming increasingly common. The common complication resulting from *P. aeruginosa* is a lung infection associated with cystic fibrosis.

In an effort to further elucidate the difference between prokaryotic and eukaryotic protein synthesis, a study was conducted on the interactions between elongation factor Tu (EF-Tu) and elongation factor Ts (EF-Ts). The studies were conducted in hopes of developing new compounds that inhibit growth of the bacteria without adversely affecting the patient.

EF-Tu has an integral role in protein synthesis by bringing the aminoacyl-tRNA (aa-tRNA) to the A-site of the ribosome during the elongation phase of translation. EF-Tu forms a ternary complex with GTP and aa-tRNA in the cytoplasm, and this complex approaches the A-site of an actively translating ribosome. Once the ternary complex is bound to the ribosome and the codon-anticodon pairing is correct, GTP is hydrolyzed to GDP by activating the GTPase activity of EF-Tu. There is a conformational change in EF-Tu, and EF-Tu-GDP dissociates from the ribosome and recycled to the EF-Tu-TP complex in an exchange catalyzed by EF-Ts. Once EF-Tu-GDP is released, the aa-tRNA fully enters the A site.

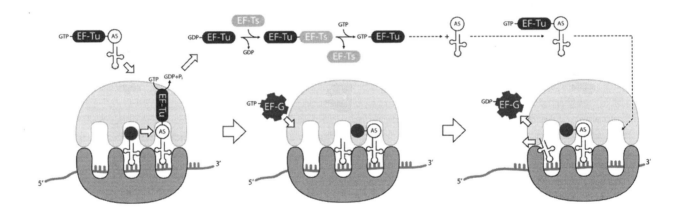

Figure 1 Elongation Phase of Translation in the Prokaryotic Cell

There are two delays offered by EF-Tu that helps to ensure translational accuracy. EF-Tu delays GTP hydrolysis if the anticodon in the A site does not match codon on the aa-tRNA and again when it frees itself from the tRNA to allow for an incorrectly paired tRNA to leave the A site.

48. Which of the following steps precedes the elongation steps described in the passage?
    A. The smaller subunit of the ribosome attaches to the cap at the 5′end of the mRNA and searches for an AUG codon by moving step-by-step in the 3′direction.
    B. With the initiating t-RNA at the P site and the second aminoacyl-tRNA tightly bound at the A site, the α amino group of the second amino acid reacts with the "activated" methionine on the initiator tRNA, forming a peptide bond.
    C. RF1 recognizes UAG, and RF2 recognizes UGA; both these factors recognize UAA. RF3, a GTP-binding protein, acts in concert with the codon-recognizing factors to promote cleavage of the peptidyl-tRNA.
    D. The fMet-tRNA enters the P site, causing a conformational change which opens the A site for the new aminoacyl-tRNA to bind.

49. Which of the following has the greatest similarity when comparing prokaryotic and eukaryotic translation?
    A. Size of ribosomes
    B. Initiator t-RNA
    C. Elongation factors
    D. Recognition sites for the smaller subunit of the ribosome

50. A molecule which does which of the following would be most effective in eliminating *Pseudomonas aeruginosa*?
    A. Inhibits the peptidyl transferase activity of the smaller subunit of the ribosome
    B. Binds to the Shine-Delgarno sequence to directly block binding of aminoacyl-tRNA at A site
    C. Binds to the 60S subunit to block translocation
    D. Binds to formylmethionyl-tRNA to prevent correct initiation

51. Which of the following laboratory procedures would be most effective in determining the concentration of GDP in EF-Tu preparation?
    A. Centrifugation
    B. Absorbance spectroscopy
    C. Extraction and filtration
    D. Fractional distillation

Passage X (Questions 52-55)

The autonomic nervous system in humans is comprised of two parts: (1) the sympathetic nervous system and (2) the parasympathetic nervous system. These two components are often referred to as "fight-or-flight" and "rest-and-digest" respectively, and explain most of the body's unconscious activity. Transmission of any signal in the autonomic nervous system is mediated by one of two types of neurons, pre-ganglionic neurons and post-ganglionic neurons. Pre-ganglionic neurons (represented by solid lines in the two figures below) originate from the thoracolumbar region of the vertebrae (T1-L2). These neurons connect with ganglia before they synapse with post-ganglionic neurons (represented by dashed lines in the figure) whose axons extend to many different target organs in the body. In general, it has been seen that the parasympathetic nervous system has long pre-ganglionic and short post-ganglionic axons, whereas the sympathetic nervous system has short pre-ganglionic and long post-ganglionic axons.

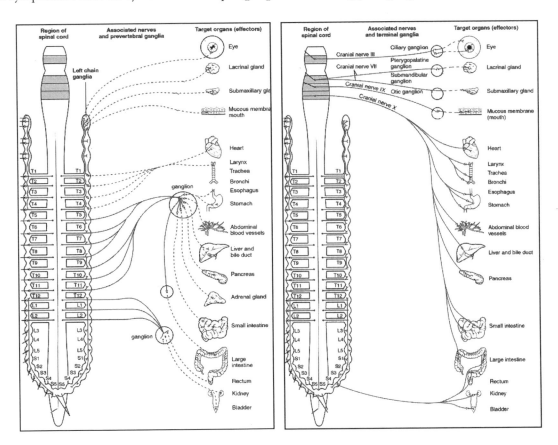

Figure 1 Organization of the Sympathetic Nervous System (left) and Parasympathetic Nervous System (right)

Two patients are brought into the neuroendocrinology wing of a hospital to participate in a study. Patient 1 is brought into a room and is asked to sit down at a dining table set with silverware. He is provided a bowl of chilled strawberry soup and is told to begin eating the soup. At the same time, Patient 2 is provided the same setup with identical instructions, but a few minutes into the meal, a wire is pulled to cause a flap of the table to collapse. This results in the bowl of cold soup suddenly and unexpectedly landing in the patient's lap, startling the patient and causing him to scream and jump out of his chair. Thirty seconds after the table collapses, the patients are both brought into a side room for observation.

52. Two nerves, one in the parasympathetic nervous system and one in the sympathetic nervous system, are both found to have myelinated pre-ganglionic cells and unmyelinated post-ganglionic cells. Compared to the overall conduction velocity of the parasympathetic nerve, the sympathetic nerve's conduction velocity will be:
    A. faster than that of the parasympathetic nerve.
    B. slower than that of the parasympathetic nerve.
    C. identical to that of the parasympathetic nerve.
    D. More information must be provided to answer this question.

53. The levels of insulin and glucagon are measured in Patient 1 and Patient 2 at the same time point in their meals, shortly after the table collapses on Patient 2. Which of the following statements regarding the hormone levels of the two patients, relative to baseline measurements, is correct?
    A. Patient 1 will have high levels of insulin, and Patient 2 will have high levels of glucagon.
    B. Patient 1 will have low levels of insulin, and Patient 2 will have low levels of glucagon.
    C. Patient 1 will have high levels of insulin, and Patient 2 will have low levels of glucagon.
    D. Patient 1 will have low levels of insulin, and Patient 2 will have high levels of glucagon.

54. Parasympathetic nervous system post-ganglionic neurons activate muscarinic receptors on target tissue through which neurotransmitter?
    A. Muscarine
    B. Serotonin
    C. Epinephrine
    D. Acetylcholine

55. It is observed that the pupils of one patient are slightly more dilated than they were during baseline observations. This is most likely:
    A. Patient 1 because his parasympathetic nervous system is activated.
    B. Patient 1 because his sympathetic nervous system is activated.
    C. Patient 2 because his sympathetic nervous system is activated.
    D. Patient 2 because his parasympathetic nervous system is activated.

Discrete Set 4 (Questions 56-59)

These questions are **NOT** related to a passage.

56. How does cDNA differ from eukaryotic DNA?
    A. It is artificially made in a lab.
    B. It has post-transcriptional modifications, such as a 5' cap.
    C. It lacks exons.
    D. It lacks introns.

57. Which of the following describes a difference between a Northern blot and a Southern blot?
    A. Northern blots are run at a lower temperature to preserve the secondary structure of the RNA.
    B. Northern blots can be used to identify many different RNA fragments, while Southern blots can identify only a few.
    C. Northern blots are used for RNA fragments, while Southern blots are used for DNA fragments.
    D. Northern blots are run under anaerobic conditions.

58. Where do post-transcriptional modifications of RNA take place?
    A. In the nucleus of the cell
    B. In the cytoplasm of the cell
    C. Mainly in the nucleus, but also in the cytoplasm
    D. Mainly in the cytoplasm, but also in the nucleus

59. Which of the following are necessary post-transcriptional modifications for export of eukaryotic mRNA to the cytoplasm?
    I. Addition of a poly-A tail
    II. 3' guanine cap
    III. Splicing

    A. I only
    B. I and II only
    C. I and III only
    D. I, II, and III

TIMED
SECTION 1
Answers and Explanations

Timed Section 1 Answer Key

Key		20	C	40	C
1	C	21	C	41	A
2	C	22	D	42	B
3	C	23	C	43	D
4	B	24	D	44	D
5	A	25	D	45	D
6	C	26	A	46	C
7	D	27	D	47	B
8	C	28	C	48	D
9	D	29	A	49	C
10	C	30	B	50	D
11	A	31	A	51	B
12	C	32	C	52	B
13	B	33	D	53	A
14	C	34	B	54	D
15	C	35	B	55	C
16	D	36	C	56	D
17	C	37	D	57	C
18	D	38	D	58	A
19	D	39	A	59	C

Passage I Explanation (Questions 1-5)

Alzheimer's disease (AD) is a common form of progressive **dementia** observed in both **familial** and **non-familial forms**. To evaluate the potential involvement of dysfunctional **intracellular Ca^{2+} mobilization** on AD-associated cognitive deficits, Ca^{2+} signaling was measured as fluorescence from human skin **fibroblasts** taken from **healthy age-matched (AC) and healthy young (YC)** donors, and from individuals with Alzheimer's disease (AD), where all cell lines were loaded with the calcium indicator **fura-2**. Fibroblasts were either untreated, treated with **bombesin**, an agent that upon binding its **G-coupled protein receptor** activates **phospholipase C (PLC)** to generate **inositol 1,4,5-trisphosphate (IP$_3$)** (which triggers release of calcium into the cytoplasm), or treated with **Ca^{2+} channel blockers**—agents that disrupt the movement of Ca^{2+} through calcium channels. **Measurements were made under the extracellular Ca^{2+} conditions indicated**, along with the results of the experiments, in **Figures 1 and 2**.

Key terms: Alzheimer's disease (AD), dementia, cognitive deficits, age-matched control donors, young control donors (YC), Alzheimer's disease donors , phospholipase C , Ca^{2+} channel blockers

Cause-and-Effect: The involvement of intracellular Ca^{2+} mobilization on AD-associated cognitive deficits was evaluated by measuring Ca^{2+} signaling from human skin fibroblasts loaded with the calcium indicator fura-2; skin fibroblasts were taken from healthy age-matched (AC) and young (YC) donors and from individuals with AD; the fibroblast were untreated or treated with either bombesin or calcium channel blockers; bombesin binds its G-coupled bombesin receptor, activating PLC and generating IP$_3$; PLC-IP$_3$ signaling increases intracellular Ca^{2+}; calcium-channel blocker treatment inhibits it

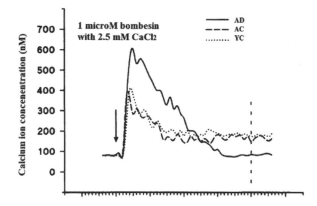

Figure 1: Ca^{2+} response induced by 1 microM bombesin in the presence of extracellular Ca^{2+}; peak Ca^{2+} signaling following bombesin application is greater in AD than in either AC or YC controls. Ca^{2+} signaling returns to baseline levels after approximately 90 seconds in AD cells, but remains elevated in control cells.

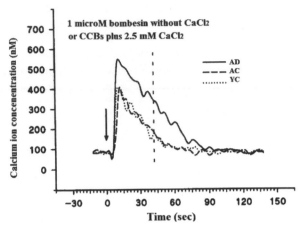

Figure 2 Ca^{2+} response induced by bombesin without extracellular Ca^{2+} present, and, when performed independently, Ca^{2+} response induced by bombesin with extracellular Ca^{2+} and calcium channel blockers (CCB) present is identical; peak Ca^{2+} in AD is slightly reduced versus the test conditions in Figure 1; AC and YC are effectively identical; the most significant difference between the signaling curves of the three test groups in Figure 2 versus Figure 1 is the lack of sustained Ca^{2+} signaling in AC or YC groups in the absence of accessible extracellular Ca^{2+}, due to either a Ca^{2+} medium, or CCB blockers preventing its influx through voltage-gated calcium channels.

Further treatment of the cell lines with **Thapisgargin**, an inhibitor of the **Ca^{2+}-ATPase** in the endoplasmic reticulum (ER), elicited the same Ca^{2+} signals from AD, AC and YC cell lines.

Key terms: Thapisgargin, Ca^{2+}-ATPase inhibitor
Cause-and-Effect: Thapisgargin, an inhibitor of the Ca^{2+}-ATPase in the endoplasmic reticulum (ER), created the same Ca^{2+} signals from AD, AC and YC cell lines

1. Under several treatment conditions shown in Figures 1 and 2, tested fibroblasts displayed a sustained phase of constant Ca^{2+} signaling above baseline levels. Which of the following statements describing this sustained signaling is NOT supported by passage information?
    A. The sustained phase elicited by bombesin from AC and YC were eliminated by the removal of extracellular Ca^{2+}.
    B. Divalent cation Ca^{2+} channel blockers eliminated the sustained phase signals in all control cells.
    C. <u>The sustained phases of fibroblast Ca^{2+} signaling do not depend on intracellularly stored calcium.</u>
    D. The Ca^{2+} signal of AD fibroblasts showed no sustained phase.

Choice **C** is correct. You are looking for the one answer NOT supported by the data. Figure 1 shows that bombesin-induced Ca^{2+} signaling returns to baseline levels after approximately 90 seconds in AD cells, but remains elevated in AC and YC control cells. It does not, however, give information to determine the dependence of the elevated AC and YC signaling on intracellular calcium stores—only that sustained-phase of Ca^{2+} signaling is dependent on the entry of extracellular Ca^{2+}.

A, B: Figures 1 and 2 demonstrate that the sustained-phase of Ca^{2+} signaling is dependent on entry of extracellular Ca^{2+}. When extracellular Ca^{2+} is unavailable, or when CCBs block extracellular Ca^{2+} from entering in response to bombesin binding, sustained signaling—demonstrated for AC and YC control cells in Figure 1, but absent in either cell type in Figure 2—does not occur. This is consistent with the true statements made in choices A and B.
D: Figure 1 shows that bombesin-induced Ca^{2+} signaling returns to baseline levels after approximately 90 seconds in AD cells, but remains elevated in AC and YC control cells, consistent with choice D.

2. The researchers concluded that AD-specific differences in initial bombesin-induced Ca^{2+} signaling in skin fibroblasts are due to dysfunction of an intracellular component of the PLC-IP_3 system. What additional findings would most *weaken* this conclusion?
    A. The thapisgargin-induced Ca^{2+} signal does not depend on extracellular Ca^{2+}.
    B. Bradykinin, another activator of PLC, elicited larger Ca^{2+} signals in AD than in YC cells.
    C. **Radioligand binding revealed a greater number of bombesin binding sites in AD fibroblasts.**
    D. Thapisgargin mobilized Ca^{2+} without a corresponding increase in inositol phosphates.

Choice **C** is correct. The initial bombesin-induced Ca^{2+} signaling in AD fibroblasts is greater than in AC and YC cells. If radioligand binding revealed a greater number of bombesin receptors on the surface of AD fibroblasts, then this could offer an alternative hypothesis to the greater bombesin-induced extracellular Ca^{2+} influence shown in AD fibroblasts being due to derangement of an intracellular-component of the PLC-IP_3 system.

A: Thapisgargin-induced Ca^{2+} signal is due to thapisgargin's inhibition of ER-embedded Ca^{2+}-ATPase. AD-specific differences in Ca^{2+} signaling is would not then be likely due to differences in stored intracellular Ca^{2+} pools.

B: The fact that another activator of PLC elicited larger Ca^{2+} signals in AD than in YC cells does not necessarily indicate dysfunction outside of the intracellular components of the PLC-IP_3 system. Bradykinin, as well as bombesin, receptors could activate the same dysfunctional components of the PLC-IP_3 system when bound. The extent of that activation could be due to differences in the extent of activation of the system by bradykinin versus bombesin.

D: If thapisgargin mobilized Ca^{2+} without a corresponding increase in inositol phosphates, and if thapisgargin-induced Ca^{2+} signaling shows no AD-specific differences, this further strengths the contention that AD-specific signaling differences are due to dysfunction of the PLC-IP_3 system.

3. Which of the following steps in bombesin-induced Ca^{2+} signaling transduction depends on the availability of a high-energy bond?
    I.   Binding of bombesin to its receptor
    II. G-protein activation
    III. Ca^{2+} reuptake into the ER
    IV. Protein kinase C kinase activity

    A. I and III only
    B. II and III only
    C. **II, III, and IV only**
    D. I, II, III, and IV

Choice **C** is correct. "High-energy" bonds include the phosphoanhydride bonds of the nucleotide triphosphates GTP and ATP. When a ligand activates a G protein-coupled receptor, such as the bombesin receptor, it induces a conformational change in the receptor that allows the receptor to function as a guanine nucleotide exchange factor (GEF) that exchanges GTP in place of GDP. Upon GTP binding, the heterotrimeric G-protein dissociates and activates other proteins in the signal transduction pathway (Roman numeral II). Active transport of Ca^{2+} against its concentration gradient by Ca^{2+}-ATPase into the ER requires the hydrolysis of ATP to power the translocation (Roman numeral III). Protein kinase enzymes, including PKC, transfer a high-energy phosphate group from a nucleoside triphosphate, typically ATP, to target enzymes (Roman numeral IV).

I: Binding of bombesin, or any substrate, to its receptor is due to binding-site specificity. Binding does not depend upon an external energy source (Roman numeral I).

4. The researchers wish to relate AD-associated cognitive deficits to the AD-specific alterations of Ca^{2+} shown in the passage. What additional finding would best support this connection?
    A. Both familial and non-familial AD skin fibroblasts display AD-specific alterations.
    B. <u>AD-specific differences in Ca^{2+} signaling have systemic expression in AD cells.</u>
    C. Ca^{2+} signaling in AD-neurons increase with greater extracellular calcium concentration.
    D. AD-specific alterations are restricted to AD skin tissue fibroblasts.

Choice **B** is correct. If AD-specific alterations in Ca^{2+} signaling extend systemically to AD cells related to cognition, then the alterations in Ca^{2+} regulation in skin fibroblasts may be offer an explanation for some aspects of AD-associated cognitive deficits.

A and D: Similarities between AD skin fibroblasts from familial and non-familial forms of the disease do not directly relate those AD-specific alterations in Ca^{2+} signaling to AD-associated cognitive deficits.

C: Increased Ca^{2+} signaling in AD-neurons with greater extracellular calcium concentrations is not alone reflective of dysfunction. In order for greater Ca^{2+} signaling to indicate a pathological cause, it would need to be shown to be unequal to control cell signaling at the same extracellular Ca^{2+} concentrations. Without such evidence, increased Ca^{2+} signaling in AD-neurons may be a normal response to increased Ca^{2+} gradients across the cell membrane.

5. Cleavage of phosphatidylinositol 4,5-bisphosphate (PIP2) by PLC results in:
    A. <u>retention of diacylglycerol (DAG) within the membrane and diffusion of IP_3 within the cell.</u>
    B. retention of IP_3 within the membrane and diffusion of diacylglycerol (DAG) within the cell.
    C. retention of diacylglycerol (DAG) and IP_3 within the membrane.
    D. diffusion of diacylglycerol (DAG) and IP_3 within the cell.

Choice **A** is correct. PLC cleaves the membrane phospholipid phosphatidylinositol 4,5-bisphosphate (PIP2) into DAG and inositol 1,4,5-trisphosphate (IP_3). DAG remains bound to the membrane, and IP_3 is released into the cytosol. IP_3 then diffuses to bind cytosolic IP_3 receptors, including those linked to calcium channels in the smooth endoplasmic reticulum (ER). DAG is a physiological activator of protein kinase C, and facilitates the translocation of PKC from the cytosol to the plasma membrane.

B, C, D: The fact that DAG is retained in the plasma membrane can be deduced from its lipophilic structures—a glyceride consisting of two fatty acid chains covalently bonded to a glycerol molecule through ester linkages. This is in contrast to the much more hydrophilic structure of IP_3, a phospholipid containing three negatively charged phosphate groups which will diffuse within the cell.

Passage II Explanation (Questions 6-10)

The heart is a muscular organ responsible for pumping nutrient- and oxygen-rich blood to every part of the body. The human heart consists of **four chambers, two atria** and **two ventricles,** separated by **valves**. The **pulmonary vein** and **artery** directly connect the heart to the **lungs**, where blood is oxygenated **prior to exiting the heart through the aorta**. Heart rate is highly susceptible to changes in hormone levels. One example of this is epinephrine, which when secreted with activation of the sympathetic nervous system, can dramatically increase heart rate. The heart also secretes its own hormone called **atrial natriuretic peptide (ANP)**. ANP is secreted by atrial myocytes in response to **high blood pressure**, causing **vasodilation** and loss of sodium from the blood. This leads to reduction in blood volume and thus **reduction in systemic blood pressure**.

Key Terms: atrium, ventricle, valves, pulmonary vein/artery, aorta, atrial natriuretic peptide (ANP), vasodilation

Contrast: The pulmonary artery brings deoxygenated blood away from the heart, and the pulmonary vein brings oxygenated blood to the heart.

Cause-and-Effect: Epinephrine secretion leads to increased heart rate. ANP secretion leads to vasodilation and loss of sodium from blood, ultimately reducing systemic blood pressure.

There are two substantial differences between the fetal heart and the adult heart. In fetal circulation, there is an **opening** between the **left and right atria** known as the **foramen ovale** that allows a portion of the blood to go **directly from the right atrium to the left atrium**, thereby **bypassing pulmonary circulation**. The blood that does not enter the left atrium is pumped into the right ventricle before entering the pulmonary artery. Fetuses also have a special connection between **the pulmonary artery and aorta** called the **ductus arteriosus**, which allows the blood that does not pass through the foramen ovale to **still bypass the lungs**. When a baby is born, changes in pulmonary pressure cause the **foramen ovale and the ductus arteriosus to close**. In rare cases, the foramen ovale **does not completely close** when the child is born, and **a hole remains between the two atria** into adulthood. This is called an **atrial septal defect**.

Key Terms: foramen ovale, pulmonary circulation, ductus arteriosus, atrial septal defect

Contrast: In the fetal heart, there are connections between the left and right atria, as well as the pulmonary artery and the aorta. These lead to the bypassing of pulmonary circulation. The adult heart does not have these connections, unless there is a congenital defect where the connections did not close.

Cause-and-Effect: The foramen ovale connects the left and right atria. The ductus arteriosus connects the pulmonary artery and the aorta. An atrial septal defect causes the left and right atria to still be connected after the child is born.

In a physiology lab at a local hospital, a researcher discovers two important **action potential recordings** collected the prior week that were accidentally put in the trash. In the experiment, **electrode recordings** were taken in **two separate muscle tissues** in a **single healthy patient**. In an effort to avoid an uncomfortable discussion with the principle investigator, the researcher **tries to match** the recordings to the appropriate muscle tissue.

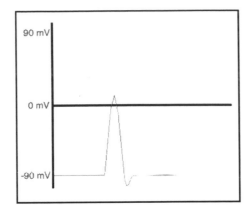

Action Potential Recording A

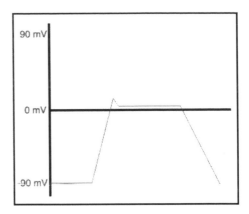

Action Potential Recording B

Key Terms: action potential, electrode recordings

Contrast: Action Potential Recording A looks like a standard action potential with a dramatic rise and fall followed by a short hyperpolarized "undershoot" period. Action Potential Recording B has a long plateau after the peak, and also has no "undershoot" at the end of the recording.

6. Upon entering the heart through the vena cava, blood travels through numerous tissues before it exits the heart. Which of the following represents the path that blood travels from the time it enters the adult heart to the time it enters systemic circulation?
    A. Right Atrium → Mitral Valve → Pulmonary Vein → Left Ventricle → Aorta
    B. Left Atrium → Tricuspid Valve → Pulmonary Artery → Right Atrium → Aorta
    C. <u>**Right Atrium → Tricuspid Valve → Pulmonary Artery → Pulmonary Vein → Left Ventricle**</u>
    D. Right Ventricle → Mitral Valve → Aorta → Tricuspid Valve → Pulmonary Vein

Choice **C** is correct. Blood enters the heart through the vena cava, and then travels through the right atrium, tricuspid valve, right ventricle, semilunar valve, pulmonary artery, lungs, pulmonary vein, left atrium, mitral valve (bicuspid valve), left ventricle, and another semilunar valve before exiting through the aorta. The passage has supplied some hints as to the order of these already, though the valves were omitted. Answer C is the only option that lists a path in this order.

A: Blood from the right atrium (after traveling through the tricuspid valve, right ventricle, semilunar valve, pulmonary artery, and lungs) would pass through the pulmonary vein before it travels through the mitral valve. This option suggests the pulmonary vein is encountered after the mitral valve.
B: Blood would pass through the tricuspid valve, pulmonary artery, and right atrium before the left atrium, not after as this answer suggests.
D: In order for this answer to be correct, mitral valve and tricuspid valve should be switched, as well as aorta and pulmonary vein. The aorta is the location where all blood exits the heart, so it naturally should be the last in this answer option.

7. The researcher in the passage believes ***Recording A*** is from cardiac muscle and ***Recording B*** is from skeletal muscle. Is this correct?

   A. Yes – cardiac muscle action potentials have no refractory period whereas skeletal muscle action potentials have both an absolute and a relative refractory period.
   B. No – skeletal muscle action potentials have a larger depolarization than cardiac muscle action potentials, so ***Recording A*** is actually skeletal muscle and ***Recording B*** is cardiac muscle.
   C. Yes – ***Recording B*** is likely from a skeletal muscle that is being flexed, which is why there is a depolarized plateau seen in the recording.
   D. <u>No – cardiac muscle has an influx of Ca^{2+} ions that balances out the outflux of K^{+} ions leading to a plateau in the action potential, so *Recording A* is actually skeletal muscle and Record B is cardiac muscle.</u>

Choice **D** is correct. Cardiac muscle has voltage-dependent calcium channels, as well as a higher concentration of calcium ions outside the cell in comparison to the inside concentration. This means that when the voltage-dependent calcium channels activate at the peak of the action potential, calcium ions flood into the cell. This temporarily counteracts the outflux of potassium ions through the voltage-dependent potassium channels that also open at the peak of the action potential, leading to a prolonged action potential with a plateau following the peak. As the voltage-dependent calcium channels close, the outflux of potassium repolarizes the cell back to its resting potential.

A: The researcher did not identify the recordings correctly, and cardiac muscle action potentials do have refractory periods just like skeletal muscle action potentials, even though they don't have an undershoot.
B: It is correct that the researcher misidentified the recordings, but not because of any difference in amount of depolarization. The two action potentials both peak around +20 mV according to the figures.
C: The researcher did not identify the recordings correctly, and flexed skeletal muscle would not have a prolonged action potential. All human skeletal muscle action potentials will have roughly the same shape attributed to Na^{+} influx causing depolarization, and K^{+} outflux causing repolarization.

8. Which of the following hormone levels would produce effects that would counteract high levels of ANP?
   I. High levels of angiotensin I
   II. Low levels of angiotensinogen
   III. High levels of aldosterone

   A. III only
   B. I and II only
   C. **I and III only**
   D. I, II, and III

Choice **C** is correct. Angiotensin I, Angiotensinogen, and Aldosterone are all part of the renin-angiotensin system. In this system, angiotensinogen is a zymogen released by the liver in response to low blood pressure. Renin cleaves the zymogen into angiotensin I. Angiotensin-Converting Enzyme (ACE) then converts Angiotensin I into Angiotensin II, which stimulates the release of aldosterone from the adrenal cortex. Aldosterone works to increase blood pressure by increasing water reabsorption and retention. It is stated in the passage that ANP reduces blood pressure through reducing blood volume. Thus, high levels of Angiotensin I (which would lead to high levels of aldosterone) and high levels of aldosterone would both counteract high levels of ANP. Options I and III are correct. High levels of angiotensinogen (leading to high levels of aldosterone) would likely also counteract high levels of ANP, not low levels of the zymogen. Thus, option II is not correct.

9. An individual born with an atrial septal defect might have which of the following symptoms?
   A. Difficulties regulating body temperature
   B. ANP deficiency
   C. Hyperactivity.
   D. **Shortness of breath when exercising**

Choice **D** is correct. The passage states that an atrial septal defect is the result of the foramen ovale not fully closing, leaving a hole between the right atrium and the left atrium. When this occurs, oxygen-rich blood can flow from the left atrium to the right atrium to mix with deoxygenated blood, or vice versa. This leads to suboptimal oxygen levels in the blood that leaves the aorta and goes to vital organs, including the brain. High intensity exercise requires significant amounts of additional oxygen, and if someone with an atrial septal defect has deficient oxygen levels at baseline, their ability to exercise will be greatly hindered by their condition.

10. The mean arterial pressure (MAP) is used to describe the average blood pressure during a single cardiac cycle in a part of the circulatory system. Where in the body is the MAP the highest?
    A. Inferior Vena Cava
    B. Right Ventricle
    C. **Aorta**
    D. Arterioles

Choice **C** is correct. The aorta is where all blood must exit the heart before it is pumped to every possible location in the body. As the blood travels away from the heart and diffuses through increasingly smaller blood vessels, the mean arterial pressure decreases. It is the pressure differential between the aorta and the right atrium that drives the flow of blood through the body. Therefore the blood will be lowest in the right atrium and highest in the aorta.

A: Mean arterial pressure will be at its lowest point near the vena cava and the right atrium.
B: Mean arterial pressure will be increasing at the right ventricle, but it will not be as high in the right ventricle as it will be in the aorta.
D: Mean arterial pressure will have decreased significantly once it has passed far away from the aorta and reached the arterioles.

Passage III Explanation (Questions 11-15)

Pancreatic ductal **adenocarcinoma** (PDAC) is a lethal cancer with extremely poor prognosis. The **role of miRNA** in other cancers have been elucidated, but due to **high tissue heterogeneity** of PDAC, studies have **not revealed** any particular pattern of **miRNA dysregulation**.

Keywords: adenocarcinoma, tissue heterogeneity, dysregulation

MiRNAs are small non-coding RNA molecules that direct post-transcriptional regulation of gene expression. Typically, miRNAs are produced either from their own transcriptional units or derived from the introns of coding genes. Both undergo different avenues of processing to produce a **miRNA/miRNA* duplex**. Only one strand is incorporated into the RNA-induced silencing complex (**RISC**), which interacts with the mRNA, while the other strand is degraded. For **partially complementary** miRNAs to recognize their targets, only nucleotides 2 through 8 in the 'seed region' have to be **perfectly complementary**, located in the 3' untranslated region (UTR). As a result of binding, the mRNA is silenced by translational repression or deadenylation. When there is perfect complementarity, the **mRNA is silenced** by endonucleolytic cleavage and degradation.

Keywords: miRNA/miRNA* duplex, RNA-induced silencing complex (RISC), partially complementary, 'seed region', deadenylation, perfect complementary, endonucleolytic

Contrast: Partially complementary miRNA recognize seed region and silence by repression, while perfectly complementary silence by cleavage and degradation.

The epithelial-mesenchymal transition (**EMT**), in which cells **lose their polarity** and adhesion, is the initial step in tumor metastasis. **Epithelial cells** are highly ordered and display polarity by adhering to one another via tight junctions, **while mesenchymal cells** differ in shape and display the capacity for migration. Studies have **demonstrated** that the miR-200 family, a group of functionally related **miRNAs, inhibits EMT** by negatively regulating transcription factors ZEB1 and ZEB2. Studies have also shown that the tumor suppressor protein E-cadherin regulates EMT through its role in cell adhesion and maintenance of cell polarity. Experiments were conducted to assess **whether** miR-200 family **expression correlates** with the **epithelial phenotype** in PDAC cell lines, and the results are below:

Keywords: EMT, epithelial, mesenchymal, cell polarity, epithelial phenotype

Contrast: Epithelial cells are highly ordered and display polarity, but mesenchymal cells differ in shape and can migrate.

Cause and Effect: miR-200 family inhibits EMT by destroying transcription factors ZEB1 and ZEB2.

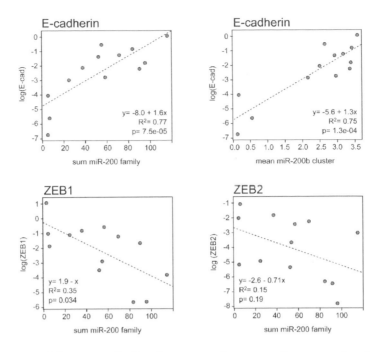

Figure 1: There is a strong positive association between the sum of expression levels of all miR-200 family members and E-cadherin expression. There is also a significant negative association between the miR-200 expression and ZEB1 levels. ZEB2 expression showed greater variance and was not significantly correlated with miR-200 expression according to the p-value, but there is a negative trend.

In prostate cancer cell lines, **miR-34a** was found to be **downregulated** and suspected to have a role similar to **E-cadherin**. A vector was used to reintroduce expression of miR-34a into PDAC lines in order to elucidate its role, and the data is shown below:

Keywords: E-cadherin

Figure 2 Growth rates of retrovirally-infected PDAC lines

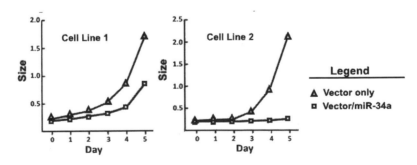

Figure 2: Expression of miR-34a in Panc-1 and MiaPaCa2 cell lines dramatically inhibited cellular proliferation demonstrating the antitumorigenic properties of miR-34a are operative in PDAC cells.

11. Anti-miRs are oligonucleotide analogs have been used therapeutically to correct any defective miRNA-mRNA interaction that contributes causally to a disease. Based on the information given in the passage, which anti-miR would be most effective at silencing the miRNA for the following mRNA transcript?

$$5'-...CUAGAGUCCCCGGCGCGCCUUUCUGCUGCUGU...-3'$$

   A. 5'-UGCUGCUGA-3'
   B. 5'-ACAGCAGCA-3'
   C. 5'-UCCCCGAUG-3'
   D. 5'-CGCGCCGGGG-3'

Choice **A** is correct. Antagomirs bind to miRNA, and miRNA pairs with its mRNA. The anti-miR would have a sequence most similar to the original mRNA transcript. According to the passage, for partially complementary miRNAs to recognize their targets, only nucleotides 2 through 8 in the 'seed region' have to be perfectly complementary, generally in the 3'-UTR. Eliminate any sequence that is complementary to the mRNA transcript. 5'-UGCUGCUGA-3' matches the mRNA transcript nearest the 3' end, and it would be able to be perfectly complementary for nucleotides 2 through 8 on the miRNA.

B: Notice how 5'-ACAGCAGCA-3' has more adenines than appears in the original mRNA transcript. By turning it around (3'-ACGACGACA-5'), it can be matched up perfectly with 3' end of the mRNA transcript.
C: 5'-UCCCCGAUG-3' is similar to the original transcript. The anti-miR differs at the AU near the 3' end, so there is no configuration that would allow for perfect complementarity for 7 consecutive nucleotides.
D: For 5'-CGCGCCGGGG-3', the four sequential guanines hint that the sequence is complementary to the mRNA transcript. By turning it around (3'-GGGGCCGCGC-5'), it can be matched up starting with the CCCC in the original transcript.

12. The 70 nucleotide hairpin structure of pre-miRNA is an example of secondary structure for nucleic acids. Which of the following structures would be similarly classified?
   A. DNA-RNA hybrid
   B. α-helix in transmembrane receptors
   C. tRNA cloverleaf
   D. disulfide bond in IgG

Choice **C** is correct. For nucleic acids, secondary structure involves base pairing interactions within a single molecule or set of interacting molecules. The cloverleaf structure in tRNA, the stem loop in rho-independent termination, and the pseudoknot of telomerase are all secondary structure elements for nucleic acids.

A: The DNA-RNA hybrid involves pairing between two strands of nucleic acids, and this would fall under tertiary structure of nucleic acids.
B, D: These are examples of structures for proteins, not nucleic acids.

13. There are certain elements on a plasmid vector that are essential for ensuring expression of a particular miRNA in the transfected cell. Which of the following is NOT an essential component?
    A. Bacterial origin of replication
    B. **Reporter gene**
    C. Restriction enzyme sites
    D. Host transcription initiating sequence

Choice **B** is correct. Some vectors may contain a reporter gene that allows for identification of plasmid that contains inserted DNA sequence. A common reporter in bacteria is the E. coli lacZ gene, which encodes the protein beta-galactosidase. This enzyme causes bacteria expressing the gene to appear blue when grown on a medium that contains the substrate analog X-gal.

A. Vectors must have a bacterial origin of replication to allow for the replication and maintenance of the vector in the host cell.
C. Vectors must have at least one restriction enzyme site to allow for the insertion of foreign DNA into the vector through ligation.
D. Expressing an RNA sequence requires transcribing it, so vectors must have at least one transcription initiating sequence to provide a site to being the transcription process.

14. Based on the growth rate charts of the retrovirally infected PDAC cell lines, what of the following statements best describes the role of miR-34a?
    A. miR-34a expression promotes extensive cell death and necrosis.
    B. miR-34a is less effective at promoting cell death in Cell Line 1.
    C. **miR-34a exhibits potent antitumorigenic or anti-tumor forming properties in PDAC cell lines.**
    D. miR-34a is strongly downregulated in a majority of the PDAC cell lines.

Choice **C** is correct. In both tumor cell lines, restoration of miR-34a dramatically inhibits cell growth. Based on these results, the antitumorigenic properties are operative in PDAC cells.

A: Restoration of miR-34a expression does not promote necrosis but perhaps apoptosis. Necrosis is the premature death of living cells by autolysis, while apoptosis is a naturally occurring programmed and targeted cause of cellular death.
B: In comparing the two cell lines, there is more tumor growth in Cell Line 1, but it cannot be inferred that miR-34a is less effective. miRNA regulation is combinatorial, so there could be other mitigating factors or miRNAs involved in counteracting miR-34a.
D: Inherent in the data is that the two cell lines start with low endogenous miR-34a expression since the vector reinstates miR-34a expression. However, it cannot be inferred that it is strongly downregulated in the other PDAC cell lines.

15. As defined by the passage, what is necessary for the maintenance of the "epithelial" phenotype?
    A. Low levels of miR-34a
    B. High levels of ZEB-1 and ZEB-2
    C. **High levels of E-cadherin**
    D. Low levels of miR-200

Choice **C** is correct. From the last question, we determined that miR-34a exhibits potent antitumorigenic properties. The data demonstrates that there is a positive correlation between miR-200 family and E-cadherin. So when miR-200 levels are high, E-cadherin levels must also be high. The passage states that E-cadherin acts as a tumor suppressor protein and has a role in cell-to-cell adhesion. Since the EMT involves loss of adhesion, high levels of E-cadherin must be necessary to maintain the epithelial phenotype

A: High levels of miR-34a prevent tumorigenesis, but do not act to maintain the epithelial phenotype.

B: MiR-200 inhibits EMT by negatively regulating transcription factors ZEB1 and ZEB2. The data confirms that negative correlation between miR-200 and ZEB, so when miR-200 levels are high, both ZEB-1 and ZEB-2 should be low.

D: The data also indicates that there is a positive correlation between miR-200 and an epithelial phenotype. Thus low levels of miR-200 would not help maintain the epithelial phenotype.

Discrete Set 1 Explanation (Questions 16-18)

16. During diastole:
    A. the ventricles contract and pump blood into the aorta and pulmonary artery.
    B. the vena cava contracts and pumps blood into the right atrium.
    C. the aorta smooth muscle stretches as it is filled with blood from the left ventricle.
    D. <u>**the ventricles relax and fill with blood from the atria.**</u>

Choice **D** is correct. The heart cycle runs between systole, during which the ventricles contract and push blood into the body and diastole, during which the ventricles relax and fill with blood from the atria.

A: This is systole.
B: The vena cava is lined with smooth muscle, but it does not actively pump blood.
C: The aorta receives blood during systole.

17. When comparing the evolutionary similarity of two organisms, biologists determine that the closest evolutionary relationship between them is reflected by the fact that they are in the same order. Two species that are even more closely related would be placed in the same:
    A. sub-kingdom.
    B. phylum.
    C. <u>**family.**</u>
    D. class.

Choice C is correct. Organisms are classified in a hierarchy: Kingdom, Phylum, Class, Order, Family, Genus, Species. The more closely related two organisms are, the farther down the hierarchy you go when grouping them. Thus two organisms in the same genus are very closely related, but two organisms in the same phylum may not be closely related at all. Here, two organisms in the same family would be more closely related that two organisms in the same order.

18. Which of the following places the components listed in the correct order, following the flow of fluid from the blood plasma to the urine?
    A. Glomerulus; distal convoluted tubule; ureter; collecting duct
    B. Renal artery; proximal convoluted tubule; ascending loop of Henle; descending loop of Henle; ureter
    C. Renal artery; glomerulus; descending loop of Henle; bladder; ureter
    D. <u>**Glomerulus; descending loop of Henle; ascending loop of Henle; bladder**</u>

Choice D is correct. The correct order for fluid moving from the blood, through the nephron and exiting the body is: Renal artery→glomerulus→proximal tubule→descending loop of Henle→ ascending loop of Henle→distal tubule→collecting duct→ureter→bladder. All the other choices fail to put these components in the proper order.

Passage IV Explanation (Questions 19-22)

Parathyroid hormone (PTH) is secreted by cells of the **parathyroid glands**. It acts to **increase** the concentration of **calcium** in the blood, whereas **calcitonin** acts to **decrease calcium** concentration. PTH promotes bone resorption by indirectly stimulating osteoclasts, the cells responsible for resorbing bone tissue. Osteoclasts lack PTH receptors, but PTH does bind osteoblasts—cells responsible for bone synthesis. Binding stimulates osteoblasts to increase their expression of **RANKL** and inhibits their expression of OPG. Binding of RANK to RANKL stimulates osteoclast **differentiation**. OPG binds to RANKL and blocks it from interacting with RANK. Additionally, PTH acts on the kidneys, where it enhances active reabsorption of Ca^{2+} and Mg^{2+}, while decreasing reabsorption of **phosphate**. PTH further acts on the kidneys to **increase** their production of the active metabolite of **Vitamin D, calcitriol**, which **increases the absorption of Ca^{2+} by the intestines**.

Key terms: parathyroid hormone (PTH), parathyroid glad, calcitonin, osteoclasts, osteoblasts, RANK, RANKL, OPG, Vitamin D, calcitriol

Contrast: PTH increases free calcium ion concentration in the blood; calcitonin decreases it

Cause-and-Effect: PTH increases calcium ion levels in the blood by promoting resorption of bone; bone resorption is stimulated by PTH binding to its receptors on osteoblasts; the binding of RANKL by its ligand, RANK, stimulates osteoclast differentiation; OPG binding blocks binding of RANK to RANKL; PTH binding causes osteoblasts to increase their expression of RANK and inhibits their expression of OPG, thereby increasing the number of active osteoclasts; PTH acts on the kidneys to increase Ca^{2+} and Mg^{2+} reabsorption, decrease phosphate reabsorption, and increase the kidneys conversion of a Vitamin D precursor to its active metabolite, calcitriol; calcitriol increases intestinal absorption of Ca^{2+}

A physician examining a 55 year old female patient complaining of abdominal pain suspected a **dysfunction of calcium regulation**. Laboratory analysis revealed a total serum **calcium of 12.3 (normal 8.4-10.2)**, a serum **phosphorous of 2.4 (normal 2.7-4.5)**, and **elevated PTH**. In order to make a diagnosis, the physician took the laboratory values into consideration along with the following information regarding PTH dysfunction:

Primary hyperparathyroidism can develop as a result of autonomous oversecretion of PTH by the parathyroid gland.

Secondary hyperparathyroidism is characterized by an appropriately elevated PTH response to low blood Ca^{2+} concentration.

Pseudohypoparathyroidism is a condition associated with **resistance of cells to PTH**.

An **inappropriately low level of PTH** in the blood due to decreased parathyroid gland function is known as hypoparathyroidism.

Key terms: primary hyperthyroidism; secondary hyperthyroidism; pseudohypoparathyroidism; hypoparathyroidism

Cause-and-Effect: the patient's lab results show elevated calcium and PTH levels; primary hyperthyroidism results from inappropriate oversecretion of PTH; secondary hyperthyroidism is an appropriately elevated PTH response to low blood calcium; hypoparathyroidism is characterized by low levels of PTH synthesis or secretion; pseudohypoparathyroidism is caused by resistance of cells to PTH

19. Secondary hyperparathyroidism is likely to be caused by all of the following EXCEPT:
    A. chronic kidney disease.
    B. decreased dietary calcium intake.
    C. elevated blood phosphate levels.
    D. <u>**a PTH secreting tumor.**</u>

Choice **D** is correct. Secondary hyperparathyroidism is the compensatory increase in parathyroid hormone (PTH) as a result of decreased calcium. A PTH secreting tumor would lead to an inappropriate elevation of PTH hormone and low serum calcium (high serum calcium is seen in primary hyperparathyroidism, as would result from the situation described in choice D).

A: Secondary hyperparathyroidism can be caused by chronic kidney disease, by decreasing the synthesis of calcitriol; when calcitriol levels are decreased, there is decreased calcium absorption from the GI tract, leading to decreased serum Ca^{2+} levels—resulting in increased PTH release
B: Secondary hyperparathyroidism can be caused by decreased dietary intake of calcium, leading to decreased serum Ca^{2+} levels—resulting in increased PTH release
C: Secondary hyperparathyroidism can be caused by elevated blood phosphate levels; phosphate binds Ca^{2+}, removing free calcium from circulation, leading to decreased serum Ca^{2+} levels—resulting in increased PTH release

20. Sarcoidosis, a disease involving the formation of nodules containing inflammatory cells, can lead to increased formation of calcitriol. Of the following, what is the most likely physiological effect of this disease?
    A. Decreased bone density
    B. Hypoparathyroidism
    C. <u>**Elevated urinary calcium**</u>
    D. Less intestinal calcium absorption

Choice **C** is correct. Calcitriol synthesis by sarcoid granulomas will cause increased calcium absorption from the GI tract, leading to increased serum Ca^{2+} levels and increased urinary calcium clearance. The increase in the filtered load of Ca^{2+} is due to both its elevated concentration in the blood and its decreased reabsorption in the tubules secondary to an appropriate decrease in PTH secretion by the parathyroid gland.

A: an appropriate PTH response should not have a negative effect on bone mineralization.
B: the passage indicates that hypoparathyroidism is due to some dysfunction of PTH secretion, most often as a consequence of surgical removal of the thyroid or parathyroid gland, or an inherited or immune-related condition; while PTH levels would be decreased in the situation described in the question stem, it would constitute an appropriate response to changes in circulating calcium levels.
D: calcitriol synthesis by sarcoid granulomas will cause increased calcium absorption from the GI tract.

21. What would result from the total surgical removal of the parathyroid gland?
    A. Enhanced bone mineralization
    B. Increased cardiac contractility
    C. <u>**Neurological complications**</u>
    D. Kidney failure

Choice **C** is correct. Extracellular calcium is required for both neurotransmitter release and is involved in the mechanism of contraction of the cells of the all muscle types. For this reason, physiological blood calcium concentrations are tightly regulated within a narrow range for proper cellular processes. Removal of the parathyroid gland—the source of PTH synthesis—would severely interfere with normal calcium homeostasis. Involuntary muscular contraction, referred to as tetany, and seizures may result from the condition.

A: Bone mineralization would not be increased by decreased PTH secretion.

B: Cardiac contractility, which depends on extracellular calcium influx as part of its mechanism of calcium-induced calcium release from the sarcoplasmic reticulum, would be decreased, rather than increased, in severe cases of depressed blood calcium.

D: While the kidneys are centrally involved in the body's various mechanisms of calcium homeostasis, their function does not depend on the maintenance of extracellular calcium

22. The following findings in a symptomatic patient are most consistent with what disorder of calcium metabolism? (Note: measurements of serum Ca^{2+}, phosphates and calcitriol concentrations and in urinary phosphorus excretion after administration of biosynthetic PTH were unchanged).

Serum [PTH]:   High
Serum [Calcitriol]: Low
Serum [Ca^{2+}]:   Low
Serum [Phosphate]: High

  A. Primary hyperparathyroidism
  B. Secondary hyperparathyroidism
  C. Hypoparathyroidism
  D. <u>Pseudohypoparathyroidism</u>

Choice **D** is correct. Pseudohypoparathyroidism is one of several unrelated genetic condition where affected individuals show a common phenotype associated with resistance to PTH. Patients have a low serum calcium and high phosphate, because of resistance to the effects of PTH at the cellular level, but an appropriate elevation of PTH in response to low blood calcium concentrations.

A: Blood [Ca^{2+}] would be elevated in primary hyperparathyroidism

B: Laboratory values such as those shown could also be due to secondary hyperparathyroidism; however, the fact that measurements of serum calcium, phosphates and calcitriol concentrations, as well as of urinary phosphorus excretion after administration of biosynthetic PTH were unchanged, indicates a primary insensitivity to PTH activity.

C: PTH would be low in hypoparathyroidism

Passage V Explanation (Questions 23-26)

Entry of **enveloped viruses** into cells can occur by **membrane fusion** or by **endocytosis**. Viral **envelope proteins** attach to receptors on the **surface of target cells** at **neutral pH**, triggering fusion with the host cell, uncoating and emptying of the viral contents into the cell. In endocytosis, **viral particles** are endocytosed by host cell endosomes. Following entry into the host cell, viral particles can be **released** from the endosomes in a **pH-dependent mechanism**, most likely because of **conformational changes** in **protein receptors** caused by the action of pH-dependent proteases during endosomal acidification.

Key terms: enveloped virus, membrane fusion, endocytosis, envelope proteins, uncoating, endosomal acidification

Cause-and-Effect: enveloped viruses can enter target cells by membrane fusion or endocytosis; envelope proteins can attach to cell-surface receptors on target cells at neutral pH, triggering membrane fusion, uncoating and the entry of viral contents in cells; in endocytosis, viral particles enter into cells in host cell endosomes; after entry in endosomes, viral particles are released because of conformation changes in protein receptors due to the action of pH-dependent proteases during endosomal acidification

Particles of **human immunodeficiency virus (HIV)**—an **enveloped virus**—produced in the presence of the **viral factor Nef** are **more infectious** than particles produced in the absence of this protein. The mechanism underlying this effect is poorly understood. In order to study Nef-mediated infectivity enhancement, HIV particles were engineered to contain envelope proteins from **CXCR4-dependent (X4)** HIV (an uncommon, receptor specific form of HIV which **requires** the cell surface protein **CD4** for viral entry), amphotropic murine leukemia virus (**ampho**), or the vesicular stomatitis virus (**VSV**). The **infectivity** of these engineered particles, as well as that of a HIV particle containing the most common envelope protein, **CCR5 (R5)**, were **measured** in the **presence or absence of Nef**. Results are given in Figure 1.

Key terms: human immunodeficiency virus (HIV), Nef, CXCR4-dependent (X4) HIV, CD4, amphotropic murine leukemia virus (ampho), vesicular stomatitis virus (VSV), CCR5 (R5)

Cause-and-Effect: HIV particles produced in the presence of Nef are more infectious than those made in its absence; the infectivity of particles with X4, ampho, VSV or R5 coat protein was tested

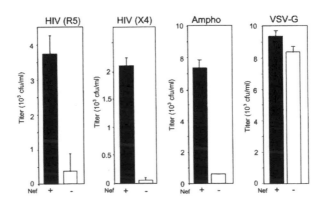

Figure 1: Nef significantly increases the infectivity of HIV particles containing all coat proteins other than VSV-G

To test the hypothesis that **Nef-mediated rate enhancement** is **specific to** envelope protein fusion at **neutral pH**, the scientists produced Nef+ and Nef− HIV hybrids with Ebola virus glycoprotein **(Ebola-GP)**, which has recently been shown to facilitate **fusion** through a **low-pH**-dependent mechanism. The **infectivity** of these particles, as well as three previously synthesized hybrids, was tested in the presence or absence of **bafilomycin A1**, an agent that **prevents** the **acidification of endosomes** by blocking the function of the vacuolar H^+ ATPase. Results are shown in Figure 2.

Key terms: Ebola virus glycoprotein (Ebola-GP), low pH-dependent mechanism; bafilomycin A1, vacuolar H^+ ATPase

Cause and effect: they tested the hypothesis that Nef-mediated rate enhancement is specific to envelope protein fusion at neutral pH; infectivity of HIV-Ebola GP hybrids (and hybrids tested previously) was tested in presence/absence of bafilomycin A1; it prevents endosomal acidification

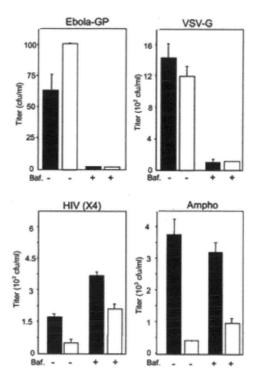

Figure 2: Nef enhanced infectivity only in HIV hybrids containing X4 and Ampho envelope proteins in the presence of the inhibitor of endosomal acidification, Baf; infectivity by Ebola-GP and VSV-G hybrids was greatly reduced by Baf treatment; infectivity was slightly increased in X4 and Ampho hybrids by the addition of Baf. Figure 1 shows that Nef significantly increases the infectivity of HIV particles containing all coat proteins other than VSV-G

23. Given passage information, target cell pH-dependent proteases required for viral release from endosomes have which of the following effects, if any, on the Ebo-GP envelope proteins of HIV particles in acidified endosomes?
    A. Reduced enzyme activity
    B. Protein dimer synthesis
    C. **Formation of smaller protein fragments**
    D. No effect

Choice **C** is correct. Figure 2 supports the conclusion that Ebo-GP hybrid particles enter the cell, like VSV-G hybrids, in a low-pH dependent pathway. The passage also states that viral particles can be released from the endosomes in a pH-dependent mechanism, most likely because of conformational changes in envelope protein receptors caused by the action of host cell pH-dependent proteases. This indicates that pH-dependent proteases act in the same fashion as do all proteases—the hydrolysis of peptide bonds in the residue sequences for which they are specific, resulting in the digestion of proteins. Only choice C is consistent with the hydrolysis of peptide bonds to form smaller proteins.

A: The passage state that the targets of pH-dependent proteases are protein receptors, not enzymes.
B: The hydrolysis of peptide bonds in the residue sequences for which the proteases are specific result in the digestion of proteins, not the synthesis of dimers.
D: The hydrolysis of peptide bonds in the residue sequences for which the proteases are specific result in the digestion of proteins.

24. The trials shown in Figure 2 that were conducted in the presence of bafilomycin A1 confirm that:
    A. all particles tested are able to enter the cell through a neutral-pH mechanism.
    B. particles containing Ebola-Gp and VSV-G envelope proteins enter the cell in a pH-independent mechanism.
    C. particles containing HIV X4 and ampho envelope proteins enter through a low-pH dependent mechanism.
    D. **particles containing Ebola-Gp and VSV-G envelope proteins enter through a low-pH dependent mechanism.**

Choice **D** is correct. Figure 2 shows that the infectivities of Ebola-GP and VSV-G containing hybrids are substantially reduced upon addition of the inhibitor of endosomal acidification bafilomycin A1 (Baf), suggesting that both enter through a low-pH dependent mechanism. This supports the hypothesis that Nef-mediated rate enhancement is specific to envelope protein fusion at neutral pH.

A and B: Ebola-GP and VSV-G containing hybrids enter cells through a low-pH dependent mechanism.
C: Because bafilomycin increases their infectivity, we can conclude that HIV X4 and ampho containing hybrids enter cells through a pH neutral mechanism.

25. It is proposed that in some instances CXCR4-dependent HIV particles initially enter the cell through an endocytic route as mentioned in the passage. Is this consistent with the results shown in Figure 2 relating bafilomycin A1 treatment's effect on Nef+ particles containing HIV X4 envelope protein??
    A. No, an increase in endosomal pH due to bafilomycin A1 would decrease the likelihood of infection due to endocytosed HIV particles.
    B. No, the fraction HIV X4-containing particles that enter cells by the endocytic route fail to survive subsequent endosomal acidification.
    C. No, Nef+ particles containing HIV X4 envelope proteins display approximately equal infectivities with or without bafilomycin A1 treatment.
    D. **Yes, treatment with bafilomycin A1 would prevent acidification and therefore could cause this usually nonproductive route of entry to become productive.**

Choice **D** is correct. Figure 2 shows that bafilomycin A1 treatment of Nef+ particles containing HIV X4 envelope proteins significantly increases infectivity. Information presented in the question supports the conclusion that these hybrids containing HIV X4 envelope proteins enter the cell in a pH-neutral pathway as described in paragraph 1. This information could be reconciled with the increased infectivity of X4 hybrids when treated with bafilomycin if bafilomycin A1-induced blockage of endosomal acidification allowed increased survival and subsequent infectivity of those particles entering the cell through endosomal route.

A and C: Figure 2 shows that an increase in endosomal pH due to baf treatment increases infectivity in both Nef+ and Nef- hybrid particles containing X4 contain proteins.

B: while it's likely that under normal conditions the fraction HIV X4-containing particles that enter cells by the endocytic route fail to survive subsequent endosomal acidification, an inhibitor of endosomal acidification such as Baf may increase the likelihood of survival for those endocytosed particles.

26. Which of the following results, together with data in Figure 2 that indicates the loss of Nef infectivity enhancement function in HIV-Ebola-GP hybrids, most strengthens the hypothesis that fusion at the cell surface is required for Nef enhancement of infectivity?

   A. In HIV particles bearing both X4 and VSV-G envelope proteins, no Nef infectivity enhancement was seen in cells lacking CD4.

   B. HIV particles containing only VSV-G envelope proteins showed the same Nef infectivity enhancement toward cells expressing CD4 as HIV particles bearing X4 and VSV-G envelope proteins.

   C. In HIV particles bearing both Ebola-GP and VSV-G, envelope proteins, greater Nef infectivity enhancement was seen in cells lacking CD4 than in cells expressing CD4.

   D. HIV particles containing only Ebola-GP envelope proteins showed greater Nef infectivity enhancement toward cells expressing CD4 than did HIV particles bearing both Ebola-V and VSV-G envelope proteins.

Choice **A** is correct. The passage states that the CXCR4-dependent (X4) HIV envelope protein binds to the cell surface protein CD4 for viral entry. Additionally, Figures 1 and 2 indicate that VSV-G hybrids enter the cell in a low-pH dependent mechanism that is not significantly influenced by Nef, while the infectivity of X4 hybrid particles is due to a pH-neutral pathway that is significantly enhanced by Nef. If a new hybrid particle was engineered to contain VSV-G and X4 envelope proteins, and if no CD4 was present on target cells to permit entry via X4-CD4 surface binding, then viral particle entry should be confined to the VSV-G endosomal pathway—a pathway which does not display Nef enhancement.

B: hybrid viral particles containing both X4 and VSV-G envelope proteins should show greater infectivity enhancement toward CD4 expressing cells than particles containing only VSV-G envelope protein, provided that the VSV-G entry pathway is not fully dominant to X4 mediated entry. In either case, however, this finding does not support the conclusion drawn in the question.

C: the finding that HIV particles bearing both Ebola-GP and VSV-G, envelope proteins displayed greater Nef infectivity enhancement in cells lacking CD4 than in cells expressing CD4 would contradict, rather than support the mechanism of Nef infectivity enhancement referenced in the question.

D: the finding that HIV particles containing only Ebola-GP envelope proteins showed greater Nef infectivity enhancement toward cells expressing CD4 than did HIV particles bearing both Ebola-V and VSV-G envelope proteins would neither strongly support, nor contradict the mechanism of Nef infectivity enhancement referenced in the question.

Discrete Set 2 Explanation (Questions 27-30)

These questions are NOT related to a passage.

27. When calcium ions are released from the sarcoplasmic reticulum:
    A. the muscle is able to repolarize after a fiber twitches.
    B. the acetylcholine in the neuromuscular junction is able to be reabsorbed by the presynaptic membrane.
    C. the myosin heads are able to disconnect from the actin filaments.
    D. <u>they bind to troponin allowing the actin filament to bind to myosin.</u>

Choice **D** is correct. This bio question is asking us about the function of Ca^{2+} in the muscle contraction cycle. Calcium binds to troponin, which allows actin and myosin bind to each other to carry out the sliding action that is contraction.

A: Repolarization is the process of cell membranes re-establishing their resting potentials, and is not linked with calcium activity.
B: Acetylcholine is one of several neurotransmitters in the autonomic nervous system. ACh acts on both the peripheral nervous system and central nervous system and is used in the motor division of the somatic nervous system. However, it is released by the synapse and is not associated with calcium activity in the neuromuscular junction.
C: This is known as the power-stroke of muscle contraction and requires ATP, not calcium.

28. Angiogenesis inhibitors can serve as an effective treatment for stopping or slowing the growth of tumors because:
    A. in the absence of a steady blood supply, the telomeres in the tumor cells will shorten, causing the tumor cells to stop dividing after approximately 50 rounds of division.
    B. lack of adequate vascularization triggers apoptosis in any cell.
    C. <u>cells or tissues that can only receive nutrients by diffusion through surrounding tissues are size limited.</u>
    D. the tumor growth factors that stimulate tumor development must be delivered via the circulatory system.

Choice **C** is correct. One of the most important underlying biological principles the MCAT will expect you to know is the importance of surface area to volume ratios. Individual cells are limited in size because nutrients must move through a cell by diffusion. Tissues of cells can grow larger because the circulatory system effectively increases the surface area across which nutrients can be delivered and waste products removed. As a tumor grows, it needs to have new blood vessels grow to provide this surface area for nutrient exchange. In the absence of such blood vessel growth, tumors are limited in volume.

29. Which of the following is the structure of pyruvate?

A.

B.

C.

D.

Choice **A** is correct. Pyruvate (IUPAC name, 2-oxopropanoic acid) has 3 carbons and a carboxylic acid group (RC(O) OH). Choices B, C, and D do not have the correct structure.

B: There are 5 total carbons here and no acid group.
C: There are 4 total carbons here and no acid group.
D: There are 2 total carbons here and no acid group.

30. Which of the following is NOT a bond that directly helps determine secondary and tertiary structure of a protein?
    A. Hydrogen bonds
    B. <u>Peptide bonds</u>
    C. Electrostatic bonds
    D. Disulfide bonds

Choice **B** is correct. Remember that peptide bonds determine primary structure, not secondary or tertiary structure. Thus choice B is correct.

A: Hydrogen bonds play a role in secondary structure
C, D: Electrostatic and disulfide bonds play a role in determining tertiary structure

Passage VI Explanation (Questions 31-34)

Mesenchymal stem cells (MSCs), which express the marker proteins **CD109** and **CD90**, are **stromal cells** that, upon terminal differentiation, yield the cells of **connective tissue**. Scientists considering the influence of transcription factors on MSC lineage commitment studied the effects of a pool of four transcription factors thought to be involved in MSC differentiation. They noticed that fourteen days after injection of mouse MSCs with a pool of the four factors, cells testing the number of CD109-positive cells declined.

Key terms: mesenchymal stem cells (MSCs), CD109, CD90, stromal cells

Cause-and-Effect: MSCs are stromal cells that express CD109 and CD190, and which differentiate to connective tissue; injection of a pool of four transcription factors caused expression of Bglap, a connective-tissue specific protein, and of osteonectin in mouse MSC cells, as well a decrease in CD109 expression cells.

Fibroblast growth factor 2 (Fgf2) has previously been shown to **reversibly inhibit differentiation** of primary mouse MSCs, but the intracellular signaling pathways that maintain cells in an undifferentiated state remain largely unexplored. To further study the effects of transcription factors on MSC differentiation, mouse **MSCs** were **cultured** for seven days in complete culture media (CCM) supplemented with 20 ng/ml **Fgf2**. This treatment was shown to **alter expression** of genes for the **four transcription factor** pool versus levels of expression in untreated cells, as shown in Figure 1.

Key terms: fibroblast growth factor 2 (Fgf2)

Cause-and-Effect: Fgf2 inhibits MSC differentiation; treatment of MSCs with Fgf2 alters expressions of the four transcription factors previously tested

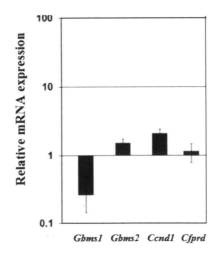

Figure 1: Fgf2 decreases expression of Gbms1 and increases Gbms2, Ccnd1 and Cfprd expression

In subsequent experiments, scientists attempted to determine the influence of those four transcription factors in the differentiation of MSC, by **removing one of four transcription factors** from the four-factor pool, and observing the presence of cells **testing positive for bone gamma-carboxyglutamic acid protein (Bglap)**, a **connective-tissue specific** non-collagenous bone protein, or **osteonectin**, a component of basement membranes, after fourteen days. Results are shown in Figure 2.

Key terms: bone gamma-carboxyglutamic acid protein (Bglap), osteonectin

Cause-and-Effect: the individual effect of the members of the four transcription factor pool are tested by measuring Bglap or osteonectin expression—markers of connective tissue—in the absence of one of the four members of the transcription factor pool.

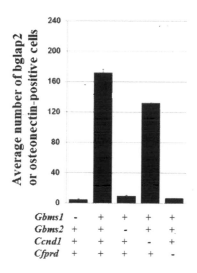

Figure 2: This figure shows the influence of individual transcription factors on MSC differentiation. The extent to which a given column shows a decrease in the number of bglap2- or osteonectin-positive cells versus the second bar, which shows the number of bglap2- or osteonectin-positive cells upon treatment with all four transcription factors, indicates the extent of the contribution of the missing factor to MSC differentiation. For this reason, Ccnd1, which is absent from the pool in the fourth column, has a relatively minor effect on differentiation, while Gbms1 (column 1), Gbms2 (column 3) and Cfprd (column 4) are all necessary for meaningful differentiation. Of those factors tested, Gbms2 has the greatest effect on MSC differentiation.

31. Fgf2 is most likely to inhibit MSC differentiation through its modulation of the expression of what transcription factor?
    A. **Gbms1**
    B. Gbms2
    C. Ccnd1
    D. Cfprd

Choice **A** is correct. Figures 1 and 2 demonstrate that Fgf2 treatment decreases only Gbms1 transcription (Figure 1) and that Gbms1 expression positively influences the number of tissues expressing a connective tissue-like phenotype. This is consistent with the passage description of Fgf2, which states that Fgf2 inhibits MSC differentiation

B, C, D: Figure 1 shows that Fgf2 enhances the rates of transcription of Gbms2 (choice B), Ccnd1 (choice C), and Cfprd (choice D). These factors all stimulate the differentiation of MSCs.

32. Based upon the results presented in the passage, which of the following factors least strongly influenced commitment of mesenchymal stem cells to the connective-tissue lineage in vitro?
    A. Gbms1
    B. Gbms2
    C. **Ccnd1**
    D. Cfprd

Choice **C** is correct. Figure 2 compares the number of bglap2- or osteonectin-positive cells upon treatment with all 4 transcription factors to the number of such cells when one of the factors is removed. Whichever transcription factor shows the least change when absent would have the least effect on commitment of mesenchymal stem cells. In the fourth column of the figure, we see that Ccnd1 was removed and the change from baseline (second column) was the smallest.

33. What is the most likely reason that the scientists chose to measure bglap2 levels in assessing the influence of transcription factors on the maintenance of MSCs in the undifferentiated state?
    A. bglap2 is expressed in all cells of mesenchymal origin.
    B. bglap2 is expressed by both connective tissue and mesenchymal stem cells.
    C. bglap 2 induces differentiation of MSCs.
    D. **bglap2 is expressed by cells with connective tissue-like phenotypes.**

Choice **D** is correct. Because bglap2, like osteonectin, is expressed by connective tissue-like phenotypes, and not undifferentiated MSCs, it is a good indicator of MSC differentiation.

A: bglap2 is not necessarily expressed in all cells of mesenchymal origin, nor does it need to be to indicate differentiation of at least a portion of the MSC population.
B: bglap2 is not expressed by MSCs. If it were, it would not be an effective indicator of MSC differentiation.
C: bglap2 is not the cause, but is an indicator, of MSC differentiation.

34. In terms of their gene activation potential, MSCs are best described as what type of progenitor cell?
    A. Unipotent
    B. **Multipotent**
    C. Pluripotent
    D. Totipotent

Choice B is correct. Multipotency describes progenitor cells which have the gene activation potential to differentiate into multiple, but limited cell types. For example, a multipotent blood stem cell is a hematopoietic cell, and this cell type can differentiate itself into several types of blood cells, such as lymphocytes, monocyte and neutrophils, but cannot differentiate into cells of other lineages. As described by the passage, MSCs are stromal cells which can give rise only to connective tissue cells: osteoblasts (bone cells), chondrocytes (cartilage cells), and adipocytes (fat cells).

A: A unipotent cell can differentiate into only one cell type. It is unclear if any truly unipotent stem cells exist.
C: A pluripotent stem cell can give rise to cells of any of the three germ layers: endoderm (tissue lining the gastrointestinal and respiratory linings), mesoderm (muscle, bone, blood, and the lining of most of the urogenital system), or ectoderm (epidermal and nervous tissues). MSCs give rise only to tissues of mesoderm origin.
D: Totipotency is the ability of a single cell to divide and produce all of the differentiated cells in an organism. Zygotes are an example of a totipotent cell.

Passage VII Explanation (Questions 35-39)

Huntington's disease (HD) is an **inherited neurodegenerative disease** caused by progressive **neuronal loss** in the **striatum** region of the brain. The **Huntingtin gene (HTT)**, which is located on the **short arm of chromosome 4** and which codes for the **cytoplasmic protein Huntingtin (Htt)**, contains a sequence of three DNA bases—cytosine-adenine-guanine (CAG)—repeated multiple times. This repeating sequence is known as a **trinucleotide repeat**. CAG codes for the amino acid **glutamine**, and the trinucleotide repeat results in the production of a chain of glutamine known as a **polyglutamine** (polyQ) tract. The **length of CAG repeat varies** between individuals and, depending upon its length, **dynamic mutation** may **increase its length between generations**. When the length of this repeated section reaches a certain **threshold**, it produces an altered form of the protein, called **mutant Huntingtin protein (mHtt)**, which is toxic to cells of the striatum.

Key terms: Huntington's disease (HD), Huntingtin (Htt) protein, trinucleotide repeat, polyglutamine (polyQ) tract, mutant Huntingtin protein (mHtt)

Cause-and-Effect: HD is caused by neuron loss in the striatum; HTT contains trinucleotide (CAG) repeats that code for the polyQ regions of repeated glutamine residues in the HTT protein; the length of CAG repeats varies between individuals; sufficiently long trinucleotide repeats are expanded (dynamic mutation) during meiosis and passed to subsequent generations; trinucleotide repeats of sufficient length code for harmful mHTT protein

Geneticists studying the inheritance pattern of HD found that it is **rare for HD to be caused by a new mutation** and noticed that the **length of the repeated sequence** influenced the **age of onset** and **progression** and **severity** of symptoms experienced by **affected individuals** and their **affected offspring**. The geneticists' findings are summarized in Table 1.

Key terms: rare for new mutation, length of sequence

Cause-and-Effect: HD is rarely caused by a new mutation and the length of repeated sequence influenced the age of onset and progression and severity of symptoms of affected individual and their affected children

Repeat Count	Disease status	Age of onset	Probability of affected offspring
< 26	Will not be affected	N/A	None
27-35	Will not be affected	N/A	Elevated, but much less than 50%
36-39	May be affected	After 40	50%
40+	Will be affected	Between 25-39; earlier with increased repeat count	50%

Table 1: Individuals with fewer than 36 CAG repeats do not display symptoms of the disease, while those with 36-39 repeats may or may not display symptoms. Those with 40 repeats or more will be symptomatic. Only those with fewer than 26 repeats have no chance of producing offspring displaying symptoms of the disease. The age of onset of the disease tends to decrease with greater repeat counts in those with more 40 or more repeats.

A pedigree showing the inheritance pattern of Huntington's disease in one affected family studied by the geneticists is shown in Figure 1.

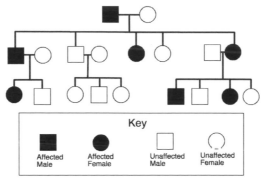

Figure 1: This pedigree suggests an autosomal dominant mode of inheritance. No generations are skipped and approximately half of the children with an unaffected and affected parent are affected. No affected children have unaffected parents. Additionally, all three children of the affected mother and father in the second generation are affected. These facts all suggest a dominant disease. Male-to-male transmission occurs and not all daughters of affected males and unaffected females are affected. Together, these show an autosomal dominant pattern of inheritance.

35. The pedigree in Figure 1 indicates that Huntington's disease displays what pattern of inheritance?
    A. Autosomal recessive
    B. **Autosomal dominant**
    C. Sex-linked recessive
    D. Sex-linked dominant

Choice **B** is correct. This pedigree strongly suggests an autosomal dominant mode of inheritance. No generations are skipped and approximately half of the children with an unaffected and affected parent are affected. No affected children have two unaffected parents. Additionally, all three children of the unaffected mother and father in the second generation are unaffected. These facts all suggest a dominant disease. Male-to-male transmission occurs and not all daughters of affected males and unaffected females are affected. Together, these show an autosomal dominant pattern of inheritance.

36. Given results of the geneticist's work, what is the maximum number of possible glutamine residues in the polyQ region of Htt in an individual displaying a normal phenotype?
    A. 25
    B. 35
    C. **39**
    D. 40

Choice **C** is correct. Individuals with fewer than 35 repeats will not show symptoms. Those with 36-39 may not be affected. Thus the maximum number of glutamine residues of Htt in a normal individual is 39.

A,B: Individuals with as many as 35 glutamine repeats will remain unaffected, while those with between 36-39 repeats may or may not affected.
D: Individuals with 40 or more repeats will be affected by the disease.

37. The geneticists concluded that the symptoms of HD generally become more severe and were diagnosed at an earlier age in affected offspring than in their affected parents. Is there a potential biological explanation for this phenomenon?
    - **A.** No, the observation is due to heightened awareness of disease symptoms within affected families.
    - **B.** No, regions of trinucleotide expansion, located on an autosome, occur only in somatic cells.
    - **C.** Yes, mutant mHtt protein is synthesized by individuals containing CAG repeats.
    - **D.** **Yes, dynamic mutation results in expanded trinucleotides associated with a more severe disease phenotype.**

Choice **D** is correct. The phenomena observed by the geneticists is referred to as genetic anticipation, whereby the symptoms of a genetic disorder become apparent at an earlier age as it is passed on to the next generation. In most cases, an increase of severity of symptoms is also noted. Genes with more than 25 trinucleotide CAG repeats are unstable during replication and this instability increases with the number of repeats present, leading to new expansions from generation to generation (dynamic mutation) rather than the passing of an exact copy of the original trinucleotide repeat. This causes the number of repeats to change in successive generations, such that an unaffected parent with an "intermediate" number of repeats (26–35), or the reduced penetrance form of the disease (36–40 repeats), may pass on a copy of the gene with an increased number of repeats to produce children with fully penetrant HD. Such increases in the number of repeats, and hence the earlier age of onset and severity of disease, could potentially be accounted for if the number of repeats not only determined whether or not symptoms of the disease occur, but also the age of onset and severity of disease symptoms.

A: Increases in the number of repeats, and hence the earlier age of onset and severity of disease, could potentially be accounted for if the number of repeats not only determined whether or not symptoms of the disease occur, but also the age of onset and severity of disease symptoms. Because choice D provides a plausible biological explanation for the geneticists' observations, choice A must be false.
B: Regions of trinucleotide expansion do occur on an autosome (the passage states that Htt is located on chromosome 4), but chromosome 4 is present in both somatic and germ line cells. In fact, its expansion during replication of germ line, not somatic, cells is responsible for the heritable nature of the disease.
C: While this choice correctly states a fact relating to HD, it does offer an explanation for the geneticists' observations.

38. What is the probability that both of the children of an affected father with two copies of the HTT allele, containing more than 40 CAG repeats, and a mother with fewer than 26 CAG repeats, will express the mHtt protein?
    - **A.** 25%
    - **B.** 50%
    - **C.** 75%
    - **D.** **100%**

Choice **D** is correct. Table 1 provides the probability that the offspring of an individual with one expanded HTT allele containing 40 or more repeats and an individual with a repeat count < 26 on either HTT allele is 50%. This probability reflects the fact that the affected offspring is affected because the allele they received from their affected parent was the parent's mutant copy of the HTT allele containing the expanded trinucleotide region. Given HD's autosomal dominant pattern of inheritance, if a parent contained two such alleles, they MUST pass a mutant copy of that allele to all offspring, all of whom would be affected.

39. The observation that not all individuals containing between 36-39 CAG repeats display clinical symptoms of Huntington's disease can be explained in terms of what property of the disease's inheritance pattern?
    A. **Incomplete penetrance**
    B. Variable expressivity
    C. Pleiotropy
    D. Genetic anticipation

Choice **A** is correct. Penetrance in genetics is the proportion of individuals carrying a particular allele that also expresses an associated phenotype. In terms of medical genetics, the penetrance of a disease-causing mutation is the proportion of individuals with the mutation who exhibit clinical symptoms of the associated disease. Some conditions are described as having incomplete penetrance. This means that clinical symptoms are not always present in individuals who have the potentially disease-causing mutation. This is consistent with the situation presented in the question stem regarding the incomplete penetrance of Huntington's disease in the cases of individuals containing 36-39 CAG trinucleotide repeats.

B: Expressivity refers to variations in a phenotype among individuals carrying a particular genotype. This differs from penetrance, which refers to the likelihood of the gene generating any associated phenotype. Variable expressivity occurs when a phenotype is expressed differently among individuals with the same genotype, an example is neurofibromatosis type 1, where patients with the same genetic mutation show different signs and symptoms of the disease.
C: Pleiotropy occurs when one gene influences multiple, seemingly unrelated phenotypic traits, an example being phenylketonuria, a disease that affects multiple systems but is caused by one gene defect.
D: As discussed previously, anticipation is a phenomenon whereby the symptoms of a genetic disorder become apparent at an earlier age and with increasing severity over succeeding generations. Anticipation is common in trinucleotide repeat disorders, where a dynamic mutation in DNA occurs.

Passage VIII Explanation (Questions 40-43)

Though the two conditions arc characterized by similar symptoms, **Diabetes Mellitus (DM) and Diabetes Insipidus (DI) have distinct and unrelated causes**. In both DM and DI, patients experience polyuria (excessive urination). It is important for physicians to differentiate between DM and DI in order to properly treat their patients.

Key terms: Diabetes Mellitus, Diabetes Insipidus, polyuria

Contrast: DI vs. DM caused by problems with ADH and insulin, respectively

Cause-and-Effect: Two conditions with similar symptoms have diff. causes

DM is caused by the **impaired action of insulin in the body**. People with **type 1 DM produce insufficient quantities of insulin or sometimes no insulin at all**. This is thought to be the result of the immune system attacking insulin-secreting cells. **In type 2 DM**, the body develops a gradual reduction in sensitivity to insulin, **resulting in little or no response to the insulin the body produces**. Type 2 DM is associated with obesity and increases the risk of many other health problems, including cardiovascular disease and nerve damage. Elevated levels of blood glucose in DM **can exceed the capacity of the kidneys to reabsorb the substance**.

Key terms: Insulin, type 1 DM, type 2 DM, insulin sensitivity

Contrast: Type 1 DM caused by low/no insulin production, type 2 DM caused by low insulin response

Cause-and-Effect: Two types of DM have different causes

DI is caused by the **impaired action of antidiuretic hormone (ADH)** on the kidneys. In **central DI**, the body **does not produce sufficient ADH**. **Nephrogenic DI** is characterized by **normal serum ADH levels** with an **impaired ability of the kidney to respond to the action of ADH**. Both types of DI can be hereditary in nature or caused by other factors.

Key terms: ADH, central DI, nephrogenic DI

Contrast: Central DI caused by low/no ADH production, nephrogenic DI caused by abnormal response to ADH in kidney

Cause-and-Effect: Two types of DI have different causes

A 15-year-old male with **polyuria and polydipsia (excessive thirst)** presents to his pediatrician. The doctor runs a series of blood and urine tests. In addition to the tests in Table 1 below, the physician performs a test to measure the **patient's response to exogenous insulin, the results of which are normal**.

Key terms: polyuria, polydipsia, exogenous insulin

Contrast: Pt has excessive urination, excessive thirst with normal insulin sensitivity

Value	Result	Normal Range
Fasting Serum Glucose	328 mg/dL	70-110 mg/dL
Serum ADH	3.6 pcg/mL	1-5 pcg/mL
Urine Glucose	Positive	Negative
Urine Osmolality	1127 mOsm/kg	50-1200 mOsm/kg

Table 1 Results of the patient's laboratory tests. All reference ranges are for an adolescent male.

Key terms: FSG, serum ADH, urine glucose, urine osmolality

Contrast: Pt has high serum glucose and abnormal glucose in urine with normal ADH and urine osmolality

Cause-and-Effect: Pt has symptoms of DM, not DI.

40. Nephrogenic DI is most plausibly caused by damage to ADH receptors in:
    A. the glomerulus.
    B. the pituitary gland.
    C. **the collecting duct.**
    D. the hypothalamus.

Choice **C** is correct. The passage states that nephrogenic DI is characterized by normal ADH levels but impaired action of ADH on the kidneys. ADH is secreted by the pituitary gland, but this is not relevant to its interaction with receptors in the kidney. ADH does not affect the glomerulus, but does affect aquaporins in the collecting duct.

A: The glomerulus does not have ADH receptors.
B: ADH is secreted by the pituitary but this is not relevant to its interaction with receptors in the kidney.
D: ADH does not interact with receptors in the hypothalamus.

41. The patient's expected result serum insulin levels are:
    A. **below normal.**
    B. normal.
    C. above normal.
    D. The answer cannot be determined without more information.

Choice **A** is correct. The passage tells us that the patient has normal insulin sensitivity (a normal response to insulin), meaning that he does not have type 2 DM. In addition, his ADH levels are normal, ruling out central DI. The abnormal presence of glucose in his urine and elevated blood glucose levels indicate that his kidneys cannot reabsorb all of it from the filtrate. Therefore, he most plausibly has type 1 DM. The passage states that type 1 DM is characterized by abnormally low (or absent) insulin production.

B: The patient would not have elevated blood sugar with normal insulin levels and sensitivity.
C: This would result in low, not high, blood glucose levels.
D: The answer can be determined with information in the passage.

42. Which of the following symptoms would be seen in DM but NOT in DI?

      I Excessive hunger (polyphagia)

      II Ketoacidosis from abnormally high fatty acid metabolism

      III Excessive thirst (polydipsia)

    A. I only

    B. **I and II only**

    C. II and III only

    D. I, II, and III

I: Correct: In DM, blood glucose is high but without the action of insulin cells cannot uptake glucose. This leads the cells to signal that they need more energy, leading to the feeling of hunger. Impaired glucose metabolism is not present in DI.

II: Correct: In DM, glucose cannot be properly utilized and so the body begins to break down fatty acids for energy, leading to the production of ketone bodies. Impaired glucose metabolism is not present in DI.

III: Incorrect: Because of the high production of dilute urine in both DI and DM, the body must replace the lost fluid by increasing intake. This answer is the only one that does not involve glucose metabolism.

43. In a healthy person, ADH is most likely to be secreted when:

    A. Blood pressure is high; blood osmolality is low.

    B. Blood pressure is high; blood osmolality is high.

    C. Blood pressure is low; blood osmolality is low.

    D. **Blood pressure is low; blood osmolality is high.**

Choice **D** is correct. ADH increases the reabsorption of water in the collecting duct of the kidney, decreasing the osmolality of the blood and conserving blood volume. Therefore, it increases blood pressure. Thus, the body will secrete it when blood pressure is low and blood osmolality is high. Answer D is correct.

A: ADH conserves fluid; it would not be released when BP is high or blood osmolality is low.

B: ADH conserves fluid; it would not be released when BP is high.

C: ADH conserves fluid; it would not be released when blood osmolality is low.

Discrete Set 3 Explanation (Questions 44-47)

These questions are **NOT** related to a passage.

44. Which of the following is NOT directly involved as a product or reactant in the conversion of pyruvate to acetyl CoA?
    A. CO_2
    B. NADH
    C. H^+
    D. <u>**ATP**</u>

Choice **D** is correct. Recall that CO_2 is cleaved from pyruvate to form acetyl CoA and NAD^+ is reduced to NADH via addition of H^+. ATP is not created as a direct result of conversion of pyruvate to acetyl CoA

A: Decarboxylation is defined as the loss of a CO_2 molecule.
B: This is the reduced form of NAD^+ created during pyruvate decarboxylation.
C: H^+ is used to reduce NAD^+

45. Which of the following is a peptide hormone?
    A. T_4
    B. Leukotrienes
    C. Testosterone
    D. <u>**ACTH**</u>

Choice **D** is correct. ACTH is a peptide hormone, comprised of amino acids.

A: T_4 is a tyrosine-derived hormone. Thyroid hormones are lipid-soluble amino acid hormones and act at the level of transcription (unlike peptide hormones).
B: Leukotrienes are eicosanoid type inflammatory mediators produced in leukocytes by the oxidation of arachidonic acid.
C: Testosterone is a steroid hormone.

46. If baldness is an X-linked recessive disorder, which of the following could NOT also have been a carrier of the gene or genes resulting in a man's baldness?
    A. The bald male's mother
    B. The bald male's maternal grandmother
    C. <u>**The bald male's paternal grandfather**</u>
    D. The bald male's maternal grandfather

Choice **C** is correct. X-linked diseases cannot pass from male to male while they can pass from female to male or female offspring. The bald male must have received his X chromosome from his mother. She in turn could have received that same X chromosome from her father or mother. The paternal side gave the bald male his Y chromosome so no one on the paternal side will have carried the same X chromosome as the affected male.

47. The heart, femur and bicep most likely arise from which of the following primary germ layers?
    A. Endoderm
    B. <u>**Mesoderm**</u>
    C. Ectoderm
    D. Morula

Choice **B** is correct. The three primary germ layers are the endoderm, mesoderm, and ectoderm. The mesoderm gives rise to connective tissue, cartilage, and bone; striated and smooth muscles; the heart walls, blood and lymph vessels and cells; the kidneys; the gonads (ovaries and testes) and genital ducts; the serous membranes lining the body cavities; the spleen; and the suprarenal (adrenal) cortices

A: The endoderm gives rise to the epithelial lining of the gastrointestinal and respiratory tracts; the parenchyma of the tonsils, the liver, the thymus, the thyroid, the parathyroids, and the pancreas; the epithelial lining of the urinary bladder and urethra.

C: The ectoderm gives rise to the central nervous system; the peripheral nervous system; the sensory epithelia of the eye, ear, and nose; the epidermis and its appendages (the nails and hair); the mammary glands; the hypophysis; the subcutaneous glands; and the enamel of the teeth.

D: The morula is a globular solid mass of 16-32 blastomeres formed by cleavage of the zygote that precedes the blastocyst. It is not a primary germ layer.

Passage IX Explanation (Questions 48-51)

Pseudomonas aeruginosa is one of the most common Gram-negative pathogen accounting for over 10% of all infections. With its increasing prevalence, **multidrug-resistant** strains are becoming increasingly common. The common complication resulting from *P. aeruginosa* is a lung infection **associated with cystic fibrosis**.

Keywords: Gram-negative, multidrug-resistant, P. aeruginosa, cystic fibrosis

In an effort to further **elucidate the difference** between prokaryotic and eukaryotic protein synthesis, a study was conducted on the **interactions between** elongation factor **Tu (EF-Tu) and elongation factor Ts (EF-Ts)**. The studies were conducted in hopes of developing new compounds that inhibit growth of the bacteria without adversely affecting the patient.

Keywords: elongation factor

EF-Tu has an integral role in protein synthesis by **bringing the aminoacyl-tRNA** (aa-tRNA) to the A site of the ribosome during the elongation phase of translation. EF-Tu forms a **ternary complex with GTP** and aa-tRNA in the cytoplasm, and this complex approaches the A-site of an actively translating ribosome. Once the ternary complex is bound to the ribosome and the **codon-anticodon** pairing is correct, GTP is hydrolyzed to GDP by activating the GTPase activity of EF-Tu. There is a **conformational change** in EF-Tu, and EF-Tu-GDP dissociates from the ribosome and recycled to the EF-Tu-TP complex in an exchange catalyzed by EF-Ts. Once EF-Tu-GDP is released, the aa-tRNA **fully enters the A site**.

Keywords: aminoacyl-tRNA, ternary complex, codon-anticodon, GTPase, EF-Tu-TP complex

Cause and Effect: Ternary complex forms and correct codon-anticodon pairing then hydrolysis of GTP to cause conformational change for dissociation of EF-Tu-GDP

Figure 1 Elongation Phase of Translation in the Prokaryotic Cell

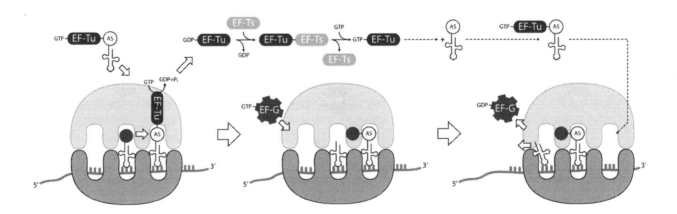

Figure 1. Diagram illustrating steps of the elongation phase of translation. From left to right, sites E, P, and A on the ribosome, and 50S and 30S for top and bottom.

There are two delays offered by EF-Tu that helps to **ensure translational accuracy**. EF-Tu delays GTP hydrolysis if the anticodon in the A site does not match codon on the aa-tRNA and again when it frees itself from the tRNA to allow for an incorrectly paired tRNA to leave the A site.

Keywords: translational accuracy

Cause and Effect: EF-Tu can delay in GTP hydrolysis and dissociation for translational accuracy

48. Which of the following steps precedes the elongation steps described in the passage?
    A. The smaller subunit of the ribosome attaches to the cap at the 5′ end of the mRNA and searches for an AUG codon by moving step-by-step in the 3′ direction.
    B. With the initiating t-RNA at the P site and the second aminoacyl-tRNA tightly bound at the A site, the α amino group of the second amino acid reacts with the "activated" methionine on the initiator tRNA, forming a peptide bond.
    C. RF1 recognizes UAG, and RF2 recognizes UGA; both these factors recognize UAA. RF3, a GTP-binding protein, acts in concert with the codon-recognizing factors to promote cleavage of the peptidyl-tRNA.
    D. **The fMet-tRNA enters the P site, causing a conformational change which opens the A site for the new aminoacyl-tRNA to bind.**

Choice **D** is correct. The question stem is asking for a step that precedes the elongation process described in the passage. Any step in initiation would suffice for an answer. Translation begins in prokaryotes with the fMet-tRNA entering the P site, causing a conformational change which opens the A site for the new aminoacyl T-RNA to bind.

A: Prokaryotic mRNA do not have a 5' cap. Prokaryotes begin translation through recognition of the Shine-Delgarno sequence.
B: The formation of the peptide bond occurs after the steps mentioned in the passage when the aminoacyl-tRNAs are in the P and A sites.
C: This describes termination and termination factors and codons involved to release the ribosome.

49. Which of the following has the greatest similarity when comparing prokaryotic and eukaryotic translation?
    A. Size of ribosomes
    B. Initiator t-RNA
    C. **Elongation factors**
    D. Recognition sites for the smaller subunit of the ribosome

Choice **C** is correct. The question stem is asking us to consider what has the greatest similarity when comparing prokaryotic and eukaryotic translation. Elongation factors are very similar in both. For prokaryotes, there are four elongation factors: EF-Tu, EF-Ts, EF-G, and EF-P, while eukaryotic have two elongation factors, eEF-1 and eEF-2. eEF1 has two subunits, and they are analogous to EF-Tu and EF-TS.

A: Ribosomes are different and pharmaceuticals can be targeted specifically for one or the other. Prokaryotes have ribosomes consisting of a 30S and 50S subunits, and eukaryotes correspondingly 40S and 60S subunits.
B: Prokaryotes use a special initiator t-RNA charged with N-formylmethionine, but eukaryotes just use methionine.
D: Recognition site for prokaryotes is the Shine-Delgarno sequence on the mRNA, but for eukaryotes 5'-methylguanosine cap.

50. A molecule which does which of the following would be most effective in eliminating *Pseudomonas aeruginosa*?
    A. Inhibits the peptidyl transferase activity of the smaller subunit of the ribosome
    B. Binds to the Shine-Delgarno sequence to directly block binding of aminoacyl-tRNA at A site
    C. Binds to the 60S subunit to block translocation
    D. **Binds to formylmethionyl-tRNA to prevent correct initiation**

Choice **D** is correct. The question stem is asking for the method most effectively at eliminating a prokaryote such as *P. aeruginosa*. Knowing the difference between prokaryotic and eukaryotic translation is important for answering this question. A drug that binds to fMet-tRNA to prevent correct initiation would prevent protein synthesis for prokaryotes.

A: Peptidyl transferase activity belongs to the larger subunit not the smaller subunit.
B: Binding to Shine-Delgarno sequence is necessary for initiation. Binding of aminoacyl-tRNA at the A site is part of elongation.
C: The 60S subunit belongs only to eukaryotes, not prokaryotes.

51. Which of the following laboratory procedures would be most effective in determining the concentration of GDP in EF-Tu preparation?
    A. Centrifugation
    B. **Absorbance spectroscopy**
    C. Extraction and filtration
    D. Fractional distillation

Choice **B** is correct. Guanosine diphosphate (GDP) consists of pyrophosphate group, ribose sugar, and the nucleoside guanine. Guanine is a fused pyrimidine-imidazole ring system with conjugated double bonds. Using UV-Vis spectroscopy, a type of absorbance spectroscopy, would be effective in determining the concentration. The concentration is determined by using Beer's law once the procedure has been performed.

A: Centrifugation will separate compounds by mass.
C: Extraction and filtration use two immiscible phases to separate a solute from one phase into another. A common use is acid-base extraction.
D: Fractional distillation is used to separate two liquids with boiling points that are close to each other; it is not a technique for assessing concentration levels of large organic molecules.

Passage X Explanation (Questions 52-55)

The autonomic nervous system in humans is comprised of two parts: (1) the **sympathetic nervous system** and (2) the **parasympathetic nervous system**. These two components are often referred to as "fight-or-flight" and "rest-and-digest" respectively, and explain most of the body's unconscious activity. Transmission of any signal in the autonomic nervous system is mediated by one of two types of neurons, **pre-ganglionic neurons** and **post-ganglionic neurons**. Pre-ganglionic neurons (represented by solid lines in the two figures below) originate from the thoracolumbar region of the vertebrae (T1-L2). These neurons connect with ganglia before they synapse with post-ganglionic neurons (represented by dashed lines in the figure) whose axons extend to many different target organs in the body. In general, it has been seen that the parasympathetic nervous system has **long pre-ganglionic** and **short post-ganglionic** axons, whereas the sympathetic nervous system has short pre-ganglionic and long post-ganglionic axons.

Key terms: sympathetic, parasympathetic, ganglia, pre- and post-ganglionic.

Contrast: The parasympathetic system is for resting state activities in the body, whereas sympathetic is for fight or flight. The parasympathetic system has long pre-ganglionic, and short post-ganglionic. The sympathetic system is the reverse.

Cause-and-Effect: Sympathetic and parasympathetic nerves innervate target organs to cause effects that regulate the body's unconscious activity.

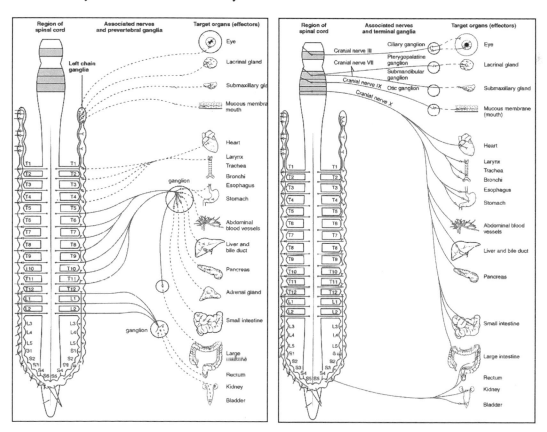

Figure 1 Organization of the Sympathetic Nervous System (left) and Parasympathetic Nervous System (right)

Two patients are brought into the neuroendocrinology wing of a hospital to participate in a study. **Patient 1** is brought into a room and is asked to sit down at a dining table set with silverware. He is provided a bowl of **chilled strawberry soup** and is told to **begin eating the soup**. At the same time, Patient 2 is provided the same setup with **identical instructions**, but a few minutes into the meal, a wire is pulled to cause a flap of the table to collapse. This results in the bowl of **cold soup suddenly and unexpectedly landing in the patient's lap, startling** the patient and causing him to **scream** and **jump** out of his chair. **Thirty seconds** after the table collapses, the patients are both brought into a side room for observation.

Key terms: neuroendocrinology, observation

Contrast: Patient 1 is relaxed and consuming a sugary substance, whereas Patient 2 has been startled and had a very physical reaction to it.

Cause-and-effect: Patient 1 is only consuming a meal, and Patient 2 has cold soup splashed on him suddenly and unexpectedly.

52. Two nerves, one in the parasympathetic nervous system and one in the sympathetic nervous system, are both found to have myelinated pre-ganglionic cells and unmyelinated post-ganglionic cells. Compared to the overall conduction velocity of the parasympathetic nerve, the sympathetic nerve's conduction velocity will be:
    A. faster than that of the parasympathetic nerve.
    B. **slower than that of the parasympathetic nerve.**
    C. identical to that of the parasympathetic nerve.
    D. More information must be provided to answer this question.

Choice **B** is correct. The passage states that parasympathetic nerves have long pre-ganglionic axons and short post-ganglionic axons, whereas sympathetic nerves have the opposite. Myelination increases the conduction velocity along an axon. Thus, the system with the myelination along the long axons (parasympathetic) will have a faster conduction velocity than the system with myelination along the short axons (sympathetic). In this question, the parasympathetic nerve's signal will have a faster conduction velocity, thus the answer is B – the sympathetic nerve's signal is slower than the parasympathetic nerve's signal.

A: As described above, the sympathetic nerve's signal will be slower than the parasympathetic's, not faster. Its myelination is along the short axon, and its long axon is unmyelinated.
C: The myelination along the long axon is not the same across the two systems, so they will not have identical speeds.

53. The levels of insulin and glucagon are measured in Patient 1 and Patient 2 at the same time point in their meals, shortly after the table collapses on Patient 2. Which of the following statements regarding the hormone levels of the two patients, relative to baseline measurements, is correct?
    A. **Patient 1 will have high levels of insulin, and Patient 2 will have high levels of glucagon.**
    B. Patient 1 will have low levels of insulin, and Patient 2 will have low levels of glucagon.
    C. Patient 1 will have high levels of insulin, and Patient 2 will have low levels of glucagon.
    D. Patient 1 will have low levels of insulin, and Patient 2 will have high levels of glucagon.

Choice **A** is correct. In the experimental setup, Patient 1 is allowed to begin eating his soup for a few minutes. This would cause his insulin levels to elevate, as the chilled strawberry soup is likely quite sugary. He is then interrupted and asked to go into the side room for observation. Patient 2 also begins eating his soup, but then the table collapses in on him and the cold soup goes into his lap. Patient 2 might have elevated insulin levels as well from eating some of the soup, but this is not relevant to the question. What is more important is the glucagon secretion caused by the activation of the sympathetic nervous system. Thus, Patient 1 will have high levels of insulin, and Patient 2 will have high levels of glucagon.

54. Parasympathetic nervous system post-ganglionic neurons activate muscarinic receptors on target tissue through which neurotransmitter?
    A. Muscarine
    B. Serotonin
    C. Epinephrine
    D. <u>**Acetylcholine**</u>

Choice **D** is correct. The primary post-ganglionic neurotransmitter of the parasympathetic nervous system is acetylcholine, and this neurotransmitter is capable of binding to the muscarinic receptors on target organs.

A: While this compound does indeed bind to muscarinic receptors (and it is why they were named as such), muscarine is not a neurotransmitter, but a product found in mushrooms.
B: This is not the primary neurotransmitter of the parasympathetic nervous system.
C: This is the primary post-ganglionic neurotransmitter of the sympathetic nervous system, and it binds to adrenergic receptors.

55. It is observed that the pupils of one patient are slightly more dilated than they were during baseline observations. This is most likely:
    A. Patient 1 because his parasympathetic nervous system is activated.
    B. Patient 1 because his sympathetic nervous system is activated.
    C. <u>**Patient 2 because his sympathetic nervous system is activated.**</u>
    D. Patient 2 because his parasympathetic nervous system is activated.

Choice **C** is correct. One of the effects of sympathetic nervous system activation is pupil dilation, and Patient 2 would likely have his sympathetic nervous system activated from having cold soup fall in his lap. Thus, the answer is C.

A: The parasympathetic nervous system being active would not create the pupil dilation effect.
B: Patient 1 would likely not have his sympathetic nervous system predominate over the parasympathetic nervous system while simply eating soup.
D: Pupil dilation is not an effect of the parasympathetic system, and Patient 2 would likely have his sympathetic nervous system dominate his parasympathetic nervous system in this scenario.

Discrete Set 4 Explanations (Questions 56-59)

These questions are **NOT** related to a passage.

56. How does cDNA differ from eukaryotic DNA?
    A. It is artificially made in a lab.
    B. It has post-transcriptional modifications, such as a 5' cap.
    C. It lacks exons.
    D. **It lacks introns.**

Choice **D** is correct. cDNA is reverse-transcribed from mRNA, and introns are removed from mature mRNA.

A: Not always. cDNA is also made by some retroviruses.
B: mRNA, not cDNA, has a 5' cap
C: Exons are the portions of the genetic code that are expressed.

57. Which of the following describes a difference between a Northern blot and a Southern blot?
    A. Northern blots are run at a lower temperature to preserve the secondary structure of the RNA.
    B. Northern blots can be used to identify many different RNA fragments, while Southern blots can identify only a few.
    C. **Northern blots are used for RNA fragments, while Southern blots are used for DNA fragments.**
    D. Northern blots are run under anaerobic conditions.

Choice **C** is correct. While they are both electrophoresis procedures; Northern blot is used to analyze RNA while Southern blot is for DNA.

58. Where do post-transcriptional modifications of RNA take place?
    A. **In the nucleus of the cell**
    B. In the cytoplasm of the cell
    C. Mainly in the nucleus, but also in the cytoplasm
    D. Mainly in the cytoplasm, but also in the nucleus

Choice **A** is correct. Post-transcriptional modifications take place in the nucleus. They are required for export to the cytoplasm.

59. Which of the following are necessary post-transcriptional modifications for export of eukaryotic mRNA to the cytoplasm?

> I. Addition of a poly-A tail
> II. 3' guanine cap
> III. Splicing

    A. I only
    B. I and II only
    C. **I and III only**
    D. I, II, and III

Choice **C** is correct. Three processes make up post-transcriptional modifications: 5' capping, addition of the poly-A tail, and splicing. The 5' capping reaction replaces the triphosphate group at the 5' end of the RNA chain with a special nucleotide that is referred to as the 5' cap. It is thought to help with mRNA recognition by the ribosome during translation. A modification also takes place at the opposite end of the RNA transcript. To the 3' end of the RNA chain 30-500 adenines are added in what is called a poly-A tail. Splicing involves excising non-coding regions (introns) while keeping coding sequences (exons).

I: This is a required post-transcriptional modification.
II: This is not a required post-transcriptional modification. The cap is placed on the 5' end.
III: This is a required post-transcriptional modification.

TIMED
SECTION 2
59 Questions, 95 Minutes

(Use the tear-out answer sheet provided in Appendix D)

Passage I (Questions 1-5)

Glioblastoma multiforme (GBM) is an aggressive malignant primary brain tumor. The highly glycolytic nature of GBM reflects their propensity to metabolize glucose to lactic acid at an elevated rate, even in the presence of abundant oxygen. Their metabolism is characterized by efflux of lactic acid from the tumor microenvironment through transmembrane transporters known as monocarboxylate transporters (MCTs). Of the four known functional MCTs (MCTs 1–4) that transport lactate, all except MCT3 are currently known to be overexpressed in tumors.

Researchers analyzed the effects of MCT inhibition on glycolytic metabolism and GBM invasiveness, by considering treating U251-MG glioma cells engineered to express enhanced green fluorescent protein (EGFP) with α-cyano-4-hydroxy-cinnamic acid (ACCA), a membrane-impermeable small-molecule inhibitor of MCTs.

To test for invasion capacity of GBM when lactate transport is inhibited, cellular assays containing pyruvate, lactate, glucose, or glucose supplemented with ACCA were tested. After 120 hours, the fluorescence of the samples was quantified using a fluorescent plate reader and the invasive capacity was calculated. Their results are shown in Figure 1.

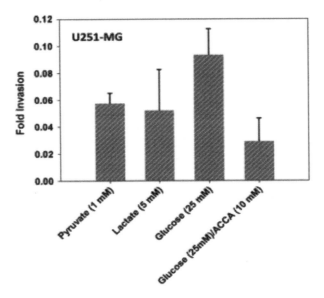

Figure 1 Invasion across coronal brain slices of U251-MG were plotted as fold invasion compared to cultures containing only U251-MG cells (Note: 0.00 fold invasion indicates invasiveness for control cells; error bars indicate standard deviation).

Measurements of oxygen consumption upon application of ACCA or digitonin, an agent that increases the permeability of plasma membranes to ACCA, were also carried out to determine the potential impact on mitochondrial respiration after in vivo application of ACCA to a glucose-containing growth medium containing U251-MG cells. Figure 2 shows the results of the measurements.

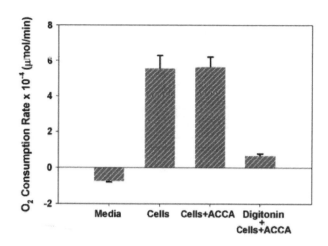

Figure 2 Rates of O$_2$ consumption in medium alone (Media), with U251-MG cells alone in medium (Cells), supplemented with ACCA (Cells + ACCA) or supplemented with ACCA and digitonin (Digitonin + Cells + ACCA) (Note: error bars indicate standard deviation).

1. Comparison across brain slice cultures reveals that U251-MG invasiveness:
    A. is not enhanced in glioma cells treated with ACCA and glucose versus in untreated glial cells.
    B. is negatively correlated with the presence of lactate in the medium.
    C. is positively correlated with enhanced glycolytic flux.
    D. demonstrates that glioma invasiveness is decreased less versus controls in glucose treated cells also treated with ACCA.

2. In addition to blocking lactate transport, what do the results shown in Figure 2 suggest might be true of ACCA's action on glioma cell respiration?
    A. Intracellular ACCA induces an increase in respiration due to the exposure of mitochondria to respiratory substrates.
    B. Extracellular ACCA interferes with glucose transport across the cell membrane.
    C. Extracellular ACCA acts to decrease O_2 permeability across the cell membrane.
    D. Intracellular ACCA blocks intracellular pyruvate entry into mitochondria.

3. Gliomas such as GBM arise from glial cells. Which of the following is a function of these cells?
    I. Maintenance of the myelin sheath in the peripheral nervous system
    II. Secretion of cerebrospinal fluid.
    III. Maintenance of the myelin sheath in the central nervous system

    A. I only
    B. I and II only
    C. I and III only
    D. I, II, and III

4. MCT4 participates in the astrocyte-neuron lactate shuttle that occurs between neurons and astrocytes during routine axonal firing. Given this, what is the most likely reason that researchers believe ACCA is a better candidate as a potential treatment for GBM than other small molecule inhibitors with greater affinity for MCTs?
    A. Its relatively lower MCT affinity implies broader activity against all MCTs overexpressed in GBM.
    B. High-affinity inhibitors may be unable to disrupt the neuron-astrocyte lactate shuttle in GBM.
    C. Other small molecule inhibitors may have few adverse effects against the elevated glycolytic metabolism of GBM.
    D. ACCA is less likely to impact normal tissue while adversely affecting cells displaying elevated rates of glycolysis.

5. The researchers hypothesized that lactate can initiate a cascade of events that up-regulate the expression of growth factors that enhance the invasive capacity of GBM. What alternative explanation for the increase in GBM invasiveness when lactate efflux is inhibited is NOT consistent with results from the passage?
    A. Tumor lactate can up-regulate expression of proteins that degrade the extracellular matrix in the tumor micro-environment.
    B. The collapse of glycolytic metabolism degraded the cellular energy pool and the invasive capacity of GBM.
    C. Lactate efflux directly modulates the tumor micro-environment in such a way as to promote GBM invasiveness.
    D. Efflux of lactate decreases an invasive GBM cell's capacity for aerobic metabolism in highly vascularized sites.

THIS PAGE LEFT

INTENTIONALLY BLANK

Passage II (Questions 6-10)

Epstein-Barr virus (EBV) infection is suspected in the development of a variety of autoimmune diseases, including multiple sclerosis (MS), arthritis, and type 1 diabetes. More than 93% of Americans are thought to be infected by the virus, which is unique in that it has the ability to infect, activate, and latently persist in B lymphocytes for the lifetime of the infected individual. Previously, the effect of EBV infection has been attributed to immunological cross-reactivity between EBV and self-antigen. Scientists instead proposed that the development of autoimmunity due to EBV infection occurs because of an impairment of CD8+ T cell control.

The hypothesis proposes that susceptibility to the development of chronic autoimmune diseases after EBV infection is dependent on a genetically determined quantitative deficiency of the cytotoxic CD8+ T cells that normally maintain tight control of EBV infection. Deprivation of sunlight and vitamin D at higher latitudes aggravates the genetic CD8+ T cell deficiency and increases the incidence and progression of autoimmune disease. The relationship between the severity of disease and the age of disease onset to the extent of genetic or environmentally-induced deficiency of CD8+ T cells is shown in Figure 1.

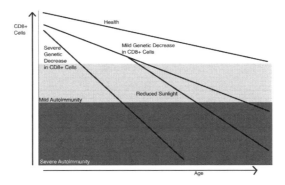

Figure 1 Relationship between the number of CD8+ T cells and the development of chronic autoimmune diseases. Each line represents the number of CD8+ T cell present with increasing age for normal individuals (Health) or under the condition indicated.

The proposal supposes that autoimmunity develops sequentially in the steps illustrated in Figure 2, ending with the development of ectopic B cell follicles, which may represent sites of clonal expansion of autoreactive B cells specific for antigens present in the target organ.

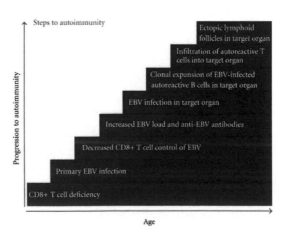

Figure 2 Proposed sequence of chronic autoimmune disease development

6. Latently infected memory B cells express proteins which mimic the mechanism of activation of antigen-selected B cells. In normal B cell differentiation, naïve B cells:
    A. differentiate exclusively to memory B cells following initial antigen exposure.
    B. require only binding of antigen to the B cell receptor for differentiation to occur.
    C. may be activated in a T cell independent pathway.
    D. require antigen presentation by helper T cells during activation.

7. CD8+ T cells normally maintain control of EBV infection in what way?
    A. Through release of cytotoxic granules following their binding of soluble antigens in the blood or lymph.
    B. By ingesting, processing and presenting antigenic components of infected B cells to natural killer T cells.
    C. Through complement-mediated marking and removing of proliferating infected B cells.
    D. By eliminating proliferating and lytically infected B cells in an antigen-specific manner.

8. CD8+ T cell deficiency has shown to be present in the healthy blood relatives of patients with autoimmune diseases. What does this most likely reflect concerning the relationship between latent EBV infection, CD8+ T cell deficiency and autoimmunity?
    A. Latent EBV infection decreases CD8+ T cell count, but does not always result in the development of autoimmune disease.
    B. CD8+ T cell deficiency alone cannot explain the progression of autoimmune disease.
    C. CD8+T cell abnormalities are genetically determined and not a consequence of EBV infection.
    D. Environmental, not genetic factors, are the primary determinant of CD8+ T cell deficiency.

9. What conclusion concerning CD8+ T cell count and the development of autoimmunity can reasonably be drawn from Figure 1?
    A. Sunlight deprivation can lead to the development of autoimmunity in individuals with normal CD8+ T cell counts.
    B. Decline in CD8+ T cell levels results only from disease-related processes.
    C. Primary CD8+ T cell deficiency is aggravated by aging.
    D. The rate of CD8+T cell count decline is equal in all individuals who develop severe autoimmunity.

10. If the mechanism for development of autoimmune disease presented in the passage is true, then which statement regarding MS is most likely to be INCORRECT?
    A. The risk of developing MS is extremely low among individuals not infected with EBV.
    B. Most individuals infected with EBV develop MS.
    C. The likelihood of EBV infection is slightly higher in MS patients than in the general population.
    D. The risk of developing MS increases following EBV infection.

Passage III (Questions 11-15)

Lambert–Eaton syndrome (LEMS) is an autoimmune disorder that is characterized by muscular weakness in the extremities. It is the result of a reaction in which antibodies are formed against presynaptic voltage-gated calcium channels, and likely other nerve terminal proteins, in the neuromuscular junction, shown in Figure 1.

LEMS contrasts with a similar neuromuscular disease, myasthenia gravis (MG), which gives rise to muscle weakness caused by circulating antibodies that impair binding of acetylcholine to its acetylcholine receptors at the postsynaptic neuromuscular junction. Some forms of the antibody impair the ability of acetylcholine to bind to receptors. Others lead to the destruction of receptors, either by complement fixation or by inducing the muscle cell to eliminate the receptors through endocytosis.

The antibodies are produced by plasma cells, which are derived from B cells. B cells convert into plasma cells by helper T cell stimulation. To carry out this activation, helper T cells must first be activated themselves, which is done by binding of the T cell receptor (TCR) to the acetylcholine receptor antigenic peptide fragment, known as an epitope, resting within the major histocompatibility complex of antigen presenting cells.

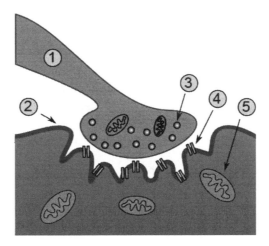

Figure 1 Neuromuscular junction. 1. Presynaptic terminal 2. Sarcolemma 3. Synaptic vesicle 4. Nicotinic acetylcholine receptor 5. Mitochondria.

11. The symptoms of patients with what disease are likely to see symptom improvement when treated with an inhibitor of acetylcholinesterase?
    A. MG only
    B. LEMS only
    C. Both MG and LEMS
    D. Neither MG nor LEMS

12. What causes the autoantibody-mediated weakness seen in LEMS?
    A. Receptor binding by acetylcholine is blocked.
    B. Calcium reuptake through voltage-gated channels is inhibited.
    C. Action potential transmission is inhibited.
    D. Pre-synaptic vesicular binding to the plasma membrane is reduced.

13. Surgical removal of what organ in MG patients is most likely to have been shown to reduce the pool of mature, circulating T cells available for B cell activation?
    A. Thyroid
    B. Spleen
    C. Thymus
    D. Pituitary gland

14. In LEMS, the velocity of action potential propagation is unchanged. Which of the following is likely to result in a decrease in the rate of action potential propagation along an individual axon?
    A. The blockage of acetylcholine receptors on neuromuscular junction endplates
    B. Demyelination of the axon
    C. Propagation between nodes along myelinated axons
    D. Increased extracellular sodium concentrations

15. Apart from skeletal muscle weakness, individuals with LEMS experience specific problems with complex muscular coordination during movement. This information is consistent with the presence of acetylcholine receptors in the:
    A. cerebellum.
    B. hypothalamus.
    C. medulla oblongata.
    D. pons.

Discrete Set 1 (Questions 16-18)

These questions are **NOT** related to a passage.

16. Which of the following is most likely to be transmitted between a neuron and skeletal muscle tissue?
    A. Epinephrine
    B. Dopamine
    C. Acetylcholine
    D. Muscarine

17. Under which of the following classifications does erythropoietin fall?
    I. Glycoprotein hormone
    II. Steroid hormone
    III. Erythrocyte precursor

    A. I only
    B. III only
    C. I and II only
    D. I, II, and III

18. Which of the following enzymes does NOT use RNA nucleotides as a part of its function?
    A. DNA ligase
    B. Primase
    C. RNA polymerase III
    D. Telomerase

THIS PAGE LEFT

INTENTIONALLY BLANK

Passage IV (Questions 19-22)

Alpha helices are an important part of the structure of most proteins. They form because of the structure of the amino acids in a protein. The functional groups of amino acids in proximity are able to form hydrogen bonds. When these hydrogen bonds consistently form between every 4th amino acid, the result is a right-handed helix. There are 3.6 residues per helical turn in an alpha helix and 5.4 Angstroms between consecutive turns.

There are many ways of depicting alpha helices in two dimensions. A Wenxiang diagram can be used to show the relative location of amino acids as they bind with one another about a central axis. Figure 1 shows a Wenxiang diagram with the letters corresponding to amino acids.

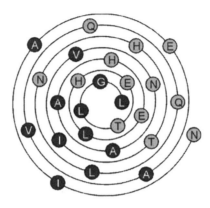

Figure 1 A Wenxiang diagram of an alpha helix

Each amino acid has a different propensity for being in an alpha helix. Alanine has the greatest propensity. Table 1 shows the relative propensities of the amino acids to be involved in an alpha helix. The values in the table represent the difference between the Gibbs free energy change of the hydrogen bond formation for each amino acid and the energy change for alanine. Thus the values are relative to the value for alanine.

There are two other forms of helices that can occur with some frequency. They are denoted the 3_{10} helix and the π-helix. Amino acids in a 3_{10} helix hydrogen bond every 3rd amino acid. Every amino acid in a 3_{10} helix represents a 120 degree rotation in the helix. In a π-helix hydrogen bonding occurs between every 5th amino acid and each amino acid corresponds to a 90 degree turn in the helix.

Table 1 the relative propensities of amino acids to form hydrogen bonds in alpha helices.

Amino Acid	Free energy change	Amino Acid	Free energy change
Alanine	0	Tyrosine	0.52
Arginine	0.21	Phenylalanine	0.54
Leucine	0.21	Histidine	0.61
Methionine	0.23	Valine	0.61
Lysine	0.27	Asparagine	0.65
Glutamine	0.38	Threonine	0.66
Glutamic acid	0.39	Cysteine	0.68
Isoleucine	0.42	Aspartic Acid	0.69
Tryptophan	0.49	Glycine	1
Serine	0.50	Proline	3.15

19. Alpha helices contribute to which of the following?
    A. Primary structure
    B. Secondary structure
    C. Tertiary structure
    D. Quaternary structure

20. Which of the following are involved in the hydrogen bonding in the alpha helix backbone?
    A. The side groups of the amino acids
    B. The amine groups from each amino acid
    C. The carbonyl groups from each amino acid
    D. The amine group from one with the carbonyl group of another

21. Starting from the center of Figure 1, which amino acids are bound to the first E?
    A. Guanine and asparagine
    B. Guanine and leucine
    C. Leucine and histidine
    D. Lysine and asparagine

22. Why might proline disrupt the formation of an alpha helix?
    A. The ring on proline causes too much strain to be bent sufficiently in the helix.
    B. The amine group from proline creates a more polar molecule than other amino acids.
    C. The aromatic portion of proline disrupts its ability to hydrogen bond.
    D. Proline is too large.

Passage V (Questions 23-26)

The artificial sweetener aspartame is the methyl ester of the dipeptide of L-phenylalanine and L-aspartic acid, whose structure is shown in Figure 1. There are two general approaches to commercially prepare this compound. The chemical approach involves reacting the methyl ester of phenylalanine with an N-protected anhydride of aspartic acid. The protecting group, either a benzyl or formyl group is then removed by mild acid hydrolysis. In addition to the desired product, a beta structural isomer is also formed due to formation of a peptide bond with the wrong carboxylate group, which must be removed since it produces a bitter taste. A second enzymatic synthesis has been developed in which proteases catalyze the selective peptide bond formation and avoids the formation of the beta isomer.

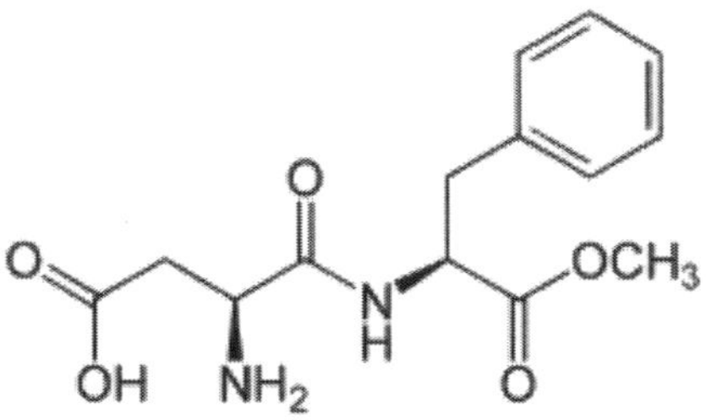

Figure 1 The structure of N-(L-α-Aspartyl)-L-phenylalanine,1-methyl ester, $pK_{a1} = 3.2$ and $pK_{a2} = 7.7$.

Upon ingestion, aspartame breaks down in the small intestines into its components, aspartic acid, phenylalanine and methanol, with the subsequent formation of metabolites such as formaldehyde and formic acid. There has been some concern that aspartame can play a role in the formation of certain cancers as a result of the formation of some of these potentially toxic compounds.

23. What is the pI of aspartame?
    A. 3.2
    B. 5 5
    C. 7.0
    D. 7.7

24. How many chiral centers are in aspartame?
    A. 1
    B. 2
    C. 3
    D. 4

25. The two amino acids that form the basis for the dipeptide structure of aspartame, aspartic acid and phenylalanine, can be classified as:
    A. hydrophilic and hydrophilic, respectively.
    B. hydrophobic and hydrophilic, respectively.
    C. hydrophilic and hydrophobic, respectively.
    D. hydrophobic and hydrophobic, respectively.

26. The pH of human gastric fluids is generally between 1 and 3. What is net charge of aspartame under these conditions?
    A. -1
    B. 0
    C. +1
    D. +2

Discrete Set 2 (Questions 27-30)

These questions are **NOT** related to a passage.

27. Which of the following amino acids is achiral?
    A. Lysine
    B. Aspartic acid
    C. Phenylalanine
    D. Glycine

28. The mean molecular weight of an amino acid residue in a protein is 110 g/mol. If a protein has a mass of approximately 50 kDa, how many amino acid residues are in the protein?
    A. 2
    B. 50
    C. 450
    D. 5500

29. The pancreas secretes pancreatic juices into the small intestine, which contain enzymes that help digest all of the following EXCEPT:
    A. starch.
    B. proteins.
    C. lipids.
    D. cellulose.

30. Which of the following best describes the production pathway for a plasma membrane-bound protein, starting with the production of the mRNA?
    A. nucleus → cytoplasm → ribosome → endosome
    B. nucleus → RER → Golgi → secretory vesicle
    C. nucleus → cytoplasm → ribosome → RER → Golgi
    D. nucleus → cytoplasm → RER

THIS PAGE LEFT

INTENTIONALLY BLANK

Passage VI (Questions 31-34)

RNA plays a key role in the translation of genetic material into protein. Messenger RNA provides the code from which the amino acid chain is formed. Ribosomal RNA provides the structure of ribosomes, where the translation is carried out. Transfer RNA brings amino acids to the ribosomes. Thus we see that RNA provides the template for transcription, the site of transcription, and all the means of transcription.

Messenger RNA needs to be processed before it is ready to bind a ribosome. On the 5' end of the sequence, a methylated guanosine is attached in a 5' – 5' triphosphate linkage. The addition of the guanine residue allows mRNA to properly bind the ribosome before translation. Additionally, a 3' poly-A tail is added to the sequence.

Transfer RNA molecules have primary, secondary, and tertiary structure due to interactions between base pairs and folding. The tRNA structure consists of a phosphate group on the 5' end, a CCA tail on the 3' end which contains a hydroxyl group where an amino acid can be added by aminoacyl tRNA synthetase. Also, the tRNA contains a unique 3 nucleotide anticodon sequence where the molecule binds opposite mRNA in the ribosome. Figure 1 shows the structure of a tRNA molecule.

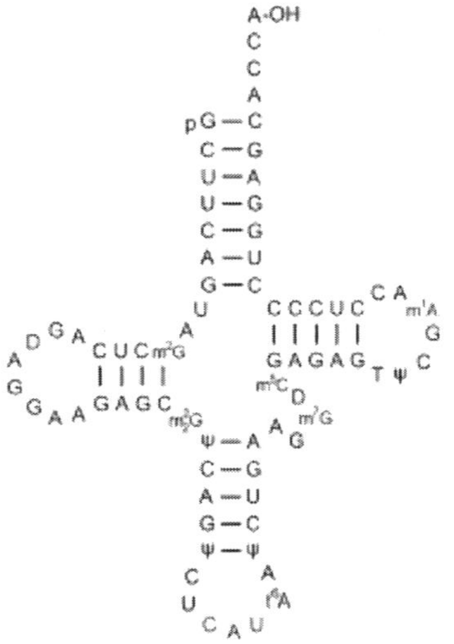

Figure 1 tRNA structure

Ribosomal RNA is the major structural component of ribosomes. Ribosomes have two subunits, labeled 60S and 40S for their sedimentation rate. The sedimentation rate is the rate at which a particle falls through a liquid and is deposited at the bottom of a sample. Sedimentation rate depends on the acceleration down and terminal velocity of the particle as it falls. The rate depends on 3 forces: gravity, the buoyant force, and the drag force. The large subunit is composed of proteins and 3 smaller rRNA molecules. The small subunit is composed of proteins as well as an 18S rRNA molecule.

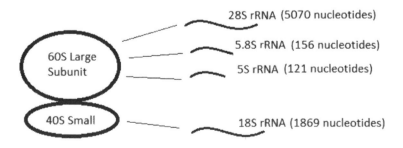

Figure 2 Subunits of a ribosome

31. In prokaryotes, translation can begin to occur before transcription has finished. Which of the following explains this?
    A. Prokaryotes have ribosomes on their nuclear envelope and need not transport mRNA before translation.
    B. Prokaryotes have no endoplasmic reticulum and exclusively use bound ribosomes for translation.
    C. Prokaryotes lack a nucleus and thus need not transport the mRNA before translation.
    D. Prokaryotes have circular DNA which allows transcribed mRNA easy access to ribosomes.

32. Which of the following is shown in Figure 1?
    I. Primary structure
    II. Secondary structure
    III. Tertiary structure

    A. I only
    B. III only
    C. I and II only
    D. I, II, and III

33. Which of the following is the approximate total length of human rRNA?
    A. 6000 nucleotides
    B. 6500 nucleotides
    C. 7000 nucleotides
    D. 8000 nucleotides

34. A human ribosome is 80S. During sedimentation analysis, which of the following best explains why the 60S and 40S subunits together do not result in a 100S ribosome?
    A. The volume of the ribosome is smaller than sum of the volumes of each subunit.
    B. The buoyant force on the ribosome is smaller than the sum of the buoyant forces on each subunit.
    C. The drag force on the ribosome is smaller than the sum of the drag forces on each subunit.
    D. The gravitation force on the ribosome is greater than the sum of the gravitational forces on each subunit.

Passage VII (Questions 35-39)

Pyruvate decarboxylation is an important process that must occur to pyruvate before continuing to be processed in the Krebs cycle. Decarboxylation occurs after pyruvate enters the mitochondrial matrix. During pyruvate decarboxylation, pyruvate is converted to acetyl CoA by the complex of three enzymes, commonly called E1, E2, and E3. The three enzymes together are called the pyruvate dehydrogenase complex (PDC).

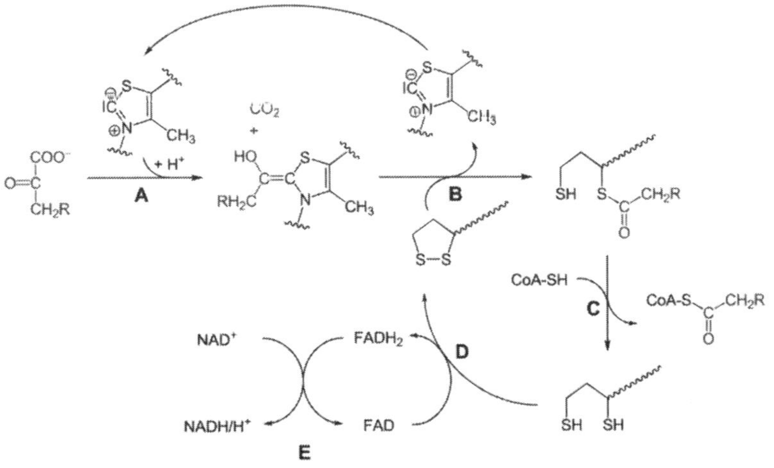

Figure 1 The mechanism of the enzymatic action of the pyruvate dehydrogenase complex

E1 contains a thiazolium ring that exists in zwitterion form. Pyruvate is added to the ring and loses CO_2. It is then transferred to a lipoate on a long lysine residue arm. The lipoate is reduced and the ring is broken as a S-C bond is formed. The arm is then able to physically translocate the intermediate to the E2 active site on the complex. This is where the intermediate is transferred to a coenzyme A molecule. Acetyl CoA is produced and released from the complex. The lysine arm then transfers the dihydrolipoate to E3, where it is oxidized to prepare for the next pyruvate molecule.

Pyruvate dehydrogenase is regulated by two enzymes, pyruvate dehydrogenase kinase (PDK), which can phosphorylate and deactivate E1, and pyruvate dehydrogenase phosphatase (PDP), which activates E1 by dephosphorylating it.

The activity of PDK and PDP is regulated by the concentrations of ATP, ADP, NADH, NAD^+, acetyl-CoA, and coenzyme A. The products of the reaction in Figure 1 activate PDK and the substrates inhibit PDK.

35. What is the product of B?
    A. A lipoate
    B. A thioacetate
    C. A lipoic acid
    D. A thioketone

36. Which of the following occurs during B?
    I. Decarboxylation of pyruvate
    II. Oxidation of a carbon on pyruvate
    III. Reduction of the lipoate arm

    A. I only
    B. III only
    C. I and II only
    D. II and III only

37. During starvation, what would be the purpose of increased production of PDK?
    A. To activate PDC to create energy in the form of ATP from pyruvate
    B. To inactivate PDC because amino acids from protein degradation provide more energy per molecule
    C. To inactivate PDC because fats are a quicker source of energy
    D. To inactivate PDC to preserve glucose metabolism for the brain

38. Muscle contraction stimulates glycolysis. Which of the following is the most reasonable explanation for how this occurs?
    A. Calcium released from the sarcoplasmic reticulum activates PDK, which results in decreased pyruvate concentrations, activating glycolysis.
    B. Calcium released from sarcoplasmic reticulum activates PDP, which results in decreased pyruvate concentrations, activating glycolysis.
    C. Calcium released from the sarcoplasmic reticulum inhibits PDK, which results in increased pyruvate concentrations, activating glycolysis.
    D. Calcium released from the sarcoplasmic reticulum inhibits PDP, which results in increased pyruvate concentrations, activating glycolysis.

39. An increase in which of the following values will stimulate PDC activity?
    I. $[NADH]/[NAD^+]$
    II. $[Acetyl\ CoA]/[CoA]$
    III. $[ADP]/[ATP]$

    A. I only
    B. III only
    C. I and II only
    D. I, II, and III

Passage VIII (Questions 40-43)

Human Immunodeficiency Virus (HIV) is a retrovirus that infects cells of the immune system, such as CD4+ T cells. Infection by HIV leads to low numbers of CD4+ T cells through apoptosis of uninfected cells, and killing of infected cells by the virus or CD8+ cytotoxic lymphocytes. When CD4+ numbers falls below a critical threshold, cell-mediated immunity is lost and the infected individual becomes increasingly vulnerable to life-threatening opportunistic infections.

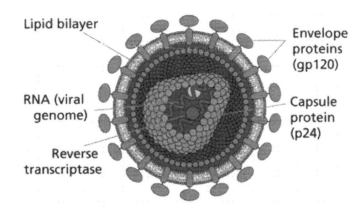

Figure 1 HIV viral particle

Though the virus's genome is coded in RNA in free viral particles, in infected cells it is reverse-transcribed to cDNA and inserted into the host cell's genome. The process of reverse-transcription is error-prone, which contributes to the virus's ability to quickly mutate to evade the immune system and resist drug treatments.

During viral replication, the virus uses host-cell machinery to replicate its genome and produce the proteins that form the structural components of the virus. Viral RNA genomes lack the post-transcriptional modifications that allow mRNA molecules to be transported out of the nucleus, therefore they require additional proteins to move into the cytoplasm, where the genomes are packaged for viral release.

The latent virus within an infected cell is activated by transcription factors, such as NF-κB, which is upregulated in active T cells. The DNA provirus is then transcribed into mRNA which is then heavily spliced. Some mRNAs produced then undergo post-transcriptional modifications and are exported to the cytoplasm where they are translated. One such protein is Rev, which is then transported back into the nucleus, where it binds unspliced viral mRNAs via a Rev Response Element (RRE). Rev contains a nuclear export signal (NES), which allows it—with the viral RNA bound—to be exported into the nucleus. Other necessary proteins are then translated from the intact viral RNA genome.

40. What type of signals would you expect Rev to contain?
   I. Nuclear Export Signal
   II. Nuclear Localization Signal
   III. ER Signal Sequence

   A. I only
   B. I and II only
   C. I and III only
   D. I, II, and III

41. Which of the following would NOT be a good method for a drug to inhibit HIV?
   A. A drug that binds to GP120 to prevent binding of the viral particle to the cell membrane
   B. A drug that inhibits reverse transcriptase
   C. A drug that inhibits DNA polymerase
   D. A drug that inhibits viral particle assembly

42. Reverse transcriptase produces a double-stranded DNA molecule from a single-stranded RNA molecule. What types of activity does this enzyme have?
   A. RNA-dependent DNA polymerase activity only
   B. RNA-dependent DNA polymerase activity, and DNA-dependent DNA polymerase activity
   C. RNA-dependent DNA polymerase activity, and DNA ligase activity
   D. DNA-dependent DNA polymerase activity only

43. The HIV viral particle has both a protein capsule and a lipid envelope. How are viral particles released from the infected cell?
   A. Viral particles are packaged in the ER-Golgi pathway and exocytosed from the infected cell.
   B. Viral particles acquire the lipid envelope while leaving the cell's nucleus and then are released by lysis of the cell.
   C. Viral particles bud off the infected cell, and the cells plasma membrane donates the lipid envelope.
   D. It is not possible to tell without more information.

Discrete Set 3 (Questions 44-47)

These questions are **NOT** related to a passage.

44. Which of the following occurs during skeletal muscle contraction?
    A. Actin filaments pull on myosin filaments, bringing them closer to the edges of the sarcomere.
    B. Actin filaments pull on myosin filaments, bringing them closer to the center of the sarcomere.
    C. Myosin filaments pull on actin filaments, bringing them closer to the edges of the sarcomere.
    D. Myosin filaments pull on actin filaments, bringing them closer to the center of the sarcomere.

45. Which of the following contains a nucleus?
    I. Erythrocytes
    II. Megakaryocytes
    III. Leukocytes

    A. I only
    B. II only
    C. III only
    D. II and III only

46. Where is DNA ligase most likely to be used in DNA replication?
    A. The leading strand of a DNA replication fork
    B. The lagging strand of a DNA replication fork
    C. As a cofactor of DNA polymerase
    D. As a cofactor of RNA polymerase

47. Which of the following is NOT a characteristic of prokaryotes?
    A. They have no endoplasmic reticulum.
    B. They have circular DNA.
    C. They have a cell wall.
    D. They lack a plasma membrane.

THIS PAGE LEFT

INTENTIONALLY BLANK

Passage IX (Questions 48-51)

Cardiac arrest is the absence of productive mechanical activity in the heart, though significant electrical activity (usually measured by electrocardiogram) may still be present. Without cardiac activity to circulate blood, tissue oxygen levels plummet and muscle activity ceases. Generally, periods of untreated cardiac arrest longer than six minutes result in permanent neurological damage due to lack of oxygen in the brain. Though myriad causes of cardiac arrest exist, the most common include hypoxia, hypoglycemia, hypovolemia (low blood volume), acidosis, thrombosis (clots), and hyperkalemia (elevated serum potassium).

The first line treatment for cardiac arrest is CPR (cardiopulmonary resuscitation). Chest compressions during CPR simulate the mechanical action of the heart by circulating blood, while artificial ventilation provides the lungs with fresh oxygen in the absence of diaphragm contractions. The administration of electric shocks to the heart (defibrillation) is used to restore productive electric activity in the heart. A common electrical rhythm during cardiac arrest is ventricular fibrillation (VF), resulting in unorganized and unproductive movement of the ventricles and no cardiac output.

Resuscitation in cardiac arrest from cold water drowning is generally more successful than warm water drowning. In one example, doctors resuscitated a two and a half year old girl after she was submerged in an icy creek for 1 hour and 6 minutes. When rescuers pulled her from the creek, she was not breathing and was in cardiac arrest. Upon arrival at the hospital, her core temperature was measured at 66°F, 22.6° below normal. Her remarkable recovery left her free of neurological deficit. At the time, her survival of over an hour without oxygen was the longest ever recorded without brain damage.

48. Which of the following physiological responses probably occurred in the patient immediately upon submersion in the creek?

   I. Peripheral vasodilation
   II. Piloerection
   III. Shivering

   A. I and II
   B. I and III
   C. II and III
   D. I, II, and III

49. Given information the passage, which of the following conditions would most plausibly result from extended cardiac arrest?
   A. Acidosis
   B. Alkalosis
   C. Hyperglycemia
   D. Hypoglycemia

50. Under normal conditions, which of the following vessels carries deoxygenated blood?
   A. Aorta
   B. Arterioles
   C. Pulmonary arteries
   D. Pulmonary veins

51. While VF is deadly if not treated immediately, many people live years with atrial fibrillation (AF). Why might this be?
   A. The atria are smaller than the ventricles.
   B. The atria are not responsible for pumping blood.
   C. The ventricles pump blood into circulation, while the atria move blood into the ventricles.
   D. The ventricles are not well-perfused by the coronary arteries, while the atria are.

Passage X (Questions 52-55)

Most of the cells in the human body are actually prokaryotes that live on or in important organ systems. *E. coli* is one bacteria that exists in huge numbers in the gut and assist with breaking down food, vitamin K_2 production, and waste disposal. Vitamin K_2's main function is to add a carboxylic acid to glutamate. This functionality affects many processes in the body. Vitamin K_2 promotes blood clotting, osteoblast activity, and breaks up calcium deposits in soft tissue. Vitamin K_2 also acts as an antioxidant.

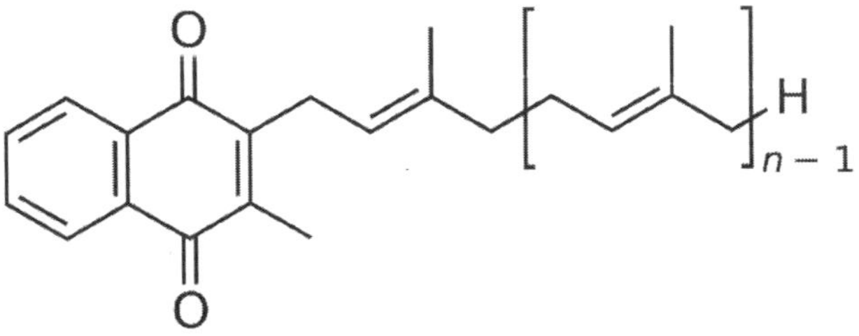

Figure 1 Vitamin K_2

E. coli is known as a gram-negative bacteria. The gram classification comes from a technique used to stain bacteria. A culture of bacteria is introduced to a stain and then washed out with an alcohol or acetone. After washing, the bacteria which were stained and retained the color of the stain are called gram positive. Bacteria which lose the color are called gram negative. Gram-positive bacteria retain the stain because of their large amount of peptidoglycan forming a shell around the cell. Gram-negative bacteria lack the thick peptidoglycan layer. Peptidoglycan is shown in figure 2 alongside methyl violet 10B, a popular gram stain.

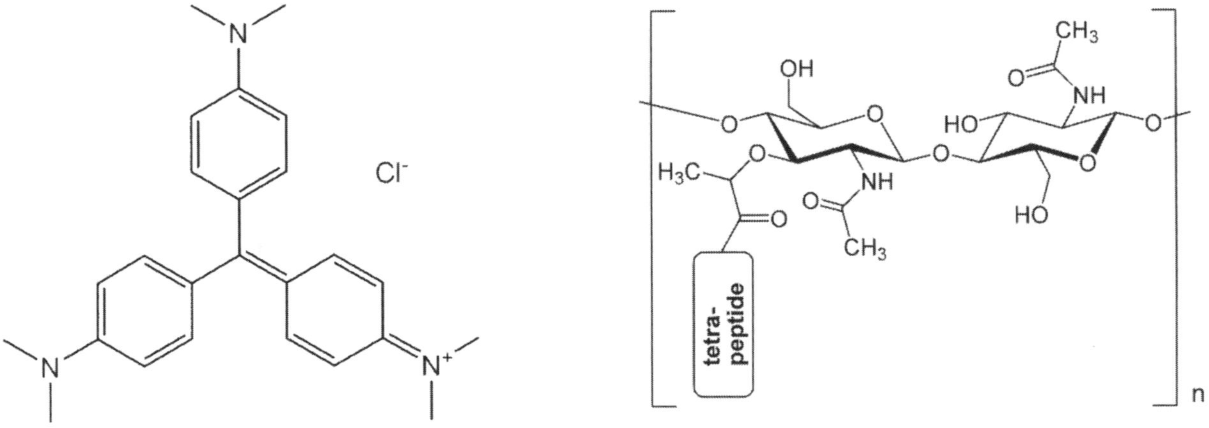

Figure 2 Methyl violet 10B and peptidoglycan monomer

At a pH of 1.0, the methyl violet 10B has two protonated nitrogens and 3 positive charges and appears yellow. The pK_a of the diprotonated molecule is 1.15 and for the monoprotonated molecule is 1.8. Above a pH of 1.8 it has a single positive charge and a violet color.

52. Visible light ranges from about 400 to 700 nm. Which of the following is most likely the absorbance maximum for methyl violet 10B at a pH of 7?
    A. 400 nm
    B. 470 nm
    C. 530 nm
    D. 590 nm

53. Why is methyl violet 10B retained by larger amounts of peptidoglycan?
    A. Peptidoglycan and methyl violet 10B are both hydrophilic.
    B. Methyl violet 10B can hydrogen bond with peptidoglycan's hydroxyl groups.
    C. Methyl violet 10B and peptidoglycan both have charges at neutral pH.
    D. Peptidoglycan and methyl violet 10B are both hydrophobic.

54. Under which of the following classifications does Vitamin K_2 fall?
    I. Lipid soluble
    II. Amphipathic
    III. Hydrophobic

    A. I only
    B. I and III only
    C. II and III only
    D. I, II, and III

55. Which of the following might result from taking an antibiotic that destroys normal intestinal flora *E. coli*?
    A. Decreased risk of osteoporosis
    B. Increased risk of spontaneous bleeding
    C. Decreased risk of cancer
    D. Decreased risk of bacterial infection by *E. coli*

Discrete Set 4 (Questions 56-59)

These questions are **NOT** related to a passage.

56. Which of the following RNA molecules forms a stable long-term RNA-protein structure?
    A. mRNA
    B. rRNA
    C. tRNA
    D. snRNA

57. Where does formation of neutrophils begin?
    A. Hepatocytes
    B. Adipose tissue
    C. Bone marrow
    D. Erythrocytes

58. Which of the following signals has highest ratio of energy/wavelength?
    A. Infrared light used in organic analysis
    B. Microwaves used to sterilize medical equipment
    C. Gamma rays released by chemo-isotopes
    D. They all have the same ratio.

59. Which of the following enzymes does NOT act concurrently with the enzyme helicase during DNA replication?
    A. Topoisomerase
    B. Telomerase
    C. DNA polymerase
    D. DNA ligase

TIMED
SECTION 2

Answers and Explanations

Timed Section 2 Answer Key

Key		20	D	40	B
1	C	21	C	41	C
2	D	22	A	42	B
3	D	23	B	43	C
4	D	24	B	44	D
5	D	25	C	45	D
6	C	26	C	46	B
7	D	27	D	47	D
8	B	28	C	48	C
9	C	29	D	49	A
10	B	30	C	50	C
11	C	31	C	51	C
12	D	32	C	52	D
13	C	33	C	53	A
14	B	34	C	54	B
15	A	35	B	55	B
16	C	36	D	56	B
17	A	37	D	57	C
18	A	38	B	58	C
19	B	39	B	59	B

Passage I Answers and Explanations (Questions 1-5)

Glioblastoma multiforme (GBM) is an aggressive malignant primary brain tumor. The highly glycolytic nature of GBM reflects their propensity to metabolize glucose to lactic acid at an elevated rate, even in the presence of abundant oxygen. Their metabolism is characterized by efflux of lactic acid from the tumor microenvironment through transmembrane transporters known as monocarboxylate transporters (MCTs). Of the four known functional MCTs **(MCTs 1–4)** that transport lactate, **all except MCT3** are currently known to be **overexpressed in tumors**.

Key terms: glioblastoma multiforme (GBM); brain tumor; monocarboxylate transporters (MCTs)

Cause-and-Effect: Glioblastoma multiforme (GBM) is an aggressive malignant primary brain tumor that metabolize glucose to lactic acid at an elevated rate, even when oxygen is available; they expel lactic acid from the tumor microenvironment through MCTs; there are four known functional MCTs, all of which, except MCT3, are overexpressed in tumors

Researchers analyzed the effects of MCT inhibition on glycolytic metabolism and GBM invasiveness, by considering **treating U251-MG glioma cells** engineered to express enhanced green fluorescent protein (EGFP) with α-cyano-4-hydroxy-cinnamic acid (**ACCA**), a membrane-impermeable small-molecule **inhibitor of MCTs**.

Key terms: U251-MG glioma cells; enhanced green fluorescent protein (EGFP); α-cyano-4-hydroxy-cinnamic acid (ACCA)

Cause-and-Effect: researchers engine to U251-MG glioma cells to express EGFP and treated them with the membrane-impermeable MCT inhibitor ACCA

To **test for invasion capacity of GBM** when lactate transport is inhibited, cellular assays containing pyruvate, lactate, glucose, or glucose supplemented with ACCA were tested. After 120 hours, the fluorescence of the samples was quantified using a **fluorescent plate reader** and the **invasive capacity** was calculated. Their results are shown in Figure 1.

Key terms: pyruvate, glucose, fluorescent plate reader, invasive capacity

Cause-and-Effect: assays containing GBM cells and pyruvate, lactate, glucose, and glucose plus ACCA were measured after 120 hours for the invasive capacity displayed by each cell type

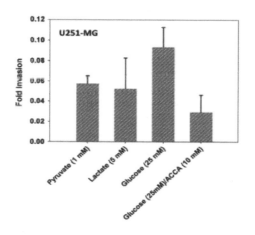

Figure 1: Invasive capacity is elevated versus control GBM for all treatment conditions; it is most elevated in the presence of glucose and is reduced versus the glucose containing media when ACCA is added

Measurements of **oxygen consumption** upon application of **ACCA or of digitonin**, an agent that **increases the permeability of plasma membranes to ACCA**, were also carried out to determine the potential impact on **mitochondrial respiration** after *in vivo* application of ACCA. Figure 2 shows the results of the measurements.

Key terms: oxygen consumption, digitonin, mitochondrial respiration

Cause-and-Effect: mitochondrial respiration was measured in cells after addition of ACCA or ACCA and digitonin, an agent that increase the permeability of the plasma membrane to ACCA.

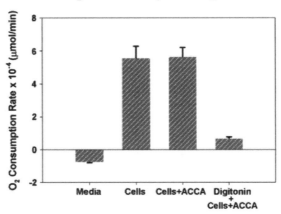

Figure 2: Rates of O₂ consumption in medium are approximately equal in the glucose-containing cellular media with and without ACCA, but are decreased versus glioma cells treated with ACCA when digitonin is also present

1. Comparison across brain slice cultures reveals that U251-MG invasiveness:
   A. is not enhanced in glioma cells treated with ACCA and glucose versus untreated cells.
   B. is negatively correlated with the presence of lactate in the medium.
   C. **is positively correlated with enhanced glycolytic flux.**
   D. demonstrates that glioma invasiveness is decreased versus controls in glucose treated cells also treated with ACCA.

Choice **C** is correct. Figure 1 shows U251-MG invasiveness is positively correlated to the presence of glucose in the growth medium, while ACCA treatment decreases lactic acid efflux, causing glioma cell invasiveness to decrease below the level shown with any other treatment. This suggests that a buildup of intracellular lactic acid, which is typically avoided by the characteristic efflux of lactic acid through MCTs described in the passage, inhibits glycolytic flux and thus glioma invasiveness.

A and B: Figure 1 shows enhanced glial cell invasiveness relative to control (0.0) levels for ACCA-treated and lactate-supplemented media.
D: Figure 1 shows that that glioma invasiveness is increased versus controls in glucose treated cells also treated with ACCA

2. In addition to blocking lactate transport, what do the results shown in Figure 2 suggest might be true of ACCA's action on glioma cell respiration?
   A. Intracellular ACCA induces an increase in respiration due to the exposure of mitochondria to respiratory substrates.
   B. Extracellular ACCA interferes with glucose transport across the cell membrane.
   C. Extracellular ACCA acts to decrease O_2 permeability across the cell membrane.
   D. <u>Intracellular ACCA blocks intracellular pyruvate entry into mitochondria.</u>

Choice **D** is correct. Figure 2 shows that rates of O_2 consumption by GBM cells in glucose-containing media are approximately equal with and without ACCA, but are decreased versus glioma cells treated with ACCA when digitonin, an agent that increases the permeability of ACCA to the plasma membrane, is also present. The fact that ACCA treatment alone does not substantially influence O_2 consumption suggests that ACCA's inhibition of aerobic respiration occurs only when ACCA, which is otherwise membrane impermeable, is able to enter the cell following digitonin treatment. Therefore, the mechanism by which ACCA mediates its inhibition of aerobic respiration must occur intracellularly.

A: ACCA decreases, rather than increases, mitochondrial activity as reflected by the changes in oxygen consumption by GBM cells shown in Figure 2.
B and C: the mechanism by which ACCA mediates its inhibition of aerobic respiration must occur intracellularly.

3. Gliomas such as GBM arise from glial cells. Which of the following is a function of these cells?
   I. Maintenance of the myelin sheath in the peripheral nervous system
   II. Secretion of cerebrospinal fluid
   III. Maintenance of the myelin sheath in the central nervous system

   A. I only
   B. III only
   C. I and III only
   D. <u>I, II, and III</u>

Choice **D** is correct. Glial cells are non-neuronal cells that maintain homeostasis, form myelin, and provide support and protection for neurons in the brain and peripheral nervous system. Oligodendrocytes are glial cells that coat axons in the central nervous system with myelin, while Schwann cells perform a similar function in the peripheral nervous system. Ependymal cells line the spinal cord and the ventricular system of the brain. These cells synthesize and secrete of cerebrospinal fluid (CSF)

4. MCT4 participates in the astrocyte-neuron lactate shuttle that occurs between neurons and astrocytes during routine axonal firing. Given this, what is the most likely reason that researchers believe ACCA is a better candidate as a potential treatment for GBM than other small molecule inhibitors with greater affinity for MCTs?
   A. Its relatively lower MCT affinity implies broader activity against all MCTs overexpressed in GBM.
   B. High-affinity inhibitors may be unable to disrupt the neuron-astrocyte lactate shuttle in GBM.
   C. Other small molecule inhibitors may have few adverse effects against the elevated glycolytic metabolism of GBM.
   D. <u>ACCA is less likely to impact normal tissue while adversely affecting cells displaying elevated rates of glycolysis.</u>

Choice **D** is correct. If ACCA is a relatively lower affinity inhibitor of MCTs, it is less likely to interfere with normal neuronal function and specifically inhibit the metabolic function of cancerous cells displaying abnormally rapid glycolytic flux.

A: lower MCT affinity does not necessarily imply broader activity against all MCTs.

B: high-affinity inhibitors are more likely to disrupt the neuron-astrocyte lactate shuttle in GBM than a lower affinity inhibitor.

C: high-affinity inhibitors are likely to disrupt all MCT-related functions to a greater extent than would a lower affinity inhibitor.

5.   The researchers hypothesized that lactate can initiate a cascade of events that up-regulate the expression of growth factors that enhance the invasive capacity of GBM. What alternative explanation for the increase in GBM invasiveness when lactate efflux is inhibited is NOT consistent with results from the passage?

   A. Tumor lactate can up-regulate expression of proteins that degrade the extracellular matrix in the tumor micro-environment.

   B. The collapse of glycolytic metabolism degraded the cellular energy pool and the invasive capacity of GBM.

   C. Lactate efflux directly modulates the tumor micro-environment in such a way as to promote GBM invasiveness.

   D. **Efflux of lactate decreases an invasive GBM cell's capacity for aerobic metabolism in highly vascularized sites.**

Choice **D** is correct. When efflux of lactate is decreased in GBM due to ACCA/digitonin co-treatment, Figure 2 shows that oxygen consumption decreases implying that aerobic metabolism had decreased. This implies that efflux of lactate maintains a basal state of aerobic activity in glioma cells either for reasons separate from or related to its promotion of glycolytic metabolism—it does not decrease the cancerous cells capacity for aerobic metabolism.

A, B and C: All three of these statements are alternate explanations for the relationship between changes in lactate efflux and changes in GBM invasiveness as indicated by the data.

Passage II Explanation (Questions 6-10)

Epstein-Barr virus (EBV) infection is suspected in the development of a variety of **autoimmune diseases**, including multiple sclerosis (MS), arthritis, and type 1 diabetes. More than **93%** of Americans are thought to be infected by the virus, which is unique in that it has the ability to infect, activate, and latently persist in B lymphocytes for the lifetime of the infected individual. Previously, the effect of EBV infection has been attributed to immunological cross-reactivity between EBV and self-antigen. Scientists instead proposed that the **development of autoimmunity due** to EBV infection **occurs because of an impairment of CD8+ T cell control**.

Key terms: EBV, multiple sclerosis (MS), arthritis, type 1 diabetes, B lymphocytes, autoimmunity, CD8+ T cell

Cause-and-Effect: EBV is linked to the development of autoimmune diseases; more than 93% of Americans are infected the virus which can persist for the lifetime of an affected individual; EBV may contribute to the development of autoimmunity by impairing control of CD8+ T cells

The hypothesis proposes that **susceptibility to the development of chronic autoimmune diseases after EBV infection** is dependent on a genetically determined quantitative deficiency of the cytotoxic CD8+ T cells that normally maintain tight control of EBV infection. Deprivation of sunlight and vitamin D at higher latitudes aggravates the genetic CD8+ T cell deficiency and increases the incidence and progression of autoimmune disease. The relationship between the severity of disease and the age of disease onset to the **extent of genetic or environmentally-induced deficiency of CD8+ T cells** is shown in **Figure 1**.

Key terms: sunlight, vitamin D

Cause-and-Effect: chronic autoimmune disease is caused by EBV infection in those with a pre-existing genetic deficiency of CD8+ T cells; CD8+ T cells normally control EBV infection; lack of sunlight or vitamin D aggravate pre-existing CD8+ T cell deficiencies and increases the incidence and progression of autoimmune disease

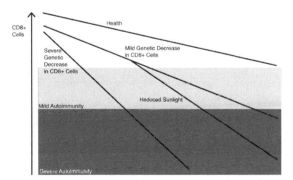

Figure 1: the figure illustrates that the number of CD8+ T cells in the body decreases with age, but that the rate of the decline is greater in individuals with a pre-existing deficiency of CD8+ T cells. Those with a more severe deficiency display a greater age-related rate of decline in CD8+ T cell count. Lack of exposure to sunlight can increase the rate of decline for individuals with a mild genetic deficiency of CD8+ T cells. Individuals with both a mild and more severe deficiency will progress through stages of mild and eventually severe immunity as CD8+ T cell counts decline; the age of onset of both severities of the condition depends on the rate of decline of CD8+ T cells and the number of CD8+ T cells initially present in the individual

The proposal supposes that autoimmunity develops sequentially in the steps illustrated in Figure 2, ending with the development of **ectopic B cell follicles**, which may represent sites of **clonal expansion of autoreactive B cells** specific for antigens present in the target organ.

Key terms: ectopic B cell follicles; clonal expansion; autoreactive B cells

Cause-and-Effect: it's proposed that autoimmunity develops sequentially as shown in Figure 2, ending with the development of B cell follicles; these follicles may represent sites of clonal expansion of B cells specific for antigens in the target organ

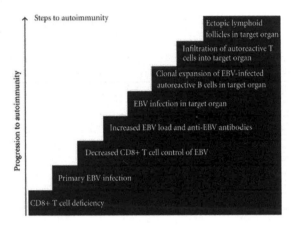

Figure 2: Sequence of steps in the development of chronic autoimmune disease development, beginning with pre-existing CD8+ T cell deficiency and ending with development of ectopic B cell follicles in target organs

6. Latently infected memory B cells express proteins which mimic the mechanism of activation of antigen-selected B cells. In normal B cell differentiation, naïve B cells:
    A. differentiate exclusively to memory B cells following initial antigen exposure.
    B. require only binding of antigen to the B cell receptor for differentiation to occur.
    C. <u>**may be activated in a T cell independent pathway.**</u>
    D. require antigen presentation by helper T cells during activation.

Choice **C** is correct. B cell recognition of antigen is not the only element necessary for B cell activation, but this activation can occur in either a T cell-dependent or -independent manner. Most antigens are T-dependent, meaning T cell help is required for maximal antibody production. With a T-dependent antigen, the first signal comes from antigen's cross-linking the B cell receptor (BCR), and the second signal comes from co-stimulation provided by a T cell. One advantage of foregoing T cell involvement is that an expedited immune response can be mobilized, however germinal center formation, isotype switching and affinity maturation do not occur during this form of activation. Also, because almost all memory B cells are derived from germinal centers, effective antibody-mediated memory is compromised by T-independent B cell activation.

A: Immature B cells may differentiate to plasma- or memory-B cells upon activation.
B: B cell recognition of antigen is not the only element necessary for B cell activation.
D: B cell activation can occur in either a T cell-dependent or -independent manner.

7. CD8+ T cells normally maintain control of EBV infection in what way?
   A. Through release of cytotoxic granules following their binding of soluble antigens in the blood or lymph.
   B. By ingesting, processing and presenting antigenic components of infected B cells to natural killer T cells.
   C. Through complement-mediated marking and removing of proliferating infected B cells.
   D. <u>**By eliminating proliferating and lytically infected B cells in an antigen-specific manner.**</u>

Choice **D** is correct. Cytotoxic T cells destroy virus-infected cells and tumor cells, by binding to a specific antigen associated with MHC class I molecules present on the surface of all nucleated cells.

A: Unlike B cells, CD8+ T cells bind only those antigens associated with MHC class I molecules.
B: NK cells—an element of the innate immune response—recognize target cells independent of any action by B or T lymphocytes. Their primary action is to eliminate cells lacking self-antigen.
C: The complement system is an element of the innate immune response that combines the actions of small blood-borne proteins, antibodies and phagocytic cells to clear pathogens from an organism—it does not involve the action of CD8+ T cells.

8. CD8+ T cell deficiency has shown to be present in the healthy blood relatives of patients with autoimmune diseases. What does this most likely reflect concerning the relationship between latent EBV infection, CD8+ T cell deficiency and autoimmunity?
   A. Latent EBV infection decreases CD8+ T cell count, but does not always result in the development of autoimmune disease.
   B. <u>**CD8+ T cell deficiency alone cannot explain the progression of autoimmune disease.**</u>
   C. CD8+T cell abnormalities are genetically determined and not a consequence of EBV infection.
   D. Environmental, not genetic factors, are the primary determinant of CD8+ T cell deficiency.

Choice **B** is correct. The fact that CD8+ T cell deficiency has shown to be present in the healthy blood relatives of patients with autoimmune diseases indicates that CD8+ T cell deficiency alone cannot explain the occurrence of autoimmune disease, as those healthy relatives were deficient but did not develop the disease.

A: The question provides no indication of whether those healthy relatives are or are not infected by EBV.
C: We have no way of knowing whether those healthy relatives are or not infected with EBV—although given the extent of EBV in the population, as described in the passage, it's not unreasonable to assume that some of the relatives are infected with EBV—and as a result we cannot determine whether genetic or other factors are solely responsible for the deficiency.
D: The information presented in the question does not address the extent to which the deficiency is environmentally influenced.

9. What conclusion concerning CD8+ T cell count and the development of autoimmunity can reasonably be drawn from Figure 1?
   A. Sunlight deprivation can lead to the development of autoimmunity in individuals with normal CD8+ T cell counts.
   B. Decline in CD8+ T cell levels results only from disease-related processes.
   C. <u>**Primary CD8+ T cell deficiency is aggravated by aging.**</u>
   D. The rate of CD8+T cell count decline is equal in all individuals who develop severe autoimmunity.

Choice **C** is correct. Figure 2 shows that CD8+ T cell counts decline with age in all individuals, including those with primary CD8+ T cell deficiency, increasing the likelihood of autoimmune, with age, for those suffering a primary deficiency.

A: Figure 2 shows that only individuals with at least a mild primary deficiency develop symptoms of autoimmunity because of decreased exposure to natural sunlight.

B: Figure 2 shows that CD8+ T cell counts decline with age in all individuals.

D: The rate of CD8+T cell count decline is greatest in individuals with the most severe primary CD8+ T cell deficiencies and in those with more mild deficiencies if deprived of natural sunlight.

10. If the mechanism for development of autoimmune disease presented in the passage is true, then which statement regarding MS is most likely to be INCORRECT?
    A. The risk of developing MS is extremely low among individuals not infected with EBV.
    B. <u>**Most individuals infected with EBV develop MS.**</u>
    C. The likelihood of EBV infection is higher in MS patients than in the general population.
    D. The risk of developing MS increases following EBV infection.

Choice **B** is correct. The passage states that more than 93% of Americans are thought to be infected by the virus and that MS is caused by the mechanism, involving EBV, described at length in the passage. Given that such a high percentage of the population are potentially infected by the virus, and that relatively fewer individuals develop MS, this suggests that most individuals do not develop MS following EBV infection if the mechanism described in the passage is correct.

A: The passage mechanism implicates EBV infection in the mechanism of autoimmune disease progression. In the absence of primary EBV infection, the risk of MS infection should be low if the mechanism proposed in the passage is correct.

C: If EBV infection is required for the progression of autoimmune diseases, including MS, than very nearly all individuals with MS should be infected with EBV.

D: If EBV infection is required for the progression of autoimmune diseases, then the risk of developing MS should increase following infection.

Passage III Explanation (Questions 11-15)

Lambert–Eaton syndrome (LEMS) is an autoimmune disorder that is characterized by muscular weakness in the extremities. It is the result of a reaction in which **antibodies are formed against** presynaptic voltage-gated calcium channels, and likely other nerve terminal proteins, in the **neuromuscular junction**, shown in Figure 1.

Key terms: Lambert-Easton syndrome (LEMS); presynaptic voltage-gated calcium channels; neuromuscular junction

Cause-and-Effect: LEMS is an autoimmune disorder characterized by muscular weakness in the extremities and caused by autoantibodies formed against presynaptic voltage-gated calcium channels

LEMS contrasts with a similar neuromuscular disease, **myasthenia gravis (MG)**, which gives rise to **muscle weakness** caused by circulating **antibodies** that **impair binding by acetylcholine to its receptors** at the postsynaptic neuromuscular junction. Some forms of the antibody **impair** the ability of acetylcholine to **bind to receptors**. Others lead to the **destruction of receptors**, either by **complement fixation** or by inducing the muscle cell to **eliminate the receptors through endocytosis**.

Key terms: myasthenia gravis (MG), postsynaptic neuromuscular junction

Cause-and-Effect: MG gives rise to muscle weakness because of circulating antibodies binding acetylcholine receptors at the postsynaptic neuromuscular junction and either blocking binding or eliminating the receptors through complement-fixation or endocytosis.

The antibodies are produced by **plasma cells,** which are derived from **B cells**. B cells convert into plasma cells by **helper T cell** stimulation. To carry out this activation, helper T cells must first be activated themselves, which is done by binding of the **T cell receptor (TCR)** to the **acetylcholine receptor antigenic peptide fragment**, known as an **epitope**, resting within the **major histocompatibility complex** of **antigen presenting cells**.

Key terms: plasma cell, B cells, helper T cell, acetylcholine receptor antigenic peptide fragment, epitope, major histocompatibility complex, antigen presenting cells

Cause-and-Effect: autoantibodies against the acetylcholine receptor are produced by plasma cells; plasma cells are derived from B cells when B cells are activated by helper T cells; helper T cells are activated by binding of a fragment of acetylcholine receptor on the major histocompatibility complex of an antigen presenting cell to the helper T cell receptor

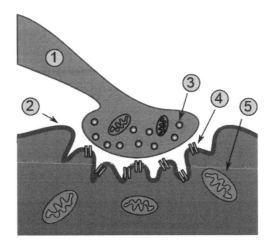

Figure 1: The figure illustrates the major parts of the neuromuscular junction. LEMS is caused by autoantibodies interfering with neurotransmitter release from the presynaptic membrane (3), while MG is caused by autoantibodies to the postsynaptic acetylcholine receptors (4).

11. The symptoms of patients with what disease are likely to see symptom improvement when treated with an inhibitor of acetylcholinesterase?
    A. MG only
    B. LEMS only
    C. <u>**Both MG and LEMS**</u>
    D. Neither MG nor LEMS

Choice **C** is correct. Acetylcholinesterase inhibitors can provide symptomatic benefits for both MG and LEMS patients by increasing the activity of what little ACh is present in the synaptic cleft.

12. What causes the autoantibody-mediated weakness seen in LEMS?
    A. Receptor binding by acetylcholine is blocked.
    B. Calcium reuptake through voltage-gated channels is inhibited.
    C. Action potential transmission is inhibited.
    D. <u>**Pre-synaptic vesicular binding to the plasma membrane is reduced.**</u>

Choice **D** is correct. In normal neuromuscular function, a nerve impulse is carried down the axon until reaching the neuromuscular junction, where the impulse is transferred to the muscle cell, leading to the opening of voltage-gated calcium channel, the influx of calcium ions into the nerve terminal, and the calcium-dependent triggering of synaptic vesicle fusion with plasma membrane. These synaptic vesicles contain acetylcholine, which is released into the synaptic cleft and stimulates the acetylcholine receptors on the muscle. In LEMS, antibodies against these channels decrease the amount of calcium that can enter the nerve ending, hence less acetylcholine can be released from the neuromuscular junction

A: Receptor binding by acetylcholine is unaffected; instead, less acetylcholine is released.
B: LEMS only interferes with the flow of extracellular calcium ions into the nerve terminal.
C: The transmission of the action potential is unaffected.

13. Surgical removal of what organ in MG patients is most likely to have been shown to reduce the pool of mature, circulating T cells available for B cell activation?
    A. Thyroid
    B. Spleen
    C. Thymus
    D. Pituitary gland

Choice **C** is correct. Within the thymus, T cells mature; specifically T cells that recognize and attack self-antigens are eliminated. This process occurs in two steps. First, T cells undergo "Positive Selection" whereby the cell comes in contact with self-MHC expressed by thymic epithelial cells; those with no interaction are destroyed. Second, the T cell undergoes "Negative Selection" by interacting with thymic dendritic cells whereby T cells with high affinity interaction are eliminated through apoptosis, avoiding autoimmunity. Only those with intermediate affinity survive, promoting the development of self-tolerance. Removal of the thymus would decrease the pool of mature, circulating T cells available for B cell activation.

A: The thyroid gland controls regulates metabolism and helps maintain calcium homeostasis via its secretion of thyroid hormone and calcitonin. It is not directly involved in T cell maturation.
B: As part of the mononuclear phagocyte system, it metabolizes removes senescent red blood cells from circulating and initiates process of the hemoglobin which they contained. The spleen also synthesizes antibodies in its white pulp and removes antibody-coated bacteria and antibody-coated blood cells by way of blood and lymph circulation, it is, however, not directly involved in T cell maturation.
D: The pituitary gland is an endocrine gland that synthesizes and stores a variety of hormones, but it is not directly involved in T cell maturation.

14. In LEMS, the velocity of action potential propagation is unchanged. Which of the following is likely to result in a decrease in the rate of action potential propagation along an individual axon?
    A. The blockage of acetylcholine receptors on neuromuscular junction endplates
    B. Demyelination of the axon
    C. Propagation between nodes along myelinated axons
    D. Increased extracellular sodium concentrations

Choice **B** is correct. Myelin is a dielectric material that forms a layer, the myelin sheath, around neuronal axons of the central and peripheral nervous system. The main purpose of a myelin sheath is to increase the speed at which impulses propagate along the myelinated fiber. Along unmyelinated fibers, impulses move continuously as waves, but, in myelinated fibers, they "hop" or propagate by saltatory conduction. Loss of myelination along previously myelinated fibers would slow the velocity of action potential propagation.

A: While blocking acetylcholine receptors would create symptoms similar to those seen in MS patients, it will not affect the rate of action potential conduction.
C: This is what occurs during saltatory conduction.
D: This would increase the rate of influx of sodium ions during action potential propagation, but would not slow the rate of conduction.

15. Apart from skeletal muscle weakness, individuals with LEMS experience specific problems with complex muscular coordination during movement. This information is consistent with the presence of acetylcholine receptors in the:
    A. **cerebellum.**
    B. hypothalamus.
    C. medulla oblongata.
    D. pons.

Choice **A** is correct. The cerebellum is a region of the brain that plays an important role in motor control. While it doesn't initiate movement, it contributes to coordination, precision, and accurate timing of that movement by receiving input from sensory systems of the spinal cord and from other parts of the brain, and integrates these inputs to fine tune motor activity. Cerebellar damage does not cause paralysis, but instead produces disorders in fine movement, equilibrium, posture, and motor learning.

B: The hypothalamus controls body temperature, hunger, important aspects of parenting and attachment behaviors, thirst, fatigue, sleep, and circadian rhythms through its regulation of neurohormone release, but hypothalamic damage would not cause specific difficulty with complex muscular movement.
C: The medulla oblongata is the lower half of the brainstem, and contains the cardiac, respiratory, vomiting and vasomotor centers. It therefore deals with the autonomic (involuntary) functions of breathing, heart rate and blood pressure control. Medullary damage would not cause isolated difficulty with complex muscular movement.
D: The pons is another portion of the brain stem that contains nuclei that relay signals from the forebrain to the cerebellum, along with nuclei that deal primarily with sleep, respiration, swallowing, bladder control, hearing, equilibrium, taste, eye movement, facial expressions and sensation, and posture. Pontine damage would not cause isolated difficulty with complex muscular movement.

Discrete Set 1 Answers and Explanations (Questions 16-18)

16. Which of the following is most likely to be transmitted between a neuron and skeletal muscle tissue?
    A. Epinephrine
    B. Dopamine
    C. **<u>Acetylcholine</u>**
    D. Muscarine

Choice **C** is correct. Remember that acetylcholine is the neurotransmitter used in the somatic nervous system.

A: Epinephrine is a hormone secreted by the medulla of the adrenal glands, which causes an increase in heart rate, muscle strength, blood pressure, and sugar metabolism. This reaction, known as the "Flight or Fight Response" prepares the body for strenuous activity. It is not a neurotransmitter.
B: In the brain, dopamine functions as a neurotransmitter—a chemical released by nerve cells to send signals to other brain cells, not muscular tissue.
D: Muscarine is a highly toxic alkaloid related to the cholines and has neurologic effects. It is isolated from certain mushrooms.

17. Under which of the following classifications does erythropoietin fall? ·
    I. Glycoprotein hormone
    II. Steroid hormone
    III. Erythrocyte precursor

    A. **<u>I only</u>**
    B. III only
    C. I and II only
    D. I, II, and III

Choice **A** is correct. I is true. Erythropoietin (EPO) is a glycoprotein hormone. It is not a precursor of erythrocytes.

II: Steroids are a group of cyclical organic compounds whose basis is a characteristic arrangement of seventeen carbon atoms in a four-ring structure. EPO is a glycoprotein-based hormone, not a steroid hormone.
III: EPO is not a precursor of erythrocytes.

18. Which of the following enzymes does NOT use RNA nucleotides as a part of its function?
    A. **<u>DNA ligase</u>**
    B. Primase
    C. RNA polymerase III
    D. Telomerase

Choice **A** is correct. DNA ligase forms a phosphodiester bond between two DNA nucleotides.

B: Primase places an RNA primer for DNA polymerase to work off of
C: RNA polymerase III uses RNA nucleotides to create an RNA molecule
D: Telomerase is an enzyme made of protein and RNA subunits that elongates chromosomes by adding TTAGGG sequences to the end of existing chromosomes.

Passage IV Answers and Explanations (Questions 19-22)

Alpha helices are an important part of the structure of most **proteins**. They form because of the structure of the **amino acids** in a protein. The functional groups of amino acids in proximity are able to form **hydrogen bonds**. When these hydrogen bonds consistently form between every **4th** amino acid, the result is a **right-handed helix**. There are **3.6 residues** per helical turn in an alpha helix and **5.4 Angstroms** between consecutive turns.

Key Terms: alpha helices, proteins, amino acids, hydrogen bonds, every 4th, right-handed, 3.6 residues, 5.4 angstroms.

There are many ways of depicting alpha helices in two dimensions. A **Wenxiang diagram** can be used to show the relative location of amino acids as they bind with one another about a central axis. Figure 1 shows a Wenxiang diagram with the letters corresponding to amino acids.

Key Terms: Wenxiang diagram.

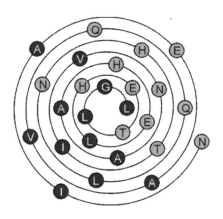

Figure 1 A Wenxiang diagram of an alpha helix

Figure 1 shows a Wenxiang diagram for an alpha helix with a given amino acid sequence.

Each amino acid has a different **propensity** for being in an alpha helix. **Alanine** has the greatest propensity. Table 1 shows the relative propensities of the amino acids to be involved in an alpha helix. The values in the table represent the difference between the **Gibbs free energy change** of the hydrogen bond formation for each amino acid and the energy change for alanine. Thus the values are relative to the value for alanine.

Key Terms: propensity, alanine, Gibbs free energy.

Cause and Effect: In this section we are told that not all amino acids have the same propensity toward participating in hydrogen bonding necessary for alpha helix formation. Alanine is the most likely to do so.

There are two other forms of helices that can occur with some frequency. They are denoted the **3_{10} helix** and the **π-helix.** Amino acids in a 3_{10} helix hydrogen bond **every 3rd** amino acid. Every amino acid in a 3_{10} helix represents a **120 degree rotation** in the helix. In a π-helix hydrogen bonding occurs between **every 5th** amino acid and each amino acid corresponds to a **90 degree turn** in the helix.

Key Terms: 3_{10} helix, π-helix, every 3rd, 120 degrees, every 5th, 90 degrees. This paragraph tells us about two other types of helices. The 3_{10} helix has 3 amino acids per turn because $360/120 = 3$ and the π -helix has 4 amino acids per turn because $360/90 = 4$.

Table 1 The relative propensities of amino acids to form hydrogen bonds in alpha helices

Table 1 shows us the propensities of amino acids to form hydrogen bonds in alpha helices compared to that of alanine.

Amino Acid	Free energy change	Amino Acid	Free energy change
Alanine	0	Tyrosine	0.52
Arginine	0.21	Phenylalanine	0.54
Leucine	0.21	Histidine	0.61
Methionine	0.23	Valine	0.61
Lysine	0.27	Asparagine	0.65
Glutamine	0.38	Threonine	0.66
Glutamic acid	0.39	Cysteine	0.68
Isoleucine	0.42	Aspartic Acid	0.69
Tryptophan	0.49	Glycine	1
Serine	0.50	Proline	3.15

19. Alpha helices contribute to which of the following?
    A. Primary structure
    B. **Secondary structure**
    C. Tertiary structure
    D. Quaternary structure

Choice **B** is correct. This question is asking us to recall what type of structures alpha helices are. Within the long protein chains there are regions in which the chains are organized into regular structures known as alpha helices which are secondary structures in proteins. These secondary structures are held together by hydrogen bonds. In an alpha helix, the protein chain is coiled like a loosely-coiled spring.

A: This term is used to describe the order of the amino acids joined together to make the protein. This primary structure is usually shown using abbreviations for the amino acid residues.
C: Tertiary structure of a protein is a description of the way the whole chain, including the secondary structures, folds itself into its final 3D shape.
D: Quaternary protein structure involves the clustering of several individual peptide or protein chains into a final specific shape. A variety of bonding interactions including hydrogen bonding, salt bridges, and disulfide bonds hold the various chains into a particular geometry.

20. Which of the following are involved in the hydrogen bonding in the alpha helix backbone?
    A. The side groups of the amino acids
    B. The amine groups from each amino acid
    C. The carbonyl groups from each amino acid
    D. The amine group from one with the carbonyl group of another.

Choice **D** is correct. This question asks us to consider what two species on an amino acid will hydrogen bond with one another. The amine group will create dipole from the N-H with a positive charge on the H that can interact with the negative dipole on the O of the carbonyl group on another residue.

A: The side groups' interactions contribute to tertiary structure, not alpha helices.
B: This does not occur as readily as choice D because the oxygen in carbonyl groups are more nucleophilic than nitrogens in amines.
C: This will not occur because there will be no positive side of a dipole with which the negative O in a carbonyl can interact.

21. Starting from the center of Figure 1, which amino acids are bound to the first E?
    A. Guanine and asparagine
    B. Guanine and leucine
    C. Leucine and histidine
    D. Lysine and asparagine

Choice **C** is correct. We are told in the passage that amino acids in an alpha helix are bound to every 4th amino acid. Looking at figure 1, you can see that the first leucine (L) is bound to the first glutamic acid (E) and then four more residues gives us a histidine (H).

22. Why might proline disrupt the formation of an alpha helix?
    A. The ring on proline causes too much strain to be bent sufficiently in the helix.
    B. The amine group from proline creates a more polar molecule than other amino acids.
    C. The aromatic portion of proline disrupts its ability to hydrogen bond.
    D. Proline is too large.

Choice **A** is correct. This question requires us to remember the general structure of proline. Proline is the only amino acid whose amine group forms a ring. This means that it is unable to twist and turn with the same fluidity as other amino acids. Below is the structure of proline

B: There is no charge on proline. It is less polar than some other charged amino acids.
C: There is no aromatic portion of proline.
D: Proline is smaller than other amino acids, such as phenylalanine, which can appear in alpha helices.

Passage V Answers and Explanations (Questions 23-26)

The artificial sweetener aspartame is the **methyl ester of the dipeptide of L-phenylalanine and L-aspartic acid**, whose structure is shown in Figure 1. There are two general approaches to commercially prepare this compound. The chemical approach involves reacting the methyl ester of phenylalanine with an **N-protected** anhydride of aspartic acid. The protecting group, either a benzyl or formyl group is then removed by mild acid hydrolysis. In addition to the desired product, a **beta structural isomer is also formed due to formation of a peptide bond with the wrong carboxylate group**, which must be removed since it produces a bitter taste. A second enzymatic synthesis has been developed in which **proteases** catalyze the selective peptide bond formation and avoids the formation of the beta isomer.

Key Terms: Dipeptide, N-protected, isomer, peptide bond, and proteases

Cause and effect: Protecting the amino group of the aspartic anhydride prevents the formation of an amide bond with the carboxylate of the phenylalanine, which would be an undesirable dipeptide product.

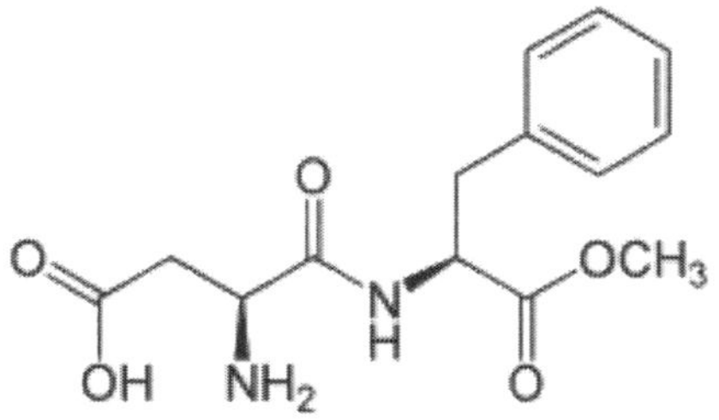

Figure 1 The structure of N-(L-α-Aspartyl)-L-phenylalanine,1-methyl ester, pK$_{a1}$ = 3.2 and pK$_{a2}$ = 7.7

Figure 1 N-(L-α-Aspartyl)-L-phenylalanine,1-methyl ester is the IUPAC name for aspartame, which can be considered a diprotic acid, with the more acidic carboxylate group having a pK$_a$ of 3.2 and the ammonium group having a pK$_a$ of 7.7. The peptide nitrogen does not have significant acid-base properties because the nitrogen lone pair is delocalized by resonance with the carbonyl group.

Upon ingestion, aspartame breaks down in the **small intestines** into its components, aspartic acid, phenylalanine and methanol, with the subsequent formation of **metabolites** such as formaldehyde and formic acid. There has been some concern that aspartame can play a role in the **formation of certain cancers as a result of the formation of some of these potentially toxic compounds.**

Key Terms: Small intestines, metabolites

Cause and effect: During the digestion of aspartame, methanol is produced which is a relatively toxic alcohol, which is metabolized to formaldehyde and formic acid and also toxic, raising concerns about the use of aspartame as an artificial sweetener.

23. What is the pI of aspartame?
    A. 3.2
    B. **5.5**
    C. 7.0
    D. 7.7

Choice B is correct. The isoelectric point of an amino acid or oligopeptide, is when the net charge is zero. Therefore the pI is the pH where the carboxylate is deprotonated and the amino group is protonated. The pI can be approximated as the average of the pK_as of the carboxylic acid and the ammonium group, which are given in the caption to Figure 1.

$$pI = (pK_{a1} + pK_{a2})/2 = (3.2 + 7.7)/2 = 10.9/2 = 5.5$$

24. How many chiral centers are in aspartame?
    A. 1
    B. **2**
    C. 3
    D. 4

Choice **B** is correct. The α-carbon atoms of the amino acids, aspartic acid and phenylalanine, are chiral and looking closely at the structure in Figure 1 we can see that these carbons are the only two chiral centers in aspartame.

25. The two amino acids that form the basis for the dipeptide structure of aspartame, aspartic acid and phenylalanine, can be classified as:
    A. hydrophilic and hydrophilic, respectively.
    B. hydrophobic and hydrophilic, respectively.
    C. **hydrophilic and hydrophobic, respectively.**
    D. hydrophobic and hydrophobic, respectively.

Choice **C** is correct. Aspartic acid is considered a hydrophilic amino acid since in its protonated form there can be hydrogen bonding interactions with water and in the deprotonated form, the anion will form ion-dipole interactions with water, both of which are relatively strong intermolecular interactions. The benzyl side group of phenylalanine is a nonpolar group, which would be expected to be significantly hydrophobic.

26. The pH of human gastric fluids is generally between 1 and 3. What is net charge of aspartame under these conditions?
    A. -1
    B. 0
    C. **+1**
    D. +2

Choice **C** is correct. The average pH of gastric juices is below the pK_{a1} of the carboxylate in aspartame, which is given in the caption of Figure 1. Therefore the carboxylate is protonated and not charged, and the amine group is also protonated and in the positively charged ammonium form. The peptide nitrogen is an extremely poor base, primarily due to the delocalization of the nitrogen lone-pair due to resonance with the carbonyl group. Therefore, the net charge of aspartame in the gastric juices will be +1.

Discrete Set 2 Answers and Explanations (Questions 27-30)

27. Which of the following amino acids is achiral?
     A. Lysine
     B. Aspartic acid
     C. Phenylalanine
     D. <u>Glycine</u>

Choice **D** is correct. An achiral molecule generally has no chiral centers (a carbon bonded to 4 different substituents). Glycine is the only naturally occurring amino acid that has only a hydrogen side chain attached to the alpha carbon and as a result it is the only achiral compound of the amino acids.

28. The mean molecular weight of an amino acid residue in a protein is 110 g/mol. If a protein has a mass of approximately 50 kiloDaltons, how many amino acid residues are in the protein?
     A. 2
     B. 50
     C. <u>450</u>
     D. 5500

Choice **C** is correct. The unit of a Dalton is essentially the same as one atomic mass unit (amu) and therefore 50 kiloDaltons is 50,000 amus. If the average molecular weight of an amino acid is 110 g/mol, then it also has a mass of 110 Daltons. The approximate number of amino acids in the protein is $50,000/110 \sim (5/1.1) \times 10^4 \times 10^{-2} \sim 4.5 \times 10^2$.

29. The pancreas secretes pancreatic juices into the small intestine, which contain enzymes that help digest all of the following EXCEPT:
     A. starch.
     B. proteins.
     C. lipids.
     D. <u>cellulose.</u>

Choice **D** is correct. Cellulose is the major component of dietary fiber and is not typically digested by enzymes produced in the human gut, due to the unreactive nature of the $\beta(1,4)$ glycosidic bonds. The $\alpha(1,4)$ glycosidic bonds in starch are much more reactive, and can be metabolized by enzymes such as amylase produced by the salivary glands and pancreas.

A: Pancreatic amylase is an enzyme that aids in starch digestion.
B: The pancreas produces enzymes that help digest proteins, such as protease.
C: The pancreas produces enzymes that digest lipids, like lipase.

30. Which of the following best describes the production pathway for a plasma membrane-bound protein, starting with the production of the mRNA?
    A. Nucleus → cytoplasm → ribosome → endosome
    B. Nucleus → RER → Golgi → secretory vesicle
    C. **Nucleus → cytoplasm → ribosome → RER → Golgi**
    D. Nucleus → cytoplasm → RER

Choice **C** is correct. mRNA is transcribed in the nucleus, exported to the cytoplasm, where it is bound by a ribosome. It will then code for a signal sequence that will cause it to be transported to the RER and then to the Golgi to be moved to the cell's plasma membrane. When presented with problems that involve ranking or ordering, identify the extreme portions of the answer 1st. This can allow you to reach the answer with less effort.

A: mRNA will not go to an endosome, a membrane-bounded compartment inside eukaryotic cells. This serves as a compartment of the endocytic membrane transport pathway from the plasma membrane to the lysosome.
B: mRNA will not go directly to the RER from the nucleus
D: mRNA will not go to the RER without being bound by a ribosome

Passage VI Answers and Explanations (Questions 31-34)

RNA plays a key role in the **translation** of genetic material into **protein**. **Messenger RNA** provides the code from which the amino acid chain is formed. **Ribosomal RNA** provides the structure of ribosomes, where the translation is carried out. **Transfer RNA** brings amino acids to the ribosomes. Thus we see that RNA provides the template for transcription, the site of transcription, and all the means of transcription.

Key Terms: RNA, translation, protein, mRNA, tRNA, rRNA.

This paragraph outlines three different types of RNA and their basic function in the body. RNA is involved in all steps of the translation process.

Messenger RNA needs to be processed before it is ready to bind a **ribosome**. On the **5' end** of the sequence, a **methylated guanosine** is attached in **a 5' − 5' triphosphate linkage**. The addition of the guanine residue allows mRNA to properly bind the ribosome before translation. Additionally, a **3' poly-A tail** is added to the sequence.

Key Terms: ribosome, 5' end, methylated guanosine, 5'-5' triphosphate linkage, 3' poly-A tail.

Transfer RNA molecules have primary, secondary, and tertiary structure due to interactions between base pairs and folding. The tRNA structure consists of a phosphate group on the 5' end, a CCA tail on the 3' end which contains a hydroxyl group where an amino acid can be added by aminoacyl tRNA synthetase. Also, the tRNA contains a unique 3 nucleotide anticodon sequence where the molecule binds opposite mRNA in the ribosome. Figure 1 shows the structure of a tRNA molecule.

Key Terms: primary, secondary, and tertiary structure, phosphate group, CCA tail, hydroxyl group, aminoacyl tRNA synthetase, anticodon.

Figure 1 tRNA structure

Figure 1 shows the base pair sequence of tRNA molecule as well as some of its secondary structure

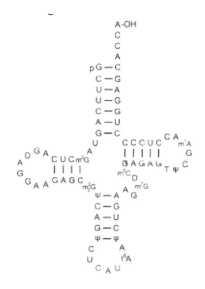

Ribosomal RNA is the major structural component of ribosomes. Ribosomes have two **subunits**, labeled **60S and 40S** for their **sedimentation rate**. The sedimentation rate is the rate at which a particle falls through a liquid and is deposited at the bottom of a sample. Sedimentation rate depends on the acceleration down and **terminal velocity** of the particle as it falls. The rate depends on 3 forces: **gravity, the buoyant force, and the drag force**. The **large subunit** is composed of proteins and 3 smaller rRNA molecules. The **small subunit** is composed proteins as well as an 18S rRNA molecule.

Key Terms: small and large subunits, 60S and 40S, sedimentation rate, terminal velocity, gravity, buoyant force, drag force.

Figure 2 Subunits of a ribosome

Figure 2 shows the breakdown of a ribosome's rRNA structural components

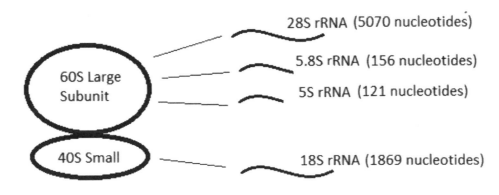

31. In prokaryotes, translation can begin to occur before transcription has finished. Which of the following explains this?
    A. Prokaryotes have ribosomes on their nuclear envelope and need not transport mRNA before translation.
    B. Prokaryotes have no endoplasmic reticulum and exclusively use bound ribosomes for translation.
    C. **Prokaryotes lack a nucleus and thus need not transport the mRNA before translation.**
    D. Prokaryotes have circular DNA which allows transcribed mRNA easy access to ribosomes.

Choice **C** is correct. This question asks us to determine what about prokaryotes allows them to move quickly from transcription of DNA to translation of the transcribed mRNA before it is completely finished being transcribed. Eukaryotes lack this ability because transcription occurs in the nucleus and mRNA needs to be transported to the cytoplasm or the ER to be translated. Prokaryotes have no nucleus and thus the mRNA can interact with ribosomes directly and quickly.

A: Prokaryotes have no nucleus.
B: Prokaryotes do not have an ER so their ribosomes would actually be free ribosomes, not bound ribosomes (which would mean ER-bound in this context).
D: The structure of the DNA is not related to the location advantage that prokaryotes have for moving from transcription to translation.

32. Which of the following is shown in Figure 1?
    I. Primary structure
    II. Secondary structure
    III. Tertiary structure

    A. I only
    B. III only
    C. **I and II only**
    D. I, II, and III

Choice **C** is correct. The primary structure is the sequence of base pairs. Secondary structure is the interaction of base pairs to create hairpin loops and other structures. Tertiary structure is the folding of the molecule that gives it an L-shape. Thus choice C is correct.
III: The folding of the tRNA is not shown.

33. Which of the following is the approximate total length of human rRNA?
    A. 6000 nucleotides
    B. 6500 nucleotides
    C. **7000 nucleotides**
    D. 8000 nucleotides

Choice **C** is correct. We need only add the nucleotides from each of the mRNA subunits that make up the large and small subunits. 5000 + 150 +120 + 1900 ~ 7170. The answer is a little over 7000.

34. A human ribosome is 80S. During sedimentation analysis, which of the following best explains why the 60S and 40S subunits together do not result in a 100S ribosome?
    A. The volume of the ribosome is smaller than sum of the volumes of each subunit.
    B. The buoyant force on the ribosome is smaller than the sum of the buoyant forces on each subunit
    C. **The drag force on the ribosome is smaller than the sum of the drag forces on each subunit**
    D. The gravitation force on the ribosome is greater than the sum of the gravitational forces on each subunit

Choice **C** is correct. The question asks us to determine why the sedimentation rate for the two subunits is not additive. The volumes are additive which means that the buoyant force on subunits is additive. The masses are additive so the gravitational force is additive as well. This means that the only remaining force must not be additive. This is the drag force. The drag force has the most to do with the shape of the falling particle, which will change when the subunits come together. Thus choice C is correct.

A: The volume of the ribosome is equal to the sum of the volumes of each subunit.
B: The buoyant force on the ribosome is equal to the sum of the buoyant forces on each subunit because the buoyant force depends on volume.
D: the gravitational force on the ribosome is equal to the sum of the gravitational forces on each subunit because the gravitational force depends on mass.

Passage VII Answers and Explanations (Questions 35-39)

Pyruvate decarboxylation is an important process that must occur to pyruvate before continuing to be processed in the Krebs cycle. Decarboxylation occurs after pyruvate enters the **mitochondrial matrix**. During pyruvate decarboxylation, pyruvate is converted to **acetyl CoA** by the complex of three enzymes, commonly called **E1, E2, and E3**. The three enzymes together are called the **pyruvate dehydrogenase complex (PDC)**.

Key Terms: pyruvate decarboxylation, mitochondrial matrix, acetyl CoA, E1, E2, E3, PDC.

Cause and Effect: We are told in the first paragraph that pyruvate decarboxylation is catalyzed by pyruvate dehydrogenase complex in the mitochondrial matrix. This must occur so that we get acetyl CoA to enter the Krebs cycle.

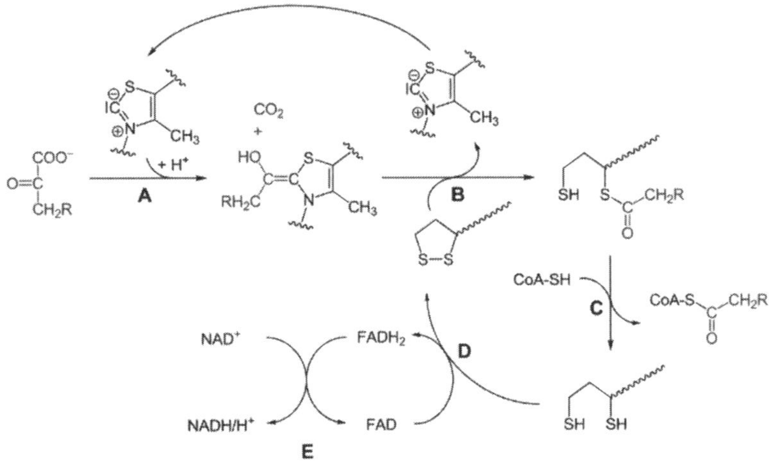

Figure 1 The mechanism of the enzymatic action of the pyruvate dehydrogenase complex

Figure 1 shows the reaction mechanism by which pyruvate is converted to acetyl CoA and how the enzyme prepares itself anew for reaction by oxidizing the lipoate arm and creating NADH + H$^+$.

E1 contains a **thiazolium** ring that exists in **zwitterion** form. Pyruvate is added to the ring and loses **CO_2**. It is then transferred to a **lipoate** on a long **lysine** residue arm. The lipoate is reduced and the ring is broken as a S-C bond is formed. The arm is then able to physically translocate the intermediate to the E2 active site on the complex. This is where the intermediate is transferred to a **coenzyme A** molecule. Acetyl CoA is produced and released from the complex. The lysine arm then transfers the **dihydrolipoate** to E3, where it is oxidized to prepare for the next pyruvate molecule.

Key Terms: thiazolium, zwitterion, CO_2, lipoate, lysine, coenzyme A, dihydrolipoate.

Cause and Effect: This paragraph is essential. It explains the workings of the PDC and basically explains in words what is shown in Figure 1.

Pyruvate dehydrogenase is regulated by two enzymes, **pyruvate dehydrogenase kinase (PDK)**, which can phosphorylate and deactivate E1, and **pyruvate dehydrogenase phosphatase (PDP)**, which activates E1 by **dephosphorylating** it.

The activity of PDK and PDP is regulated by the concentrations of **ATP, ADP, NADH, NAD$^\pm$, acetyl-CoA, and coenzyme A**. The products of the reaction in Figure 1 activate PDK and the substrates inhibit PDK.

Key Terms: PDK, PDP, phosphorylation and dephosphorylation, products, substrates. This last section tells of the regulation of PDC by PDK and PDP and the regulation of PDK and PDP by certain molecules. ATP, NADH, and Acetyl-CoA are all products of PDC's activity and thus inhibit it by activating PDK. ADP, NAD$^+$, and coenzyme A all inhibit PDC by inhibiting PDK.

35. What is the product of B?
    A. A lipoate
    B. **A thioacetate**
    C. A lipoic acid
    D. A thioketone

Choice **B** is correct. This question requires us to know what thio and acetate refer to. A thioacetate is an ester with a sulfur instead of the non-carbonyl oxygen.

A: A lipoate molecule, the conjugate base of lipoic acid ($C_8H_{14}O_2S_2$) requires a ring with two sulfurs.
C: A lipoic acid $C_8H_{14}O_2S_2$ is what we had as the product of step A, prior to step B.
D: A thioketone is a ketone with the carbonyl O replaced by a S.

36. Which of the following occurs during B?
    I. Decarboxylation of pyruvate
    II. Oxidation of a carbon on pyruvate
    III. Reduction of the lipoate arm

    A. I only
    B. III only
    C. I and II only
    D. **II and III only**

Choice **D** is correct. This question requires us to determine what is happening at step B in the reaction shown in figure 1. Figure 1 shows that a hydroxyl group is being turned into a ketone group and that both sulfurs on the lipoate arm is being reduced.

I: The decarboxylation (loss of carbon dioxide) occurred in step A

37. During starvation, what would be the purpose of increased production of PDK?
    A. To activate PDC to create energy in the form of ATP from pyruvate
    B. To inactivate PDC because amino acids from protein degradation provide more energy per molecule
    C. To inactivate PDC because fats are a quicker source of energy
    D. **To inactivate PDC to preserve glucose metabolism for the brain**

Choice **D** is correct. This question requires us to reason why we would want more PDK during starvation. More PDK will result in less glucose metabolism, this is desirable because glucose needs to be conserved for the brain, which is unable to metabolize other molecules that the rest of the body's tissue is. Thus choice D is correct.

A: Increased production of PDK will inactivate PDC.
B: Protein metabolism is not as efficient as glucose metabolism.
C: Fats are a slower source of energy.

38. Muscle contraction stimulates glycolysis. Which of the following is the most reasonable explanation for how this occurs?
    A. Calcium released from the sarcoplasmic reticulum activates PDK, which results in decreased pyruvate concentrations, activating glycolysis.
    B. **Calcium released from sarcoplasmic reticulum activates PDP, which results in decreased pyruvate concentrations, activating glycolysis**
    C. Calcium released from the sarcoplasmic reticulum inhibits PDK, which results in increased pyruvate concentrations, activating glycolysis.
    D. Calcium released from the sarcoplasmic reticulum inhibits PDP, which results in increased pyruvate concentrations, activating glycolysis.

Choice **B** is correct. This question asks us to determine how calcium release might stimulate glycolysis. Calcium can bind either PDK or PDP. Activating PDP will result in decreased pyruvate concentrations, which will stimulate glycolysis.

A: Activating PDK will result in increased pyruvate concentrations.
C, D: Increased pyruvate will inhibit glycolysis

39. An increase in which of the following values will stimulate PDC activity?
    I. $[NADH]/[NAD^+]$
    II. $[Acetyl CoA]/[CoA]$
    III. $[ADP]/[ATP]$

    A. I only
    B. **III only**
    C. I and II only
    D. I, II, and III

Choice **B** is correct. Since ATP is a product of respiration due to the processing of pyruvate, a decrease in ATP or an increase in ADP will stimulate PDC activity.

I: NADH is a product of PDC, thus this choice would inhibit PDC activity.
II: Acetyl CoA is a product of PDC, thus this choice would inhibit PDC activity.

Passage VIII Answers and Explanations (Questions 40-43)

Human Immunodeficiency Virus (HIV) is a retrovirus that infects cells of the immune system, such as **CD4+ T cells**. Infection by HIV leads to low numbers of CD4+ T cells through apoptosis of uninfected cells, and killing of infected cells by the virus or CD8+ cytotoxic lymphocytes. When CD4+ numbers falls below a critical threshold, cell-mediated immunity is lost and the infected individual becomes increasingly **vulnerable to life-threatening opportunistic infections.**

Key terms: Human Immunodeficiency Virus (HIV), retrovirus, CD4+ T cells, apoptosis, cell-mediated immunity, opportunistic infection

Cause and effect: HIV infection causes immunodeficiency

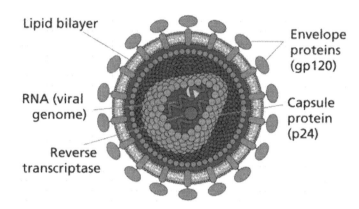

Figure 1 HIV viral particle

Though the **virus's genome is coded in RNA** in free viral particles, in infected cells it is **reverse-transcribed to cDNA** and inserted into the host cell's genome. The process of reverse-transcription is error-prone, which contributes to the virus's ability to quickly mutate to evade the immune system and resist drug treatments.

Key terms: RNA genome, reverse-transcribed, cDNA

During viral replication, the virus **uses host-cell machinery** to replicate its genome and produce the proteins that form the structural components of the virus. Viral RNA genomes lack the post-transcriptional modifications that allow mRNA molecules to be transported out of the nucleus, therefore **they require additional proteins to move into the cytoplasm**, where the genomes are packaged for viral release.

Key terms: host-cell machinery, post-transcriptional modifications

The latent virus within an infected cell is **activated by transcription factors**, such as **NF-κB**, which is upregulated in active T cells. The DNA provirus is then transcribed into mRNA which is then heavily spliced. Some mRNAs produced then undergo post-transcriptional modifications and are exported to the cytoplasm where they are translated. One such protein is **Rev, which is then transported back into the nucleus, where it binds unspliced viral mRNAs** via a Rev Response Element (RRE). **Rev contains a nuclear export signal (NES)**, which allows it—with the viral RNA bound—to be exported into the nucleus. Other necessary proteins are then translated from the intact viral RNA genome.

Key terms: NF-κB, provirus, Rev, Rev Response Element (RRE), nuclear export signal (NES)

Cause and effect: Rev (viral protein) is transcribed and translated, which allows the viral genome to be exported from the nucleus.

40. What type of signals would you expect Rev to contain?
     I. Nuclear Export Signal
     II. Nuclear Localization Signal
     III. ER Signal Sequence

     A. I only
     B. I and II only
     C. I and III only
     D. I, II, and III

Choice **B** is correct. After being translated, Rev must be transported into the nucleus to bind viral RNA genomes (requires NLS) and then transported out of the nucleus with the genome bound (requires NES).

A: True, but not the only signal
C, D: This protein is not translated into the ER so it would not have an ER signal sequence

41. Which of the following would NOT be a good method for a drug to inhibit HIV?
     A. A drug that binds to GP120 to prevent binding of the viral particle to the cell membrane
     B. A drug that inhibits reverse transcriptase
     C. A drug that inhibits DNA polymerase
     D. A drug that inhibits viral particle assembly

Choice **C** is correct. Inhibition of DNA polymerase would negatively affect all cells, not just infected cells.

A: This would be a good drug target as it would prevent the virus from entering cells.
B: This is a common drug target and would help inhibit HIV retroviral activity.
D: This would prevent the viruses from budding off and infecting other cells.

42. Reverse transcriptase produces a double-stranded DNA molecule from a single-stranded RNA molecule. What types of activity does this enzyme have?
     A. RNA-dependent DNA polymerase activity only
     B. RNA-dependent DNA polymerase activity, and DNA-dependent DNA polymerase activity
     C. RNA-dependent DNA polymerase activity, and DNA ligase activity
     D. DNA-dependent DNA polymerase activity only

Choice **B** is correct. The single stranded RNA genome is first used as a template to create a double-stranded DNA-RNA hybrid. The RNA is then degraded and the resulting single stranded DNA is used as a template to create double-stranded DNA.

A: This would result in double-stranded RNA-DNA hybrids.
C: DNA ligase does not form a double-stranded DNA molecule from single-stranded DNA molecules, it joins the phosphate backbone of separate DNA molecules.
D: This would not be functional on an RNA genome.

43. The HIV viral particle has both a protein capsule and a lipid envelope. How are viral particles released from the infected cell?

   A. Viral particles are packaged in the ER-Golgi pathway and exocytosed from the infected cell.

   B. Viral particles acquire the lipid envelope while leaving the cell's nucleus and then are released by lysis of the cell.

   C. <u>**Viral particles bud off the infected cell, and the cells plasma membrane donates the lipid envelope.**</u>

   D. It is not possible to tell without more information.

Choice **C** is correct. You know from the passage that the viral particles are assembled in the cytoplasm. The host-cell plasma membrane is the only reasonable source of the viral envelope.

A: This would not result in the viral particles having a lipid envelope. The lipid bilayer that surrounds vesicles to be exocytosed becomes part of the host cell's plasma membrane.

B: Viral particles are not assembled in the nucleus.

D: This answer is not true, with the given information we can make a deduction.

Discrete Set 3 Answers and Explanations (Questions 44-47)

44. Which of the following occurs during skeletal muscle contraction?
    A. Actin filaments pull on myosin filaments, bringing them closer to the edges of the sarcomere.
    B. Actin filaments pull on myosin filaments, bringing them closer to the center of the sarcomere.
    C. Myosin filaments pull on actin filaments, bringing them closer to the edges of the sarcomere.
    D. <u>**Myosin filaments pull on actin filaments, bringing them closer to the center of the sarcomere.**</u>

Choice **D** is correct. Prior to skeletal muscle contraction, a muscle must receive an incoming nervous stimulus. Once the cell is sufficiently stimulated, the cell's calcium, which then interacts with the protein troponin. Calcium-bound troponin undergoes a conformational shift that leads to the movement of tropomyosin, exposing the myosin-binding sites on actin. This allows for myosin and actin ATP-dependent cross-bridge cycling and shortening of the muscle. The myosin filaments will "pull" on actin filaments. Since the sarcomere is shortening, they must be pulled toward the center. See the figure below.

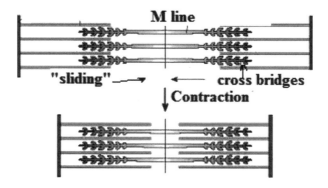

45. Which of the following contains a nucleus?
    I. Erythrocytes
    II. Megakaryocytes
    III. Leukocytes

    A. I only
    B. II only
    C. III only
    D. <u>**II and III only**</u>

Choice **D** is correct. II and III are true.

I: Erythrocytes, red blood cells, are designed to carry oxygen and as a result, do not have nuclei.
II: Megakaryocytes are large bone marrow cells with a large nucleus which are responsible for the production of platelets, which are necessary for normal blood clotting.
III: White blood cells, also called leukocytes, are the cells of the immune system that are involved in protecting the body against both infectious disease and foreign invaders. All leukocytes are nucleated when they are produced stem cells in the bone marrow.

46. Where is DNA ligase most likely to be used in DNA replication?
    A. The leading strand of a DNA replication fork
    B. **The lagging strand of a DNA replication fork**
    C. As a cofactor of DNA polymerase
    D. As a cofactor of RNA polymerase

Choice **B** is correct. DNA ligase is a special type of ligase, which is an enzyme that repairs single-stranded breaks in double stranded DNA molecules. This would only need to occur on the lagging strand where replication is not performed continuously.

A: The leading strand is replicated continuously and doesn't need ligase.
C: DNA polymerases are enzymes that create nucleic acids by assembling nucleotides. These enzymes are essential to DNA replication and usually work in pairs to create two identical DNA strands from a single original DNA molecule. It does not require DNA ligase as a co-factor.
D: RNA polymerase is an enzyme that produces RNA. It is requires for constructing RNA chains using DNA genes as templates (the process of transcription). It does not require DNA ligase as a co-factor.

47. Which of the following is NOT a characteristic of prokaryotes?
    A. They have no endoplasmic reticulum.
    B. They have circular DNA.
    C. They have a cell wall.
    D. **They lack a plasma membrane.**

Choice **D** is correct. Prokaryotes do have a plasma membrane and a cell wall.
A: Prokaryotes do not have endoplasmic reticulum.
B: Prokaryotes do have circular, double stranded DNA.
C: Prokaryotes do have a cell wall.

Passage IX Answers and Explanations (Questions 48-51)

Cardiac arrest is the absence of **productive mechanical activity in the heart**, though significant electrical activity (usually measured by electrocardiogram) may still be present. Without cardiac activity to circulate blood, tissue **oxygen levels plummet** and **muscle activity ceases**. Generally, periods of untreated cardiac arrest longer than six minutes result in **permanent neurological damage** due to lack of oxygen in the brain. Though myriad causes of cardiac arrest exist, the most common include **hypoxia, hypoglycemia, hypovolemia** (low blood volume), **acidosis, thrombosis** (clots), and **hyperkalemia** (elevated serum potassium).

Key terms: cardiac arrest, hypoxia, hypovolemia, acidosis, thrombosis, hyperkalemia

Cause-and-Effect: Cardiac arrest is lack of blood circulation by heart, damages brain and tissues due to lack of O$_2$

The first line treatment for cardiac arrest is CPR (cardiopulmonary resuscitation). Chest compressions during CPR simulate the **mechanical action of the heart by circulating blood**, while artificial ventilation provides the lungs with **fresh oxygen in the absence of diaphragm contractions**. The administration of electric shocks to the heart (defibrillation) is used to restore productive electric activity in the heart. A common electrical rhythm during cardiac arrest is ventricular fibrillation (VF), resulting in unorganized and unproductive movement of the ventricles and **no cardiac output**.

Key terms: CPR, VF, cardiac output

Cause-and-Effect: CPR and defibrillation are used to treat cardiac arrest

Resuscitation in cardiac arrest from **cold water drowning** is generally **more successful** than warm water drowning. In one example, doctors resuscitated a two and a half year old girl after she was submerged in an icy creek for 1 hour and 6 minutes. When rescuers pulled her from the creek, she was not breathing and was in **cardiac arrest**. Upon arrival at the hospital, her core temperature was measured at 66° F, **22.6° below normal**. Her remarkable recovery left her **free of neurological deficit**. At the time, her survival of over an hour without oxygen was the longest ever recorded without brain damage.

Key terms: cold water drowning, neurological deficit

Contrast: cold water drowning easier to survive than warm water drowning

Cause-and-Effect: Longest survival of cardiac arrest was over an hour in cold water.

48. Which of the following physiological responses probably occurred in the patient immediately upon submersion in the creek?

    I. Peripheral vasodilation
    II. Piloerection
    III. Shivering

  A. I and II
  B. I and III
  C. **II and III**
  D. I, II, and III

Choice **C** is correct. As the girl is submerged in the icy creek, her body would immediately respond to the cold by attempting to increase thermogenesis (heat production) and heat conservation. This can be accomplished by peripheral vasoconstriction, piloerection, shivering, or non-shivering thermogenesis.

I: Peripheral vasodilation is a response to hyperthermia, not hypothermia.
II: Piloerection is the erection of the hair of the skin due to contraction of the tiny muscles that elevate the hair follicles above the rest of the skin to trap heat.
III: Shivering is a bodily response to hypothermia. When the body temperature drops, shivering is triggered to maintain heat. Skeletal muscles begin to shake in small movements, generating heat by expending energy.

49. Given information the passage, which of the following conditions would most plausibly result from extended cardiac arrest?
    A. **Acidosis**
    B. Alkalosis
    C. Hyperglycemia
    D. Hypoglycemia

Choice **A** is correct. The passage states that cardiac arrest results in the cessation of muscular activity, including that of the diaphragm. This would result in reduced gas exchange, increased serum $[CO_2]$ (respiratory acidosis) and increased lactic acid production (due to anaerobic metabolism). Both of these factors would decrease blood pH, otherwise known as acidosis.

B: The opposite would occur.
C: The passage does not mention anything about hyperglycemia.
D: Though hypoglycemia may be a cause of cardiac arrest, the passage does not suggest that it would be a result.

50. Under normal conditions, which of the following vessels carries deoxygenated blood?
    A. Aorta
    B. Arterioles
    C. **Pulmonary arteries**
    D. Pulmonary veins

Choice **C** is correct. Of all the options listed, the pulmonary arteries are the only vessels that carry deoxygenated blood. They carry blood from the right side of the heart to the lungs to be reoxygenated.

A: The aorta carries oxygenated blood to the arteries from the heart.
B: The arterioles carry oxygenated blood to the capillaries from the arteries.
D: The pulmonary veins carry oxygenated blood to the left side of the heart from the lungs.

51. While VF is deadly if not treated immediately, many people live years with atrial fibrillation (AF). Why might this be?
    A. The atria are smaller than the ventricles.
    B. The atria are not responsible for pumping blood.
    C. **The ventricles pump blood into circulation, while the atria move blood into the ventricles.**
    D. The ventricles are not well-perfused by the coronary arteries, while the atria are.

Choice **C** is correct. The passage states that VF is chaotic and unproductive movement of the ventricles, so one can reasonably infer that AF is unproductive movement of the atria. This question basically asks why someone can survive with poor atrial function but not with poor ventricular function. This is because the ventricles are the workhorses that pump blood into pulmonary and systemic circulation at high pressure, while the atria do the much less taxing job of moving blood into the ventricles in the first place. Answer choice C most closely matches this explanation.

A: While this may be true, it does not answer the question nearly as well as choice C.
B: This is false; the atria pump blood into the ventricles.
C: This is false; the ventricles must be well-perfused with oxygen due to their heavy workload.

Passage X Answers and Explanations (Questions 52-55)

Most of the cells in the human body are actually **prokaryotes** that live on or in important organ systems. ***E. Coli*** is one **bacteria** that exists in huge numbers in the gut and assist with breaking down **food, vitamin K**$_2$ production, and waste disposal. Vitamin K$_2$'s main function is to add a carboxylic acid to glutamate. This functionality affects many processes in the body. Vitamin K$_2$ promotes blood **clotting, osteoblast** activity, and breaks up **calcium deposits** in soft tissue. Vitamin K$_2$ also acts as an **antioxidant**.

Key terms: prokaryotes, *E. Coli*, bacteria, gut, food, vitamin K$_2$, clotting, osteoblast, calcium, antioxidant.

Cause and Effect: This first paragraph outlines the function of E. Coli in the gut as well as the function of vitamin K$_2$.

Figure 1 shows the structure of Vitamin K$_2$

E. Coli is known as a **gram-negative bacteria**. The **gram** classification comes from a technique used to **stain** bacteria. A culture of bacteria is introduced to a stain and then washed out with an **alcohol or acetone**. After washing, the bacteria which were stained and retained the color of the stain are called gram positive. Bacteria which lose the color are called gram negative. Gram-positive bacteria retain the stain because of their large amount of **peptidoglycan** forming a shell around the cell. Gram-negative bacteria lack the thick peptidoglycan layer. Peptidoglycan is shown in figure 2 alongside **methyl violet 10B**, a popular gram stain.

Key Terms: gram-negative, gram-positive, stain, alcohol, acetone, peptidoglycan, methyl violet 10B.

Cause and Effect: This paragraph explains the gram staining technique used to distinguish between bacteria with a thick outer peptidoglycan layer. We are introduced to the idea of the staining as well as methyl violet 10B, which is used as a stain.

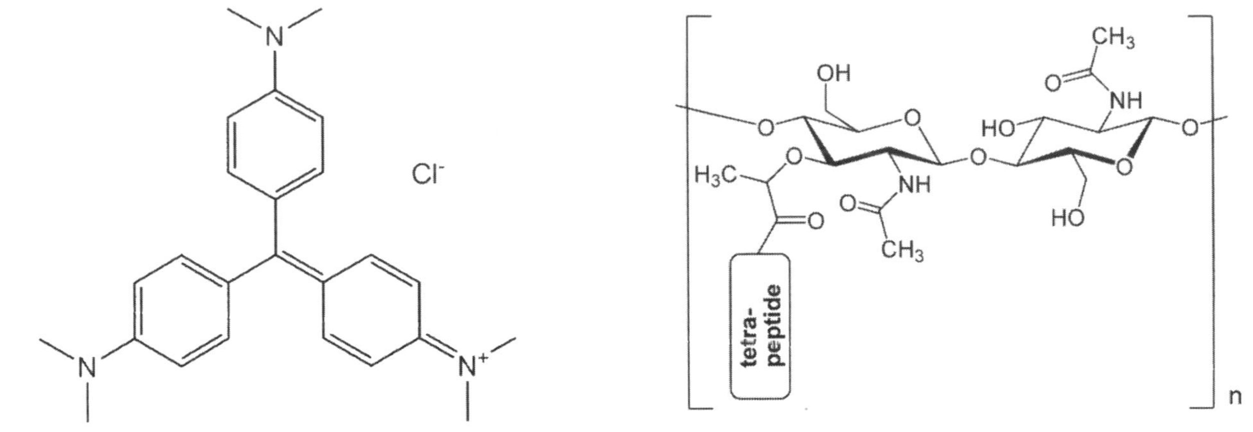

Figure 2 Methyl violet 10B and peptidoglycan monomer

Figure 2 shows the structures of methyl violet 10B and peptidoglycan

At a pH of 1.0, the methyl violet 10B has two protonated nitrogens and 3 positive charges and appears yellow. The pK_a of the diprotonated molecule is 1.15 and for the monoprotonated molecule is 1.8. Above a pH of 1.8 it has a single positive charge and a violet color.

Key terms: protonated nitrogens, yellow, pK_a.

Cause and Effect: We are told a little more about the pK_a of the protonated forms of methyl violet 10B and how pH affects the color of the molecule.

52. Visible light ranges from about 400 to 700 nm. Which of the following is most likely the absorbance maximum for methyl violet 10B at a pH of 7?
    A. 400 nm
    B. 470 nm
    C. 530 nm
    D. 590 nm

Choice **D** is correct. We know that at a pH of 7, methyl violet 10B appears violet (400nm). This means that the absorbance of the molecule should occur on the other side of the visible spectrum, farther from 400 nm.

53. Why is methyl violet 10B retained by larger amounts of peptidoglycan?
    A. Peptidoglycan and methyl violet 10B are both hydrophilic.
    B. Methyl violet 10B can hydrogen bond with peptidoglycan's hydroxyl groups.
    C. Methyl violet 10B and peptidoglycan both have charges at neutral pH.
    D. Peptidoglycan and methyl violet 10B are both hydrophobic.

Choice **A** is correct. This question requires us to think about why peptidoglycan and methyl violet 10B will interact. Peptidoglycan is formed from amino acids and sugars and is hydrophilic because of it. Methyl violet 10B is also hydrophilic because it is charged.

B: Methyl violet 10B cannot hydrogen bond because it contains no N-H bonds at a near-neutral pH.
C: Peptidoglycan will not have a charge at neutral pH.
D: Both of these molecules are shown to be hydrophilic.

54. Under which of the following classifications does Vitamin K_2 fall?
    I. Lipid soluble
    II. Amphipathic
    III. Hydrophobic

    A. I only
    B. **I and III only**
    C. II and III only
    D. I, II, and III

Choice **B** is correct. As shown in figure 1, Vitamin K_2 is shown to be lipid (aka fat) soluble due to its hydrophobic structure.

II: Amphipathic means containing both polar and nonpolar regions. This does not apply to vitamin K_2

55. Which of the following might result from taking an antibiotic that destroys normal intestinal flora *E. coli*?
    A. Decreased risk of osteoporosis
    B. **Increased risk of spontaneous bleeding**
    C. Decreased risk of cancer
    D. Decreased risk of bacterial infection by *E. coli*

Choice **B** is correct. This question asks us to determine the effects of killing *E. coli*. *E. coli* creates vitamin K_2, which is essential in the clotting cascade.

A: Decreased vitamin K_2 will result in increased risk of osteoporosis by decreased osteoblast activity.
C: Decreased vitamin K_2 will result in increased risk of cancer because it is an antioxidant.
D: The *E. coli* in our colon is not dangerous as long as it stays in the colon. Killing it will not decrease the risk of infection.

Discrete Set 4 Answers and Explanations (Questions 56-59)

56. Which of the following RNA molecules forms a stable long-term RNA-protein structure?
    A. mRNA
    B. <u>**rRNA**</u>
    C. tRNA
    D. snRNA

Choice **B** is correct. Ribosomal RNA and proteins combine to form a nucleoprotein called a ribosome which is made up of both protein and RNA. The ribosome serves as the site and carries the enzymes necessary for protein synthesis. Thus, rRNA forms most of the structure of ribosomes.

A: mRNA is synthesized from DNA which contains the information on the primary sequence of amino acids in a protein to be synthesized. The messenger RNA carries the code into the cytoplasm where protein synthesis occurs.
C: tRNA reads the mRNA code and carries the amino acid to be incorporated into the assembled protein. On one end the amino acid is attached. On the opposite end, a specific base triplet, called the anticodon, is used to read the codons on the mRNA.
D: Small nuclear RNA (snRNA) is a small RNA species confined to the nucleus. snRNAs are involved in splicing and other RNA processing reactions.

57. Where does formation of neutrophils begin?
    A. Hepatocytes
    B. Adipose tissue
    C. <u>**Bone marrow**</u>
    D. Erythrocytes

Choice **C** is correct. Neutrophils are white blood cells. Neutrophils are produced in the bone marrow from stem cells that proliferate and differentiate to mature neutrophils. At sites of infection, endothelial cells capture passing neutrophils and guide them. Once in tissues, neutrophils kill microorganisms.

A: A hepatocyte is a cell of the tissue of the liver.
B: Adipose tissue, or fat, is loose connective tissue composed of adipocytes. It acts to store energy in the form of fat. It also cushions and insulates the body.
D: Erythrocytes are red blood cells.

58. Which of the following has highest ratio of energy/wavelength?
    A. Infrared light used in organic analysis
    B. Microwaves used to sterilize medical equipment
    C. <u>**Gamma rays released by chemo-isotopes**</u>
    D. They all have the same ratio.

Choice **C** is correct. $E = hc/\lambda$. This means $E/\lambda = hc/\lambda^2$. This value is largest when λ is small. Recall that gamma rays have the highest frequency and lowest wavelength along the EM spectrum.

B and D: These both have longer wavelengths than gamma rays.

59. Which of the following enzymes does NOT act concurrently with the enzyme helicase during DNA replication?
    A. Topoisomerase
    B. Telomerase
    C. DNA polymerase
    D. DNA ligase

Choice **B** is correct. Telomeres are repetitions of a DNA sequence located at the ends of chromosomes. They act as protective caps to maintain stability and integrity of the chromosomes, Telomerase is active during embryonic development, enabling the rapid cell division that supports normal growth. Telomerase acts after DNA replication is completed.

A: Topoisomerases are enzymes that regulate the overwinding or underwinding of DNA. Thus, this enzyme does work concurrently during the replication of a DNA strand.
C: DNApol serves to create DNA molecules by assembling nucleotides together. This enzyme is essential to DNA replication. Thus, this enzyme must work concurrently during the replication of a DNA strand.
D: DNA ligase is an enzyme that helps to close nicks in the backbone of DNA. This is essential for the joining of Okazaki fragments during DNA replication. Thus, this enzyme does work concurrently during the replication of a DNA strand.

TIMED
SECTION 3
59 Questions, 95 Minutes

(Use the tear-out answer sheet provided in Appendix D)

Passage I (Questions 1-5)

The Triple Sugar Iron, or TSI, test is useful for identifying bacterial genera, known collectively as enterics, commonly found in the human large intestine.

The test is performed in a tube containing agar, phenol red (a pH-sensitive dye), 1% lactose, 1% sucrose, 0.1% glucose, and ferrous sulfate ($FeSO_4$). The slanted shape of the medium provides an array of surfaces that are either exposed to oxygen-containing air in varying degrees (the upper slant) or not exposed to air (the lower butt). Fermentation of any of the three sugars in the tube will produce byproducts, resulting in an observed color change of the dye from red to yellow. Because there is so little glucose in the medium, those bacteria which are able to metabolize glucose will exhaust the glucose supply and turn to alternative substrates. Byproducts of the oxidation of those substrates will increase the pH of the medium, returning the plate to its original red color. Many bacteria that can ferment sugars in the anaerobic butt of the tube are enterobacteria.

Under anaerobic conditions, as occurs at the bottom of the test tube, certain bacteria utilize thiosulfate anion as a terminal electron acceptor, reducing it to sulfide. If this occurs, the newly formed hydrogen sulfide (H_2S) gas may escape or react with ferrous sulfate in the medium to form ferrous sulfide, which is visible as a black precipitate.

A laboratory technician attempting to identify four unknown enteric pathogens noted the results of a bacterial culture shown in Table 1. The technician noticed no color change in the butt region of Unknown B during the initial TSI test, but, upon repeat testing in a modified tube lacking ferrous sulfate, noticed a marked color change.

Unknown Bacterium	Slant	Butt	Precipitate	H2S gas
A	R	Y	-	-
B (trial 1)	R	R	+	+
B (trial 2)	R	Y	-	+
C	R	R	+	-
D	Y	R	-	+

Table 1 Reactions of enteric bacteria in TSI media (Note: R = red color, Y = yellow, +/ (-) indicates formation (or absence) of a black precipitate and/or gas formation).

1. Based upon the results shown in Table 1, bacterium A is best described as a(n):
    A. facultative anaerobe capable of fermenting sucrose or lactose.
    B. obligate anaerobe capable of fermenting sucrose or lactose.
    C. obligate aerobe incapable of fermenting sucrose or lactose.
    D. facultative anaerobe incapable of fermenting sucrose or lactose.

2. Which of the following regarding the two trials of bacterium B is the most likely explanation for the difference in results noted by the technician?
    A. The formation of H_2S gas inhibited anaerobic respiration.
    B. Ferrous sulfide provided an oxygen source for aerobic respiration.
    C. In trial 1, blackening of the medium obscured the color change.
    D. The presence of H_2S gas, a weak acid, acidified the medium.

3. What single test would best be able to distinguish bacterium D from the other unknown bacteria tested?
    A. Culture in a vacuum-sealed dish containing 1% lactose and sucrose and 0.1% glucose
    B. Culture in a vacuum-sealed dish containing only 0.1% glucose
    C. Culture in an open dish containing only 1% lactose and sucrose
    D. Culture in an open dish containing only 0.1% glucose

4. All four of the bacteria tested are described as Gram negative. Gram negative bacteria are distinguished from Gram positive bacteria in that:
    A. Gram negative bacteria lack a membrane-bound nucleus.
    B. Gram negative bacteria have a thinner peptidoglycan layer than do Gram positive bacteria.
    C. Gram positive bacteria lack a cell wall.
    D. Gram negative bacteria have an exclusively rod-shaped morphology.

5. The enzymes responsible for electron transport in aerobically growing bacteria are found within what region or structure of the cell?
    A. Inner mitochondrial membrane
    B. Cytoplasm
    C. Mitochondrial matrix
    D. Plasma membrane

Passage II (Questions 6-10)

Chronic arterial hypertension (HTN), otherwise known as high blood pressure, is a condition that affects millions. Blood pressure is measured while the patient is sitting, often in the brachial artery on the anterior part of the elbow, as the artery is superficial in this location. A blood pressure measurement has two components, usually reported in mmHg: the systolic pressure (when the heart is contracting) and the diastolic pressure (when the heart is relaxed). Through exact cutoffs may vary, repeated systolic measurements above 140 mmHg and/or diastolic measurements above 90 mmHg are generally considered abnormally high. Blood pressure is equal to the product of cardiac output (CO) and total peripheral resistance (TPR), as shown in Equation 1 below.

$$BP = CO \times TPR$$

Equation 1

Primary hypertension (PHTN) is not caused by another medical condition, while secondary hypertension (SHTN) is diagnosed when the cause of the elevated blood pressure is suspected to be a concurrent condition or medication side effect. Risk factors for PHTN include sedentary lifestyle, hereditary factors, a diet high in salt, and high alcohol consumption. Because of the kidneys' role in maintaining fluid balance in the body, renal and endocrine pathophysiology is often a cause of SHTN.

Regardless of cause, untreated HTN increases the risk of cardiovascular disease, heart attack, stroke and kidney disease. Thus, its management is an important priority in health care. In a clinical trial to compare treatments for HTN, patients were randomized to 4 groups. The results of the study are shown in Table 1 below. The blood pressure readings are in mmHg.

Group	Mean BP pre-study (systolic/diastolic)	Mean BP post-study (systolic/diastolic)	Change (systolic)
Placebo	158/94	162/95	+4
Medication A	154/93	143/85	-11
Low sodium diet	158/96	151/90	-7
Aerobic exercise	155/92	146/87	-9

Table 1 Results of blood pressure study

6. Because of a mistake in the clinical study, subjects in the low sodium diet group had their pre-study brachial blood pressure measured while lying down instead of sitting down. How did this likely affect the results of the study?
   A. The reduction in BP over the course of the study in the low sodium diet group was actually larger than reported.
   B. The reduction in BP over the course of the study in the low sodium diet group was actually smaller than reported.
   C. The patients in the low sodium diet group probably did not have HTN.
   D. This mistake probably did not affect the result of the study.

7. During aerobic exercise, cardiac output increases by a factor of 5. Why doesn't blood pressure increase by the same factor?
   A. Vasoconstriction in all vessels
   B. Vasoconstriction in working muscles
   C. Vasodilation in all vessels
   D. Vasodilation in working muscles

8. In which of the following vessels is blood pressure likely to be highest?
   A. Capillaries
   B. Aorta
   C. Arteries
   D. Veins

9. Beta-blockers are medications that reduce blood pressure by antagonizing beta-adrenergic receptors in the heart and blood vessels. They mimic the effects of:
   A. epinephrine.
   B. norepinephrine.
   C. the parasympathetic nervous system.
   D. the sympathetic nervous system.

10. The results of the placebo group suggest that:
    A. HTN does not need to be treated.
    B. HTN may be a progressive condition.
    C. the subjects were not exercising in the first place.
    D. the subjects should eat less salt.

Passage III (Questions 11-15)

Congenital hemophilia (CH) is a chronic, X-linked, recessive disease that affects thousands worldwide. Acquired hemophilia (AH) is much less common than CH; it is a rare, acute condition with a few hundred cases in the United States a year. While both diseases affect the same proteins, their causes and treatments are distinct.

The most common type of hemophilia, type A CH, results from a mutation in the gene coding for factor VIII (FVIII), a protein that is critical in the blood clotting process. It is typically treated with infusions of normal FVIII. Type B CH is the result of mutation in the gene for factor IX (FIX), also involved in the clotting process. Similarly, people with type B CH receive infusions of FIX to maintain normal hemostasis. Depending on the severity of the mutation, symptoms of CH may be as mild as prolonged bleeding during dental visits or as severe as spontaneous bleeds that occur without trauma. CH is infamous for its prevalence in royal families, including the descendants of Queen Victoria in the British, Spanish and Russian royalty of the 19th century. A variety of mutations including point mutations may cause CH. These mutations may be spontaneous or inherited.

As the name suggests, AH occurs in people who have normal genes for FVIII and FIX. Patients are not born with AH; instead, they begin producing antibodies that attack the FVIII or FIX that their bodies produce. Because both AH and CH are characterized by abnormally low or absent FVIII or FIX activity, their symptoms are generally similar. Treatment of AH involves immunosuppression, reversal of underlying cause (if any), and administration of bypassing agents that can activate the blood-clotting cascade without FVIII or FIX.

11. If historical research reveals that none of Queen Victoria's ancestors had evidence of a bleeding disorder such as hemophilia even though she was a carrier for CH, this could be because:

    I. she did not inherit the mutation that causes hemophilia; it was spontaneous.

    II. her ancestors were carriers for hemophilia but the mutation was not severe enough to cause noticeable symptoms.

    III. her ancestors were carriers for CH Type B.

    A. I only
    B. I and II
    C. II and III
    D. I, II and III

12. Based on the passage, the vast majority of symptomatic hemophiliacs are:
    A. overweight.
    B. Caucasian.
    C. male.
    D. female.

13. In some cases, congenital hemophiliacs develop antibodies (inhibitors) to the factor treatments they receive, resulting in reduced efficacy of treatment. The treatment for these patients is most likely:
    A. factor infusions.
    B. whole blood.
    C. fresh frozen plasma.
    D. bypassing agents.

14. Which of the following factors would increase the prevalence of hemophilia in future generations of a royal family where the queen is a carrier?
    A. The presence of mutagenic paint in the royal castle
    B. The development of inhibitors by her son
    C. Inbreeding
    D. The prince engaging in a high activity lifestyle

15. Which of the following could explain the survival of hemophilia over many generations, even though those afflicted have shorter life expectancies than healthy people?
    A. Increased presence of carcinogens in 19th century Europe
    B. Increased fitness and reproductive success in carriers
    C. Decreased presence of carcinogens in 19th century Europe
    D. Decreased fitness and reproductive success in carriers

Discrete Set 1 (Questions 16-18)

These questions are **NOT** related to a passage.

16. How many distinct codons code for amino acids?
    A. 64
    B. 61
    C. 31
    D. 21

17. Which of the following is responsible for the formation of beta-pleated sheets?
    A. Disulfide bonds between two cysteine residues
    B. Side group interactions between amino acids
    C. Hydrogen bonds in backbone of peptide
    D. Van der Waals forces between peptides

18. Which of the following has the greatest number of complete waves in a 1000 nm length?
    A. Ultraviolet light used in the treatment of skin diseases
    B. Yellow light that is emitted from neonatal heat lamps
    C. Red light used in pain therapy for severe arthritis
    D. Microwaves used to treat a swollen prostate

THIS PAGE LEFT

INTENTIONALLY BLANK

Passage IV (Questions 19-22)

Studies have documented a strong association between smoking and depression. Cigarette smoke has been reported to modulate monoamine oxidase (MAO) A levels in vitro and in animals. MAO exists in two subtypes, MAO A and B. In the brain, MAO A oxidizes serotonin and norepinephrine, whereas MAO B oxidizes benzylamine and phenethylamine and is localized in serotonergic neurons and in glial cells. Both forms oxidize dopamine. Serotonin and norepinephrine levels in the thalamus have been linked to the maintenance of mood. Deficiency of either neurotransmitter is associated with the development of depression.

Researchers compared MAO A levels in the brains of nonsmokers and current smokers using ^{11}C-labeled clorgyline (^{11}C]clorgyline), a radiotracer which binds specifically and irreversibly to brain MAO A, and positron emission tomography (PET) of both groups. Four of the nonsmokers were also treated with a MAO inhibitor (MAOI), tranylcypromine after the baseline PET scan and then rescanned to assess the sensitivity of ^{11}C]clorgyline binding to MAO inhibition. MAO A levels were quantified by using the model term λk3, which is a function of and increases along with the concentration of enzymatically activated MAO A in the brain. A comparison of MAO A levels in the thalamus for those tested is shown in Figure 1.

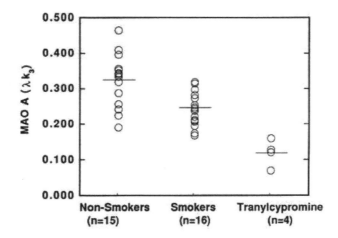

Figure 1 Comparison of MAO A levels in the thalamus (as expressed by the model term λk3 ($cc_{brain} (ml_{plasma})^{-1} min^{-1}$)) for nonsmokers (n = 15), smokers (n = 16), and nonsmokers who were treated with tranylcypromine (n = 4).

19. Tranylcypromine is a competitive inhibitor of MAO enzymes. According to the Michaelis-Menten model of enzyme kinetics, what changes in the kinetic parameters of MAO activity occur due to the addition of tranylcypromine?
    A. K_m increases and V_{max} is unchanged.
    B. K_m is unchanged and V_{max} decreases.
    C. K_m is unchanged and V_{max} increases.
    D. K_m decreases and V_{max} is unchanged.

20. Tranylcypromine treatment is expected to have which of the following effects on thalamic neurotransmitter levels in non-smokers?
    A. Decreased norepinephrine and serotonin
    B. Increased dopamine
    C. Decreased benzylamine and phenethylamine
    D. Increased benzylamine and phenethylamine

21. Which of the following possibilities relating cigarette smoking to MAO A or depression is best supported by the passage?
    A. Smoking may increase the risk of developing a depressive disorder.
    B. Tranylcypromine reduces the concentration of the biologically active form of nicotine in the brains of smokers.
    C. Mood stabilizing neurotransmitter levels are likely higher in non-smokers after tranylcypromine treatment than are levels in smokers after the same treatment.
    D. The inhibition of MAO A by smoking may contribute to the difficulty of smoking cessation.

22. The researchers concluded that smoking exerted an inhibitory influence on MAO A enzymes present in the thalamus. Which additional finding, if true, most challenges this assertion?
    A. The activity of both MAO A and MAO B are reduced in animals exposed to tobacco smoke.
    B. MAO activity in cultured thalamic cells is unchanged by direct application of nicotine.
    C. Local vasoconstriction reduces MAO A delivery to the thalamus.
    D. [^{11}C]clorgyline binding is reduced when preceded by treatment of the thalamus with an MAOI.

Passage V (Questions 23-26)

Alzheimer's Disease is a neurodegenerative disorder that predominantly affects individuals over the age of 65. One of the first and most common symptoms is difficulty remembering events stored in short term memory. As the disease progresses, patients often become irritable and withdrawn, and eventually lose much of their long term memory. On the molecular level, many researchers believe that most of the disease's symptoms are attributed to one of two proteins: amyloid-beta (A_β) or tau (τ).

The A_β theory suggests that the A_β peptide, which consists of around 40 amino acids, aggregates to form extracellular clumps called "plaques" in brain tissue. It has been shown in mouse models that overexpression of the A_β gene leads to behaviors and memory loss resembling the effects of Alzheimer's in humans. The natural function of A_β is not well understood, but it has been potentially implicated in oxidative stress protection and kinase activation. A_β becomes dangerous when misfolding in the tertiary structure leads to accumulation of the protein at neurotoxic levels.

The τ theory suggests that Alzheimer's symptoms are attributed to hyperphosphorylation of τ. This protein has several isomers, the longest of which has around 440 amino acids. The normal function of τ is to stabilize microtubules. It is hypothesized that in Alzheimer's disease, the hyperphosphorylation leads to tangles of τ inside nerve cell bodies that cause microtubule collapse. Another hypothesis involves proline, a unique amino acid that has a distinctive cyclic structure that prevents typical protein geometry. Many other theories to explain Alzheimer's disease have been proposed, and it is possible that it is not necessarily one microbiological entity that is responsible for the disease, but rather concerted destruction caused by multiple genes or proteins gone awry.

23. The τ protein is likely to cause disruptions in which of the following cellular processes?
    I. Mitosis
    II. Translation
    III. Intracellular transport

    A. I only
    B. I and III
    C. II and III
    D. I, II, and III

24. Which organelle is the site of A_β and τ translation?
    A. Ribosome
    B. Smooth Endoplasmic Reticulum
    C. Mitochondrion
    D. Nucleus

25. Given that memory loss is often one of the earliest symptoms of Alzheimer's disease, which part of the brain most likely suffers damage soon after onset of the disease?
    A. Cerebellum
    B. Prefrontal Cortex
    C. Pons
    D. Hippocampus

26. Suppose researchers have implicated another protein in causing Alzheimer's disease. This protein is found to be made up of 35 amino acids, including 18 proline residues. The secondary structure will most likely have a(n):
    A. large number of alpha helices.
    B. large number of beta sheets.
    C. alternative secondary structure.
    D. even number of alpha helices and beta sheets.

Discrete Set 2 (Questions 27-30)

These questions are **NOT** related to a passage.

27. When creating a clone library, why is an antibiotic resistance gene included on the plasmid to be used?
    A. Antibiotic resistance is needed in case of contamination of the media that the clones will grow on.
    B. Bacteria only take up plasmids that confer a selective advantage to them.
    C. The clones will be plated on media containing antibiotics and only successfully transformed clones will grow.
    D. Antibiotic resistance differentiates plasmids that have inserts from those that do not.

28. How many possible codons are there?
    A. 48
    B. 12
    C. 81
    D. 64

29. Nondisjunction during meiosis can result in a gamete that is diploid for a given chromosome rather than haploid, and another gamete that has no copies of that chromosome. If a diploid gamete fuses with a normal haploid gamete, a zygote results with three copies, or trisomy. Most trisomies are not survivable, but several notable ones are. Which of the following represents a survivable trisomy of the sex chromosome?
    A. Down Syndrome
    B. Turner Syndrome
    C. Klinefelter Syndrome
    D. Phenylketonuria

30. In normal patients, a membrane bound chloride channel in epithelial cells near sweat glands is responsible for chloride uptake from the sweat into the cytoplasm. In cystic fibrosis patients, this channel is defective. What is most likely to happen to sodium ions in sweat in cystic fibrosis patients?
    A. Taken into epithelial cells
    B. Released along with the sweat
    C. Reabsorbed into the sweat gland
    D. Adhere to the negatively charged cell membrane of the epithelial cells

THIS PAGE LEFT

INTENTIONALLY BLANK

Passage VI (Questions 31-34)

The liver is the second largest organ in the body by weight, smaller only than the skin. It performs many functions as part of the digestive system, aided by the hepatic portal system, one of two portal systems in the body. In these systems, blood is carried from one capillary bed to another without returning to the heart in between. The hepatic portal system allows nutrient-rich blood coming from the gastrointestinal tract and spleen to take an express path via the hepatic portal vein to the liver. The nutrients, which largely consist of monosaccharides absorbed by the first bed of capillaries, can be quickly processed and any toxins that may have been ingested can be filtered out.

Glycogen Storage Disease (GSD) Type IV is a hereditary metabolic disorder resulting from enzymatic defects affecting glycogen processing, and can take a variety of forms. In the most common form, the progressive hepatic type, an affected baby is born with no apparent health defects but soon shows difficulty gaining weight and enlargement of the liver, leading to cirrhosis (i.e., scarring of the liver tissue) and hypertension (i.e., high blood pressure) in the hepatic portal. The disease is usually fatal within the first few years of life.

A two-month old girl born to healthy parents begins exhibiting such symptoms and is eventually diagnosed with GSD Type IV. The child's father remembers that his brother died of a rare disease at the age of two, and quickly learns from his parents that this resulted from the same disease. The child's mother does not have any siblings.

31. Which of the following is NOT a role performed by the liver?
    A. Breakdown of caffeine
    B. Insulin storage
    C. Bile production
    D. Angiotensinogen synthesis

32. The hepatic portal system is one of two portal systems and it carries blood through a second set of capillaries in the liver before returning to the heart. Where does the other portal system bring blood?
    A. Kidneys
    B. Heart
    C. Feet
    D. Brain

33. Based on information provided in the passage, which of the following would be likely symptoms for someone born with the progressive hepatic type of GSD Type IV?
    I. Increased bone strength
    II. Toxin buildup in the brain
    III. Hepatomegaly

    A. I only
    B. II only
    C. II and III
    D. I, II, and III

34. What type of inheritance does GSD Type IV display, and if the same parents were to have a son, what is the likelihood that he will also suffer from GSD Type IV?
    A. X-linked dominant; 100%
    B. Autosomal recessive; 25%
    C. Autosomal recessive; 6.25%
    D. X-linked recessive; 50%

Passage VII (Questions 35-39)

In cap-dependent translation initiation, the open reading frame (ORF) of mRNA is established by the placement of the start codon and initiator tRNA in the ribosomal peptidyl (P) site. Methionine-charged initiator tRNA is brought to the P-site of the small ribosomal subunit by eukaryotic eIF2 and utilizes GTP. Internal ribosome entry sites (IRES), present within regions of some viral genomes, promote translation of mRNAs in a cap-independent manner, avoiding many of the complex controls placed on eukaryotic host cell translational initiation and allowing translation to be initiated within an ORF. The Taura syndrome virus (TSV) contains an ORF which includes an intragenic region (IGR). The IGR contains an IRES that drives translation of a second ORF without the aid of initiation factors. Virologists studying TSV proposed a mechanism for translational initiation at the IRES within the IGR region of TSV, shown in Figure 1.

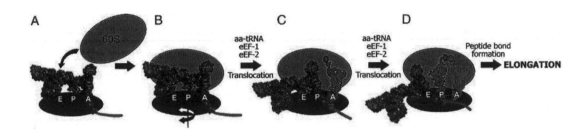

Figure 1 Schematic of translational initiation within the IGR region of TSV mRNA

Step A
Formation of the 40S-IRES complex at pseudoknot I (PKI). PKI is a distinct secondary structural element present at the IRES that resembles and functionally mimics the anticodon stem loop of tRNA bound to a cognate mRNA codon. PKI serves to position the 40S-IRES complex within the ORF in a cap-independent manner.

Step B
Large ribosomal subunit binding and spontaneous 40S subunit rotation.

Step C
Translocation of PKI allows accommodation of the first aminoacyl-tRNA (aa-tRNA), alanyl-tRNA^{Ala} in the aminoacyl (A) site, catalyzed by eukaryotic elongation factors eEF-1 and eEF-2.

Step D
PK1 remains bound following a second translocation, allowing accommodation of an aa-tRNA. Step D is followed by peptide bond formation and elongation.

35. Crystallographic studies revealed that the codon-like region of PKI strongly resembles the trinucleotide tRNA anticodon 5'-UCC-3'. What is the trinucleotide sequence within the IGR region of TSV mRNA most likely to be bound by PKI?
    A. 5'-AAG-3'
    B. 5'-CAA-3'
    C. 5'-GGA-3'
    D. 5'-AAC-3'

36. Binding of the large ribosomal subunits at the IRES of TGV mRNA is powered by hydrolysis of the same nucleoside triphosphate as is hydrolyzed in cap-dependent eukaryotic initiation. This molecule is:
    A. ATP
    B. CTP
    C. GTP
    D. UTP

37. According to the virologists' mechanism, the initiation of translation in the IGR region of TSV mRNA is most likely to include which of the following events?
    A. Binding of the 40s ribosomal subunit to an AUG codon within the IGR region of TSV mRNA.
    B. PKI binding to the unoccupied 40s ribosomal subunit P site.
    C. Completed assembly of the 70s ribosome in eukaryotic hosts.
    D. Reversible association of PKI and the A site of the 40s ribosomal subunit.

38. During the normal process of eukaryotic translation, the start codon codes for:
    A. methionine and is contained on a mature transcript containing a methylated purine nucleobase cap.
    B. methionine and lacking a mature transcript containing a methylated purine nucleobase cap.
    C. N-formylmethionine and is contained on a mature transcript containing a methylated purine nucleobase cap.
    D. N-formylmethionine and lacking a mature transcript containing a methylated purine nucleobase cap.

39. What statement concerning movement of mRNA along the ribosome describes the mechanisms of cap-dependent initiation of translation in eukaryotes and the proposed mechanism of initiation in TSV mRNA?
    A. Two TSV mRNA translocation events must occur prior to formation of the first peptide bond; a single translocation event must occur prior to formation of the first peptide bond in cap-dependent translation.
    B. Two TSV mRNA translocation events must occur prior to formation of the first peptide bond; two translocation events must also occur prior to formation of the first peptide bond in cap-dependent translation.
    C. One TSV mRNA translocation event must occur prior to formation of the first peptide bond; one translocation events must also occur prior to formation of the first peptide bond in cap-dependent translation.
    D. One TSV mRNA translocation event must occur prior to formation of the first peptide bond; two translocation events must also occur prior to formation of the first peptide bond in cap-dependent translation.

Passage VIII (Questions 40-43)

Obesity is characterized by excessive circulating fatty acids, giving rise to many metabolic complications including insulin resistance. A strong correlation exists between intramuscular lipid (IML) concentration and the onset and severity of insulin resistance in both humans and rodents. It has previously been hypothesized that elevated IML levels are responsible for insulin insensitivity in the obese.

DGAT1 is a key enzyme in intramuscular triglyceride (ITAG) synthesis, catalyzing the conversion of diacylglycerol (DAG) and fatty acyl-CoA, formed from circulating fatty acids, into ITAG. Scientists examined the impact of DGAT1 in skeletal muscle lipid metabolism and muscle-specific insulin sensitivity by transiently overexpressing DGAT1 in the left tibialis anterior (TA) muscle of adult rats, fed either a standard rat dietary mix (chow) or a high fat diet, while using the right leg of the same animal as an untreated control.

The effect of DGAT1 overexpression on IML levels in rats fed a high-fat (HFD) or rodent chow diet is shown in Figure 1.

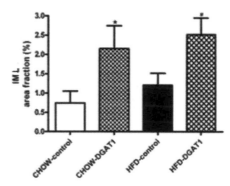

Figure 1 IML levels after three weeks of dietary intervention in rats fed CHOW and HFD diets (Note: error bars give standard deviation)

To determine whether IML content in TA muscle overexpressing DGAT1 was correlated with intramuscular DAG concentrations, DAG was measured in TA muscle overexpressing DGAT1 as well as in the untreated muscle. These measurements are shown in Figure 2.

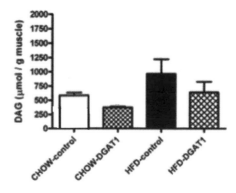

Figure 2 DAG content in the TA muscle of rats fed CHOW and HFD diets (Note: error bars give standard deviation)

One week after introduction of DGAT1, TA muscle insulin sensitivity was assessed in vivo by measuring the rate of radioisotope-labeled infusion of 2-deoxy-[3H]glucose (2DG) uptake. The results in TA muscle are given in Figure 3.

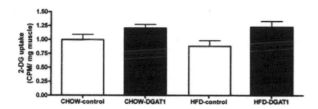

Figure 3 2DG uptake in TA muscle of CHOW- and HFD-fed rats (Note: error bars give standard deviation)

40. Based on passage information, which pair of factors would be LEAST likely to demonstrate an inverse relationship?
    A. Circulating fatty acid concentration and IML concentration
    B. Insulin sensitivity and dietary fat intake
    C. Fatty acyl-CoA and intramuscular DGAT1 concentration
    D. Insulin sensitivity and intramuscular DAG concentration

41. Molecules such as DAG are absorbed in the digestive tract:
    A. after chemical digestion in the mouth and stomach by gastric lipases.
    B. through active transport by transmembrane proteins in the brush border of the small intestine.
    C. only if a person has a fully functioning gall bladder and normal recycling of bile salts.
    D. following emulsification by bile salts, formation into micelles, and transport through lacteals.

42. Based upon the results of the trials, when compared to rats fed a normal diet, the muscle tissue of rats fed a high fat diet expressing DGAT1 normally will likely demonstrate:
    A. an increased rates of lipolysis.
    B. decreased oxidative breakdown of fatty acids.
    C. an increased rate of entry of glucose into glycolysis.
    D. a decreased rate of glycogen utilization.

43. Which statement correctly describes a relationship between the carbon-chain lengths of IMLs and a physical property of those lipids?
    A. As the number of carbons decreases, IML melting point is unchanged.
    B. As the number of carbons increases, IML boiling point increases.
    C. As the number of carbons decreases, IML boiling point is unchanged.
    D. As the number of carbons increases, IML melting point decreases.

Discrete Set 3 (Questions 44-47)

These questions are **NOT** related to a passage.

44. Which of the following will NOT be added to a protein during post-translational modification?
    A. Sugars
    B. Lipids
    C. Phosphate groups
    D. Chaperone proteins

45. What is the function of the nucleolus?
    A. It is the site of ribosome production in eukaryotes.
    B. It is the site of active DNA replication.
    C. It is the site of protein synthesis for nuclear proteins.
    D. It is the site of translation.

46. Which of the following processes is characterized by the formation of a sperm's pronucleus?
    A. Spermatogenesis
    B. Fertilization
    C. Puberty
    D. Meiosis

47. In a fall off a ladder, a woman hits her head on a rock and suffers damage to her cerebellum. Which of the following activities is most likely to be affected?
    A. Voluntary movement of the hands to grasp and pick up objects
    B. Producing speech that has semantic content
    C. Playing the piano
    D. Pain sensation in the feet

THIS PAGE LEFT

INTENTIONALLY BLANK

Passage IX (Questions 48-51)

Septic shock syndrome can be triggered by endotoxins, specifically by lipopolysaccharide (LPS), the major component of the outer membrane of all Gram-negative bacteria. LPS contains three components: the variable O antigen on the membrane surface, the core domain and lipid A. The lipid A domain, buried within the core of the bacterial cell membrane, anchors LPS to the membrane, and is responsible for much of the toxicity of Gram-negative bacteria.

In Gram-negative sepsis, the LPS antigen attaches to a circulating LPS-binding protein, and the complex then binds to a specific receptor on monocytes, macrophages, and neutrophils, leading to the release of potent cytokine proteins such as IL-6, MCP-1, and TNF-α. While these cytokines trigger the immune system to attempt to clear the microbial pathogens, if the infection is not brought under control, these secondary mediators can lead to the signs of septic shock: vasodilation, diminished cardiac output, decreased cardiac output, fever, and damage to the endothelium of capillaries in the lung.

One novel approach to the treatment of septic shock involves EVK-203, an alkylpolyamine compound that specifically binds to and neutralizes circulating LPS. In order to test the ability of EVK-203 to sequester LPS, mice received graded doses of EVK-203. Then, following injection of a lethal dose of LPS, plasma levels of LPS-induced cytokines were measured.

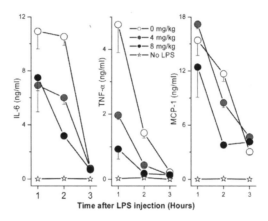

Figure 1 Time-course of cytokine profiles in the plasma of mice receiving graded doses of EVK-203 and a lethal dose of LPS.

Ten mice were also administered the same dose of EVK-203 at various times before and after the administration of a LPS dose lethal to 50% of untreated-mice. Dose-dependent survival rates are shown in Figure 2.

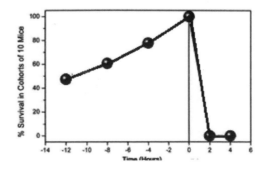

Figure 2 Percent survival of ten mice administered EVK-203 at times prior to, and following, LPS administration (Note: LPS was administered at time = 0 hours).

48. Like Gram-negative septic shock, Waterhouse-Friderichsen syndrome is due to the effects of bacterial endotoxins and, because of acute adrenal failure, can lead to septic shock. An individual suffering from the syndrome would NOT be expected to show what symptom?

    A. Low blood sugar

    B. Low blood pressure

    C. Decreased circulating potassium concentration

    D. Decreased circulating sodium concentration

49. The immune response leading to Gram-negative septic shock is most likely to be initiated when:

    A. exposed O antigen is bound by specific host antibodies.

    B. LPS secretes bacterial cytokines that precipitate an exaggerated immune response.

    C. bacterial cells are lysed and lipid A-containing membrane fragments are released into the circulation.

    D. bacterially-mediated endothelial damage causes activation of a local immune response.

50. Information presented in the passage most *challenges* what conclusion concerning the protective effects of EVK-203 against LPS exposure in the mouse model?

    A. Plasma concentrations sufficient to provide some protection against LPS-lethality persist for up to 12 hours.

    B. Its protective effects are reflected by a reduction in circulating LPS-induced cytokines levels.

    C. It is maximally effective in mouse models when administered concurrently with LPS administration.

    D. EVK-203 must be present prior to activation of the innate immune response to provide protection from LPS-lethality.

51. Release of TNF-α leads to the activation of multiple transcription factors. One such factor, NFAT, increases pro-inflammatory calcium signaling by increasing expression of a protein product through binding downstream of its transcriptional start site. The region of DNA bound by NFAT can best characterized as a(n):

    A. enhancer.

    B. co-repressor.

    C. promoter.

    D. activator.

Passage X (Questions 52-55)

For most adolescent girls, the onset of puberty occurs around age 11 or 12. This period is marked by a number of physical changes, including body hair growth and the onset of menstruation. The menstrual cycle is broken into three phases. The first phase, the follicular phase, begins with gonadotropin releasing hormone (GnRH) secretion from the hypothalamus. GnRH then stimulates the release of follicle stimulating hormone (FSH), the hormone responsible for follicular development, from the anterior pituitary gland. As the follicle develops, it releases large amounts of estrogen. Rising levels of estrogen in the blood signal the release of luteinizing hormone (LH) from the anterior pituitary gland, commencing the next phase of menstruation, ovulation. FSH and LH surges stimulate the developed follicle to rupture and eject an egg into the Fallopian tube where it may be fertilized before reaching the uterus. The final stage, the luteal phase, is characterized by the transformation of the ruptured follicle into the corpus luteum. The corpus luteum releases progesterone and a small amount of estrogen. Progesterone causes the thickening of the endometrial lining. If the egg is not fertilized, the corpus luteum atrophies, progesterone levels fall, and the endometrium is shed, allowing the cycle to begin again.

As women age into their late 40s and early 50s, they enter a period called menopause characterized by the cessation of menstruation and the woman's ability to reproduce. Menopausal women often experience significant estrogen deficiency and bone loss. These two physiological effects may be related – it is believed that estrogen acts through high affinity receptors on osteoblasts and osteoclasts, the cells responsible for bone growth and breakdown, respectively, to regulate bone density and prevent osteoporosis. Once this regulation is removed through menopause, dramatic increases in porosity of the bone are seen (See Figure 1).

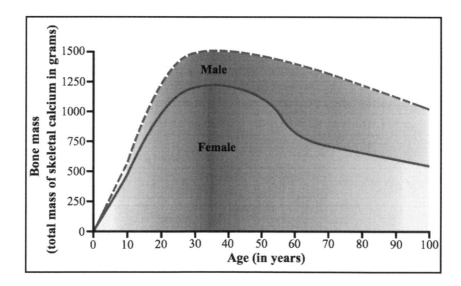

Figure 1 Bone mass as a function of age and sex

52. In what phase of meiosis is an egg when it is traveling down the Fallopian tube prior to contact with a sperm cell?
    A. Prophase I
    B. Anaphase I
    C. Metaphase II
    D. It is not undergoing meiosis at that point.

53. Which of the following choices represents a valid combination of a menstrual cycle hormone and its effect in a man?
    A. LH stimulates Leydig cells to produce estrogen.
    B. FSH stimulates Sertoli cells to produce sperm.
    C. Estrogen stimulates the development of male secondary sex characteristics (e.g., body hair and voice deepening).
    D. Prolactin leads to lactation in men.

54. Which of the following osteoblast and osteoclast activity levels would result in the porosity of bone seen in patients suffering from osteoporosis?
    A. High levels of osteoblast activity and low levels of osteoclast activity
    B. High levels of osteoblast activity and high levels of osteoclast activity
    C. Low levels of osteoblast activity and low levels of osteoclast activity
    D. Low levels of osteoblast activity and high levels of osteoclast activity

55. According to the passage, the rate of bone mass loss is highest, on average, during which years of a woman's life?
    A. From age 20 to 30
    B. From age 30 to 40
    C. From age 50 to 60
    D. From age 80 to 90

Discrete Set 4 (Questions 56-59)

These questions are **NOT** related to a passage.

56. Menstruation is preceded by which of the following hormone changes?
    A. A surge in luteinizing hormone
    B. A decrease in estrogen and an increase in progesterone
    C. A decrease in estrogen and progesterone
    D. An increase in aldosterone

57. Which of the following is NOT a chiral molecule?
    A. Alpha-hydroxybutyric acid
    B. Beta-hydroxybutyric acid
    C. Gamma-hydroxybutyric acid
    D. 3-hydroxybutyric acid

58. Which of the following is a six carbon molecule?
    A. Oxaloacetate
    B. Citrate
    C. Acetyl-CoA
    D. Ribose

59. During which phase of meiosis does crossing over occur?
    A. Prophase I
    B. Anaphase I
    C. Metaphase II
    D. Anaphase II

TIMED
SECTION 3
Answers and Explanations

Timed Section 3 Answer Key

Key		20	B	40	A
1	A	21	D	41	D
2	C	22	C	42	A
3	C	23	B	43	B
4	B	24	A	44	D
5	D	25	D	45	A
6	B	26	C	46	B
7	D	27	C	47	C
8	B	28	D	48	C
9	C	29	C	49	C
10	B	30	B	50	A
11	B	31	B	51	A
12	C	32	D	52	C
13	D	33	C	53	B
14	C	34	B	54	D
15	B	35	C	55	C
16	B	36	C	56	C
17	C	37	D	57	C
18	A	38	A	58	B
19	A	39	A	59	A

Passage I Answers and Explanations (Questions 1-5)

The **Triple Sugar Iron**, or TSI, test is useful for identifying bacterial genera, known collectively as **enterics**, commonly found in the human large **intestine**.

Key terms: TSI test, enterics, large intestine

Cause-and-Effect: TSI test is useful for identifying enteric bacteria

The test is performed in a tube containing agar, **phenol red** (a pH-sensitive dye), **1% lactose, 1% sucrose, 0.1% glucose**, and ferrous sulfate ($FeSO_4$). The slanted shape of the medium provides an array of surfaces that are either exposed to **oxygen**-containing air in varying degrees (the **upper slant**) or **not exposed to air** (the **lower butt**). Fermentation of any of the three sugars in the tube will produce byproducts, resulting in an observed color change of the dye from red to yellow. Because there is so little glucose in the medium, those bacteria that are able to metabolize glucose will exhaust the glucose supply and turn to alternative substrates. Byproducts of the oxidation of those substrates will increase the pH of the medium, returning the plate to its original red color. Many bacteria that can ferment sugars in the anaerobic butt of the tube are enterobacteria.

Key terms: phenol red, lactose, sucrose, glucose, ferrous sulfate, slant, butt

Cause-and-Effect: test tube contains a pH-sensitive dye (phenol red), 1% lactose, 1% sucrose, 0.1% glucose, and ferrous sulfate; the slant is the region exposed to oxygen; anaerobic fermentation results in a color change from red to yellow; a reverse color change back to red will occur if bacteria are not able to metabolize sucrose or lactose when glucose is exhausted

Under **anaerobic** conditions, as occurs at the bottom of the test tube, certain bacteria utilize **thiosulfate** anion as a terminal electron acceptor, reducing it to sulfide. If this occurs, the newly formed **hydrogen sulfide** (H_2S) gas may escape or react with ferrous sulfate in the medium to form **ferrous sulfide**, which is visible as a black precipitate.

Key terms: butt region, thiosulfate anion, hydrogen sulfide (H_2S), ferrous sulfide

Cause-and-Effect: under anaerobic conditions, which occur at the bottom of the test tube (the butt), some bacteria reduce thiosulfate to hydrogen sulfide; the gas produced may escape or react with ferrous sulfate to form ferrous sulfide; ferrous sulfide creates a visible, black precipitate

A laboratory technician attempting to identify **four unknown enteric pathogens** noted the results of a bacterial culture shown in Table 1. The technician noticed no color change in the butt region of Unknown B during the initial TSI test, but, upon repeat testing in a modified tube lacking ferrous sulfate, noticed a marked color change.

Cause-and-Effect: when identifying four unknown enteric pathogens, the technician initially noted no color change in the butt region; repeat testing in a tube lacking ferrous sulfate gave a color change

Table 1 Only unknown D gives a positive color change under the aerobic conditions of the slant, while unknown A and B (trial 2) do so under anaerobic conditions in the butt; gas is evolved in unknowns B and D; black precipitate forms from unknown B (trial 1) and C.

Unknown Bacterium	Slant	Butt	Precipitate	H_2S gas
A	R	Y	-	-
B (trial 1)	R	R	+	+
B (trial 2)	R	Y	-	+
C	R	R	+	-
D	Y	R	-	+

1. Based upon the results shown in Table 1, bacterium A is best described as a:
   A. **facultative anaerobe capable of fermenting sucrose or lactose.**
   B. obligate anaerobe capable of fermenting sucrose or lactose.
   C. obligate aerobe incapable of fermenting sucrose or lactose.
   D. facultative anaerobe incapable of fermenting sucrose or lactose.

Choice **A** is correct. A facultative anaerobe is an organism that makes ATP by aerobic respiration if oxygen is present, but is capable of switching to fermentation or anaerobic respiration if oxygen is absent. Table 1 shows that under exclusively anaerobic conditions, bacterium A is capable of sustained metabolism of glucose in addition to either sucrose or lactose, as evidenced by the color change noted in the butt region. Combined with the fact that no change is noted in the slant region in which oxygen is available, despite the fact that the color change in butt indicates that sucrose or lactose fermentation can occur, you can determine that bacterium A must be capable of both aerobic and anaerobic metabolism as well as lactose or sucrose fermentation.

B, C: An obligate aerobe cannot make ATP in the absence of oxygen as it is incapable of fermentation. If bacterium A were an obligate anaerobe, no color change would have been noted in the butt region.
D: If bacterium A was incapable of metabolizing either or both of sucrose or lactose, no color change would have been noted in the butt region.

2. Which of the following regarding the two trials of bacterium B is the most likely explanation for the difference in results noted by the technician?
   A. The formation of H_2S gas inhibited anaerobic respiration.
   B. Ferrous sulfide provided an oxygen source for aerobic respiration.
   C. **In trial 1, blackening of the medium obscured the color change.**
   D. The presence of H_2S gas, a weak acid, acidified the medium.

Choice **C** is correct. The formation of black precipitate could create a yellow solution that appears red within the medium. This possibility is consistent with the appearance of the red solution upon removal of the ferrous sulfate in the modified test tube of trial 2. Without ferrous sulfate, no black precipitate—ferrous sulfite—can be produced in reaction with the H_2S produced by the metabolism of unknown B.

A: H_2S gas was formed in both trial 1 and trial 2 and could not have accounted for the differing color changes seen in the butt region.
B: Ferrous sulfide (FeS) lacks oxygen.
D: Acidification of the medium would promote, rather than prevent, the red-to-yellow color change.

3. Based on the results of the experiments performed in the passage, which test would best distinguish bacterium D from the other unknown bacteria tested?
    A. Culture in a vacuum-sealed dish containing 1% lactose and 1% sucrose and 0.1% glucose
    B. Culture in a vacuum-sealed dish containing only 0.1% glucose
    C. **Culture in an open dish containing only 1% lactose and sucrose**
    D. Culture in an open dish containing only 1% glucose

Choice **C** is correct. In the slant region in which oxygen is present, bacterium D is the only bacterium tested which gives a color change. This indicates that, in the presence of oxygen, only bacterium D is capable of metabolizing lactose or sucrose and will engage in fermentation. For this reason, only bacterium D should appear yellow when inoculated in a culture containing lactose and sucrose where oxygen is available.

A, B: In a vacuum-sealed dish where little, if any, oxygen is available, bacteria D and C may give similar results, as shown in results from the butt region in Table 1.

D: In a medium containing glucose where oxygen is available, several outcomes are possible, depending upon the unknown organisms' possible modes of metabolism and preference for aerobic versus anaerobic metabolism. The most likely outcome of culturing in dilute glucose, based on the results shown in Table 1, is that no organism would demonstrate a color change, as the color change requires continued anaerobic metabolism of either glucose or lactose or sucrose—none are available beyond the small amount of glucose which the passage indicates is insufficient to permit a sustained color change.

4. All four of the bacteria tested are described as Gram negative. Gram negative bacteria are distinguished from Gram positive bacteria in that:
    A. Gram negative bacteria lack a membrane-bound nucleus.
    B. **Gram negative bacteria have a thinner peptidoglycan layer than do Gram positive bacteria.**
    C. Gram positive bacteria lack a cell wall.
    D. Gram negative bacteria have an exclusively rod-shaped morphology.

Choice **B** is correct. Gram-negative bacteria are a broad class of bacteria that do not retain the crystal violet stain used in the Gram staining method of bacterial differentiation, because they possess only a thin peptidoglycan layer sandwiched between an inner cell membrane and a bacterial outer membrane. Gram-positive bacteria, in contrast, have a thicker peptidoglycan layer in their cell wall outside the cell membrane, which retains the crystal violet stain during the alcohol wash. This question can still be answered without being specifically aware of these facts via a process of elimination.

A: All bacteria lack a membrane-bound nucleus; the lack of such a membrane-bound nucleus could not be a basis for differentiating between bacterial types.

C: All bacteria possess a cell wall, present, ordinarily, on the outside of the cytoplasmic membrane.

D: Bacteria display a wide diversity of shapes and sizes, called morphologies. Most bacterial species are either spherical, referred to as cocci, or rod-shaped, called bacilli.

5. The enzymes responsible for electron transport in aerobically growing bacteria are found within what region or structure of the cell?
   A. Inner mitochondrial membrane
   B. Cytoplasm.
   C. Mitochondrial matrix
   D. **Plasma membrane**

Choice **D** is correct. In prokaryotes, the enzymes of electron transport chains are localized to the cell's plasma membrane.

A, C: Prokaryotes lack mitochondria as well as all other membrane-bound organelles.
B: The enzymes of bacterial electron transport chains are found in the plasma membrane. A common requirement of all electron transport chains is the need for a membranous barrier across which protons can be pumped to create a transmembrane proton gradient.

Passage II Answers and Explanations (Questions 6-10)

Chronic arterial hypertension (HTN), otherwise known as high blood pressure, is a condition that affects millions. Blood pressure is measured while the patient is sitting, often in the brachial artery on the anterior part of the elbow, as the artery is superficial in this location. A blood pressure measurement has two components, usually reported in mmHg: the systolic pressure (when the heart is contracting) and the diastolic pressure (when the heart is relaxed). Through exact cutoffs may vary, repeated systolic measurements above **140 mmHg** and/or diastolic measurements above **90 mmHg** are generally considered abnormally high. Blood pressure is equal to the **product of cardiac output (CO) and total peripheral resistance (TPR)**, as shown in Equation 1 below.

Key terms: HTN, systolic pressure, diastolic pressure, cardiac output, total peripheral resistance

Contrast: Diastolic pressure is when the heart is relaxed, systolic is when it's contracting

Cause-and-Effect: BP measured while sitting and in brachial artery, HTN > 140/90 mmHg

$$BP = CO \times TPR$$
Equation 1

Equation 1 is very simple: BP is proportional to both CO and TPR

Primary hypertension (PHTN) is not caused by another medical condition, while **secondary hypertension (SHTN)** is diagnosed when the cause of the elevated blood pressure is suspected to be a concurrent condition or medication side effect. Risk factors for PHTN include sedentary lifestyle, hereditary factors, a diet high in salt, and high alcohol consumption. Because of the kidneys' role in maintaining fluid balance in the body, renal and endocrine pathophysiology is often a cause of SHTN.

Key terms: PHTN, SHTN

Contrast: PHTN not caused by medical condition, SHTN is.

Cause-and-Effect: HTN caused by other medical conditions, lack of exercise, too much salt/alcohol

Regardless of cause, untreated HTN increases the **risk of cardiovascular disease, heart attack, stroke and kidney disease**. Thus, its management is an important priority in health care. In a clinical trial to **compare treatments for HTN, patients were randomized to 4 groups**. The results of the study are shown in Table 1 below. The blood pressure readings are in mmHg.

Key terms: Untreated HTN

Cause-and-Effect: Untreated HTN dangerous, clinical trial done to compare treatments

Table 1 Results of blood pressure study

Group	Mean BP pre-study (systolic/diastolic)	Mean BP post-study (systolic/diastolic)	Change (systolic)
Placebo	158/94	162/95	+4
Medication A	154/93	143/85	-11
Low sodium diet	158/96	151/90	-7
Aerobic exercise	155/92	146/87	-9

Table 1 shows that patients in all four groups started with HTN, and in the three treatment groups BP was successfully reduced to varying degrees. Medication A was most effective, exercise second most effective, and the diet the third most effect. BP increased in the untreated group.

6. Because of a mistake in the clinical study, subjects in the low sodium diet group had their pre-study brachial blood pressure measured while lying down instead of sitting down. How did this likely affect the results of the study?
    A. The reduction in BP over the course of the study in the low sodium diet group was actually larger than reported.
    B. **The reduction in BP over the course of the study in the low sodium diet group was actually smaller than reported.**
    C. The patients in the low sodium diet group probably did not have HTN.
    D. This mistake probably did not affect the result of the study.

Choice **B** is correct. The subject's blood pressure in the arteries of the arm, including the brachial artery, would be higher while lying down than sitting up due to a shift of blood from the lower half of the body to the upper half when lying down. Thus, in the low sodium diet group, their pre-study BP was artificially elevated (it was actually lower than in Table 1). This would lead to a greater measured change over the course of the study.

A: The opposite is true.
C: This cannot be reasonably inferred from information in the answer stem or passage; you don't know what their BP would be sitting up, just that it would be lower.
D: The opposite is true.

7. During aerobic exercise, cardiac output increases by a factor of 5. Why doesn't blood pressure increase by the same factor?
    A. Vasoconstriction in all vessels
    B. Vasoconstriction in working muscles
    C. Vasodilation in all vessels
    D. **Vasodilation in working muscles**

Choice **D** is correct. The question asks us why BP does not increase 5 fold during exercise while CO does. Based on Equation 1, this must mean that TPR goes down. This eliminates choices A and B, because vasoconstriction would increase TPR. The body shunts blood to working muscles to supply them with oxygen during exercise. This is accomplished through vasodilation in working muscles.

A: This would increase TPR.
B: This would increase TPR.
C: This would increase blood flow to all tissues, not just the muscles. Choice D would specifically supply the working tissue with more blood and is more plausible.

8. In which of the following vessels is blood pressure likely to be highest?
    A. Capillaries
    B. **Aorta**
    C. Arteries
    D. Veins

Choice **B** is correct. BP is higher in arteries than veins and capillaries, so you can eliminate choices A and D. BP would be highest closest to the heart, where blood has not had an opportunity to diffuse into low-pressure capillaries. The aorta is the closest to the heart on the arterial side.

A: BP is lower in the capillaries than aorta.
C: BP is lower in the arteries than aorta.
D: BP is lower in the veins than aorta.

9. Beta-blockers are medications that reduce blood pressure by antagonizing beta-adrenergic receptors in the heart and blood vessels. They mimic the effects of:
    A. Epinephrine
    B. Norepinephrine
    C. **The parasympathetic nervous system**
    D. The sympathetic nervous system

Choice **C** is correct. The question states that beta-blockers reduce blood pressure. This is associated with the 'rest and digest' action of the parasympathetic nervous system.

A: Epinephrine is a neurotransmitter in the sympathetic nervous system, not parasympathetic.
B: Norepinephrine is a neurotransmitter in the sympathetic nervous system, not parasympathetic.
D: The opposite is true.

10. The results of the placebo group suggest that:
    A. HTN does not need to be treated.
    B. **HTN may be a progressive condition.**
    C. The subjects were not exercising in the first place.
    D. The subjects should eat less salt.

Choice B is correct. Table 1 shows that mean BP increased in the placebo group over the course of the study, suggesting that those subjects' HTN was worsening.

A: This is the opposite of what is stated in the passage: Regardless of cause, untreated HTN increases the risk of cardiovascular disease, heart attack, stroke and kidney disease. Thus, its management is an important priority in health care.
C: This is out of the scope of the passage; you do not know about the placebo group's lifestyle.
D: This is out of the scope of the passage; you do not know about the placebo group's lifestyle.

Passage III Answers and Explanations (Questions 11-15)

Congenital hemophilia (CH) is a chronic, **X-linked, recessive disease** that affects thousands worldwide. **Acquired hemophilia (AH)** is much less common than CH; it is a rare, acute condition with a few hundred cases in the United States a year. While both diseases affect the same proteins, their causes and treatments are distinct.

Key terms: Congenital hemophilia, X-linked, recessive, acquired hemophilia

Contrast: CH is genetic, chronic. AH is not genetic, acute, rarer

Cause-and-Effect: Two diff types of hemophilia affect same proteins

The most common type of hemophilia, **type A CH**, results from a **mutation in the gene coding for factor VIII** (FVIII), a protein that is critical in the blood clotting process. It is typically treated with **infusions of normal FVIII. Type B CH** is the result of **mutation in the gene for factor IX** (FIX), also involved in the clotting process. Similarly, people with type B CH receive infusions of FIX to maintain normal hemostasis. Depending on the severity of the mutation, symptoms of CH may be as mild as prolonged bleeding during dental visits or as severe as spontaneous bleeds that occur without trauma. CH is infamous for its prevalence in royal families, including the descendants of Queen Victoria in the British, Spanish and Russian royalty of the 19th century. A variety of mutations including **point mutations** may cause CH. These mutations may be **spontaneous or inherited**.

Key terms: Type A CH, FVIII, Type B CH, FIX, Queen Victoria, point mutation, spontaneous, inherited

Contrast: Type A CH is lack of or not enough FVIII, type B CH is lack of or not enough FIX

Cause-and-Effect: Genetic abnormalities in CH cause abnormalities in clotting.

As the name suggests, **AH** occurs in people who have **normal genes for FVIII and FIX**. Patients are not born with AH; instead, they begin **producing antibodies that attack the FVIII or FIX** that their bodies produce. Because both AH and CH are characterized by **abnormally low or absent FVIII or FIX activity**, their symptoms are generally similar. Treatment of AH involves **immunosuppression**, reversal of underlying cause (if any), and administration of **bypassing agents** that can activate the blood-clotting cascade without FVIII or FIX.

Key terms: AH, antibodies, immunosuppression, bypassing agents

Contrast: Unlike CH, AH is not genetic

Cause-and-Effect: AH is body attacking its own FVIII or FIX that it produces.

11. If historical research reveals that none of Queen Victoria's ancestors had evidence of a bleeding disorder such as hemophilia even though she was a carrier for CH, this could be because:

    I. She did not inherit the mutation that causes hemophilia; it was spontaneous.

    II. Her ancestors were carriers for hemophilia but the mutation was not severe enough to cause noticeable symptoms.

    III. Her ancestors were carriers for CH Type B.

    A. I only
    B. I and II
    C. II and III
    D. I, II and III

Choice **B** is correct. The question asks why Queen Victoria could be a carrier of hemophilia if none of her relatives had symptoms of the disease. This could be for two reasons. The most likely is that she was the first one in her family to be a carrier, meaning that the mutation arose spontaneously and was not inherited from one her parents. This is choice I. The other possibility is that she did inherit the gene for hemophilia, but it was such a mild mutation that it did not result in symptoms of hemophilia. This is choice II.

A: Choice II is also correct.
C: Choice III is incorrect. In fact, if her ancestors were carriers for a type of hemophilia, they would have likely been symptomatic. This contradicts the question stem.
D: See explanation for choice C.

12. Based on the passage, the vast majority of symptomatic hemophiliacs are:
    A. overweight.
    B. Caucasian.
    C. male.
    D. female.

Choice **C** is correct. The passage states that hemophilia is an X-linked, recessive disease. Thus, one copy of the normal gene for FVIII or FIX is sufficient to produce normal clotting. Males are much more likely to be affected by an X-linked disease because they only have one copy of the X chromosome. For a female to be affected, she would have to have two mutated copies of the hemophilia gene, one each from her mother and father. This would be exceptionally rare.

A: This is not relevant to hemophilia.
B: Though genetic diseases may have different prevalence in different races, this cannot be concluded about hemophilia from the passage.
D: The opposite is true.

13. In some cases, congenital hemophiliacs develop antibodies (inhibitors) to the factor treatments they receive, resulting in reduced efficacy of treatment. The treatment for these patients is most likely:
    A. factor infusions.
    B. whole blood.
    C. fresh frozen plasma.
    D. **bypassing agents.**

Choice **D** is correct. Congenital hemophilia with inhibitors is analogous to acquired hemophilia as it is described in the passage: in both cases, the body produces antibodies that attack FVIII or FIX (endogenous or exogenous). Thus, one can infer that the treatment for CH with inhibitors would be the same as AH. As stated in the final paragraph, bypassing agents can activate the blood-clotting cascade without FVIII or FIX.

A: This would not be effective due to the presence of antibodies that will attack the factor.
B: This would not be effective due to the presence of antibodies that will attack the factor in the whole blood.
C: This would not be effective due to the presence of antibodies that will attack the factor dissolved in the FFP.

14. Which of the following factors would increase the prevalence of hemophilia in future generations of a royal family where the queen is a carrier?
    A. The presence of mutagenic paint in the royal castle
    B. The development of inhibitors by her son
    C. **Inbreeding**
    D. The prince engaging in a high activity lifestyle

Choice **C** is correct. The question asks us to pick a choice that would make future members of the royal family MORE likely to be hemophiliacs. If relatives were to mate with each other (for instance, a hemophiliac male with a carrier female), their children would be much more likely to get hemophilia than if the prince and princess were to reproduce with people outside the royal family. For instance, the daughter of a carrier mother and a hemophiliac father must be a carrier, whereas the daughter of a carrier mother and normal father has a ~50% chance of being a carrier.

A: Though hemophilia could plausibly be caused by a mutagen, it could also cause many other deleterious or harmless mutations. The passage does not support this answer.
B: This would not change the likelihood of hemophilia in future generations.
D: This might make the prince have more bleeds if he has hemophilia, but would not affect the prevalence of hemophilia in future generations.

15. Which of the following could explain the survival of hemophilia over many generations, even though those afflicted have shorter life expectancies than healthy people?
    A. Increased presence of carcinogens in 19th century Europe
    B. **Increased fitness and reproductive success in carriers**
    C. Decreased presence of carcinogens in 19th century Europe
    D. Decreased fitness and reproductive success in carriers

Choice **B** is correct. Why might hemophilia survive generation after generation if those afflicted with it die younger? The answer must be that there is something adaptive about being a carrier for hemophilia.

A: One cannot conclude from the passage if this would affect hemophilia carriers or suffers disproportionately. This answer is a misuse of detail from the passage.
C: See answer explanation for choice A.
D: This would make hemophilia LESS likely to survive for many generations.

Discrete Set 1 Answers and Explanations (Questions 16-18)

16. How many distinct codons code for amino acids?
    A. 64
    B. <u>61</u>
    C. 31
    D. 21

Choice **B** is correct. There are 4 possible RNA bases, A G C U. Each codon is 3 bases in sequence. Thus, there are (4x4x4 = 64) possibilities of arranging them in groups of 3. However, there are 3 stop codons, UAA, UAG, UGA, that do not code for amino acids. Thus only 61 code for amino acids.

17. Which of the following is responsible for the formation of beta-pleated sheets?
    A. Disulfide bonds between two cysteine residues
    B. Side group interactions between amino acids
    C. <u>Hydrogen bonds in backbone of peptide</u>
    D. van der Waals forces between peptides

Choice **C** is correct. The two most commonly encountered secondary structures of a polypeptide chain are α-helices and beta-pleated sheets. Secondary structure refers to the shape of a folding protein due exclusively to hydrogen bonding between its backbone amide and carbonyl groups. Secondary structure does not include bonding between the R-groups of amino acids, hydrophobic interactions, or other interactions associated with tertiary structure.

A: These forces contribute to tertiary structure.
B: These interactions contribute to tertiary structure.
D: van der Waals forces do not contribute to secondary structure.

18. Which of the following has the greatest number of complete waves in a 1000 nm length?
    A. <u>Ultraviolet light used in the treatment of skin diseases</u>
    B. Yellow light used in neonatal heat lamps
    C. Red light used in pain therapy for severe arthritis
    D. Microwaves used to treat swollen prostates

Choice **A** is correct. The question is essentially asking which of the choices has the shortest wavelength. As one travels across the electromagnetic spectrum, from longest to shortest wavelength are as follows: radio waves, infrared, visible light (ROYGBIV), UV, gamma rays. Choices B, C, and D all have longer wavelength radiation than ultraviolet light.

Passage IV Answers and Explanations (Questions 19-22)

Studies have documented a strong **association between smoking and depression. Cigarette smoke** has been reported to modulate monoamine oxidase (MAO) A levels in vitro and in animals. MAO exists in two subtypes, **MAO A** and **B**. In the brain, **MAO A oxidizes serotonin and norepinephrine**, whereas MAO B oxidizes benzylamine and phenethylamine and is localized in serotonergic neurons and in glial cells. Both forms oxidize dopamine. Serotonin and norepinephrine levels in the thalamus have been linked to **the maintenance of mood. Deficiency** of either neurotransmitter is associated with the **development of depression**.

Key terms: cigarette smoke; monoamine oxidase (MAO) A and B; serotonin; norepinephrine; benzylamine; phenethylamine; serotonergic neurons; glial cells; dopamine; thalamus; depression

Cause-and-Effect: an association between smoking and depression has been documented; cigarette smoke modulates MAO A levels; MAO A oxidizes serotonin and norepinephrine; MAO B oxidizes benzylamine and phenthylamine and is localized mainly to serotonergic neurons and glial cells; MAO A and B both oxidize dopamine; serotonin and norepinephrine levels in the thalamus are linked to the maintenance of mood; deficiency of either is associated with the depression

Researchers compared **MAO A levels in the brains of nonsmokers and current smokers** using **^{11}C-labeled clorgyline ([^{11}C]clorgyline)**, a radiotracer which binds specifically and irreversibly to brain MAO A, and **positron emission tomography (PET)** scans of both groups. Four nonsmokers were also treated with the MAO inhibitor (MAOI), tranylcypromine after receiving baseline PET scans and then rescanned to assess the sensitivity of [^{11}C]clorgyline binding to **MAO inhibition**. MAO A levels were **quantified** by using the **model term λk_3**, which is a **function of, and increases along with the concentration of enzymatically activated MAO A** in the brain. A comparison of MAO A levels in the thalamus for those tested is shown in Figure 1.

Key terms: [^{11}C]clorgyline, positron emission tomography (PET), MAO inhibitor (MAOI), tranylcypromine, $\lambda k3$

Cause-and-Effect: researchers compared MAO levels in the brains of smokers, non-smokers and non-smokers treated with an MAOI received PET scans assessing for the presence of the MAO binding compound [^{11}C]clorgyline; MAO A levels were quantified by using the model term $\lambda k3$; $\lambda k3$

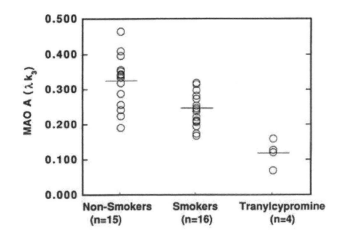

increases along with brain MAO A concentration
Figure 1: MAO A levels are decreased in both smokers and non-smokers treated with

tranylcypromine versus untreated non-smokers

19. Tranylcypromine is a competitive inhibitor of MAO enzymes. According to the Michaelis-Menten model of enzyme kinetics, what changes in the kinetic parameters of MAO activity occur due to the addition of tranylcypromine?
    A. **K_m increases and V_{max} is unchanged**
    B. K_m is unchanged and V_{max} decreases
    C. K_m is unchanged and V_{max} increases
    D. K_m decreases and V_{max} is unchanged

Choice **A** is correct. Competitive inhibitors compete with substrate for the active site of enzymes. V_{max} for such reactions is unchanged, as at high substrate concentrations, there is sufficient substrate present to out-compete inhibitors for access to the active site. At non-saturating substrate concentrations, competitive inhibitors meaningfully impact the rate of the catalyzed reaction. This leads to an increased K_m value—a measure of the substrate concentration required to reach the half-maximal reaction velocity.

B: Competitive inhibitors lead to an increased K_m value and an unchanged V_{max}.
C: Competitive inhibitors lead to an increased K_m value and an unchanged V_{max}.
D: These changes do not correspond to the changes in V_{max} and K_m seen in competitive inhibitors.

20. Tranylcypromine treatment is expected to have which of the following effects on thalamic neurotransmitter levels in non-smokers?
    A. Decreased norepinephrine and serotonin
    B. **Increased dopamine**
    C. Decreased benzylamine and phenethylamine
    D. Increased benzylamine and phenethylamine

Choice **B** is correct. The passage states that MAO A oxidizes serotonin and norepinephrine, whereas MAO B oxidizes benzylamine and phenethylamine. Dopamine is metabolized by both MAO A and B. The passage further states that tranylcypromine is a selective MAO A inhibitor. Inhibition of MAO A is therefore expected to cause an increase in dopamine.

A: Inhibition of MAO A by tranylcypromine should lead to an increase in norepinephrine and serotonin.
C, D: Benzylamine and phenethylamine are not metabolized by MAO A; its inhibition would, at least within the context of passage information, not change their expected concentration

21. Which of the following possibilities relating cigarette smoking to MAO A or depression is best supported by the passage?
    A. Smoking may increase the risk of developing a depressive disorder.
    B. Tranylcypromine reduces the concentration of the biologically active form of nicotine in the brains of smokers.
    C. Mood stabilizing neurotransmitter levels are likely higher in non-smokers after tranylcypromine treatment than are levels in smokers after the same treatment.
    D. **The inhibition of MAO A by smoking may contribute to the difficulty of smoking cessation.**

Choice **D** is correct. MAO A inhibition increases norepinephrine and serotonin, both of which are MAO A-specific substrates, in addition to dopamine, which is a substrate for both MAO subtypes. If the monoamines norepinephrine and serotonin are linked to mood, the inhibition of human brain MAO A by smoke may contribute to the difficulty of smoking cessation in depression, as the withdrawal from cigarettes would not only represent withdrawal from nicotine but also withdrawal from MAO A inhibitory substances in smoke.

A: MAO A inhibition increases norepinephrine and serotonin, the deficiency of which are linked to the development of depression. It is unlikely to lead to an increased risk of depression for this reason.

B: The passage provides no specific indication as to tranylcypromine's relationship to nicotine function.

C: Baseline MAO A level of non-smokers are higher than those of smokers; it can be expected, then, that serotonin and norepinephrine levels are lower in non-smokers than in smokers—at least on the basis of information presented in the passage. There is no direct indication that tranylcypromine levels would result in a decline in MAO A levels for non-smokers below those of smokers, leading to an increase in serotonin and norepinephrine levels in non-smokers above the level of those found in smokers.

22. The researchers concluded that smoking exerted an inhibitory influence on MAO A enzymes present in the thalamus. Which additional finding, if true, most challenges this assertion?
    A. The activity of both MAO A and MAO B are reduced in animals exposed to tobacco smoke.
    B. MAO activity in cultured thalamic cells is unchanged by direct application of nicotine.
    C. **Local vasoconstriction reduces MAO A delivery to the thalamus.**
    D. [^{11}C]clorgyline binding is reduced when preceded by treatment of the thalamus with an MAOI.

Choice **C** is correct. The researchers conclusion that smoking exerted an inhibitory influence on MAO A enzymes present in the thalamus rests on the assumption that the extent of [^{11}C]clorgyline binding reflects the concentration of enzymatically active MAO A in the thalamus, and that smoking-related changes in the amount of enzymatically active MAO A able to bind [^{11}C]clorgyline are due to smoking's inhibition of MAO A. If, however, smoking caused local vasoconstrictive changes that decreased delivery of MAO A to the thalamus, an alternative explanation for decreased [^{11}C]clorgyline binding could be offered apart from smoking's direct modulation of MAO A activity.

A: The fact that MAO B activity, in addition to that of MAO A, is reduced in animals exposed to tobacco smoke does not challenge the researchers' conclusion.

B: Likewise, the researchers do not conclude that the effects of cigarette smoke are directly due to nicotine.

D: [^{11}C]clorgyline binding depends upon the presence of active MAOI, which should be reduced versus control levels in a thalamus pre-treated with an MAOI.

Passage V Answers and Explanations (Questions 23-26)

Alzheimer's disease is a **neurodegenerative** disorder that predominantly affects individuals over the age of 65. One of the first and most common symptoms is **difficulty remembering events** stored in **short term memory**. **As the disease progresses**, patients often become **irritable** and withdrawn, and eventually lose much of their long term memory. On the molecular level, many researchers believe that most of the disease's symptoms are attributed to one of two proteins: ***amyloid-beta (A_β) and tau (τ)***.

Key Terms: Alzheimer's Disease, neurodegenerative, short term memory, long term memory, amyloid-beta (A_β), and tau (τ)

Cause-and-Effect: It is believed that amyloid-beta (A_β) and tau (τ) cause changes in the brain responsible for the symptoms displayed in Alzheimer's patients

The **A_β theory** suggests that the A_β peptide, which consists of around 40 **amino acids**, aggregates to form **extracellular clumps** called "**plaques**" in brain tissue. It has been shown in mouse models that **overexpression of the A_β gene** leads to behaviors and **memory loss** resembling the effects of Alzheimer's in humans. The natural function of A_β is not well understood, but it has been potentially implicated in **oxidative stress protection and kinase activation**. A_β becomes dangerous when **misfolding** in the **tertiary structure** leads to accumulation of the protein at **neurotoxic levels**.

Key Terms: A_β theory, peptide, amino acids, plaques, overexpression, oxidative stress, kinase activation, tertiary structure, neurotoxic

Contrast: A_β protein naturally is involved in oxidative stress protection and kinase activity, and when it is misfolded causes neurotoxic accumulations of protein (whereas the τ theory below suggests an alternative culprit)

Cause-and-Effect: A_β plaques in extracellular space are caused by misfolding of tertiary structure, and lead to accumulation of protein in neurotoxic levels.

The **τ theory** suggests that Alzheimer's symptoms are attributed to **hyperphosphorylation** of τ. This protein has several isomers, the longest of which has around **440 amino acids**. The normal function of τ is to **stabilize microtubules**. It is hypothesized that in Alzheimer's disease, the hyperphosphorylation leads to **tangles of τ inside nerve cell bodies that cause microtubule collapse**. Another hypothesis involves proline, a unique amino acid that has a distinctive cyclic structure that prevents typical protein geometry. Many other theories to explain Alzheimer's disease have been proposed, and it is possible that it is not necessarily one microbiological entity that is responsible for the disease, but rather **concerted destruction** caused by **multiple genes or proteins** gone awry.

Key Terms: τ theory, hyperphosphorylation, microtubules

Contrast: τ also causes protein aggregates but they are inside the cell instead of extracellular like in A_β plaques, and they cause death through microtubule collapse, not neurotoxicity.

Cause-and-Effect: τ tangles are caused by hyperphosphorylation of the protein, and tangles cause microtubule collapse.

23. The τ protein is likely to cause disruptions in which of the following cellular processes
    I. Mitosis
    II. Translation
    III. Intracellular transport

    A. I only
    B. **I and III**
    C. II and III
    D. I, II, and III

Choice **B** is correct. The τ protein disrupts microtubule stabilization, and leads to microtubule collapse. Microtubules are involved in mitosis because they are the fundamental component of the mitotic spindles. Microtubules are also used heavily in intracellular transport through the motor proteins dynein and kinesin. Transport would be affected by microtubule collapse. Microtubules are not involved in translation, and so this process would likely be unaffected.

A: I is correct, but III is correct as well.
C: III is correct, but II is not.
D: I and III are correct, but II is not.

24. Which organelle is the site of A_β and τ translation?
    A. **Ribosome**
    B. Smooth Endoplasmic Reticulum
    C. Mitochondrion
    D. Nucleus

Choice **A** is correct. The ribosome is the site of protein synthesis in the cell. Translation is the process of converting RNA into protein, thus the ribosome is where A_β and τ translation would occur.

B: The ribosomes are located on the rough endoplasmic reticulum, not the smooth endoplasmic reticulum. The smooth endoplasmic reticulum is responsible for synthesizing lipids and steroids, not proteins.
C: The mitochondrion is not involved in protein synthesis. Mitochondria generate most of the cell's energy supply in the form of ATP.
D: The nucleus is where transcription occurs, not translation.

25. Given that memory loss is often one of the earliest symptoms of Alzheimer's disease, which part of the brain most likely suffers damage soon after onset of the disease?
    A. Cerebellum
    B. Prefrontal Cortex
    C. Pons
    D. **Hippocampus**

Choice **D** is correct. The passage states that one of the first and most common symptoms in Alzheimer's patients is short term memory loss. The hippocampus plays an important role in information consolidation for short-term memory.

A: The cerebellum is not very involved in memory, but plays a significant role in motor control.
B: The prefrontal cortex is not very involved in memory, but rather in complex cognitive behaviors and decision making.
C: The pons is not involved in memory. It is mostly involved in the autonomic nervous system.

26. Suppose researchers have implicated another protein in causing Alzheimer's disease. This protein is found to be made up of 35 amino acids, including 18 proline residues. The secondary structure will most likely have a(n):
    A. large number of alpha helices.
    B. large number of beta sheets.
    C. **an alternative secondary structure.**
    D. even numbers of alpha helices and beta sheets.

Choice **C** is correct. As stated in the final paragraph, proline is a unique amino acid in that it has a distinctive cyclic structure that prevents standard geometry. This forces proteins to adopt secondary structures that are not alpha helices or beta sheets. It is commonly found in "turns," an alternative secondary structure.

A, D: Due to proline's unique nature, it will not give rise to alpha helices.
B: Due to proline's unique nature, it will not give rise to beta sheets.

Discrete Set 2 Answers and Explanations (Questions 27-30)

27. When creating a clone library, why is an antibiotic resistance gene included on the plasmid to be used?
    A. Antibiotic resistance is needed in case of contamination of the media that the clones will grow on.
    B. Bacteria only take up plasmids that confer a selective advantage to them.
    C. The clones will be plated on media containing antibiotics and only successfully transformed clones will grow.
    D. Antibiotic resistance differentiates plasmids that have inserts from those that do not.

Choice **C** is correct. This is the first level of selection to make sure the clones have been transformed with the correct plasmid.

A: The clones are grown on media containing antibiotics.
B: This is not true. Bacteria can't "know" if a plasmid will give them an advantage.
D: This only differentiates clones that have plasmids from those that don't.

28. How many possible codons are there?
    A. 48
    B. 12
    C. 81
    D. 64

Choice **D** is correct. There are 4 possible nucleotides and 3 positions within the codon, therefore there are $4^3 = 64$ possible codons.

29. Nondisjunction during meiosis can result in a gamete that is diploid for a given chromosome rather than haploid, and another gamete that has no copies of that chromosome. If a diploid gamete fuses with a normal haploid gamete, a zygote results with three copies, or trisomy. Most trisomies are not survivable, but several notable ones are. Which of the following represents a survivable trisomy of the sex chromosome?
    A. Down Syndrome
    B. Turner Syndrome
    C. Klinefelter Syndrome
    D. Phenylketonuria

Choice **C** is correct. The MCAT will expect you to be familiar with the classic aneuploidies – genetic disorders where the person doesn't have the normal diploid set of chromosomes. Klinefelter syndrome is XXY, a trisomy of the sex chromosomes.

A: Down syndrome is trisomy 21, a trisomy of the autosomal chromosomes.
B: Turner syndrome is XO, a monosomy of the sex chromosomes.
D: Phenylketonuria is not an aneuploidy disorder.

30. In normal patients, a membrane bound chloride channel in epithelial cells near sweat glands is responsible for chloride uptake from the sweat into the cytoplasm. In cystic fibrosis patients, this channel is defective. What is most likely to happen to sodium ions in sweat of cystic fibrosis patients?
    A. Taken into epithelial cells
    B. **Released along with the sweat**
    C. Reabsorbed into the sweat gland
    D. Adhere to the negatively charged cell membrane of the epithelial cells

Choice **B** is correct. If the chloride ions (negatively charged) cannot enter the epithelial cells, then sodium ions (positively charged) could not enter as well to maintain charge neutrality. Choice B is correct.

A, C, D: The ions would not re-enter the sweat gland nor adhere to the epithelial cell membrane because ions are soluble molecules dissolved in sweat.

Passage VI Answers and Explanations (Questions 31-34)

The **liver** is the second largest organ in the body by weight, smaller only than the skin. It performs many functions as part of the **digestive system**, aided by the **hepatic portal system**, one of two portal systems in the body. In these systems, blood is carried from one **capillary** bed to another without returning to the **heart** in between. The hepatic portal system allows nutrient-rich blood coming from the **gastrointestinal tract** and **spleen** to take an express path via the **hepatic portal vein** to the liver. The nutrients, which largely consist of **monosaccharides** absorbed by the first bed of capillaries, can be quickly processed and any **toxins** that may have been ingested can be filtered out.

Key Terms: liver, hepatic portal system, capillary, gastrointestinal tract, spleen, hepatic portal vein, monosaccharide

Contrast: A portal system is different because it goes from one capillary bed to another without returning to the heart in between

Cause-and-Effect: The hepatic portal system shunts blood coming from the GI tract and spleen to the liver before returning to the heart.

Glycogen Storage Disease (GSD) Type IV is a **hereditary metabolic disorder** resulting from enzymatic defects affecting **glycogen** processing, and can take a variety of forms. In the most common form, the **progressive hepatic type**, an affected baby is born with no apparent health defects but soon shows difficulty gaining weight and enlargement of the liver, leading to **cirrhosis** (i.e., scarring of the liver tissue) and **hypertension** (i.e., high blood pressure) in the hepatic portal. The disease is usually fatal within the first few years of life.

Key Terms: Glycogen Storage Disease Type IV, glycogen, cirrhosis, hypertension

Contrast: GSD Type IV babies have difficulty gaining weight, enlargement of the liver, cirrhoses, and are hypertensive.

Cause-and-Effect: GSD Type IV causes downstream developmental issues that usually end in early death.

A two-month old girl born to healthy parents begins exhibiting such symptoms and is eventually diagnosed with **GSD Type IV**. The child's father remembers that his brother died of a rare disease at the age of two, and quickly learns from his parents that this resulted from the same disease. The child's mother does not have any siblings.

Key Terms: GSD type IV genetics

Cause-and-Effect: Parents' genes caused daughter to be born with GSD Type IV.

31. Which of the following is NOT a role performed by the liver?
    A. Breakdown of caffeine
    B. **Insulin storage**
    C. Bile production
    D. Angiotensinogen synthesis

Choice **B** is correct. Insulin is stored in beta cells in the pancreas. The other three options, breakdown of caffeine, bile production, and angiotensinogen synthesis, are all well-established functions of the liver.

A: The liver is responsible for the breakdown of toxins, which include caffeine and alcohol.
C: Bile is produced in the liver before being transported to the gallbladder to be stored and concentrated.
D. Angiotensinogen is the zymogen precursor to angiotensin, a peptide hormone that leads to vasoconstriction. It is produced in the liver.

32. The hepatic portal system is one of two portal systems in humans and it carries blood through a second set of capillaries in the liver before returning to the heart. Where does the other portal system bring blood?
    A. Kidneys
    B. Heart
    C. Feet
    D. <u>Brain</u>

Choice **D** is correct. This requires the reader to know that the other portal system is the hypophyseal portal system, which connects the hypothalamus to the anterior pituitary in the brain allowing for quick transport of hormones leading to rapid effects.

A: A renal portal system is not present in humans, and is exclusively found in non-mammals.
B: By definition, a portal system consists of two capillary beds, in which blood travels from the first capillary bed to the second without first returning to the heart. This is explicitly stated in the passage.
C: There is no portal system that extends to the feet, nor would this be a logical explanation, as no organs that would necessitate such rapid transport of material via blood are present there.

33. Based on information provided in the passage, which of the following would be likely symptoms for someone born with the progressive hepatic type of GSD Type IV?
    I. Increased bone strength
    II. Toxin buildup in the brain
    III. Hepatomegaly

    A. I only
    B. II only
    C. <u>II and III</u>
    D. I, II, and III

Choice **C** is correct. Enough information is stated in the passage to allow for the reasonable conclusion that both toxin buildup in the brain and hepatomegaly (enlarged liver) could occur as a result of GSD Type IV and resulting cirrhosis. Bone strength may be decreased as a result of cirrhosis, but not enough information is given to conclude this. No evidence is provided that may allude to an increase in bone strength.

A: As stated above, the passage does not provide any information that may allow a reasonable deduction to be made regarding bone strength, and if it had, it would point toward the possibility of decreased bone strength as a result of cirrhosis, not increased bone strength.
B: Toxin buildup in the brain is a likely symptom for someone suffering from cirrhosis, as implied in the passage when it stated that one of the roles of the liver is to filter out ingested toxins. However, this answer is not correct because it excludes another correct answer.
D: Since increased bone strength is not a likely symptom for someone born with progressive hepatic GSD Type IV, as described above, this answer is not correct.

34. What type of inheritance does GSD Type IV display, and if the same parents were to have a son, what is the likelihood that he will also suffer from GSD Type IV?

    A. X-linked dominant; 100%

    B. **Autosomal recessive; 25%**

    C. Autosomal recessive; 6.25%

    D. X-linked recessive; 50%

Choice **B** is correct. This is a two-part question. Since both parents are healthy but clearly carry the gene leading to GSD Type IV, the disease must be recessive. The key piece of information that points toward the disease being autosomal rather than X-linked is that the father is a carrier of the disease, but does not have it. If it were X-linked and he had an allele for the disease, he would present symptoms and likely not be alive today. This means the disease is autosomal recessive, and both parents must be heterozygous for the mutation leading to disease. The probability of two heterozygous parents producing a child homozygous for the mutation is 1 in 4.

A: This answer can be eliminated immediately. If the disease gene were dominant, at least one of the child's parents would have had the disease.

C: While the disease gene is autosomal recessive, the likelihood of a child homozygous for it would be 1 in 4, not 1 in 16. Be careful not to calculate the probability of having two children both with the disease, as this is not what the question asks.

D: This answer implies that the female child has one copy of the disease gene from each parents. However, if this gene was on the X chromosome, her father would be affected by the disease since he only carries one X chromosome.

Passage VII Answers and Explanations (Questions 35-39)

In **cap-dependent translation initiation**, the open reading frame (ORF) of mRNA is established by the placement of the start codon and **initiator tRNA** in the ribosomal **peptidyl (P) site**. Methionine-charged initiator **tRNA** is brought to the P-site of the small ribosomal subunit by eukaryotic eIF2 and utilizes GTP. Internal ribosome entry sites (IRES) present within regions of some viral genomes **promote translation** of mRNAs in a **cap-independent** manner, avoiding many of the complex controls placed on eukaryotic host cell translational initiation and allowing translation to be initiated within an ORF. The **Taura syndrome virus (TSV)** contains two ORFs separated by an intragenic region (IGR). The Taura syndrome virus (TSV) contains an ORF which includes an intragenic region (IGR). The IGR contains an IRES that drives **translation of a second ORF without the aid of initiation factors.** Virologists studying TSV proposed a mechanism for translational initiation at the IRES within the IGR region of TSV, shown in Figure 1.

Key terms: cap-dependent translation initiation; open reading frame (ORF); start codon; initiator tRNA; peptidyl (P) site; internal ribosome entry sites (IRES); cap-independent translation initiation; Taura syndrome virus (TSV); intragenic region (IGR); initiation factor

Cause-and-Effect: normal, cap-dependent initiation begins at the start codon, the position of which defines the position at which the associated ORF begins, and attracts the initiator tRNA; this initiator tRNA binds the P site; some viral genomes contain an IRES; an IRES, located within the IGR of TSV promotes the initiation of transcription mid-ORFT at the IRES, driving translation also of a second ORF without initiation factors

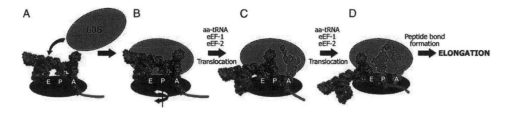

Figure 1 Schematic of translational initiation within the IGR region of TSV mRNA

Figure 1: Schematic of translation initiation, the steps of which are detailed below.

Step A. Formation of the **40S-IRES** complex at **pseudoknot I (PKI). PKI is a distinct secondary structural element** present at the IRES that resembles and functionally mimics the anticodon stem loop of tRNA bound to a cognate mRNA codon. PKI serves to **position the 40S-IRES** complex **within the ORF** in a **cap-independent manner.**

Key terms: 40S-IRES, pseudoknot I (PKI), anticodon stem loop

Cause-and-Effect: PKI is a secondary structural element which forms at the IRES and which mimics the structure of a charged-tRNA; PKI serves to position the 40S-IRES complex within the ORF in cap-independent initiation

Step B. **Large ribosomal subunit binding** and spontaneous 40S subunit rotation.

Step C. **Translocation of PKI** allows accommodation of the first **aminoacyl-tRNA (aa-tRNA), alanyl-tRNA^Ala** in the **aminoacyl (A) site**, catalyzed by eukaryotic elongation factors eEF-1 and eEF-2.

Key terms: aminoacyl-tRNA (aa-tRNA), alanyl-tRNA^{Ala}, aminoacyl (site; eEF-1, eEF-2)

Cause-and-Effect: Translocation of PKI precedes alanyl-tRNA^{Ala} binding to the A site; this reaction is catalyzed by eEF-1 and eEF-2

Step D. **PK1 remains bound following a second translocation**, allowing **accommodation** of an **aa-tRNA**. Step D is followed by peptide bond formation and elongation. followed by peptide bond formation and elongation.

Key terms: elongation

Cause-and-Effect: the second translocation event is followed by formation of the first peptide bond and the beginnings of elongation

35. Crystallographic studies revealed that the codon-like region of PKI strongly resembles the trinucleotide tRNA anticodon 5'-UCC-3'. What is the trinucleotide sequence within the IGR region of TSV mRNA most likely to be bound by PKI?
    A. 5'-AGG-3'
    B. 5'-CAA-3'
    C. 5'-GGA-3'
    D. 5'-AAC-3'

Choice **C** is correct. mRNA is read in the 5' to 3' direction by the ribosome; the mRNA sequence complementary to the anticodon sequence 5'-UCC-3', is then, in the 5' to 3' direction 5'-GGA-3'

36. Binding of the large ribosomal subunits at the IRES of TGV mRNA is powered by hydrolysis of the same nucleoside triphosphate as is hydrolyzed in cap-dependent eukaryotic initiation. This molecule is:
    A. ATP
    B. CTP
    C. GTP
    D. UTP

Choice **C** is correct. The first paragraph tells you that during eukaryotic translational initiation, methionine-charged initiator tRNA is brought to the P-site of the small ribosomal subunit by eukaryotic eIF2. Once there, GTP is hydrolyzed, signaling the dissociation of several factors from the small ribosomal subunit, which results in the association of the large subunit.

A: Adenosine triphosphate is not hydrolyzed as an energy source during cap initiation.
B: Cytidine triphosphate is an energy molecule similar to ATP, but its role as an energy coupler is limited to a much smaller subset of metabolic reactions. It serves as a coenzyme in metabolic reactions like the glycosylation of proteins.
D: Uridine triphosphate is a nucleotide involved in RNA synthesis but it is not utilized during cap-dependent initiation.

37. According to the virologists' mechanism, the initiation of translation in the IGR region of TSV mRNA is most likely to include which of the following events?
    A. Binding of the 40s ribosomal subunit to an AUG codon within the IGR region of TSV mRNA.
    B. PKI binding to the unoccupied 40s ribosomal subunit P site.
    C. Completed assembly of the 70s ribosome in eukaryotic hosts.
    D. Reversible association of PKI and the A site of the 40s ribosomal subunit.

Choice **D** is correct. The passage states that translocation of PKI allows accommodation of the first aminoacyl-tRNA at the A site. The mechanism presented in the passage further states that following two translocation events, PKI remains bound, and that those two translocation events allow for the binding of two charged-tRNA molecules—first by alanyl-tRNA^{Ala}, followed by a second aa-tRNA. This suggests that PKI must initially have been reversibly bound to the 40s ribosomal subunit A site.

A: The start codon AUG would not be present at the IRES of TSV mRNA, which the passage states is located within a TSV ORF.

B: The passage suggests that PKI must initially have been reversibly bound to the 40s ribosomal subunit A site.

C: The completed eukaryotic ribosome is the 80s ribosome.

38. During the normal process of eukaryotic translation, the start codon codes for:

   A. **methionine and is contained on a mature transcript containing a methylated purine nucleobase cap.**
   B. methionine and lacking a mature transcript containing a methylated purine nucleobase cap.
   C. N-formylmethionine and is contained on a mature transcript containing a methylated purine nucleobase cap.
   D. N-formylmethionine and lacking a mature transcript containing a methylated purine nucleobase cap.

Choice **A** is correct. During eukaryotic translational initiation, methionine-charged initiator tRNA is brought to the P-site of the small ribosomal subunit. Further, the 5' cap, found on the 5' end of eukaryotic mRNA molecules containing the codon, consists of a guanine nucleotide connected to the primary mRNA transcript via an unusual 5' to 5' triphosphate linkage. This guanosine residue is methylated at the 7 position directly after capping.

B: All mature eukaryotic mRNA molecules contain a 7-methylguanosine cap.

C, D: N-formylmethionine is the starting residue in the synthesis of proteins in bacteria and certain organellar genes.

39. What statement concerning movement of mRNA along the ribosome describes the mechanisms of cap-dependent initiation of translation in eukaryotes and the proposed mechanism of initiation in TSV mRNA?

   A. **Two TSV mRNA translocation events must occur prior to formation of the first peptide bond; a single translocation event must occur prior to formation of the first peptide bond in cap-dependent translation.**
   B. Two TSV mRNA translocation events must occur prior to formation of the first peptide bond; two translocation events must also occur prior to formation of the first peptide bond in cap-dependent translation.
   C. One TSV mRNA translocation event must occur prior to formation of the first peptide bond; one translocation events must also occur prior to formation of the first peptide bond in cap-dependent translation.
   D. One TSV mRNA translocation event must occur prior to formation of the first peptide bond; two translocation events must also occur prior to formation of the first peptide bond in cap-dependent translation.

Choice **A** is correct. The passage indicates that two translocation events must occur in order to situate two amino acids in adjacent A and P sites of the small ribosomal subunit during cap-independent initiation in TNV. Only then can the ribosomal peptidyl synthase activity catalyze their linkage in a peptide bond. In cap-dependent initiation, the initiator tRNA occupies the P site in the ribosome at the end of initiation, and the A site is ready to receive an aminoacyl-tRNA. After a single translocation event releasing the initiator tRNA and shifting the amino acid previously seated in the A site, a peptide bond is formed with the newly delivered amino acid residue of the A site.

Passage VIII Answers and Explanations (Questions 40-43)

Obesity is characterized by excessive circulating fatty acids, giving rise to many metabolic complications including insulin resistance. A strong correlation exists between intramuscular lipid (IML) concentration and the onset and severity of insulin resistance in both humans and rodents. It has previously been hypothesized that **elevated IML levels are responsible for insulin insensitivity** in the obese.

Key terms: intramuscular lipids (IML), insulin resistance

Cause-and-Effect: obesity involves excess circulating fatty acids and insulin resistance; IML concentration is correlated to increased risk and severity of insulin resistance in humans and rodents; some have hypothesized that IML elevation is responsible for insulin insensitivity

DGAT1 is a key enzyme in **intramuscular triglyceride (ITAG) synthesis**, catalyzing the **conversion** of diacylglycerol (DAG) and fatty acyl-CoA, formed from circulating fatty acids, into ITAG. Scientists examined the impact of DGAT1 in skeletal muscle lipid metabolism and muscle-specific insulin sensitivity by transiently overexpressing DGAT1 in the left tibialis anterior (TA) muscle of adult rats, fed either a standard rat dietary mix (chow) or a **high fat diet**, while using the **right leg of the same animal** as an **untreated control**.

Key terms: DGAT, intramuscular triglyceride (ITAG); diacylglycerol (DAG), fatty acyl-CoA, tibialis anterior (TA), chow

Cause-and-Effect: DGAT1 catalyzes the synthesis of triglycerides, including ITAG, from DAG and fatty acyl CoA; rats artificially overexpressing DGAT1 in their TA muscle were tested

The **effects of DGAT1 overexpression on IML** levels in rats fed a high-fat (HFD) or rodent chow diet is shown in Figure 1.

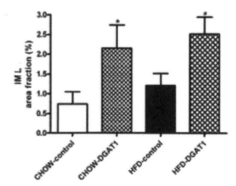

Figure 1: IML levels are greater in rats eating a high-fat diet than in those fed a normal diet; IML levels in both control groups are less than those in DGAT overexpressing TA muscle; IML levels are highest when DGAT is overexpressed in rats fed a high-fat diet

To determine whether IML content in TA muscle overexpressing DGAT1 was correlated with intramuscular DAG concentrations, DAG was measured in TA muscle overexpressing DGAT1 as well as in the untreated muscle. These measurements are shown in Figure 2.

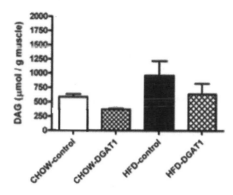

Figure 2 DAG content in the TA muscle of rats is greater in those fed high-fat (HFD) diets than those fed CHOW diets; increasing DGAT expression leads to a decrease in DAG for rats fed either diet

One week after introduction of DGAT1, **TA muscle insulin sensitivity** was assessed in vivo by measuring the **rate of radioisotope-labelled infusion of 2-deoxy-[3H]glucose (2DG) uptake**. The results in TA muscle are given in Figure 3.

Key terms: insulin sensitivity; 2-deoxy-[3H]glucose (2DG) uptake

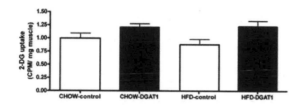

Figure 3: 2DG uptake in TA muscle is greater in CHOW-fed than in HFD-fed rats; uptake is increased versus control groups in TA muscle overexpressing DGAT1 for rats fed either diet

40. Based on passage information, which pair of factors would be LEAST likely to demonstrate an inverse relationship?
    A. **Circulating fatty acid concentration and IML concentration**
    B. Insulin sensitivity and dietary fat intake
    C. Fatty acyl-CoA and intramuscular DGAT1 concentration
    D. Insulin sensitivity and intramuscular DAG concentration

Choice **A** is correct. Circulating fatty acids are converted to fatty acyl-CoA, which is a substrate for the production of ITAG—of which IMLs are composed—in the reaction catalyzed by DGAT1. Increasing the concentration of the reaction substrate should lead to a subsequent increase in product—IML—concentration. This does not represent an inverse relationship.

B: Figure 3 shows that increasing dietary fat intake decreases insulin sensitivity. This is an inverse relationship.
C: Increasing intramuscular DGAT1 concentration should increase the rate of conversion of fatty acyl-CoA molecules into ITAG. This is an inverse relationship.
D: Figures 2 and 3 indicate that an increasing DGAT1 expression decreases intramuscular DAG concentration and increases insulin sensitivity. Additionally, the figures also show that mice fed a high-fat diet have higher intramuscular DAG and lower insulin sensitivity.

41. Molecules such as DAG are absorbed in the digestive tract:
    A. after chemical digestion in the mouth and stomach by gastric lipases.
    B. through active transport by transmembrane proteins in the brush border of the small intestine.
    C. only if a person has a fully functioning gall bladder and normal recycling of bile salts.
    D. <u>**following emulsification by bile salts, formation into micelles, and transport through lacteals.**</u>

Choice **D** is correct. Dietary fats are absorbed after being broken into monoacylglycerol and free fatty acids by pancreatic lipase. These lipid-soluble molecules can freely diffuse into intestinal cells and contribute to the formation of micelles, which then move into lacteals (specialized lymphatic vessels) and are moved into circulation.

A: Gastric lipase would contribute to digestion in the stomach only, not the mouth (one would hope not to regurgitate stomach digestive enzymes into the mouth!).
B: Lipid-soluble molecules are absorbed through diffusion directly through the plasma membrane of intestinal cells. Active transport is used for things like carbohydrate monomers and some amino acids.
C: The liver produces bile salts, so a person can still absorb some fats even after having had the gall bladder removed.

42. Based upon the results of the trials, when compared to rats fed a normal diet, the muscle tissue of rats fed a high fat diet and expressing DGAT1 normally will likely demonstrate:
    A. <u>**an increased rate of lipolysis.**</u>
    B. decreased oxidative breakdown of fatty acids.
    C. an increased rate of entry of glucose into glycolysis.
    D. a decreased rate of glycogen utilization.

Choice **A** is correct. Figure 3 shows that control rats expressing DGAT1 and fed a high fat diet are less insulin sensitive than those fed a normal diet. This suggests that lipolysis, normally inhibited by insulin, would occur at an increased rate.

B: Insulin inhibits the beta oxidation of fatty acids and promotes lipid synthesis. Insulin desensitization would increase the rate of fatty acid oxidation.
C: Insulin promotes glucose entry into insulin-sensitive tissue, including skeletal muscle, and further promotes entry of sugars into glycolysis. Insulin desensitization would decrease glycolytic flux.
D: Insulin promotes glycogenesis and inhibits glycogenolysis. Insulin desensitization would increase, rather than decrease, the rate of glycogen utilization.

43. Which statement correctly describes a relationship between the carbon-chain lengths of IMLs and a physical property of those lipids?

    A. As the number of carbons decreases, IML melting point is unchanged.

    B. <u>**As the number of carbons increases, IML boiling point increases.**</u>

    C. As the number of carbons decreases, IML boiling point is unchanged.

    D. As the number of carbons increases, IMFL melting point decreases.

Choice **B** is correct. The carbon-chain length of fatty acids is related to increased intermolecular forces between the atoms of the chain, and thus, an increase in the boiling and melting points of fats.

A: As the number of carbons decreases, IML melting point will decrease.

C: As the number of carbons increases, IML boiling point will increase.

D: As the number of carbons increases, IML melting point increases.

Discrete Set 3 Answers and Explanations (Questions 44-47)

44. Which of the following will NOT be added to a protein during post-translational modification?
    A. Sugars
    B. Lipids
    C. Phosphate groups
    D. **Chaperone proteins**

Choice **D** is correct. Chaperone proteins are not added to a protein, they help guide the protein as it is folded. These molecular chaperones assist the non-covalent folding and the assembly of other macromolecules. Chaperones are not present when the finished proteins perform their normal biological functions and have correctly completed the processes of folding and/or assembly.

A, B, C: These functional groups are all routinely added to a protein during post-translational modification.

45. What is the function of the nucleolus?
    A. **It is the site of ribosome production in eukaryotes.**
    B. It is the site of active DNA replication.
    C. It is the site of protein synthesis for nuclear proteins.
    D. It is the site of translation.

Choice **A** is correct. The nucleolus is the nuclear subdomain that assembles ribosomal subunits in eukaryotic cells. The nucleolar organizer regions of chromosomes, which contain the genes for pre-ribosomal ribonucleic acid (rRNA), serve as the foundation for nucleolar structure.

B: This occurs in the nucleus.
C: Proteins are synthesized in the cytoplasm.
D: Translation occurs at the ribosomes.

46. Which of the following processes is characterized by the formation of a sperm's pronucleus?
    A. Spermatogenesis
    B. **Fertilization**
    C. Puberty
    D. Meiosis

Choice **B** is correct. In fertilization, the cell membranes of the oocyte and sperm fuse. Each forms a pronucleus, which migrate towards each other in preparation for the first mitotic division.

A, C, D: These are all processes associated with the production of sperm, but the sperm does not form a pronucleus unless and until it actually fertilizes the egg.

47. In a fall off a ladder, a woman hits her head on a rock and suffers damage to her cerebellum. Which of the following activities is most likely to be affected?
    A. Voluntary movement of the hands to grasp and pick up objects
    B. Producing speech that has semantic content
    C. <u>**Playing the piano**</u>
    D. Pain sensation in the feet

Choice **C** is correct. The cerebellum controls coordinated movements that a person doesn't have to actively "think about" to achieve – things like walking, writing with a pen, juggling, or playing the piano.

A: Specific conscious voluntary movements are controlled by the motor cortex.
B: Wernicke's area is associated with tying meaning to speech.
D: Pain sensation is mediated by nociceptors.

Passage IX Answers and Explanations (Questions 48-51)

Septic shock syndrome can be triggered by **endotoxins,** specifically by **lipopolysaccharide (LPS)**, the major component of the **outer membrane** of all Gram-negative bacteria. LPS contains three components: the variable O antigen on the membrane surface, the core domain and lipid A. The lipid A domain, buried within the core of the bacterial cell membrane, **anchors LPS to the membrane**, and is responsible for much of the toxicity of Gram-negative bacteria.

Key terms: septic shock syndrome, endotoxins, lipopolysaccharide (LPS), Gram-negative bacteria, O antigen, core domain, lipid A

Cause-and-Effect: Gram-negative septic shock is due to the lipid A region of LPS in Gram-negative bacteria

In Gram-negative sepsis, the **LPS antigen attaches to a circulating LPS-binding protein**, and the **complex** then **binds** to a specific receptor on monocytes, macrophages, and neutrophils, leading to the release of potent cytokine proteins such as IL-6, MCP-1, and TNF-α. While these cytokines trigger the immune system to attempt to clear the microbial pathogens, if the infection is **not brought under control**, these secondary mediators can lead to the signs of septic shock: vasodilation, diminished cardiac output, decreased cardiac output, fever, and lung damage.

Key terms: LPS-binding protein, monocytes, macrophages, neutrophils, cytokines, IL-6, MCP-1, TNF-α

Cause-and-Effect: LPS antigen binds circulating LPS-binding proteins, which, as a complex with the binding protein, then binds receptors on specific white blood cells; this binding leads to the release of cytokines which trigger an immune response; if the infection is not cleared these cytokines and secondary mediators can lead to septic shock

One novel approach to the treatment of septic shock involves **EVK-203**, an **alkylpolyamine** compound that specifically binds to and neutralizes circulating LPS. In order to test the ability of EVK-203 to sequester LPS, mice received graded doses of **EVK-203**. Then, **following injection** of a **lethal dose of LPS**, plasma **levels of LPS-induced cytokines were measured**.

Key terms: EK-203, alkylpolyamine

Cause-and-Effect: EVK-203 binds LPS and removes it from circulation; levels of LPD-induced cytokines were measured to test the effectiveness of EVK-203

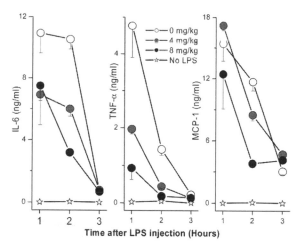

Figure 1: EVK-203 decreased LPS-related cytokine levels; the extent of cytokine inhibition generally increases with greater EVK-203 dosage

Ten mice were also administered the same dose of EVK-203 at various times before and after the administration of a LPS dose lethal to 50% of untreated-mice. Dose-dependent survival rates are shown in Figure 2.

Cause-and-Effect: survival rates for mice administered EVK-203 at various times before or after administration of a LPS dose lethal to 50% of untreated mice were measured

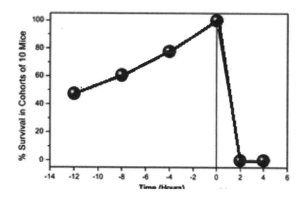

Figure 2: Percent survival of the mice was greater than the expected 50% survival rate for untreated mice administered the same LPS dose when EVK-203 was administered between 8 hours prior to LPS administration and concurrently with LPS administration; all mice survived when LPS and EVK-203 were administered concurrently; none survived if EVK-203 was administered following LPS administration

48. Like Gram-negative septic shock, Waterhouse-Friderichsen syndrome is due to the effects of bacterial endotoxins and, because of acute adrenal failure, can lead to septic shock. An individual suffering from the syndrome would NOT be expected to show what symptom?
    A. Low blood sugar
    B. Low blood pressure
    C. **<u>Decreased circulating potassium concentration</u>**
    D. Decreased circulating sodium concentration

Choice **C** is correct. WF syndrome is characterized by failure of the adrenal gland following systemic hemorrhage due to infection. As a result of the adrenal gland failure, there is no response to ACTH stimulation, and circulating mineralocorticoid and glucocorticoid levels drop precipitously. Deficiency of the glucocorticoids result in hypoglycemia (low blood sure), and lack of the mineralocorticoids —specifically aldosterone—causes both hyponatremia (low blood Na$^+$ concentrations) and hyperkalemia (elevated blood K$^+$ concentration).

A, B, D: Aldosterone's function is to act on the principal cells of the distal tubule and the collecting duct of the nephron, to upregulate and activate the basolateral Na$^+$/K$^+$ pumps, which pump three sodium ions out of the cell into the interstitial fluid, and two potassium ions into the cell from the interstitial fluid. This creates a concentration gradient which results in reabsorption of Na+ and water into the blood, and the secretion of K$^+$ into the lumen of collecting duct and eventually the urine. For the reasons described above, each of these symptoms could be seen in a patient suffering from WF syndrome.

49. The immune response leading to Gram-negative septic shock is most likely to be initiated when:
    A. exposed O antigen is bound by specific host antibodies.
    B. LPS secretes bacterial cytokines that precipitate an exaggerated immune response.
    C. **<u>bacterial cells are lysed and lipid A-containing membrane fragments are released into the circulation.</u>**
    D. bacterially-mediated endothelial damage causes activation of a local immune response.

Choice **C** is correct. The passage states that the pathway of Gram-negative sepsis initiation begins with attachment of the LPS antigen to a circulating LPS-binding protein, followed by binding of the complex to a specific receptor on monocytes, macrophages, and neutrophils. The passage additionally states that the lipid A domain is responsible for most of the toxic effects of LPS in Gram-negative shock, and that the domain, which serves to anchor LPS within the membrane, is buried within the core of the bacterial cell membrane. Taken together, these facts suggest that circulating LPS-binding protein must be able to access the lipid A domain of LPS. While under normal circumstances the lipid A domain is buried within the bacterial membrane, it could become accessible to circulating LPS-binding protein if bacterial cells are lysed and lipid A-containing membrane fragments are released into the circulation, as is stated in choice C.

A: The passage states LPS is primarily responsible for the toxic effects of Gram-negative sepsis—not O antigen—and that the pathway of Gram-negative sepsis begins with attachment of the LPS antigen to a circulating LPS-binding protein.
B: LPS does not secrete cytokines directly. Cytokines are released from leukocytes activated by binding the LPS-LPS binding protein complex.
D: The passage states that Gram-negative sepsis initiation begins with attachment of the LPS antigen to a circulating LPS-binding protein.

50. Information presented in the passage most *challenges* what conclusion concerning the protective effects of EVK-203 against LPS exposure in the mouse model?
    A. **Plasma concentrations sufficient to provide some protection against LPS-lethality persist for up to 12 hours.**
    B. Its protective effects are reflected by a reduction in circulating LPS-induced cytokines levels.
    C. It is maximally effective in mouse models when administered concurrently with LPS administration.
    D. EVK-203 must be present prior to activation of the innate immune response to provide protection from LPS-lethality.

Choice **A** is correct. Figure 2 shows that the percent survival of the mice tested was greater than the expected 50% survival rate for untreated mice only when EVK-203 was administered 0-8 hours prior to LPS administration. Between 8-12 hours prior, survival rates are below the 50% survival rate seen in untreated mice receiving the same dose of LPS.

B: Figure 1 shows that levels of all three LPS-related cytokines, which the passage indicates are largely-responsible for the pathologically consequences of septic shock—are reduced more quickly in the presence, than in the absence of LPS. And that the rate of that reduction is generally positively correlated with increased EVK-203 dosage.
C: Figure 2 shows 100% survival when LPS and EVK-203 were administered concurrently.
D: Figure 2 gives a near 0% survival rate when LPS is administered prior to EVK-203 treatment; it would not be unreasonable to conclude that the protective effects of EVK-203 require its presence prior to activation of the innate immune response to LPS.

51. Release of TNF-α leads to the activation of multiple transcription factors. One such factor, NFAT, increases pro-inflammatory calcium signaling by increasing expression of a protein product through binding downstream of its transcriptional start site. The region of DNA bound by NFAT can best characterized as a(n):
    A. **enhancer.**
    B. co-repressor.
    C. promoter.
    D. activator.

Choice **A** is correct. An enhancer is a short segment of DNA that can be bound by transcription factors (activators) to enhance transcription of a gene or genes. Enhancers are generally cis-acting, but can be upstream or downstream from the transcriptional start site.

B: A corepressor is a small molecule or protein that represses the expression of genes by binding to and activating a repressor transcription factor. The repressor in turn binds to a gene promoter (a sequence of DNA adjacent to the regulated gene), thereby blocking transcription of that gene. The question refers to the region of DNA bound by NFAT.
C: A promoter is a region of DNA that initiates transcription of a particular gene. Promoters are located near the transcription start sites of genes, on the same strand and upstream on the DNA (towards the 5' region of the sense strand). The question indicates that NFAT binds a region of DNA downstream of the transcriptional start site.
D: An activator is a protein that increases gene transcription of a gene or set of genes. Most activators are DNA-binding proteins that bind to enhancers or promoter-proximal elements. The question refers to the region of DNA bound by NFAT.

Passage X Answers and Explanations (Questions 52-55)

For most adolescent girls, the onset of **puberty** occurs around age 11 or 12. This period is marked by a number of physical changes, including body hair growth and the onset of **menstruation**. The **menstrual cycle** is broken into **three phases**. The first phase, the follicular phase, begins with Gonadotropin releasing hormone (GnRH) secretion from the hypothalamus. GnRH then stimulates the release of follicle stimulating hormone (FSH), the hormone responsible for follicular development, from the anterior pituitary gland. As the follicle develops, it releases large amounts of estrogen. Risings levels of estrogen in the blood signal the release of luteinizing hormone (LH) from the anterior pituitary gland, commencing the next phase of menstruation, ovulation. FSH and LH surges stimulate the developed follicle to rupture and eject an egg into the Fallopian tube where it may be fertilized before reaching the uterus. The final stage, the luteal phase, is characterized by the transformation of the ruptured follicle into the corpus luteum. The corpus luteum releases progesterone and a small amount of estrogen. Progesterone causes the thickening of the endometrial lining. If **the egg is not fertilized**, the corpus luteum atrophies, progesterone levels fall, and the endometrium is shed, allowing the cycle to begin again.

Key Terms: puberty, menstruation, follicular phase, GnRH, FSH, anterior pituitary gland, estrogen

Contrast: FSH causes follicles to develop, whereas the LH surge leads to follicular rupture.

Cause-and-Effect: GnRH secretion leads to FSH release, rising estrogen levels lead to LH release, LH surge causes the developed follicle to rupture leaving behind the corpus luteum, progesterone release causes the thickening of the endometrium, lack of fertilization leads to corpus luteum atrophy

As women age into their late 40s and early 50s, they enter a period called **menopause** characterized by the cessation of menstruation and the woman's ability to reproduce. Menopausal women often experience significant estrogen deficiency and bone loss. These two physiological effects may be related – it is believed that estrogen acts through high affinity **receptors** on **osteoblasts** and **osteoclasts**, the cells responsible for bone growth and breakdown, respectively, to regulate bone density and prevent **osteoporosis**. Once this regulation is removed through menopause, **dramatic increases in porosity of the bone are seen** (See Figure 1)

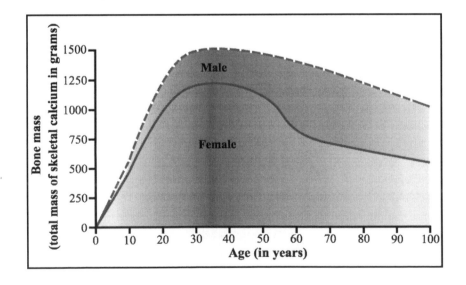

Figure 1 Bone Mass as a Function of Age and Sex

Key Terms: menopause, osteoblast, osteoclast, osteoporosis

Contrast: Osteoblasts build up bone, whereas osteoclasts break it down.

Cause-and-Effect: Menopause appears to lead to dramatic losses in bone density.

52. In what phase of meiosis is an egg when it is traveling down the Fallopian tube prior to contact with a sperm cell?
    A. Prophase I
    B. Anaphase I
    C. **Metaphase II**
    D. It is not undergoing meiosis at that point.

Choice **C** is correct. A female baby is born with roughly all the eggs she will ever have (i.e., mitosis of oocytes ends at birth), but they are all halted in Prophase I of meiosis until the child reaches puberty. After puberty, each month an egg develops in the follicle of the ovary but remains in Metaphase II of meiosis until it is fertilized in the Fallopian Tube by a sperm cell. Then meiosis finishes.

A: Oocytes are in Prophase I until one begins to mature during a particular menstrual cycle. By the time they are traveling down the Fallopian Tube, they have progressed to Metaphase II.
B: The egg would have already completed Anaphase I by this point, and would be halted in Metaphase II.
D: Meiosis is definitely occurring in the egg cell. It is occurring throughout the entire period a female is capable of reproducing – most egg cells are in Prophase I unless the egg is maturing during a particular menstrual cycle, at which point it will progress to Metaphase II and stay there until it is fertilized.

53. Which of the following choices represents a valid combination of a menstrual cycle hormone and its effect in a man?
    A. LH stimulates Leydig cells to produce estrogen
    B. **FSH stimulates Sertoli cells to produce sperm**
    C. Estrogen stimulates the development of male secondary sex characteristics (e.g., body hair and voice deepening)
    D. Prolactin leads to lactation in men

Choice **B** is correct. FSH in men does cause the Sertoli cells of the seminiferous tubules to produce sperm, which then go on to mature in the epididymis.

A: LH causes the Leydig cells in the testicles to produce testosterone, not estrogen.
C: Testosterone stimulates the development of male secondary sex characteristics, not estrogen.
D: Prolactin release can cause male lactation, but prolactin is not a menstrual cycle hormone.

54. Which of the following osteoblast and osteoclast activity levels would result in the porosity of bone seen in patients suffering from osteoporosis?
    A. High levels of osteoblast activity and low levels of osteoclast activity
    B. High levels of osteoblast activity and high levels of osteoclast activity
    C. Low levels of osteoblast activity and low levels of osteoclast activity
    D. **Low levels of osteoblast activity and high levels of osteoclast activity**

Choice **D** is correct. Osteoporosis is the loss of bone density/mass. According to the passage, osteoblasts build bone while osteoclasts break it down. Thus, high levels of osteoclast activity, without high levels of osteoblast activity to build bone back up, would result in increasing porosity of bone.

A: This would result in increasing bone mass over time, not decreasing bone mass.
B: The high activity levels of both of these cells would have opposing effects, resulting in an insignificant net change in bone mass.
C: The low activity levels of both of these cells would have opposing effects, resulting in an insignificant net change in bone mass.

55. According to the passage, the rate of bone mass loss is highest, on average, during which years of a woman's life?
    A. From age 20 to 30
    B. From age 30 to 40
    C. **From age 50 to 60**
    D. From age 80 to 90

Choice **C** is correct. According to the chart provided in the figure, the slope is most negative for women between ages 50 and 60 years.

A: Bone mass is steadily increasing during this period, not decreasing.
B: Bone mass has just begun to decrease during this period, but the rate of decrease is not yet at its maximum.
D: The rate of bone mass loss is not as high here as it is between the ages of 50 and 60 years.

Discrete Set 4 Answers and Explanations (Questions 56-59)

56. Menstruation is preceded by which of the following hormone changes?
    A. A surge in luteinizing hormone
    B. A decrease in estrogen and an increase in progesterone
    C. **A decrease in estrogen and progesterone**
    D. An increase in aldosterone

Choice **C** is correct. A drop in progesterone leads to menstruation, the sloughing off of the endometrial wall.

A: The LH surge precedes ovulation, not menstruation.
B: The increase in progesterone leads to a build up of the endometrial wall, not sloughing off.
D: Aldosterone is associated with salt/water balance, not the menstrual cycle.

57. Which of the following is NOT a chiral molecule?
    A. Alpha-hydroxybutyric acid
    B. Beta-hydroxybutyric acid
    C. **Gamma-hydroxybutyric acid**
    D. 3-hydroxybutyric acid

Choice **C** is correct. This question relies solely on your being able to reproduce or think about what the answer choice molecules look like. They are all butyric acid which has the following form: $CH_3CH_2CH_2COOH$. The alpha, beta and gamma carbons are carbons 2, 3, and 4 respectively on the butyric acid. Thus, if there is a hydroxyl group on the gamma carbon, the molecule will not be chiral, so choice C is correct.

A: This molecule has a stereogenic center at C-2.
B: This molecule has a stereogenic center at C-3.
D: This molecule is the same as beta-hydroxybutyric acid and has a stereogenic center at C-3.

58. Which of the following is a six carbon molecule?
    A. Oxaloacetate
    B. **Citrate**
    C. Acetyl-CoA
    D. Ribose

Choice **B** is correct. This question is asking us to remember a bit about the Krebs cycle and ribose. Citrate is formed from the combination of oxaloacetate with acetyl CoA, forming a six carbon compound.

A: Oxaloacetate is a four carbon compound.
C: Acetyl CoA is a four carbon compound.
D: Ribose is a 5 carbon sugar.

59. During which phase of meiosis does crossing over occur?
    A. **Prophase I**
    B. Anaphase I
    C. Metaphase II
    D. Anaphase II

Choice **A** is correct. This question requires us to remember that crossing over occurs when homologous chromosomes are lined up in meiosis I. Homologous pairs form chiasmata and swap genetic material during prophase I.

B: In anaphase I of meiosis chromosomes move to the opposite cell poles. Similar to mitosis, microtubules such as the kinetochore fibers interact to pull the chromosomes to the cell poles.
C: In metaphase II of meiosis, the chromosomes line up at the metaphase II plate at the cell's center. Also, the kinetochore fibers of the sister chromatids point toward opposite poles.
D: In anaphase II, sister chromatids separate and begin moving to opposite ends (poles) of the cell. Once the paired sister chromatids separate from one another, each is considered a full chromosome. They are referred to as daughter chromosomes. in preparation for the next stage of meiosis, the two cell poles also move further apart during the course of anaphase II. At the end of anaphase II, each pole contains a complete compilation of chromosomes.

TIMED
SECTION 4
59 Questions, 95 Minutes

(Use the tear-out answer sheet provided in Appendix D)

Passage I (Questions 1-5)

The first step in the metabolism of heme released from degraded red blood cells is its oxidation by the microsomal enzyme heme oxygenase, resulting in the green pigment biliverdin. The next step is the reduction of biliverdin to a yellow tetrapyrol pigment called bilirubin. This "unconjugated" bilirubin is bound to albumin and transported through the bloodstream to the liver. In the liver, it is conjugated with glucuronic acid by the enzyme glucuronyl transferase, forming bilirubin diglucuronide—"conjugated bilirubin." From the liver, this solubilized form of bilirubin is excreted, initially as part of bile, and eventually, from the body.

In neonates, benign "physiological" jaundice is of least concern clinically, and tends to develop after the first 24 hours of life because of an accumulation of unconjugated bilirubin in the blood (hyperbilirubinemia). This leads to the symptoms of jaundice, including a pronounced yellowing of the skin and sclera. Alternatively, neonatal jaundice may be of greater concern if a pathological condition is responsible for an elevation of bilirubin. Severe hyperbilirubinemia, especially elevation of conjugated bilirubin, may cause accumulation of bilirubin in the brain leading to irreversible neurological damage—a condition referred to as kernicterus.

A pediatrician evaluating the cases of two newborns made the observations recorded below (Note: In infants, normal total serum bilirubin (conjugated + unconjugated) < 12 mg/dL, conjugated bilirubin < 2 mg/dL, unconjugated bilirubin < 10 mg/dL).

Case 1
A 3-day-old male infant born exhibiting yellow discoloration of the skin, most notably of the forehead and neck.

Case 2
A 2-week-old, healthy female infant is slightly jaundiced. Labs show a total bilirubin of 18 mg/dl and a conjugated bilirubin of 0.8 mg/dl.

1. The increased susceptibility of neonates to the development of jaundice or kernicterus is LEAST likely to be due to what factor?

    A. The blood–brain barrier is not fully functional in neonates.

    B. Fetal red blood cells are rapidly degraded and replaced by adult red blood cells shortly before birth.

    C. Decreased synthesis of albumin versus adults increases the fraction of free bilirubin solubilized in the blood.

    D. Relatively immature hepatic metabolic pathways are unable to conjugate bilirubin as quickly as those of adults

2. Jaundice can occur during pregnancy in mothers with an inherited increase in the binding affinity of a particular class of nuclear receptors present in liver cells. A peak in the concentration of the substrate for these receptors elsewhere in the body triggers ovulation. This substrate is:

    A. estrogen.

    B. FSH.

    C. LH.

    D. progesterone.

3. Which of the following individual findings would be most concerning and prompt further evaluation of the infant in Case 1?

    A. Total serum bilirubin level of 14 mg/dL

    B. Appearance of the infant's jaundice first occurring 48 hours after birth

    C. Unconjugated bilirubin of 12 mg/dL

    D. Conjugated bilirubin of 4 mg/dL

4. What diagnosis is most consistent with the information considered by the pediatrician in Case 2?

    A. Defective hepatic bilirubin excretion

    B. Deficiency of glucuronyl transferase

    C. Lack of a fully-developed gallbladder

    D. Blockage of the common bile duct

5. The contents of bilirubin-containing bile serve which of the following digestive functions when released into the duodenum?

    A. To solubilize ingested fats and decrease duodenal pH

    B. To cleave ester linkages in ingested fat molecules and decrease duodenal pH

    C. To solubilize ingested fats and increase duodenal pH

    D. To cleave ester linkages in ingested fat molecules and increase duodenal pH

Passage II (Questions 6-10)

The pituitary gland is a major hub in the body's endocrine system. The gland is split into two parts called the anterior pituitary and posterior pituitary gland, which differ in the hormones they release. The anterior pituitary contains five types of cells, each secreting a different hormone. Those cells are called corticotropes, thyrotropes, prolactins, gonadotropes, and somatotropes.

The anterior pituitary's secretion of hormones is regulated by hormones released by the hypothalamus. This is possible because the hypothalamus and anterior pituitary are connected in the hypophyseal portal system, a system of blood vessels connecting the two glands. This system is illustrated in Figure 1.

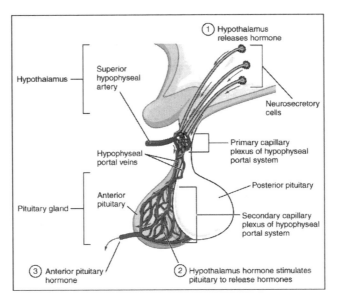

Figure 1 The anterior pituitary and hypothalamus

Some hormones secreted by the hypothalamus include gonadotropin releasing hormone, corticotropin releasing hormone, prolactin releasing hormone, and GH releasing hormone.

Hormone secretion from the anterior pituitary can also be regulated by other body systems. The molecule gamma-aminobutyric acid can stimulate the secretion of growth hormone, luteinizing hormone, and thyroid stimulating hormone.

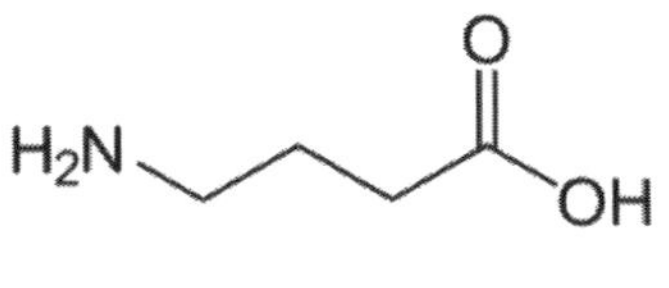

Figure 2 Gamma aminobutyric acid

Prostaglandins are a class of lipids that inhibit ACTH release and stimulate TSH, GH and LH release. Prostaglandins always contain 20 carbons and have a 5-carbon ring.

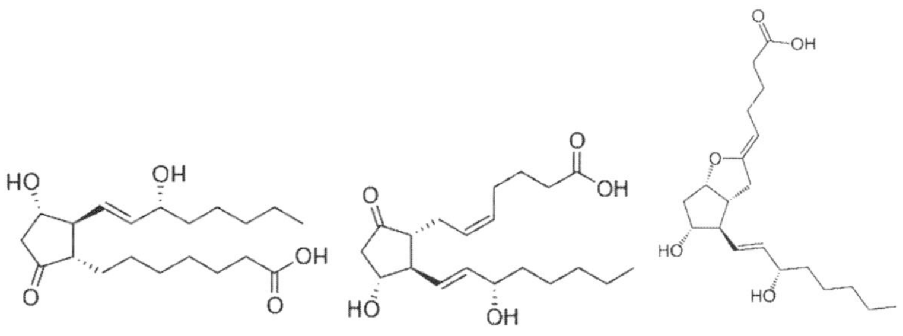

Figure 3 Prostaglandins E1, E2, and I2 (left to right)

6. What is another name for gamma-amino butyric acid?
   A. amino 4-butyric acid
   B. 4-carboxy butanamine
   C. 4-amino butanoic acid
   D. 1-hydroxy 4-amino butanone

7. Which of the following is the LEAST likely effect of an increase in GH secretion from the anterior pituitary?
   A. Increased bone growth
   B. Increased secretion of GHRH
   C. Decreased secretion of calcitonin
   D. Decreased activity of prostaglandins on somatotropes

8. Which type of cell most likely releases LH and FSH from the anterior pituitary?
   A. Gonadotropes
   B. Somatotropes
   C. Corticotropes
   D. Thyrotropes

9. What is the significance of the number given in the name of prostaglandins E1, E2, and I2?
   A. It is an indication of the number of ring structures in the molecule.
   B. It is an indication of the size of the prostaglandin.
   C. It is an indication of the number of double bonds in the molecule.
   D. It is an indication of the number of acidic functional groups.

10. Which of the following could cause an increase in T3 production?
    I. A tumor in the thyrotropes of the anterior pituitary
    II. A decrease in TRH production
    III. A decrease in gamma-aminobutyric acid production

    A. I only
    B. I and II only
    C. II and III only
    D. I and III only

Passage III (Questions 11-15)

Recombination is the exchange of genes between homologous chromosomes. This commonly occurs as a result of crossing over during meiosis I. The likelihood of crossing over appears to be correlated with the size of the chromosome. Crossing over results from the formation of Holliday junctions, a junction between four strands of DNA.

Two common forms of genetic recombination involving Holliday junctions occur during prophase and metaphase of meiosis I. The first occurs when corresponding strands on each chromosome are broken. A single strand cleavage on each homolog will result in the Holliday junction shown in Figure 1. There are two ways to resolve the Holliday junction. The first is for enzymes to cut the strands at point B or at points A and C. The latter is shown in Figure 1.

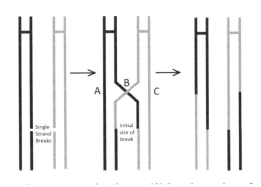

Figure 1 A single Holliday junction formed by single strand breaks in homologous chromosomes

A second common form of Holliday junction recombination that occurs during meiosis I is shown in Figure 2. This occurs when there is a double strand break in one chromosome. After several enzymatic attempts to rectify the situation, the chromosomes have a chance of ending up with the structure shown in the middle of Figure 2 with two Holliday junctions.

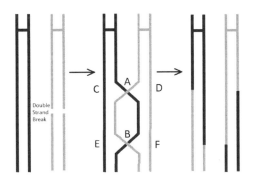

Figure 2 A double Holliday junction formed by a double strand break in one chromosome

In order to rectify this system of Holliday junctions, the DNA must be cleaved in two locations. There are two ways of doing this. The first is to cleave the DNA at A and B. This will result in nonrecombinant chromosomes. The second option is to cleave first at A or B and second at C and D together or E and F together. When this happens we will get two recombinant chromosomes that have exchanged a significant amount of genetic material.

11. Why will cleaving at A and B in Figure 2 result in nonrecombinant chromosomes?
    A. There would be no interchange of genetic material
    B. The segment of DNA that is interchanged will not likely contain any significant number of genes
    C. The cleavage would result in the exchange of the whole sister chromatids
    D. The cleavage would result in two free-floating segments of DNA

12. Which of the following is the most likely result if the Holliday junction in Figure 1 is cleaved at point B?

    A.

    B.

    C.

    D.

13. Which chromosome is most likely to experience crossing over?
    A. 1 (2000 genes)
    B. 18 (200 genes)
    C. X (800 genes)
    D. Y (50 genes)

14. Is it possible for genetic recombination to occur during meiosis II?
    A. Yes, sister chromatids on one chromosome can exchange genetic material
    B. Yes, slight overlap of adjacent chromosomal arms makes it possible for crossing over to occur between two nonhomologous chromosomes
    C. No, recombination requires two homologous but nonidentical chromosomes
    D. No, sister chromatids cannot get close enough during metaphase II

15. Which of the following combinations of DNA cuts will result in the greatest amount of base pairs exchanged between the two chromosomes in figure 2?
    A. Cleaving at A, E, and F
    B. Cleaving at A, C, and D
    C. Cleaving at B, E, and F
    D. Cleaving at B, C, and D

Discrete Set 1 (Questions 16-18)

These questions are **NOT** related to a passage.

16. Which of the following is likely to have gap junctions in its cell membrane?
    A. Erythrocyte
    B. Motor neuron
    C. Sperm cell
    D. Skin cell

17. Which of the following is most directly responsible for initiating skeletal muscle contraction?
    A. K^+
    B. Cl^-
    C. Na^+
    D. Ca^{2+}

18. Which of the following is NOT a function of carbonic anhydrase?
    A. Maintain a pH balance in the blood
    B. Transport carbon dioxide out of tissue
    C. Allow carbon dioxide to diffuse into the lungs
    D. Regulate hemoglobin's affinity for oxygen

Passage IV (Questions 19-22)

The average length of a human protein-coding gene is 27 kbp, but the average mRNA exported to the cytosol consists of only 1340 nt coding sequence, 1070 nt UTRs, and a poly-A tail. Only about 10% of the average pre-mRNA is exonic sequences, joined by pre-mRNA splicing. This splicing is carried out by a spliceosome, which is composed of five small nuclear RNAs (snRNAs) and associated protein complexes. Assembly of the spliceosome on a pre-mRNA is initiated by recognition of specific sequence elements such as 5'- and 3'-end splice sites, and the branch point sequence. The spliceosome then catalyzes the excision of introns and the ligation of exons.

Which sequences are expressed as exons is not always the same: one gene can code for multiple proteins as a result of alternative splicing. This process is estimated to affect more than 88% of human protein-coding genes. More than 25% of alternative exons include stop codons, which results in translation of truncated proteins or degradation of the mRNA. Because of their ubiquity, it is not surprising that changes in alternative splicing are frequently found in cases of human diseases.

Hutchinson-Gilford progeria syndrome (HGPS) is a rare disorder clinically characterized by features of premature aging such as postnatal growth retardation, premature atherosclerosis, lack of subcutaneous fat, and alopecia. The median age to which a person with HGPS lives is 13.4 years. Changes in splicing of the nuclear lamin A/C (LMNA) gene have been identified in cases of HGPS. This gene normally codes for a structural protein called prelamin A, which becomes lamin A when its farnesyl group binds the nuclear rim and is cleaved from the molecule. Lamin A, along with lamin B and lamin C, make up the nuclear lamina and provide structural support for the nucleus. A mutation in exon 11 of the nuclear lamin A/C (LMNA) gene that activates a cryptic splice site results in production of a truncated protein called progerin that acts in a dominant fashion.

19. A mutation in splicing factors PRPF31/U4-61k and PRP8 is the cause of the autosomal dominant form of retinis pigmentosa. What is likely the reason that diseases caused by mutations in core elements of splicing machinery, such as in this case, are rare?
    A. Signals on mRNA splice sites are read by the ribosome, which will therefore not translate introns.
    B. Any one splicing factor is not necessary for proper cell functioning because of systemic redundancy.
    C. Genes for splicing machinery are highly conserved across species.
    D. Defects in general splicing machinery are not usually compatible with life.

20. The farnesyl group of the progerin protein cannot be removed and the protein remains bound to the nuclear rim. How might this lead to the symptoms of HGPS?
    A. Killer T cells recognize progerin and induce the cells to apoptose.
    B. This weakens the nuclear lamina, which limits the cell's ability to divide.
    C. Progerin binding alters the nuclear membrane, making it less permeable to exiting mRNA molecules.
    D. Progerin cannot translocate into the cytoplasm to aid in translation of other proteins.

21. You must design an experiment to study alternative splicing in HGPS and choose to use E. coli as the model organism. Why will this experiment not be successful?
    I. HGPS symptoms are a result of lack of structural support for the nucleus.
    II. Prokaryotes lack a spliceosome.
    III. Prokaryotic RNA polymerase cannot transcribe human genes.

    A. II
    B. I and II
    C. I and III
    D. I, II, and III

22. Given its inheritance pattern, would you expect HGPS to be a prevalent condition?
    A. Yes. Any disease caused by mutated DNA will be passed on.
    B. Yes. Both alleles have to be mutated to produce disease, and this is unlikely to occur in one generation.
    C. No. It is caused by errors in splicing, not errors in the DNA itself, and only DNA is inherited.
    D. No. The condition causes death at a young age and is therefore unlikely to be passed on.

Passage V (Questions 23-26)

Carbonic anhydrase is an enzyme found in almost all human tissue, but most abundantly in red blood cells. Carbonic anhydrase catalyzes the formation of carbonic acid from CO_2 and H_2O as well as the dehydration of carbonic acid to form CO_2 and H_2O.

Reaction 1 $\qquad\qquad\qquad CO_2 + H_2O \leftrightarrow H_2CO_3 \leftrightarrow HCO_3^- + H^+$

The enzyme works via the activation of a water molecule by a zinc ion held in place by three histidine residues. When CO_2 is introduced into the active site, the activated water initiates a nucleophilic attack on the carbon atom. The mechanism is aided by a threonine residue as well as an amino acid that activates the hydroxyl group on threonine. The mechanism is shown in Figure 1.

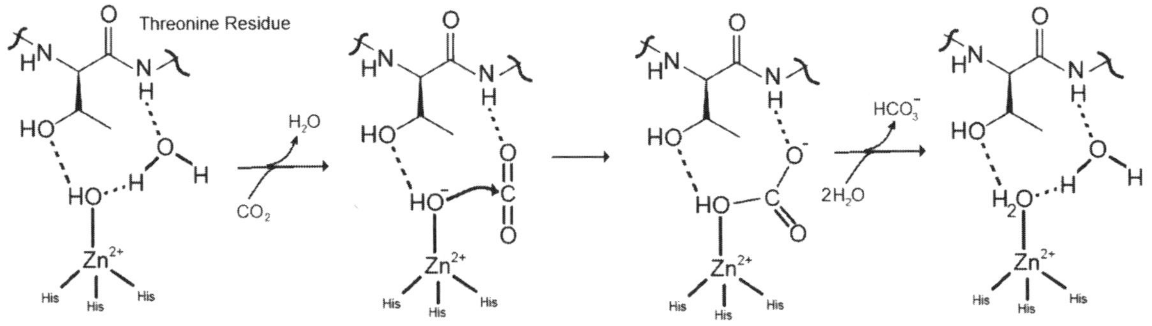

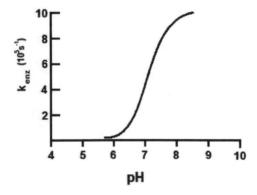

Figure 1 Forward reaction mechanism of carbonic anhydrase

The reaction rate of carbonic anhydrase is extremely fast. About 10^6 reactions per second can be performed in the forward or reverse directions. The rate of reaction of the enzyme is dependent on the surrounding pH. Activity is at a maximum at or above a pH of 8. Below a pH of 8, the rate decreases in a sigmoidal fashion.

Figure 2 The activity of carbonic anhydrase as a function of pH

23. Why is the forward reaction favored in tissues?
    A. There is more carbonic anhydrase in tissue than in the lungs
    B. There is more carbonic anhydrase near the lungs than in the tissue.
    C. There is more CO_2 in the lungs than in the tissue.
    D. There is more CO_2 in the tissue than in the lungs.

24. Which of the following would inhibit the forward reaction of carbonic anhydrase most effectively via competitive inhibition?
    A. D_2O
    B. Cl^-
    C. H_2CO_3
    D. CO_2

25. Which of the following would best help to activate the oxygen in the hydroxyl group of the side group of threonine?
    A. Lysine
    B. Histidine
    C. Proline
    D. Glutamic acid

26. Which of the following enzymes could most likely replace threonine in the mechanism shown in Figure 1 without the enzyme losing its functionality?
    A. Cysteine
    B. Serine
    C. Tyrosine
    D. Glutamic acid

Discrete Set 2 (Questions 27-30)

These questions are **NOT** related to a passage.

27. Which of the following are modes of transport for CO_2?
    I. Binding hemoglobin
    II. Dissolving in the plasma
    III. Binding red blood cell membranes

    A. I only
    B. II only
    C. I and II only
    D. II and III only

28. If the recessive phenotype is expressed in 32 out of 200 individuals in a population. How many individuals in this population would be carriers of the disease?
    A. 32
    B. 48
    C. 96
    D. 128

29. Which of the following are true about *Clostridium perfringens*, the bacterium responsible for gangrene?
    I. *Clostridium perfringens* can undergo mitosis.
    II. *Clostridium perfringens* can undergo meiosis.
    III. *Clostridium perfringens* contains a single circular chromosome.

    A. I only
    B. II only
    C. III only
    D. I and III only

30. How many distinct stop codons does the human genome possess?
    A. 1
    B. 3
    C. 61
    D. 64

THIS PAGE LEFT

INTENTIONALLY BLANK

Passage VI (Questions 31-34)

The perception of color is a process regulated by many factors. The first event in neurological chain that allows us to perceive color is a photon of light entering the eye. When focused correctly, the wave should strike the back of the eye at the retina. In the center of the retina, the fovea, humans have three kinds of cone cells. These cells are responsible for transmitting the signal for color vision to our brain. These cones are designated L, M, and S which stand for long, medium and short. The names represent the wavelength of light that the cone is receptive to. The peak wavelengths for L, M, and S cone responses are about 570, 540, and 450 nm respectively. The brain will receive signals of varying strength from these three cones, which when blended will allow the brain to interpret the signal as a color.

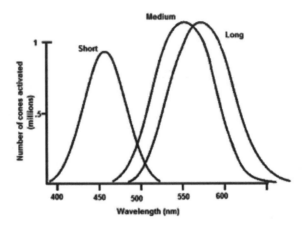

Figure 1 Activation of S, M, and L cones as a function of light wavelength

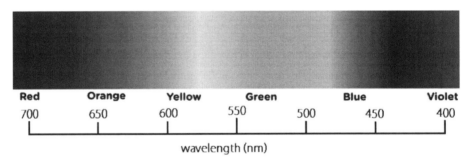

Figure 2 The spectrum of visible light

Cone cells are sensitive only to brighter levels of light than those to which rod cells will respond. When vision is employing cones, we can see much more accurately and can tell when two stimuli are separated. This lends to a greater visual acuity. This is the case because cone cells each have individual connections to the optic nerve as opposed to rod cells, which are bundled together.

Rhodopsin is the protein in rod cells that undergoes a change to propagate a signal when struck by light. In cones, there are other photopsins, called photopsin I, II, and III. These photopsins differ in only a few amino acids from rhodopsin and function the same way. Photopsin I responds to yellow-green light, photopsin II to yellow light, and photopsin III to bluish-violet light.

Deuteranopia is a color vision deficiency in which the medium photoreceptors are absent. The discrimination of red and green hues is affected by this while discrimination of blues and violets is not significantly affected. It is an X-linked disorder.

31. Why is a person with deuteranopia still able to see blues and violets?
    A. Their perception of blues and violets depends more on the amount of short cone cells that are activated than the mixture of S, M, and L cone cells activated.
    B. Their perception of blues and violets depends more on the mixture of short and medium cone cells activated than the mixture of short and long.
    C. Their perception of blues and violets depends more on long cone cells than medium cone cells.
    D. Their perception of blues and violets is compensated for by medium cone cells.

32. Which photopsin is present in most abundance in short cone cells?
    A. Photopsin I
    B. Photopsin II
    C. Photopsin III
    D. Rhodopsin

33. Which of the following best allows the human brain to produce more complex or intricate interpretations of stimuli from light?
    A. The strength of the electrochemical impulse propagated through each nerve on the way to the brain
    B. The quantity of impulses received by the brain at one time
    C. The speed with which the brain receives a neurochemical transmission
    D. A mixture of the strength and speed of the axonal signals sent to the brain

34. Which of the following graphs most closely represents the total absorbance of all 3 types of cones as a function of wavelength?

    A.

    B.
    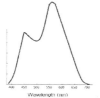

    C.
    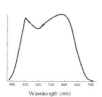

    D.
    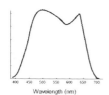

Passage VII (Questions 35-39)

The kidney can, in a sense, be considered two separate organs. Glucose utilization occurs predominantly in the renal medulla, whereas glucose release is confined to the renal cortex. This functional partition is a result of differences in the distribution of enzymes along the nephron. Therefore, the release of glucose by the normal kidney is mainly, if not exclusively, a result of renal cortical gluconeogenesis, whereas glucose uptake and utilization occur in other parts of the kidney.

Animal and in vitro experiments indicate that insulin, growth hormone, free fatty acids, and cortisol all influence glucose release from the kidneys. Cortisol and free fatty acids containing an even-number of carbons in their chain have both been shown to stimulate renal gluconeogenesis, while in normal humans, a physiological increase in circulating insulin during hyperglycemic (high blood glucose concentration) states suppresses renal glucose release and increase renal glucose uptake. This suppression of renal glucose release is thought to be due to more than only a simple reduction in gluconeogenic substrate availability in the kidneys.

To help clarify the relationship between hormones and glucose balance in the body, normal volunteers were injected with either glucagon or epinephrine at levels equal to those seen during states of hypoglycemia (low blood glucose concentration). The infusion of glucagon had no measureable effect on renal glucose release or uptake. Changes in glucose release systemically, as well as in the liver and kidneys, due to epinephrine infusion are shown in Figure 1.

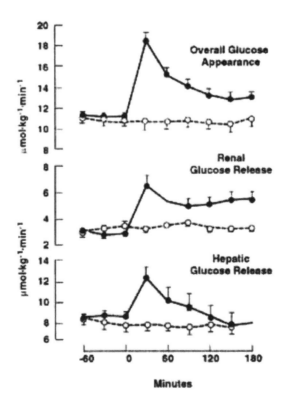

Figure 1 Effect of epinephrine infusion on overall, renal (kidney) and hepatic (liver) glucose release in normal volunteers (Note: infusion administered at time = 0 minutes, the open circles represent controls and the black circles represent epinephrine injection.)

35. Which of the following findings, if true, would most support the idea that insulin's suppression of renal glucose release is NOT due to an insulin-mediated reduction in substrate availability alone?
    A. Insulin infusion does not significantly alter total renal uptake of alanine and lactate.
    B. The rate of glycerol uptake in the renal cortex decreases in response to insulin.
    C. Insulin reduces renal uptake of even-chained free fatty acids.
    D. Insulin shunts gluconeogenic precursors into an oxidative pathway.

36. The transient increase in hepatic glucose release during a trial shown in Figure 1 reflects a change in which of the following conditions in the liver cells tested?
    A. Decreased protein kinase A activity
    B. Phosphorylation and inactivation of phosphofructokinase-2 (PFK-2)
    C. Decreased fructose 1,6-bisphophastase activity
    D. Phosphorylation and activation of phosphofructokinase-2 (PFK-2)

37. Researchers hypothesized that stimulation of lipolysis by epinephrine cause the sustained increase in systemic glucose release shown in Figure 1. Given the mechanisms of metabolic regulation in healthy adults and information presented in the passage, does this hypothesis offer a potential explanation for the effect seen in Figure 1?
    A. No, two hours following epinephrine infusion nearly all of the increase in systemic glucose resulted from renal glucose release.
    B. No, epinephrine increases the rate of fatty acid uptake and utilization in peripheral tissues.
    C. Yes, during prolonged fasting, glucose released from the kidneys is the predominate source of circulating glucose.
    D. Yes, epinephrine stimulates lipolysis and free fatty acid release, which could increase the rate of renal gluconeogenesis.

38. Given information presented in the passage, which of the following enzymes is most likely to be found in greater concentration in the renal cortex than in the renal medulla?
    A. Hexokinase
    B. Phosphoglycerate mutase
    C. Phosphoglucoisomerase
    D. Glucose-6-phosphatase

39. If not properly compensated for by other physiological responses, sustained hyperglycemia promotes cellular dehydration in what way?
    A. Glucose co-transport accelerates the rate of plasma membrane ion exchange.
    B. Glucose-water antiport during cellular uptake of glucoses increases cellular osmotic pressure.
    C. Cellular glucose is used to form glycogen in dehydration synthesis reactions.
    D. Glucose increases the osmotic pressure of the extracellular space.

Passage VIII (Questions 40-43)

Phenylketonuria (PKU) is a recessive metabolic genetic disorder characterized by an inability to metabolize the amino acid phenylalanine to the amino acid tyrosine. In classical PKU, mutations in the PAH gene on the short arm of chromosome 12, which encodes for the liver enzyme phenylalanine hydroxylase (PAH), leading to an accumulation of phenylalanine. As it accumulates, it is converted through a minor transaminase pathway with glutamate to phenylpyruvate which can be detected in the urine of affected individuals. If untreated, PKU can lead to intellectual disability, seizures, and other serious medical problems.

A rarer variant form of PKU occurs when the PAH enzyme is normal, but a defect is found in the enzyme dihydrobiopterin reductase. The enzyme is responsible for the regeneration of 5,6,7,8-tetrahydrobiopterin (BH4) from pterin-4a-carbinolamine. BH4 is an important cofactor for a number of reactions of amino acid metabolism, not only as a cofactor for PAH, but also as a cofactor required for the production of L-DOPA, a dopamine precursor, from tyrosine and 5-hydroxy-L-tryptophan, a precursor of serotonin and melatonin, from tryptophan. The degradation of phenylalanine to tyrosine, including those enzymes affected in PKU, is shown in Figure 1. The transaminase pathway in which phenylalanine is metabolized to phenylpyruvate is shown in Figure 2.

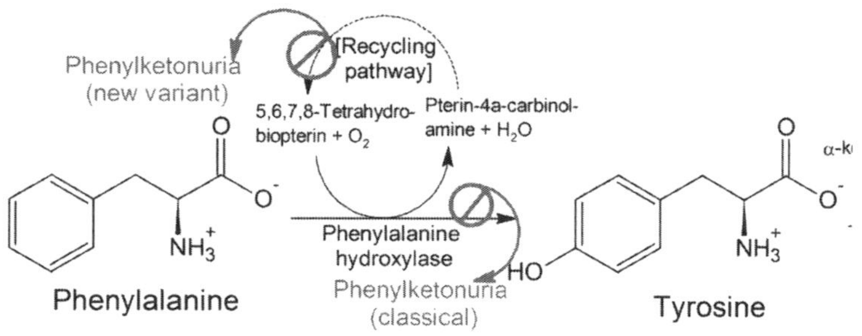

Figure 1 Initial reaction of phenylalanine degradation

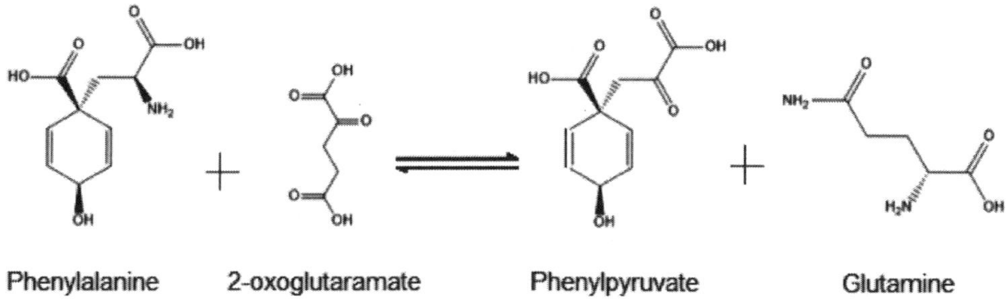

Figure 2 Transamination reaction of phenylalanine and 2-oxoglutaric acid

In addition to adhering to a diet low in phenylalanine, it is also suggested that those with PKU supplement their diet with foods rich in large neutral amino acids (LNAAs). Because of similarities in their side chain properties, LNAAs compete with phenylalanine for specific carrier proteins that transport LNAAs across the intestinal mucosa into the blood and across the blood-brain barrier into the brain.

40. When observing the inheritance pattern of the mutant form of the PAH allele within a family, which of the following is LEAST likely to be seen over a large number of generations?
    A. Generations without the appearance of individuals with symptoms of PKU
    B. Affected males with fathers who also showed symptoms of PKU
    C. An approximately equal number of males and females displaying symptoms of PKU
    D. Appearance of individuals with symptoms of PKU in each generation

41. The blood–brain barrier's relative impermeability is formed by capillary endothelial cells connected by what type of cell-cell junctions?
    A. Adherens junctions
    B. Tight junctions
    C. Anchoring junctions
    D. Gap junctions

42. Dopamine inhibits release of prolactin from the anterior pituitary. Given this, which of the following statements is most likely to be true of an individual suffering from either classical PKU or variant PKU with BH4 reductase deficiency?
    A. Prolactin release will be increased in an individual with classical PKU.
    B. Prolactin release will be decreased in an individual with classical PKU.
    C. Prolactin release will be increased in an individual variant PKU.
    D. Prolactin release will be decreased in an individual variant PKU.

43. A similar transaminase reaction to that shown in Figure 2 catalyzes the transformation of L-glutamate and pyruvate ($CH_3C(O)COOH$; shown below) into α-ketoglutarate and what amino acid?

    A. L-glycine
    B. L-alanine
    C. L-glutamine
    D. L-aspartate

Discrete Set 3 (Questions 44-47)

These questions are **NOT** related to a passage.

44. Which of the following is the amino acid that is coded for by the start codon, AUG, in humans?
    A. Cysteine
    B. Alanine
    C. Methionine
    D. Glycine

45. What is the target tissue of the hormone ACTH?
    A. Renal tissue
    B. The adrenal gland
    C. Hepatic tissue
    D. Blood vessels

46. How might glucagon affect the rate of pyruvate decarboxylation?
    A. It would increase the rate of pyruvate decarboxylation.
    B. It would decrease the rate of pyruvate decarboxylation.
    C. It would not affect the rate of pyruvate decarboxylation.
    D. There is not enough information to answer the question.

47. What tissue is most likely to use glucose as a source of energy in a state of fasting?
    A. The digestive tract
    B. Skeletal muscle
    C. The brain
    D. Cardiac muscle

THIS PAGE LEFT

INTENTIONALLY BLANK

Passage IX (Questions 48-51)

Immediately after fertilization, the human embryo undergoes rapid and drastic changes. These changes are largely driven by mitosis, the process through which cells replicate their chromosomes and divide. Mitosis is broken into four main steps – prophase, metaphase, anaphase, and telophase. During prophase, cells condense their chromosomes and begin to form the mitotic spindles used to separate the chromosomes evenly into the two daughter cells. During metaphase, the chromosomes align along the metaphase plate and begin to be pulled apart by the mitotic spindles. In anaphase, the chromosomes are separated, forming two identical sister chromatids, and are pulled to opposite ends of the dividing cell. Finally, in telophase, the two daughter cells pull apart followed by the formation of a new nucleus in each cell. Both daughter cells are genetically identical to the original cell. This cascade of events occurs in all body cells, including germ (reproductive) cells.

	No treatment	Docetaxel	Ibrutinib
Cell Line 1	25 hr	44 hr	24 hr
Cell Line 2	34 hr	36 hr	52 hr

Table 1 Doubling times for the two inhibitors with both cell lines

Cancer cells are known for their unregulated, continuous mitotic division. A cancer researcher performs an experiment in which she tests various molecules used in chemotherapy to see their effect on two cancer cell lines she has obtained. The first inhibitor she tries is docetaxel, a mitotic inhibitor that binds reversibly to microtubules, drastically increasing the doubling time of Cell Line 1. The second inhibitor she tries is ibrutinib, an inhibitor of Bruton's tyrosine kinase (BTK), an enzyme involved in B cell development. It dramatically increases the doubling time of Cell Line 2. The doubling times for the two inhibitors with both cell lines are provided in Table 1.

48. Chromosomal crossover, or the exchange of genetic information between homologous chromosomes, occurs in which stage of mitosis?
    A. Prophase
    B. Metaphase II
    C. Anaphase
    D. None of these

49. Among non-cancerous cells in the human body, which cells are likely to undergo mitosis at the fastest rate?
    A. Neurons
    B. Muscle cells
    C. Skin cells
    D. Germ cells

50. The restriction point, or the point at which a cell is committed to undergoing mitosis, is located in which stage of interphase?
    A. G0
    B. S
    C. G1
    D. G2

51. If the researcher looks at Cell Line 1 being grown in the presence of docetaxel under a microscope, would she find the majority of them in interphase or a mitotic phase?
    A. Interphase, because docetaxel will prevent the microtubule-organizing center (MTOC) from developing during this stage.
    B. A mitotic phase, because docetaxel will prevent formation of the cleavage furrow during cytokinesis.
    C. Interphase, because docetaxel will prevent DNA duplication.
    D. A mitotic phase, because docetaxel will arrest the cells in mitosis prior to anaphase.

Passage X (Questions 52-55)

The cells of eukaryotic organisms consist of a membrane comprised of phospholipids, which encases a cytosol populated by a number of organelles. One such organelle is the mitochondrion. The mitochondrion has an outer membrane and an inner membrane, separated by the intermembrane space. The space enclosed by the inner membrane is referred to as the mitochondrial matrix. The mitochondrion as a whole serves as an "energy powerhouse." It is within the mitochondrion that pyruvate decarboxylation, the Krebs cycle (i.e., the citric acid cycle), and the electron transport chain occur, all processes of aerobic respiration in cells. Pyruvate decarboxylation is a biochemical reaction occurring in the mitochondrial matrix that converts pyruvate (a product of glycolysis) into acetyl coenzyme A (Ac-CoA). Ac-CoA can then be used in the Krebs cycle (also in the mitochondrial matrix) to generate energy. Finally, the majority of the energy from aerobic respiration is generated in the electron transport chain, which occurs at the mitochondrial inner membrane. In the electron transport chain, redox reactions occur in which electrons are transferred to an acceptor molecule from a donor molecule.

While the majority of DNA in a eukaryotic cell is isolated inside the nucleus, it has been discovered that a small amount of non-nuclear DNA resides within the mitochondria. This mitochondrial DNA (mtDNA) is different from other inherited DNA in that it is inherited solely from the mother. Upon fertilization of a human zygote, the sperm's mitochondria do enter the egg, but do not provide genetic information to the embryo.

It has been seen that in rare cases mitochondria do not function properly, leading to "mitochondrial diseases" in a small subset of the population. Neuropathy, ataxia, and retinitis pigmentosa (NARP) syndrome is an example of this. Upon entering early adulthood, most people with NARP syndrome begin to experience tingling and/or pain in their extremities and problems with balance. As the disease advances, it also can lead to light sensitivity and eventually vision loss.

52. A mother with NARP syndrome has two children, a son and a daughter. Which child is more likely to inherit the disease?
    A. The son
    B. The daughter
    C. The son and daughter have equal likelihood of inheriting the disease.
    D. Information about the father's disease status must also be provided to answer this question.

53. Many scientists believe in the "endosymbiotic theory," which states that the mitochondrion developed evolutionarily when a prokaryote entered a eukaryotic cell through endocytosis and led to a symbiotic relationship where both organisms were able to thrive. If this were true, what is a plausible size of the ribosomes coded for by mtDNA?
    A. 40S
    B. 50S
    C. 70S
    D. 80S

54. What is the final electron acceptor molecule in the electron transport chain?
    A. Oxygen
    B. Water
    C. ATP
    D. Calcium

55. In an individual free of mitochondrial disease, which of the following cell types would lack functioning mitochondria?
    A. Red blood cells
    B. Muscle cells
    C. Neurons
    D. White blood cells

301

Discrete Set 4 (Questions 56-59)

These questions are **NOT** related to a passage.

56. Which of the following are most likely found in the interior of a protein?
   I. Lysine
   II. Valine
   III. Glutamic Acid

   A. I only
   B. II only
   C. I and II only
   D. I and III only

57. By which of the following processes do prokaryotes usually reproduce?
   A. Binary fission
   B. Bacterial conjugation
   C. Transduction
   D. Transformation

58. Positron emission tomography (PET) scan is an imaging test that uses a radioactive tracer to look for disease in the body. Which of the following correctly describes positron emission?
   A. A proton is converted to a neutron and a positron.
   B. A neutron is converted to an electron and a proton.
   C. A neutron is converted to a proton and a positron.
   D. A proton is converted to an electron and a neutron.

59. Which of the following does NOT contribute to genetic diversity in gamete reproduction?
   A. Random chromosomal arrangement along the metaphase plate during metaphase I
   B. Random chromosomal arrangement along the metaphase plate during metaphase II
   C. Random chromosomes are replicated during meiosis I.
   D. Crossing over during prophase I

TIMED
SECTION 4
Answers and Explanations

Timed Section 4 Answer Key

Key		20	B	40	D
1	C	21	B	41	B
2	A	22	D	42	C
3	D	23	D	43	B
4	B	24	B	44	C
5	C	25	D	45	B
6	C	26	B	46	B
7	B	27	C	47	C
8	A	28	C	48	D
9	C	29	C	49	C
10	A	30	B	50	C
11	B	31	A	51	D
12	A	32	C	52	C
13	A	33	B	53	C
14	C	34	B	54	A
15	B	35	C	55	A
16	D	36	B	56	B
17	D	37	D	57	A
18	C	38	D	58	A
19	D	39	D	59	C

Passage I Answers and Explanations (Questions 1-5)

The **first step** in the **metabolism of heme** released from **degraded red blood cells** is its **oxidation** by the **microsomal enzyme heme oxygenase**, resulting in the **green pigment biliverdin**. The next step is the reduction of biliverdin to a yellow tetrapyrol pigment called bilirubin. This "unconjugated" bilirubin is bound to albumin and transported through the bloodstream to the liver. In the liver, it is conjugated with glucuronic acid by the enzyme glucuronyl transferase, forming bilirubin **diglucuronide—"conjugated bilirubin."** From the liver, this **solubilized form of bilirubin** is **excreted, initially as part of bile**, and eventually, from the body.

Key terms: heme, red blood cells, heme oxygenase, biliverdin, tetrapyrol, pigment, bilirubin, unconjugated bilibrubin, albumin,

Cause-and-Effect: heme is released from degraded, senescent red blood cells; that heme is then oxidized by the enzyme heme oxygenase, yielding biliverdin; biliverdin is further oxidized to unconjugated bilirubin; unconjugated bilirubin is transported along with albumin to the liver where it is conjugated with glucuronic acid by glucuronosyl transferase to form soluble conjugated bilirubin; conjugated bilirubin is released from the liver in bile and eventually excreted from the body

In neonates, **benign "physiological" jaundice** is of **least concern** clinically, and tends to **develop after the first 24 hours** of life because of an accumulation of unconjugated bilirubin in the blood (hyperbilirubinemia). This leads to the symptoms of jaundice, including a pronounced yellowing of the skin and sclera. Alternatively, neonatal jaundice may be of greater concern if a pathological condition is responsible for the elevated bilirubin. Severe hyperbilirubinemia in neonates may cause **bilirubin** to **accumulate in the brain**, potentially **causing irreversible neurological damage**—a condition referred to as **kernicterus**.

Key terms: physiological jaundice, hyperbilirubinemia, sclera, kernicterus

Cause-and-Effect: physiological jaundice of the neonate, which develops after the first 24 hours of life and which leads to an accumulation of unconjugated bilirubin in the blood, is relatively benign and is of lesser concern than other causes; kernicterus can occur when bilirubin accumulates to toxic levels on the brain

A pediatrician evaluating the cases of two newborns made the observations recorded below (Note: In infants, **normal total serum bilirubin** (conjugated + unconjugated) < 12 mg/dL, conjugated bilirubin < 2 mg/dL, unconjugated bilirubin < 10 mg/dL).

Case 1

A **3-day-old male infant** born **exhibiting yellow discoloration of the skin**, most notably of the forehead and neck.

Case 2

A 2-week-old, healthy female infant is slightly jaundiced. Labs show **a total bilirubin of 18 mg/dl** and a **conjugated bilirubin of 0.8 mg/dl.**

Cause-and-Effect: total bilirubin of 18 mg/dl ; conjugated bilirubin of 0.8 mg/dl.

1. The increased susceptibility of neonates to the development of jaundice or kernicterus is LEAST likely to be due to what factor?
    A. The blood–brain barrier is not fully functional in neonates.
    B. Fetal red blood cells are rapidly degraded and replaced by adult red blood cells shortly before birth.
    C. **Decreased synthesis of albumin versus adults increases the fraction of free bilirubin solubilized in the blood.**
    D. Relatively immature hepatic metabolic pathways are unable to conjugate bilirubin as quickly as those of adults.

Choice **C** is correct. The passage indicates that bilirubin is relatively insoluble in the blood. This is suggested, in part, by the requirement for albumin to act as a carrier of bilirubin during its transport to the liver. Conjugation of bilirubin increases its water solubility and thus enabling its eventual excretion. Decreasing the pool of available albumin would decrease, rather than increase, the amount of bilirubin solubilized in the blood.

A: If the blood–brain barrier is not fully functional in neonates, increasing the ease with which bilirubin can cross the barrier and increasing the likelihood of kernicterus in infants due to the accumulation of bilirubin in grey matter of the CNS.
B: Neonates have much higher levels of bilirubin in their blood because of the rapid breakdown of fetal red blood cells immediately prior to birth and the subsequent replacement of those cells by adult hemoglobin-containing red blood cells. This breakdown of fetal red blood cells releases large amounts of bilirubin, increasing the likelihood of neonates developing physiological jaundice.
D: Any decrease in neonates' ability to conjugate and excrete bilirubin relative to adults would increase the likelihood of hyperbilirubinemia, and thus also the likelihood of developing a physiological jaundice.

2. Jaundice can occur during pregnancy in mothers with an inherited increase in the binding affinity of a particular class of nuclear receptors present in liver cells. A peak in the concentration of the substrate for these receptors elsewhere in the body triggers ovulation. This substrate is:
    A. **estrogen.**
    B. FSH.
    C. LH.
    D. progesterone.

Choice **A** is correct. The actions of estrogen are mediated by the estrogen receptor (ER), a dimeric intracellular receptor that binds to DNA and controls the expression of relevant gene products. During the female menstrual cycle, estrogen levels peak towards the end of the follicular phase, which causes a surge in levels of luteinizing hormone (LH) and follicle-stimulating hormone (FSH). This lasts from 24 to 36 hours, and results in the rupture of the ovarian follicles, causing the oocyte to be released from the ovary.

B: FSH is a glycoprotein hormone which stimulates the growth and recruitment of immature ovarian follicles in the ovaries of females, by binding a cell surface, rather than an intracellular receptor.
C: LH is a glycoprotein hormone responsible for, in women, the triggering of ovulation and the development of the corpus luteum. Like FSH, LH binds cell-surface receptors.
D: During the female menstrual cycle, progesterone levels substantially increase until the luteal phase, following ovulation and peaks in the concentrations of both LH and estrogen.

3. Which of the following individual findings would be most concerning and prompt further evaluation of the infant in Case 1?
    A. Total serum bilirubin level of 14 mg/dL
    B. Appearance of the infant's jaundice first occurring 48 hours after birth
    C. Unconjugated bilirubin of 12 mg/dL
    D. **Conjugated bilirubin of 4 mg/dL**

Choice **D** is correct. The passage states that unconjugated hyperbilirubinemia leading to a "physiological" form of jaundice is not uncommon in infants after the first 24 hours of life, and that is of lesser clinical concern than other forms of jaundice caused by a pathological elevation of bilirubin. The passage further indicates that kernicterus arises most often due to conjugated hyperbilirubinemia. For these reasons, an infant presenting with serum conjugated bilirubin outside of the reference range provided in the passage (< 2 mg/dL) warrants the most immediate attention.

A: The passage states that in neonates, benign "physiological" jaundice is of least concern clinically, and tends to develop after the first 24 hours of life because of an accumulation of unconjugated bilirubin. While an elevated total serum bilirubin above the reference range indicated in the passage is of concern, it is consistent with the possibility of developing only physiological jaundice.
B and C: This is consistent with a physiological jaundice that is of lesser clinical concern then conjugated hyperbilirubinemia.

4. What diagnosis is most consistent with the information considered by the pediatrician in Case 2?
    A. Defective hepatic bilirubin excretion
    B. **Deficiency of glucuronosyl transferase**
    C. Lack of a fully-developed gallbladder
    D. Blockage of the common bile duct

Choice **B** is correct. Laboratory results for the patient in case 2 support a probable finding of unconjugated hyperbilirubinemia. Only choice B, deficiency of glucuronosyl transferase, the enzyme described by the passage as being responsible for the glucuronidation of bilirubin in the liver, could account for the isolated elevation of unconjugated bilirubin.

A, D: The conditions listed in both choices A and D would result in an elevation of conjugated bilirubin.
C: Lack of a fully-developed gallbladder could not account for an elevation of conjugated or unconjugated bilirubin.

5. The contents of bilirubin-containing bile serve which of the following digestive functions when released into the duodenum?
    A. To solubilize ingested fats and decrease duodenal pH
    B. To cleave ester linkages in ingested fat molecules and decrease duodenal pH
    C. **To solubilize ingested fats and increase duodenal pH**
    D. To cleave ester linkages in ingested fat molecules and increase duodenal pH

Choice **C** is correct. Bile acts in part as a surfactant, helping to emulsify ingested lipids by disrupting intermolecular attractions among lipids. Anionic bile salts contain both hydrophobic and hydrophilic components. As a result, they aggregate around lipids droplets of triglycerides and phospholipids to form micelles. These dispersions greatly increase the surface area of lipids available for the action of the enzyme pancreatic lipase, which actually digests the triglycerides. Additionally, bile is alkaline because of its bicarbonate content. The relatively alkalinity of bile functions to neutralize excess gastric acid entering the duodenum from the stomach, thereby increasing duodenal pH.

A: Bile increases, rather than decreases, duodenal pH.

B: Pancreatic lipase is secreted from the pancreas, and is responsible for the hydrolysis of dietary fat molecules in the human digestive system, converting triglyceride substrates found in ingested oils to monoglycerides and free fatty acids via cleavage of ester linkages.

D: Pancreatic lipase is responsible for the hydrolysis of dietary fat molecules via cleavage of ester linkages.

Passage II Answers and Explanations (Questions 6-10)

The pituitary gland is a major hub in the body's **endocrine** system. The gland is split into two parts called the **anterior** pituitary and **posterior** pituitary glands which differ in the hormones they release. The anterior pituitary contains five types of cells, each secreting a different hormone. Those cells are called **corticotropes, thyrotropes, prolactins, gonadotropes, and somatotropes**.

Key Terms: pituitary gland, endocrine, anterior, posterior, corticotropes, thyrotropes, prolactins, gonadotropes, somatotropes.

Cause and Effect: We are told a little about the pituitary gland and what types of cells the anterior pituitary contains. It is reasonable to think that corticotropes release ACTH, thyrotropes release TSH, prolactins release prolactin, gonadotropes release FSH and LH, and somatotropes must release GH.

The anterior pituitary's secretion of hormones is regulated by hormones released by the **hypothalamus**. This is possible because the hypothalamus and anterior pituitary are connected in the **hypophyseal portal system**, a system of blood vessels connecting the two glands. This system is illustrated in Figure 1.

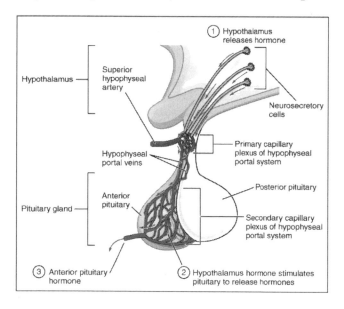

Figure 1 The anterior pituitary and hypothalamus

Figure 1 shows a schematic of the function of the anterior pituitary in conjunction with the hypothalamus.

Some hormones secreted by the hypothalamus include **gonadotropin releasing hormone, corticotropin releasing hormone, prolactin releasing hormone, and GH releasing hormone**.

Key Terms: hypothalamus, hypophyseal portal system.

Cause and Effect: We are told about the hypothalamus's regulatory control of the anterior pituitary and the hypophyseal portal system. We are reminded of the hypothalamic hormones that operate to regulate anterior pituitary hormone secretion. They are GnRH, CRH, PRH, GHRH

Hormone secretion from the anterior pituitary can also be regulated by other body systems. The molecule **gamma-aminobutyric acid** can stimulate the secretion of growth hormone, luteinizing hormone, and thyroid stimulating hormone.

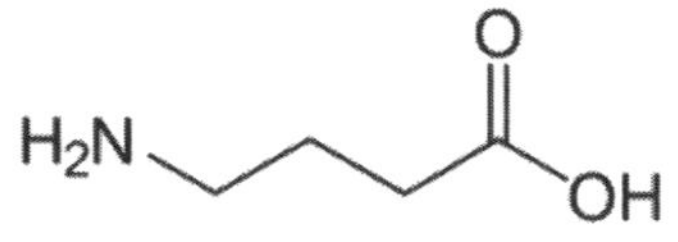

Figure 2 Gamma aminobutyric acid

Figure 2 shows the structure of gamma aminobutyric acid

Prostaglandins are a class of lipids that inhibit ACTH release and stimulate TSH, GH and LH release. Prostaglandins always contain **20** carbons and have a **5-carbon ring**.

Key Terms: gamma aminobutyric acid, prostaglandins, 20 carbons, 5-carbon ring.

Cause and Effect: gamma aminobutyric acid down-regulates GH, LH, TSH while prostaglandins down-regulate ACTH but stimulate TSH, GH, and LH

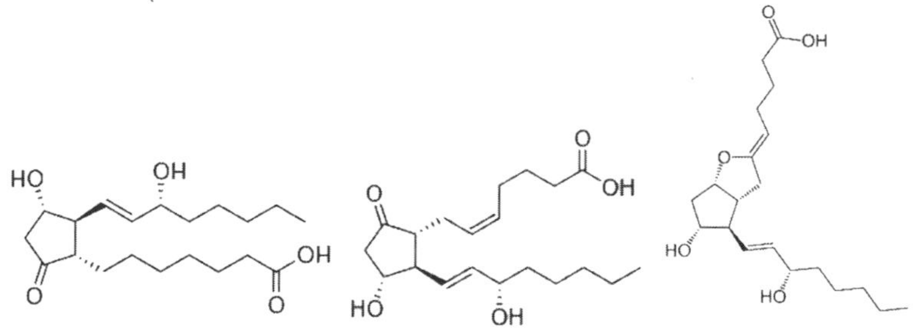

Figure 3 Prostaglandins E1, E2, and I2 (left to right)

Figure 3 shows the structure of 3 prostaglandins, labeled E1, E2, and I2 from left to right

6. What is another name for gamma-amino butyric acid?
    A. Amino 4-butyric acid
    B. 4-carboxy butanamine
    C. **4-amino butanoic acid**
    D. 1-hydroxy 4-amino butanone

Choice **C** is correct. Remember that the carboxylic acid takes priority so our answer must contain 4-amino.

A: The correct name is 4-amino butyric acid.
B: Functional group priority is given to carboxylic acids.
D: The highest priority group here is not a ketone. There is no ketone group (RC(O)R).

7. Which of the following is the LEAST likely effect of an increase in GH secretion from the anterior pituitary?
   A. Increased bone growth
   B. Increased secretion of GHRH
   C. Decreased secretion of calcitonin
   D. Decreased activity of prostaglandins on somatotropes

Choice **B** is correct. This question asks us to determine the effects of increased GH secretion. It is not likely that this would stimulate more GHRH production because GHRH acts to stimulate GH secretion. This type of positive feedback loop is not a common biological process.

A: GH stimulates growth.
C: Calcitonin would not likely be directly affected at first but it is more likely to occur than choice B because GH takes calcium from the blood.
D: Somatotropes secrete GH. It is likely that there will be less activity of prostaglandins on somatotropes because prostaglandins stimulate GH secretion.

8. Which type of cell most likely releases LH and FSH from the anterior pituitary?
   A. Gonadotropes
   B. Somatotropes
   C. Corticotropes
   D. Thyrotropes

Choice **A** is correct. This question asks us to reason which cell likely produces the gonadotropins LH and FSH.

B: Somatotropes secrete GH.
C: Corticotropes secrete ACTH.
D: Thyrotropes secrete TSH.

9. What is the significance of the number given in the name of prostaglandins E1, E2, and I2?
   A. It is an indication of the number of ring structures in the molecule.
   B. It is an indication of the size of the prostaglandin.
   C. It is an indication of the number of double bonds in the molecule.
   D. It is an indication of the number of acidic functional groups.

Choice **C** is correct. This question asks us to reason from Figure 3 why the prostaglandins have the classification of 1 or 2 as in E1, E2, and I2. The structures of the molecules would suggest that the number has to do with the number of double bonds in the structure.

A: Prostaglandin E2 has one ring.
B: The sizes of the prostaglandins are all the same. They have 20 carbons each.
D: The prostaglandins all have one carboxylic acid and two hydroxyl groups.

10. Which of the following could cause an increase in T3 production?
    I. A tumor in the thyrotropes of the anterior pituitary
    II. A decrease in TRH production
    III. A decrease in gamma-aminobutyric acid production

    A. **I only**
    B. I and II only
    C. II and III only
    D. I and III only

Choice **A** is correct. This question asks us to determine the plausible causes of an increase in T3 production. Since T3 is a thyroid hormone, an increase in TSH would do it. Choice I corresponds with an increased secretion of the thyrotropic hormone, TSH.

II: A decrease in TRH production would only decrease TSH and T3 production.
III: A decrease in GABA production would only decrease TSH secretion.

Passage III Answers and Explanations (Questions 11-15)

Recombination is the exchange of **genes** between **homologous chromosomes**. This commonly occurs as a result of **crossing over during meiosis I**. The likelihood of crossing over appears to be correlated with the size of the chromosome. Crossing over results from the formation of **Holliday junctions**, a junction between four strands of DNA.

Key Terms: recombination, genes, homologous chromosomes, crossing over, meiosis I, Holliday junctions. This first paragraph gives a brief intro to genetic recombination as it might occur during meiosis I. Holliday junctions are introduced.

Two common forms of genetic recombination involving Holliday junctions occur during prophase and metaphase of meiosis I. The first occurs when corresponding strands on each chromosome are broken. A **single strand cleavage** on each homolog will result in the Holliday junction shown in Figure 1. There are two ways to resolve the Holliday junction. The first is for enzymes to cut the strands at **point B or at points A and C**. The latter is shown in Figure 1.

Key Terms: single strand cleavage, resolve. This paragraph gives a scenario that will result in a single Holliday junction. We are told that the junction needs to be resolved, meaning that the chromosome come apart again. There are two ways of doing this and one is illustrated.

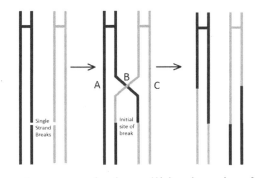

Figure 1 A single Holliday junction formed by single strand breaks in homologous chromosomes

Figure 1 shows a single Holliday junction formed by single strand breaks. The result when the strands are cut at A and C is shown.

A second common form of Holliday junction recombination that occurs during meiosis I is shown in Figure 2. This occurs when there is a **double strand break** in one chromosome. After several enzymatic attempts to rectify the situation, the chromosomes have a chance of ending up with the structure shown in the middle of Figure 2 with **two Holliday junctions**.

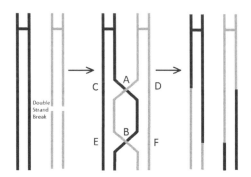

Figure 2 A double Holliday junction formed by a double strand break in one chromosome

Figure 2 shows a possible scenario where a double Holliday junction may form between chromosomes. One way of resolving it is illustrated here.

In order to rectify this system of Holliday junctions, the DNA must be cleaved in two locations. There are two ways of doing this. The first is to cleave the DNA at A and B. This will result in **nonrecombinant** chromosomes. The second option is to cleave first at A or B and second at C and D together or E and F together. When this happens we will get two **recombinant** chromosomes that have exchanged a significant amount of genetic material.

Key Terms: double strand break, two Holliday junctions, nonrecombinant, recombinant. A second scenario is presented, this time more complicated. The mechanism for the formation of the two Holliday junctions is not mentioned as much as the mechanism for resolving the system.

11. Why will cleaving at A and B in Figure 2 result in nonrecombinant chromosomes?
    A. There would be no interchange of genetic material.
    B. **The segment of DNA that is interchanged will not likely contain any significant number of genes.**
    C. The cleavage would result in the exchange of the whole sister chromatids.
    D. The cleavage would result in two free-floating segments of DNA.

Choice **B** is correct. If cleaved at points A and B, the homologous chromosomes would simply exchange that short segment of DNA between A and B to get something like this:

There will be some exchange of DNA but the chromosomes will not be recombinant because there will be no exchange of genes.

A: There will be a small interchange.
C: This is not true, the Holliday junctions are nowhere near the centromeres of the chromosomes.
D: Cleavage at this site will not result in completely separate DNA strands.

12. Which of the following is the most likely result if the Holliday junction in Figure 1 is cleaved at point B?

A.

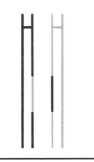

B.

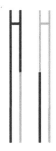

C.

D.

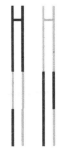

Choice **A** is correct. This question requires us to consider Figure 1 and what change will occur given the circumstance in the stem. If cleaved at point B, the strands will rectify themselves by joining their original chromosomes and there will be a small segment of DNA that has transferred between chromosomes. The result is two non-recombinant chromosomes.

13. Which chromosome is most likely to experience crossing over?
    A. **1 (2000 genes)**
    B. 18 (200 genes)
    C. X (800 genes)
    D. Y (50 genes)

Choice A is correct. Paragraph 1 informs you that crossing over has a certain probability of occurring based on the size of the chromosomes in question. Since chromosome 1 is significantly larger than the other three options, it will be most likely to undergo crossing over.

B: Chromosome 18 is smaller than chromosome 1 and thus is not as likely to experience crossing over during meiosis I.
C: Chromosome X is smaller than chromosome 1 and thus is not as likely to experience crossing over during meiosis I.
D: Chromosome Y is smaller than chromosome 1 and thus is not as likely to experience crossing over during meiosis I.

14. Is it possible for genetic recombination to occur during meiosis II?
    A. Yes, sister chromatids on one chromosome can exchange genetic material.
    B. Yes, slight overlap of adjacent chromosomal arms makes it possible for crossing over to occur between two nonhomologous chromosomes.
    C. **No, recombination requires two homologous but nonidentical chromosomes.**
    D. No, sister chromatids cannot get close enough during metaphase II.

Choice C is correct. This question requires us to know what recombination entails. Recombination is the exchange of genetic material to create new genetic possibilities. Exchange of genetic material between sister chromatids, if possible, would have no effect on genetic variance because sister chromatids are exactly identical base pair per base pair.

A: It is not possible to recombine two perfectly identical chromosomal arms.
B: Genetic machinery cannot recombine chromosomes unless they are homologous.
D: This statement is false. Sister chromatids are attached to each other and arranged along the metaphase plate in metaphase II.

15. Which of the following combinations of DNA cuts will result in the greatest amount of base pairs exchanged between the two chromosomes in figure 2?
    A. Cleaving at A, E, and F
    B. **Cleaving at A, C, and D**
    C. Cleaving at B, E, and F
    D. Cleaving at B, C, and D

Choice B is correct. This question requires us to visualize the results of the four possible cuts on the two Holliday junctions in Figure 2.

Discrete Set 1 Answers and Explanations (Questions 16-18)

16. Which of the following is likely to have gap junctions in its cell membrane?
    A. Erythrocyte
    B. Motor neuron
    C. Sperm cell
    D. **Skin cell**

Choice **D** is correct. Gap junctions are used to transmit materials quickly and efficiently from one cell's cytoplasm to that of an adjacent cell. Skin cells are found adjacent to many other skin cells and would need to be able to transfer molecules quickly between themselves.

A: Erythrocytes are not found adjacent to other cells, they are flowing through the blood
C: Motor neurons use synapses as their form of cell to cell signaling and are less likely to have gap junctions
D: Sperm cells are independent much like erythrocytes.

17. Which of the following is most directly responsible for initiating skeletal muscle contraction?
    A. K^+
    B. Cl^-
    C. Na^+
    D. **Ca^{2+}**

Choice **D** is correct. Remember that calcium is released from the sarcoplasmic reticulum and binds troponin to initiate muscle contraction.

18. Which of the following is NOT a function of carbonic anhydrase?
    A. Maintain a pH balance in the blood
    B. Transport carbon dioxide out of tissue
    C. **Allow carbon dioxide to diffuse into the lungs**
    D. Regulate hemoglobin's affinity for oxygen

Choice **C** is correct. Carbon dioxide easily diffuses into the lungs along its concentration gradient. Carbonic anhydrase itself has no part in this diffusion.

A: The creation of bicarbonate from CO_2 and H_2O also creates a H^+. Thus carbonic anhydrase can regulate the H^+ concentration in the blood.
B: Bicarbonate and carbonic acid are more soluble than CO_2 and can be more easily transported in the blood.
D: CO_2 is an allosteric inhibitor of hemoglobin binding O_2

Passage IV Answers and Explanations (Questions 19-22)

The average length of a human protein-coding gene is 27 kbp, but the average mRNA exported to the cytosol consists of only 1340 nt coding sequence, 1070 nt UTRs, and a poly-A tail. Only about **10% of the average pre-mRNA is exonic** sequences, which are joined by pre-mRNA splicing. This splicing is carried out by a spliceosome, which is composed of **five small nuclear RNAs (snRNAs)** and associated protein complexes. Assembly of the spliceosome on a pre-mRNA is initiated by recognition of specific sequence elements such as **5'- and 3'-end splice sites, and the branch point sequence**. The spliceosome then catalyzes the excision of introns and the ligation of exons.

Key terms: exon, intron, pre-mRNA, small nuclear RNA (snRNA), spliceosome

Cause and effect: Spliceosomes recognize 5'- and 3'-end splice sites and catalyze splicing

Which sequences are expressed as exons is not always the same: **one gene can code for multiple proteins** as a result of **alternative splicing**. This process is estimated to affect more than 88% of human protein-coding genes. More than 25% of **alternative exons include stop codons,** which results in translation of truncated proteins or degradation of the mRNA. Because of their ubiquity, it is not surprising that changes in alternative splicing are frequently found in cases of human diseases.

Key terms: alternative splicing, truncated

Cause and effect: alternative splicing can lead to disease

Hutchinson-Gilford progeria syndrome (HGPS) is a rare disorder clinically characterized by features of **premature aging** such as postnatal growth retardation, premature atherosclerosis, lack of subcutaneous fat, and alopecia. The median age to which a person with HGPS lives is 13.4. **Changes in splicing of the nuclear lamin A/C (LMNA) gene** have been identified in cases of HGPS. This gene normally codes for a structural protein called prelamin A, which becomes lamin A when its farnesyl group binds the nuclear rim and is cleaved from the molecule. **Lamin A, along with lamin B and lamin C, make up the nuclear lamina and provide structural support for the nucleus.** A mutation in exon 11 of the nuclear lamin A/C (LMNA) gene that activates a cryptic splice site results in production of a **truncated protein called progerin that acts in a dominant fashion**.

Key terms: HGPS, nuclear lamin A/C (LMNA) gene, prelamin, nuclear lamina, progerin

Cause and effect: alternative splicing of LMNA results in a truncated protein (progerin), causing HGPS

19. A mutation in splicing factors PRPF31/U4-61k and PRP8 is the cause of the autosomal dominant form of retinis pigmentosa. What is likely the reason that diseases caused by mutations in core elements of splicing machinery, such as in this case, are rare?
    A. Signals on mRNA splice sites are read by the ribosome, which will therefore not translate introns.
    B. Any one splicing factor is not necessary for proper cell functioning because of systemic redundancy.
    C. Genes for splicing machinery are highly conserved across species.
    D. **Defects in general splicing machinery are not usually compatible with life.**

Choice **D** is correct. Splicing is necessary for survival, so mutations in core splicing machinery usually don't allow development of the organism.

A: Ribosomes will translate any introns that are not spliced out of the mRNA. Translation will continue until a stop codon is reached.

B: Individual splicing factors are each necessary for proper splicing. This may be a tempting answer because two splicing factors are mutated in the case given.

C: Although this is true, this does not answer the question.

20. The farnesyl group of the progerin protein cannot be removed and the protein remains bound to the nuclear rim. How might this lead to the symptoms of HGPS?
    A. Killer T cells recognize progerin and induce the cells to apoptose.
    B. **This weakens the nuclear lamina, which limits the cell's ability to divide.**
    C. Progerin binding alters the nuclear membrane, making it less permeable to exiting mRNA molecules.
    D. Progerin cannot translocate into the cytoplasm to aid in translation of other proteins.

Choice **B** is correct. The structure of the nucleus is important for condensation of chromatin, so damage to this structure will make cell division more difficult.

A: Progerin binds to the nuclear membrane, which is inside the cell and therefore not accessible to Killer T cells

C: There is no evidence in the passage to support this statement.

D: This is not the normal function of lamin, which is the normal form of the progerin protein.

21. You must design an experiment to study alternative splicing in HGPS and choose to use E. coli as the model organism. Why will this experiment not be successful?
    I. HGPS symptoms are a result of lack of structural support for the nucleus.
    II. Prokaryotes lack a spliceosome.
    III. Prokaryotic RNA polymerase cannot transcribe human genes.

    A. II
    B. **I and II**
    C. I and III
    D. I, II, and III

Choice **B** is correct.

I: This is true because E. coli are prokaryotic and therefore lack the nucleus necessary to be affected.

II: This is true because HGPS is the result of improper splicing, and prokaryotes lack the spliceosome to replicate this.

III: This is false because prokaryotic RNAP can transcribe human genes.

22. Given its inheritance pattern, would you expect HGPS to be a prevalent condition?
    A. Yes. Any disease caused by mutated DNA will be passed on.
    B. Yes. Both alleles have to be mutated to produce disease, and this is unlikely to occur in one generation.
    C. No. It is caused by errors in splicing, not errors in the DNA itself, and only DNA is inherited.
    D. **No. The condition causes death at a young age and is therefore unlikely to be passed on.**

Choice D is correct. The passage states that the median age reached of a person with HGPS is 13.4, which is before the reproductive years.

A: Only mutations to gametes are passed on, and still this requires reproduction.

B: The passage states this condition is dominant so only one allele must mutate.

C: The errors in splicing are the result of a mutation in a gene for a splicing protein.

Passage V Answers and Explanations (Questions 23-26)

Carbonic anhydrase is an enzyme found in almost all human tissue, but most abundantly in **red blood cells**. Carbonic anhydrase catalyzes the formation of **carbonic acid** from CO_2 and H_2O as well as the dehydration of carbonic acid to form CO_2 and H_2O.

Key Terms: carbonic anhydrase, red blood cells, carbonic acid. This first paragraph tells us what carbonic anhydrase is and what reaction it catalyzes.

Reaction 1 $\qquad\qquad CO_2 + H_2O \langle\rangle H_2CO_3 \leftrightarrow HCO_3^- + H^+$
Reaction 1 is the reaction catalyzed by carbonic anhydrase

The enzyme works via the **activation of a water** molecule by a **zinc** ion held in place by three **histidine residues**. When CO_2 is introduced into the active site, the activated water initiates a **nucleophilic** attack on the carbon atom. The mechanism is aided by a **threonine** residue as well as an amino acid that activates the **hydroxyl** group on threonine. The mechanism is shown in Figure 1.

Key Terms: activating of water, zinc, histidine, nucleophilic attack, threonine, hydroxyl. This paragraph tells us of the action of the enzyme and how water is used as a nucleophile to attack CO_2. We are told that threonine and other amino acids play a part in the enzyme's activity.

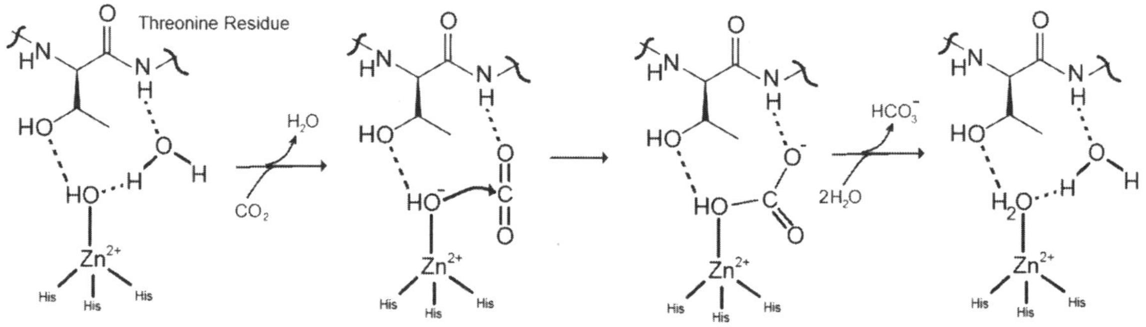

Figure 1 Forward reaction mechanism of carbonic anhydrase

Figure 1 shows the forward reaction of carbonic anhydrase and how bicarbonate is produced.

The reaction rate of carbonic anhydrase is extremely fast. About 10^6 **reactions** per second can be performed in the forward or reverse directions. The rate of reaction of the enzyme is dependent on the surrounding **pH**. Activity is at a maximum at or above a pH of 8. Below a pH of 8, the rate decreases in a sigmoidal fashion.

Key Terms: 10^6 reactions per second, pH.

Cause and Effect: the rate of reaction of carbonic anhydrase depends on the surrounding pH. We also see from the graph of figure 2 that the midpoint of the enzyme's efficiency is at a pH of about 7.

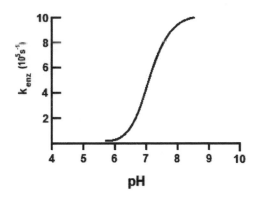

Figure 2 the activity of carbonic anhdrase as a function of pH

Figure 2 shows the rate of reaction of carbonic anhydrase as a function of pH.

23. Why is the forward reaction favored in tissues?

    A. There is more carbonic anhydrase in tissue than in the lungs
    B. There is more carbonic anhydrase near the lungs than in the tissue
    C. There is more CO_2 in the lungs than in the tissue
    D. <u>**There is more CO_2 in the tissue than in the lungs**</u>

Choice **D** is correct. This question asks us to determine why a reaction would favor the forward direction. Le Châtelier's principle tells us that the abundance of a substrate will cause the forward reaction to be favored. There is CO_2 buildup in the tissue that needs to be transported.

A: The abundance of an enzyme does not affect the equilibrium of the reaction.
B: The abundance of an enzyme does not affect the equilibrium of the reaction.
C: This is false for the reason given above.

24. Which of the following would inhibit the forward reaction of carbonic anhydrase most effectively via competitive inhibition?
    A. D_2O
    B. <u>**Cl^-**</u>
    C. H_2CO_3
    D. CO_2

Choice **B** is correct. The active site of the enzyme is a cation. A small anion is best suited to inhibit the enzyme by binding to the zinc.

A: D_2O would simply act the same as water to bring about the action of the enzyme.
C: While this would inhibit the forward reaction of the enzyme, it would not likely do so via competitive inhibition.
D: CO_2 is a substrate of the forward reaction and would only activate the enzyme.

25. Which of the following would best help to activate the oxygen in the hydroxyl group of the side group of threonine?
    A. Lysine
    B. Histidine
    C. Proline
    D. **Glutamic Acid**

Choice **D** is correct. This question asks us to determine which amino acid in carbonic anhydrase might be causing the oxygen in the hydroxyl group mentioned to draw a hydrogen atom towards it. The amino acid will have to contribute to the nucleophilic nature of the oxygen, meaning that the amino acid itself must be drawing away the hydrogen connected to the oxygen. At physiological pH, glutamic acid has a negative charge that will attract this hydrogen, lending to oxygen's nucleophilic action in the enzyme.

A: Lysine is positively charged at physiological pH and will not activate the hydroxyl group in the way desired.
B: Histidine is positively charged at physiological pH and will not activate the hydroxyl group in the way desired.
C: Proline is neutral at physiological pH and will not activate the hydroxyl group in the way desired.

26. Which of the following enzymes could most likely replace threonine in the mechanism shown in Figure 1 without the enzyme losing its functionality?
    A. Cysteine
    B. **Serine**
    C. Tyrosine
    D. Glutamic acid

Choice **B** is correct. Serine is very similar to threonine except it lacks the extra methyl group that threonine has. Since this methyl group seems to contribute very little, serine is the best choice.

A: Cysteine is similar to serine but with the oxygen replaced with sulfur. This could work but is not as good an option as serine.
C: Tyrosine contains a hydroxyl group but is larger than threonine and contains a benzene ring.
D: Glutamic acid is fundamentally different in structure from threonine.

Discrete Set 2 Answers and Explanations (Questions 27-30)

27. Which of the following are modes of transport for CO_2?
    I. Binding hemoglobin
    II. Dissolving in the plasma
    III. Binding red blood cell membranes

    A. I only
    B. II only
    C. <u>**I and II only**</u>
    D. II and III only

Choice **C** is correct. This question asks us to determine how CO_2 might be traveling through the blood. We know that CO_2 can bind hemoglobin and that it can dissolve to some degree in the plasma.

III: CO_2 is a gas molecule, and there are no CO_2 binding receptors on the RBC membrane. There is no reason to think that this is a viable option for CO_2.

28. If the recessive phenotype is expressed in 32 out of 200 individuals in a population. How many individuals in this population would be carriers of the disease?
    A. 32
    B. 48
    C. <u>**96**</u>
    D. 128

Choice **C** is correct. According to the Hardy Weinberg equations, $q^2 = .16$ so $q = .4$ so $p = .6$ so $2pq = 2(.24) = .48$. So 48% of the population will be heterozygotes, meaning 96 individuals.

29. Which of the following are true about the *Clostridium perfringens*, the bacterium responsible for gangrene?
    I. *Clostridium perfringens* can undergo mitosis.
    II. *Clostridium perfringens* can undergo meiosis.
    III. *Clostridium perfringens* contains a single circular chromosome.

    A. I only
    B. II only
    C. <u>**III only**</u>
    D. I and III only

Choice **C** is correct. Clostridium perfringens, like most bacteria, has a single circular chromosome. C. perfringens is actually made up of approximately 3.6 million base pairs.

I: Remember that prokaryotes replicate via binary fission and do not replicate via mitosis or meiosis.
II: Remember that prokaryotes replicate via binary fission and do not replicate via mitosis or meiosis.
III: Clostridium perfringens, like most bacteria, has a single circular chromosome.

30. How many distinct stop codons does the human genome possess?
   A. 1
   B. **3**
   C. 61
   D. 64

Choice **B** is correct. There are 4 amino acids so 64 possibilities of arranging them in groups of 3 base pairs (aka a codon). There is 1 start codon, AUG and 3 stop codons (UAA, UGA, UAG).

Passage VI Answers and Explanations (Questions 31-34)

The perception of color is a process regulated by many factors. The first event in neurological chain that allows us to perceive color is a **photon** of light entering the eye. When focused correctly, the wave should strike the back of the eye at the **retina**. In the center of the retina, the **fovea**, humans have three kinds of **cone cells**. These cells are responsible for transmitting the signal for color vision to our brain. These cones are designated **L, M, and S** which stand for **long, medium and short**. The names represent the wavelength of light that the cone is receptive to. The peak wavelengths for L, M, and S cone responses are about **570, 540, and 450 nm** respectively. The brain will receive signals of varying strength from these three cones, which when blended will allow the brain to interpret the signal as a color.

Key Terms: photon, retina, fovea, cone cells, L, M, S, long, medium, short, 570, 540, 450 nm. This first paragraph introduces us to the function of the three types of cone cells in the eye and how our brain interprets their signals to produce color vision.

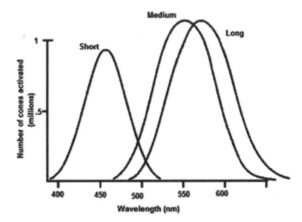

Figure 1 activation of S, M, and L cones as a function of light wavelength

Figure 1 shows the degree to which each of the three types of cone cells are sensitive to each wavelength of light.

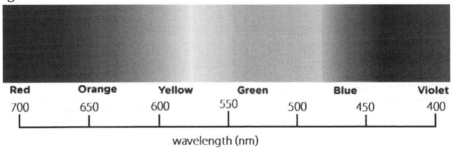

Figure 2 The spectrum of visible light

Figure 2 shows the spectrum of visible light wavelengths and their colors

Cone cells are sensitive only to brighter levels of light than those to which **rod cells** will respond. When vision is employing cones, we can see much more accurately and can tell when two stimuli are separated. This lends to a greater **visual acuity**. This is the case because cone cells each have individual connections to the optic nerve as opposed to rod cells, which are bundled together.

Key Terms: rod cells, visual acuity, optic nerve. This paragraph tells us a little bit about how cone cells differ from rod cells.

Rhodopsin is the protein in rod cells that undergoes a change to propagate a signal when struck by light. In cones, there are other photopsins, called **photopsin I, II, and III**. These photopsins differ in only a few amino acids from rhodopsin and function the same way. Photopsin I responds to yellow-green light, photopsin II to yellow light, and photopsin III to bluish-violet light.

Deuteranopia is a color vision deficiency in which the **medium** photoreceptors are absent. The discrimination of red and green hues is affected by this while discrimination of blues and violets is not significantly affected. It is an **X-linked** disorder.

Key Terms: rhodopsin, photopsin I, II, and III, deuteranopia, medium, X-linked.

Cause and Effect: a lack of medium photoreceptors leads to deuteranopia.

31. Why is a person with deuteranopia still able to see blues and violets?
    A. **Their perception of blues and violets depends more on the amount of short cone cells that are activated than the mixture of S, M, and L cone cells activated.**
    B. Their perception of blues and violets depends more on the mixture of short and medium cone cells activated than the mixture of short and long.
    C. Their perception of blues and violets depends more on long cone cells than medium cone cells.
    D. Their perception of blues and violets is compensated for by medium cone cells.

Choice **A** is correct. The passage states that people with deuteranopia lack the medium cone cell functionality, yet they are still able to see blues and violets. Figure 1 suggests that blues and violets, with wavelengths at 450 or less, are perceived solely as a function of the quantity of short cone cells that respond to the light.

B: If this were true, a person with deuteranopia would not see blues and violets correctly.
C: Figure 1 suggests that medium cone cells will play a larger role in blues perception than long cone cells.
D: According to the passage, people with deuteranopia lack medium cone cell functionality.

32. Which photopsin is present in most abundance in short cone cells?
    A. Photopsin I
    B. Photopsin II
    C. **Photopsin III**
    D. Rhodopsin

Choice **C** is correct. The passage states that short cone cells respond to short wavelengths of light and that photopsin III responds to bluish-violet light, which is short wavelength light.

A: According to the passage, types I and II are the photopsins found in long and medium cone cells respectively.
B: According to the passage, types I and II are the photopsins found in long and medium cone cells respectively.
D: Rhodopsin is found in rod cells, not cone cells.

33. Which of the following best allows the human brain to produce more complex or intricate interpretations of stimuli from light?
    A. The strength of the electrochemical impulse propagated through each nerve on the way to the brain
    B. <u>The quantity of impulses received by the brain at one time</u>
    C. The speed with which the brain receives a neurochemical transmission
    D. A mixture of the strength and speed of the axonal signals sent to the brain

Choice **B** is correct. This question asks us to interpret the information in the passage to determine why some scenarios allow us to see with more accuracy. The passage states that our daytime vision is enhanced because more cones are sending signals to the brain and each cone sends an individual neurological impulse through the optic nerve. With more information, the brain is able to create a better more accurate interpretation of the information.

A: The strength, or amplitude, of a nervous response is fixed.
C: There is no reason to think that the speed with which the brain receives signals affects its interpretation of them.
D: The reasoning for A and C applies here as well.

34. Which of the following graphs most closely represents the total absorbance of all 3 types of cones as a function of wavelength?

A.

B.

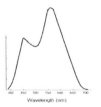

C.

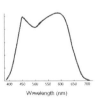

D.

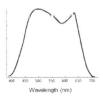

Choice **B** is correct. This question requires us to consider the sum of all the cone cells in Figure 1 as one body clumped together. At a wavelength of around 560 nm. we should see a large increase.

Passage VII Answers and Explanations (Questions 35-39)

The **kidney** can, in a sense, be considered two separate organs. Glucose utilization occurs predominantly in the renal medulla, whereas glucose release is confined to the renal cortex. This functional partition is a result of differences in the distribution of enzymes along the nephron. Therefore, the release of glucose by the normal kidney is mainly, if not exclusively, a **result** of renal **cortical gluconeogenesis**, whereas **glucose uptake** and **utilization** occur in other parts of the kidney.

Key terms: kidney, renal medulla, renal cortex, nephron, cortical gluconeogenesis

Cause-and-Effect: glucose use by the kidneys occurs primarily in the renal medulla while glucose release occurs from the renal cortex due to gluconeogenesis; the difference in glucose utilization between regions of the kidneys is due to differences in the distribution of enzymes along the nephron

Animal and in vitro experiments indicate that **insulin, growth hormone, free fatty acids, and cortisol** all **influence glucose release** from the kidneys. Cortisol and free fatty acids containing an even-number of carbons in their chain have both been shown to stimulate renal gluconeogenesis, while in normal humans, a physiological increase in circulating insulin during hyperglycemic (high blood glucose concentration) states suppresses renal glucose release and increase renal glucose uptake. This **suppression** of renal glucose release is thought to be **due** to **more than** only a **simple reduction** in **gluconeogenic substrate availability in the kidneys**.

Key terms: insulin, growth hormone, free fatty acids, cortisol

Cause-and-Effect: cortisol and free fatty acids stimulate renal gluconeogenesis; insulin suppresses renal glucose release and uptake; suppression of renal glucose release is not due to a reduction of gluconeogenic substrate availability alone

To help clarify the **relationship** between **hormones** and **glucose balance** in the body, normal volunteers were injected with either glucagon or epinephrine at levels equal to those seen during states of hypoglycemia (low blood glucose concentration). The infusion of glucagon had no measureable effect on renal glucose release or uptake. **Changes** in **glucose release systemically**, as well as in the liver and kidneys, due to epinephrine infusion are **shown in Figure 1**.

Key terms: hypoglycemia, liver

Cause-and-Effect: normal volunteers were injected with either glucagon or epinephrine; glucagon effected no significant change in renal glucose release or uptake; epinephrine caused changes in glucose release from the liver, as well from the kidneys

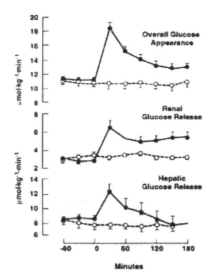

Figure 1: epinephrine infusion causes an increase in overall, renal (kidney) and hepatic (liver) glucose release in normal volunteers following infusion at time equals zero minutes; this effect is sustained beyond 2 hours in the kidneys and systemically, but returns to baseline levels in the liver by 120 minutes post-infusion; the extent of systemic glucose elevation and renal glucose elevation above baseline levels (t = 0 minutes) are approximately equal, suggesting that elevation of glucose appearance is due to renal changes in glucose release alone

35. Which of the following findings, if true, would most support the idea that insulin's suppression of renal glucose release is NOT due to an insulin-mediated reduction in substrate availability alone?

    A. Insulin infusion does not significantly alter total renal uptake of alanine and lactate.

    B. The rate of glycerol uptake in the renal cortex decreases in response to insulin.

    C. <u>Insulin reduces renal uptake of even-chained free fatty acids.</u>

    D. Insulin shunts gluconeogenic precursors into an oxidative pathway.

Choice **C** is correct. Paragraph 1 states that renal glucose release is almost entirely due to gluconeogenesis in the renal cortex. A statement that supports the contention presented in the question should demonstrate that some factor other than a reduction in the pool of available gluconeogenic substrate is causing the decreased cortical gluconeogenesis. In humans, gluconeogenesis results in the generation of glucose from non-carbohydrate carbon substrates such as pyruvate, lactate, glycerol, and glucogenic amino acids including alanine and glutamine. This gluconeogenic pathway cannot typically act on even-chain fatty acids as a substrate. Combined with the passage statement that free fatty acids stimulate gluconeogenesis, a reduction in renal free fatty acid uptake supports the possibility that insulin's suppression of renal glucose release is not due to an insulin-mediated reduction in substrate availability alone, but due to other intra-renal factors as well.

A: This indicates a lack of change in gluconeogeneic substrate to the kidney, which does not provide evidence in support of insulin's suppression of renal glucose release being due to factors beyond an insulin-mediated reduction in substrate availability.

B: This indicates change in gluconeogeneic substrate to the kidney, which does not provide evidence in support of insulin's suppression of renal glucose release being due to factors beyond an insulin-mediated reduction in substrate availability.

C: This indicates change in gluconeogeneic substrate to the kidney, which does not provide evidence in support of insulin's suppression of renal glucose release being due to factors beyond an insulin-mediated reduction in substrate availability.

36. The transient increase in hepatic glucose release during a trial shown in Figure 1 most likely reflects a change in which of the following conditions in the liver cells tested?
    A. Decreased protein kinase A activity
    B. __Phosphorylation and inactivation of phosphofructokinase-2 (PFK-2)__
    C. Decreased fructose 1,6-bisphophastase activity
    D. Phosphorylation and activation of phosphofructokinase-2 (PFK-2)

Choice **B** is correct. The question asks for the most likely explanation for the increase in glucose production seen in the figure. We are told that prior to that time, epinephrine was administered. Thus, the increase in hepatic glucose release shown in Figure 1 is likely due to an increase in hepatic gluconeogenesis caused by epinephrine injection. Epinephrine acts to increase the rate of substrate flux in liver cells through the gluconeogenic pathway and away from the glycolytic pathway. This is achieved by stimulating the cAMP regulated kinase, protein kinase A, which acts to phosphorylate and inactivate the phosphofructokinase-2 (PFK-2) domain of the bi-functional enzyme responsible for the formation of fructose-2,6-bisphosphate, a potent allosteric activator of phosphofructokinase-1 (PFK-1)—an important regulated step in glycolysis. This could explain the temporary rise in gluconeogenic products of that time period.

A: Epinephrine stimulates protein kinase A, furthermore, decreased protein kinase A activity would disfavor gluconeogenesis.
C: Fructose 1, 6-bisphosphatase is an enzyme that converts fructose-1,6-bisphosphate to fructose 6-phosphate in gluconeogenesis and aids in glucose production. Thus, a decrease in this enzyme activity would not explain a transient period of elevated glucose production.
D: Epinephrine disfavors PFK-2 activation through PKA signaling; additionally, the activation of PFK-2 would disfavor gluconeogenesis.

37. Researchers hypothesized that stimulation of lipolysis by epinephrine cause the sustained increase in systemic glucose release shown in Figure 1. Given the mechanisms of metabolic regulation in healthy adults and information presented in the passage, does this hypothesis offer a potential explanation for the effect seen in Figure 1?
    A. No, two hours following epinephrine infusion nearly all of the increase in systemic glucose resulted from renal glucose release.
    B. No, epinephrine increases the rate of fatty acid uptake and utilization in peripheral tissues.
    C. Yes, during prolonged fasting, glucose released from the kidneys is the predominate source of circulating glucose.
    D. __Yes, epinephrine stimulates lipolysis and free fatty acid release, which could increase the rate of renal gluconeogenesis.__

Choice **D** is correct. According to the passage, free fatty acids stimulate renal gluconeogenesis. Figure 1 also shows that the extent of the sustained, systemic glucose and renal glucose elevations above baseline levels (t = 0 minutes) are approximately equal, suggesting that elevation of glucose appearance is due to renal changes in glucose release alone. Together these facts suggest that the stimulation of lipolysis by epinephrine and a subsequent increase in free fatty acid release could act on the renal cortices and be responsible for the elevation in sustained overall glucose appearance shown in Figure 1.

A: While Figure 1 is consistent with the statement that nearly all of the increase in systemic glucose resulted from renal glucose release, this, combined with the information referenced in the argument above tends to strengthen, rather than weaken the hypothesis presented in the question stem.
B: While there are a number of systemic and tissue-specific physiological effects to administration of epinephrine, including increased heart and respiratory rate, changes in vascular tone, and increased lipolysis and glycogenolysis, it

does not directly affect the rate of free fatty acid uptake in peripheral tissue.

C: If this were true, it would not address the hypothesized relationship between stimulation of lipolysis by epinephrine and the changes in glucose appearance shown in Figure 1

38. Given information presented in the passage, which of the following enzymes is most likely to be found in greater concentration in the renal cortex than in the renal medulla?
    A. Hexokinase
    B. Phosphoglycerate mutase
    C. Phosphoglucoisomerase
    D. **Glucose-6-phosphatase**

Choice **D** is correct. The passage states that glucose utilization occurs predominantly in the renal medulla, while glucose release is confined to the renal cortex. The passage additionally says that these differences are due to the differential distribution of enzymes along the nephron and that nearly all glucose release in the renal cortices is due to renal gluconeogenesis. These facts suggest that the enzymes specific to gluconeogenesis should be found in relatively greater quantity in the renal cortex than in the renal medulla. Of the enzymes listed in the choices, only glucose-6-phosphatase is specific to gluconeogenesis. The enzyme itself is responsible for the hydrolysis of glucose-6-phosphate to free glucose in the final step of gluconeogenesis, and would be required for export of glucose, via glucose transporter membrane proteins, from the renal cortex.

A: Glucokinase catalyzes the reverse of the reaction catalyzed by glucose-6-phosphatase—the phosphorylation of glucose (or other hexose sugars) to glucose-6-phosphate (or other hexose phosphate sugars) in the initial step of glycolysis.
B and C: Both phosphoglycerate mutase and phosphoglucoisomerase are non-regulated enzymes common to both glycolysis and gluconeogenesis.

39. If not properly compensated for by other physiological responses, sustained hyperglycemia promotes cellular dehydration in what way?
    A. Glucose co-transport accelerates the rate of plasma membrane ion exchange
    B. Glucose-water antiport during cellular uptake of glucoses increases cellular osmotic pressure
    C. Cellular glucose is used to form glycogen in dehydration synthesis reactions
    D. **Glucose increases the osmotic pressure of the extracellular space**

Choice **D** is correct. An increased concentration of circulating blood glucose, to which cell membranes are relatively impermeable, causes the osmotic pressure of the extracellular fluid to rise, in turn causing water to leave the cell. This movement of water promotes cellular dehydration.

A: In addition to entry into cells by facilitated diffusion through the GLUT family of plasma membrane transport proteins, glucose also enters the cells of certain tissue, including the proximal tubule of the nephron and enterocytes of the small intestine, via a co-transport mechanism—specifically by way of the glucose symporter SGLT1, which co-transports one glucose (or galactose) molecule into the cell for every two sodium ions it imports into the cell. However, increased activity of this co-transport mechanism promotes hydration, rather than dehydration, of cells through an increase in intracellular osmotic pressure.
B: water enters cells via diffusion or through water-specific channels (aquaporins). It does not participate in antiport mechanisms.
C: The biological synthesis of glycogen, glycogenesis, from glucose-1-phosphate, which is further converted to UDP-glucose and added to a glucosyl residue of a growing glycogen chain, does not require the net input of water.

Passage VIII Answers and Explanations (Questions 40-43)

Phenylketonuria (PKU) is a **recessive metabolic genetic disorder** characterized by an **inability to metabolize** the amino acid phenylalanine to the amino acid tyrosine. In classical PKU, mutations in the PAH gene on the short arm of chromosome 12, which encodes for the liver enzyme phenylalanine hydroxylase (PAH), leading to an accumulation of phenylalanine. As it accumulates, it is converted through a minor transaminase pathway with **glutamate to phenylpyruvate** which can be **detected in the urine** of affected individuals. If untreated, **PKU can lead to intellectual disability, seizures**, and other serious medical problems.

Key terms: Phenylketonuria (PKU), phenylalanine, tyrosine, phenylalanine hydroxylase (PAH), transaminase, glutamate, phenylpyruvate

Cause-and-Effect: PKU is an autosomal recessive disorder characterized by an inability to metabolize Phe to Tyr; it can be caused by a mutation in the PAH gene which encodes the liver enzyme PAH; in PKU, Phe accumulations and is converted into phenylpyruvate in a transaminase reaction shown in Figure 2; phenylpyruvate can be detected in the urine and its build-up can lead to medical problems

A rarer, **variant form of PKU** occurs when the PAH enzyme is normal, but a defect is found in the enzyme dihydrobiopterin reductase. The enzyme is **responsible** for **the regeneration** of **5,6,7,8-tetrahydrobiopterin (BH4)** from pterin-4a-carbinolamine. BH4 is an important cofactor for a number of reactions of amino acid metabolism, not only as a cofactor for PAH, but also as a cofactor required for the production of L-DOPA, a dopamine precursor, from tyrosine and **5-hydroxy-L-tryptophan**, a **precursor of serotonin and melatonin, from tryptophan**.

The degradation of **phenylalanine to tyrosine**, including those enzymes affected in PKU, is shown in Figure 1. The transaminase pathway in which phenylalanine is metabolized to phenylpyruvate is shown in Figure 2.

Key terms: variant form of PKU, 5,6,7,8-tetrahydrobiopterin (BH4), pterin-4a-carinolamine, L-DOPA, dopamine, 5-hydroxy-L-tryptophan, serotonin, melatonin

Cause-and-Effect: a variant for of PKU exists wherein the PAH enzyme is normal but dihydrobiopterin reductase is deficient, leading to a deficiency in the cofactor BH4; without sufficient BH4, the production of phenylalanine accumulates leading to PKU, and, separately, the production of L-DOPA and 5-hydroxy-L-trypotphan are impaired

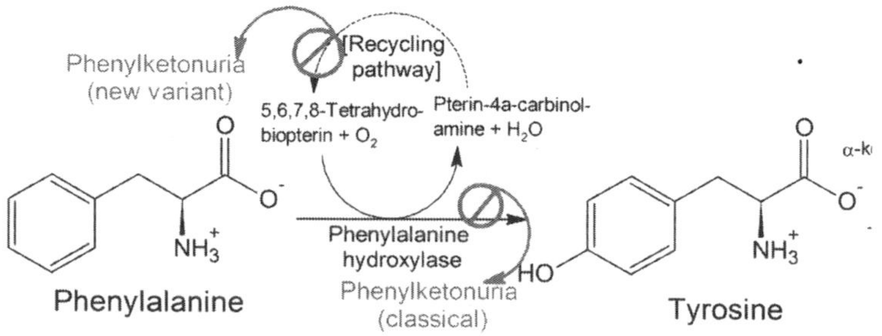

Figure 1 Deficiencies of PAH (classic PKU) or BH4 reductase (variant PKU) causes an accumulation of phenylalanine

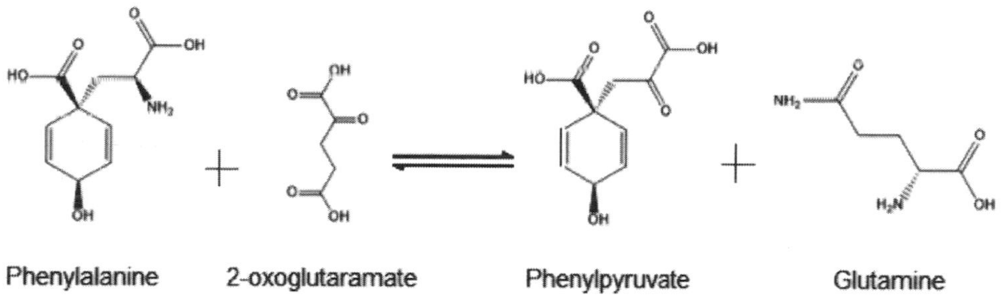

Figure 2 Phenylalanine, which accumulates in PKU, and 2-oxoglutaric acid react in a transamination reaction to yield phenylpyruvate and glutamine

In addition to adhering to a **diet low in phenylalanine**, it is also suggested that those with PKU supplement their diet with large neutral amino acids (LNAAs). Because of similarities in their side chain properties, LNAAs compete with phenylalanine for specific carrier proteins that **transport LNAAs** across the intestinal mucosa into the blood and **across the blood-brain barrier** into the brain.

Key terms: large-neutral amino acids (LNAAs), intestinal mucosa, blood-brain barrier

Cause-and-Effect: those with PKU should maintain a diet low in Phe and supplement it with LNAAs, with compete with Phe for carrier proteins that transport it across the intestinal mucosa and blood brain barrier into the blood, and brain, respectively

40. When observing the inheritance pattern of the mutant form of the PAH allele within a family, which of the following is LEAST likely to be seen over a large number of generations?
    A. Generations without the appearance of individuals with symptoms of PKU
    B. Affected males with fathers who also showed symptoms of PKU.
    C. An approximately equal number of males and females displaying symptoms of PKU
    D. **Appearance of individuals with symptoms of PKU in each generation**

Choice **D** is correct. The passage states that PKU is a recessive disorder. It further states that the mutant form of the PAH allele responsible for classical PKU is found on chromosome 12, indicating that the disease is inherited in an autosomal recessive fashion. After a large number of generations have passed, it is likely that a disease with such an inheritance pattern will show a number of generations with no affected family members.

A: Autosomal recessive disorders often skip generations.
B: Male-to-male transmission is possible in autosomally inherited disorders.
C: Autosomal disorders show a relatively equal numbers of affected males and females.

41. The blood brain barrier's relative impermeability is formed by capillary endothelial cells connected by what type of cell-cell junctions?
    A. Adherens unction
    B. **Tight junctions**
    C. Anchoring junctions
    D. Gap junctions

Choice **B** is correct. The blood–brain barrier is an extremely selective permeability barrier that separates the circulating blood from the brain extracellular fluid in the central nervous system. It is formed by capillary endothelial cells, which are connected by tight junctions—closely associated regions of adjacent cells that form a virtually impermeable barrier to fluid.

A: Adherens junction are a type of anchoring junction that link the cytoplasmic face of cells to actin of the cytoskeleton.

C: Anchoring junctions are complexes in which anchoring proteins extend through the plasma membrane to link cytoskeletal proteins in one cell to the cytoskeletal proteins of a neighboring cell as well as to proteins in the extracellular matrix. These junctions include adherens junctions, hemidesmosomes and desmosomes.

D: Gap junctions are communicating junctions that directly connect the cytoplasm of two cells, allowing passage of molecules, ions and electrical impulses between cells through a regulated gate.

42. Dopamine inhibits release of prolactin from the anterior pituitary. Given this, which of the following statements is most likely to be true of an individual suffering from either classical PKU or variant PKU with BH4 reductase deficiency?
    A. Prolactin release will be increased in an individual with classical PKU.
    B. Prolactin release will be decreased in an individual with classical PKU.
    C. **Prolactin release will be increased in an individual with variant PKU.**
    D. Prolactin release will be decreased in an individual with variant PKU.

Choice **C** is correct. According to the passage, a deficiency of the enzyme BH4 reductase leads to a deficiency in BH4, a cofactor required for the synthesis of L-DOPA, a synthetic precursor to dopamine. BH4 reductase deficient individuals, then, should be expected to have less dopamine available for the inhibition of prolactin release, and, as a consequence, greater release of prolactin.

A: The passage does not provide information to directly indicate how prolactin release could be changed in an individual with classical PKU.

B: The passage does not provide information to directly indicate how prolactin release could be changed in an individual with classical PKU.

D: Prolactin release will be increased, not increased, in an individual with variant PKU.

43. A similar transaminase reaction to that shown in Figure 2 catalyzes the transformation of L-glutamate and pyruvate ($CH_3C(O)COOH$; shown below) into α-ketoglutarate and what amino acid?

    A. L-glycine
    B. **L-alanine**
    C. L-glutamine
    D. L-aspartate

Choice **B** is correct. Transamination of L-glutamate and pyruvate is analogous to the reaction shown in Figure 2 and results in the transfer of an amino group from L-glutamate to pyruvate, resulting in the formation of the α-keto acid α-ketoglutarate and alanine, shown below. The reaction is catalyzed by the enzyme alanine amino transferase and allows muscles to use pyruvate for transamination to give alanine, which is carried by the bloodstream to the liver (the overall reaction being termed glucose-alanine cycle). Here other transaminases regenerate pyruvate, which provides a valuable precursor for gluconeogenesis in the liver.

Discrete Set 3 Answers and Explanations (Questions 44-47)

44. Which of the following is the amino acid that is coded for by the start codon in humans?
   A. Cysteine
   B. Alanine
   C. **Methionine**
   D. Glycine

Choice **C** is correct. Remember that AUG is the start codon. All further AUG after the initial sequence codes for methionine.

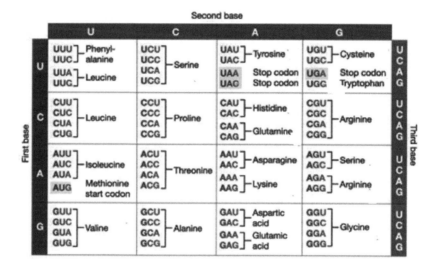

A: AUG, the start codon, does not code for cysteine.
B: AUG, the start codon, does not code for alanine.
D: AUG, the start codon, does not code for glycine.

45. What is the target tissue of the hormone ACTH?
   A. Renal tissue
   B. **The adrenal gland**
   C. Hepatic tissue
   D. Blood vessels

Choice **B** is correct. ACTH is the hormone that induces secretion of cortisol from the adrenal gland. The secretion of ACTH by the pituitary is itself regulated by another polypeptide, corticotropin-releasing hormone (CRH), which is discharged from the hypothalamus in response to impulses transmitted by the nervous system.

46. How might glucagon affect the rate of pyruvate decarboxylation?
   A. It would increase the rate of pyruvate decarboxylation
   B. **It would decrease the rate of pyruvate decarboxylation**
   C. It would not affect the rate of pyruvate decarboxylation
   D. There is not enough information to answer the question

Choice **B** is correct. Glucagon has several physiological effects. It stimulates the conversion of stored glycogen (stored in the liver) to glucose which can be released into the bloodstream. This process is called glycogenolysis. It promotes the production of glucose from amino acid molecules. This process is called gluconeogenesis. It reduces glucose consumption by the liver so that as much glucose as possible can be secreted into the bloodstream to maintain blood glucose levels. Glucagon also acts on adipose tissue to stimulate the breakdown of fat stores into the bloodstream.

A: Glucagon will decrease glucose uptake into the cells which will decrease the amount of pyruvate in the mitochondria which will decrease the rate of pyruvate decarboxylation to produce acetyl CoA.
C: Glucagon will decrease glucose uptake into the cells which will decrease the amount of pyruvate in the mitochondria which will decrease the rate of pyruvate decarboxylation to produce acetyl CoA.
D: Glucagon will decrease glucose uptake into the cells which will decrease the amount of pyruvate in the mitochondria which will decrease the rate of pyruvate decarboxylation to produce acetyl CoA.

47. What tissue is most likely to use glucose as a source of energy in a state of fasting?
    A. The digestive tract
    B. Skeletal muscle
    C. The brain
    D. Cardiac muscle

Choice **C** is correct. The body responds to reduced energy intake by burning fat reserves and consuming muscle and other tissues. Specifically, the body burns fat after first exhausting the contents of the digestive tract along with glycogen reserves stored in muscle and liver cells. After prolonged periods of starvation, the body will utilize the proteins within muscle tissue as a fuel source. After the exhaustion of the glycogen reserve, fatty acids are the principal metabolic fuel. At first, the brain continues to use glucose, because, if a non-brain tissue is using fatty acids as its metabolic fuel, the use of glucose in the same tissue is switched off. Thus, when fatty acids are being broken down for energy, all of the remaining glucose is made available for use by the brain. Remember that the brain is unable to use fats or other sources of energy. Glucose is preserved specifically for the brain when glucose intake is low.

A: This tissue can oxidize fatty acids or break down proteins for energy during fasting states.
B: Skeletal muscle can oxidize fatty acids or break down proteins for energy during fasting states.
D: Cardiac muscle can oxidize fatty acids or break down proteins for energy during fasting states.

Passage IX Answers and Explanations (Questions 48-51)

Immediately after **fertilization**, the human **embryo** undergoes rapid and drastic changes. These changes are largely driven by **mitosis**, the process through which cells replicate their **chromosomes** and divide. Mitosis is broken into **four main steps** – prophase, metaphase, anaphase, and telophase. During prophase, cells condense their chromosomes and begin to form the mitotic spindles used to separate the chromosomes evenly into the two daughter cells. During metaphase, the chromosomes align along the metaphase plate and begin to be pulled apart by the mitotic spindles. In anaphase, the chromosomes are separated, forming two identical sister chromatids, and are pulled to opposite ends of the dividing cell. Finally, in telophase, the two daughter cells pull apart followed by the formation of a new nucleus in each cell. Both daughter cells are genetically identical to the original cell. This cascade of events occurs in all body cells, including germ (reproductive) cells.

Key terms: fertilization, mitosis, chromosomes, prophase, metaphase, anaphase, telophase, daughter cells, metaphase plate, chromatids

Contrast: 4 stages of mitosis

Cause-and-Effect: Mitosis causes cells to replicate their chromosomes and divide – it's a way for tissues to repair and grow.

Cancer cells are known for their **unregulated, continuous mitotic division**. A cancer researcher performs an experiment in which she tests various molecules used in chemotherapy to see their effect on two cancer cell lines she has obtained. The first inhibitor she tries is **docetaxel**, a **mitotic inhibitor** that binds reversibly to microtubules, drastically **increasing the doubling time of Cell Line 1**. The second **inhibitor** she tries is **ibrutinib**, an inhibitor of Bruton's tyrosine kinase (BTK), an enzyme involved in **B cell development**. It dramatically increases the doubling time of Cell Line 2. The **doubling times** for the two inhibitors with both cell lines are provided in Table 1.

	No treatment	Docetaxel	Ibrutinib
Cell Line 1	25 hr	44 hr	24 hr
Cell Line 2	34 hr	36 hr	52 hr

Key terms: chemotherapy, cancer cell lines, docetaxel, mitotic inhibitor, microtubules, doubling time, ibrutinib, B cell development

Contrast: Docetaxel is a mitotic inhibitor that binds reversibly to microtubules and increases the doubling time of Cell Line 1. Ibrutinib is an inhibitor of BTK and increases the doubling time of Cell Line 2.

Cause-and-Effect: Docetaxel increases the doubling time of Cell Line 1, Ibrutinib increases the doubling time of Cell Line 2.

48. Chromosomal crossover, or the exchange of genetic information between homologous chromosomes, occurs in which stage of mitosis?
    A. Prophase
    B. Metaphase II
    C. Anaphase
    D. **None of these**

Choice **D** is correct. This question asks for which stage of mitosis. Crossing over is unique to meiosis, a specialized type of cell division that occurs only in germ cells. It occurs in Prophase I of meiosis. This question asks for which stage of mitosis.

A: Crossover occurs during Prophase I of meiosis, not mitosis.
B: Crossover occurs during Prophase I of meiosis, not metaphase II. In metaphase II of meiosis, the chromosomes line up at the metaphase II plate at the cell's center and the kinetochore fibers of the sister chromatids point toward opposite poles.
C: Crossover occurs in meiosis, not anaphase of mitosis. During anaphase, sister chromatids separate and begin moving to opposite ends of the cell. Spindle fibers not connected to chromatids lengthen and elongate the cell.

49. Among non-cancerous cells in the human body, which cells are likely to undergo mitosis at the fastest rate?
    A. Neurons
    B. Muscle cells
    C. **Skin cells**
    D. Germ cells

Choice **C** is correct. Due to constant exposure to the environment where it is subjected to cuts, scratches, and abrasions, the skin must not only continuously grow but it must also repair. This leads to the epithelial cells of the skin having the highest rate of mitosis among non-cancerous cells.

A: Neurons are typically in a state of G0, and are among the slowest dividing cells in the body, not the fastest.
B: Muscle cells are typically in a state of G0, and divide at a rate lower than skin cells.
D: Germ cells, aka gametes do not divide as fast as skin cells.

50. The restriction point, or the point at which a cell is committed to undergoing mitosis, is located in which stage of interphase?
    A. G0
    B. S
    C. **G1**
    D. G2

Choice **C** is correct. The restriction point is a point in G1 of the cell cycle, and after it is passed the cell is committed to division.

A: A cell in G0 phase of interphase has not yet reached the restriction point.
B: A cell in S phase has already passed the restriction point, and is beginning to prepare for mitosis.
D: A cell in G2 has already passed the restriction point, and is committed to division.

51. If the researcher looks at Cell Line 1 being grown in the presence of docetaxel under a microscope, would she find the majority of them in interphase or a mitotic phase?
    A. Interphase, because docetaxel will prevent the microtubule-organizing center (MTOC) from developing during this stage.
    B. A mitotic phase, because docetaxel will prevent formation of the cleavage furrow during cytokinesis.
    C. Interphase, because docetaxel will prevent DNA duplication.
    D. <u>**A mitotic phase, because docetaxel will arrest the cells in mitosis prior to anaphase.**</u>

Choice **D** is correct. The key information needed to answer this question is found in the second paragraph of the passage, which states that docetaxel binds reversibly to microtubules and as a result inhibits mitosis. Microtubules are responsible for the movement of fully duplicated chromosomes away from each other from the metaphase plate, and therefore it is likely that this will not proceed in the event of microtubule disruption due to docetaxel.

A: This is a tempting choice because it involves microtubules and it is true that the microtubule-organizing center develops during interphase. However, disruption of the microtubule-organizing center will not prevent the cell from entering mitosis, but will begin affecting the cell during mitosis, when the chromosomes are to be separated.
B: Actin and myosin, and not microtubules, are involved in the formation of the cleavage furrow. As nothing in the passage suggests an effect of docetaxel on actin or myosin, this answer is not correct.
C: No information in the passage indicates that docetaxel would have any effect on DNA duplication.

Passage X Answers and Explanations (Questions 52-55)

The **cells of eukaryotic** organisms consist of a **membrane** comprised of **phospholipids**, which encases a **cytosol** populated by a number of organelles. One such organelle is the mitochondrion. The mitochondrion has an outer membrane and an inner membrane, separated by the intermembrane space. The space enclosed by the inner membrane is referred to as the mitochondrial matrix. The mitochondrion as a whole serves as an "energy powerhouse." It is within the mitochondrion that pyruvate decarboxylation, the Krebs cycle (i.e., the citric acid cycle), and the electron transport chain occur, **all processes of aerobic respiration** in cells. Pyruvate decarboxylation is a biochemical reaction occurring in the mitochondrial matrix that converts pyruvate (a product of glycolysis) into acetyl coenzyme A (Ac-CoA). Ac-CoA can then be used in the Krebs cycle (also in the mitochondrial matrix) to generate energy. Finally, the majority of the energy from aerobic respiration is generated in the electron transport chain, which occurs at the mitochondrial inner membrane. In the electron transport chain, redox reactions occur in which electrons are transferred to an acceptor molecule from a donor molecule.

Key Terms: pyruvate decarboxylation, Krebs cycle, electron transport chain, redox

Contrast: Eukaryotic organisms have mitochondria with inner and outer membranes. Inside the inner membrane is the matrix, where pyruvate decarboxylation and Krebs cycle both occur (small amount of energy), and along the inner membrane is where the electron transport chain occurs (large amount of energy).

Cause-and-Effect: Together, the electron transport chain and Krebs cycle generate a large amount of energy for the cell within the mitochondria.

While the majority of DNA in a eukaryotic cell is **isolated inside the nucleus**, it has been discovered that a **small amount** of non-nuclear DNA resides within the **mitochondria**. This mitochondrial DNA (**mtDNA**) is different from other inherited DNA in that it is **inherited solely from the mother**. Upon fertilization of a human zygote, the sperm's mitochondria do enter the egg, **but do not** provide genetic information to the embryo.

Key Terms: non-nuclear DNA, mtDNA

Contrast: mtDNA is only inherited from the mother, and it is not located in the nucleus. It is located in the mitochondria.

Cause-and-Effect: Mitochondria have their own DNA to code for their proteins, and that is called mtDNA.

It has been seen that in rare cases mitochondria **do not function properly**, leading to "**mitochondrial diseases**" in a small subset of the population. Neuropathy, ataxia, and retinitis pigmentosa **(NARP) syndrome** is an example of this. Upon entering early adulthood, most people with NARP syndrome begin to experience **tingling and/or pain in their extremities and problems with balance**. As the disease advances, it also can lead to light sensitivity and eventually vision loss.

Key Terms: mitochondrial diseases, NARP syndrome

Cause-and-Effect: Non-functioning mitochondria can lead to neuropathies and coordination issues, as well as loss of vision.

52. A mother with NARP syndrome has two children, a son and a daughter. Which child is more likely to inherit the disease?
    A. The son
    B. The daughter
    C. **The son and daughter have equal likelihood of inheriting the disease.**
    D. Information about the father's disease status must also be provided to answer this question.

Choice **C** is correct. The passage states that mtDNA is exclusively inherited from the mother. If the mother has NARP syndrome, then she has an equal likelihood of passing it on to her children. The passage does not state any higher incidence in males vs. females, or vice versa.

A: The passage does not state that there is a higher incidence in males vs. females. Both children are equally likely to inherit the disease.
B: The passage does not state that there is a higher incidence in females vs. males. Both children are equally likely to inherit the disease.
D: mtDNA is exclusively inherited from the mother. The father's disease status is irrelevant.

53. Many scientists believe in the "endosymbiotic theory," which states that the mitochondrion developed evolutionarily when a prokaryote entered a eukaryotic cell through endocytosis and led to a symbiotic relationship where both organisms were able to thrive. If this were true, what is a plausible size of the ribosomes coded for by mtDNA?
    A. 40S
    B. 50S
    C. **70S**
    D. 80S

Choice **C** is correct. The question suggests that the mitochondria evolved evolutionarily from a prokaryote entering a eukaryote. The passage also provides evidence for this, by suggesting that the mitochondria have their own set of DNA that is separate from nuclear DNA. Prokaryotic ribosomes are 70S, comprised of a small (30S) subunit and a large (50S) subunit.

A: This is the size of the small subunit in a eukaryotic ribosome.
B: This is the size of the large subunit in a prokaryotic ribosome.
D: This is the size of the eukaryotic ribosome.

54. What is the final electron acceptor molecule in the electron transport chain?
    A. **Oxygen**
    B. Water
    C. ATP
    D. Calcium

Choice **A** is correct. In the electron transport chain, electrons are transferred in a series of redox reactions at the mitochondrial inner membrane. These redox reactions are coupled with transfer of protons across the membrane to drive ATP synthesis by ATP synthase. The final electron transfer is from Complex IV to oxygen, and oxygen is reduced to water.

B: Oxygen is converted to water after accepting the electrons.
C: ATP is generated throughout the electron transport chain, but it is not the final electron acceptor.
D: Calcium is not an acceptor in the electron transport chain.

55. In an individual free of mitochondrial disease, which of the following cell types would lack functioning mitochondria?
    A. **Red blood cells**
    B. Muscle cells
    C. Neurons
    D. White blood cells

Choice **A** is correct. In order to provide maximum space for hemoglobin, red blood cells lack a nucleus and most organelles, including mitochondria. Thus, they must only generate ATP through anaerobic respiration (glycolysis and lactic acid fermentation).

B: Muscle cells require a high amount of energy, and thus definitely must undergo aerobic respiration and have mitochondria.
C: Neurons require a high amount of energy, and thus definitely must undergo aerobic respiration and have mitochondria.
D: White blood cells are unlike red blood cells in that they have organelles and a nucleus (since they do not need to accommodate high amounts of hemoglobin).

Discrete Set 4 Answers and Explanations (Questions 56-59)

56. Which of the following are most likely found in the interior of a protein?
    I. Lysine
    II. Valine
    III. Glutamic Acid

    A. I only
    B. **II only**
    C. I and II only
    D. I and III only

Choice **B** is correct. Remember that non-polar (hydrophobic) amino acids are more likely to be found in the interior of a protein, thus protecting them from the aqueous environment of the body. Valine has a non-polar isopropyl group as its side chain.

I: This amino acid is charged. At physiological pH, lysine has a quaternary ammonium ion on its side chain.
III: This amino acid is charged. At physiological pH, glutamic acid has a carboxylate ion on its side chain.

57. By which of the following processes do prokaryotes usually reproduce?
    A. **Binary fission**
    B. Bacterial conjugation
    C. Transduction
    D. Transformation

Choice **A** is correct. Remember that prokaryotes reproduce by binary fission.

B: This is not a form of reproduction. Bacterial conjugation is the transfer of genetic material between bacterial cells by direct cell-to-cell contact or by a bridge-like connection between two cells.
C: This is not a form of reproduction. During transduction genes from a host bacteria are incorporated into the genome of a bacterial virus (bacteriophage) and then carried to another host cell when the bacteriophage initiates another cycle of infection.
D: This is not a form of reproduction. The purpose of transformation is to introduce a foreign plasmid into bacteria and to use that bacteria to amplify the plasmid in order to make large quantities of it.

58. Positron emission tomography (PET) scan is an imaging test that uses a radioactive tracer to look for disease in the body. Which of the following correctly describes positron emission?
    A. **A proton is converted to a neutron and a positron.**
    B. A neutron is converted to an electron and a proton
    C. A neutron is converted to a proton and a positron
    D. A proton is converted to an electron and a neutron

Choice **A** is correct. Positron emission or beta plus decay is when a proton inside a radionuclide nucleus is converted into a neutron while releasing a positron and an electron neutrino.

B: This is beta-minus decay, not positron emission.
C, D: These are not any kind of radioactive emission (a neutral thing emitting a positive and becoming positive itself violates the law of conservation of charge, as does starting with a positive thing and turning into a neutral thing and emitting a negative thing).

59. Which of the following does NOT contribute to genetic diversity in gamete reproduction?
    A. Random chromosomal arrangement along the metaphase plate during metaphase I
    B. Random chromosomal arrangement along the metaphase plate during metaphase II
    C. **Random chromosomes are replicated during meiosis I**
    D. Crossing over during prophase I.

Choice **C** is correct. Prior to meiosis I, cells will copy all of their genetic information prior to meiosis. These homologous chromosomes always pair up. There is nothing random about this process.

A: During metaphase I, the division of homologous chromosomes is random, for each chromosome, each daughter cell has a 50% chance of getting the father's chromosome and 50% chance of getting the mother's.
B: Sister chromatids will not be exactly identical due to crossing over in meiosis I. For each chromosome, each daughter cell has a 50% chance of getting one chromatid over the other.
D: Crossing over is a definite source of genetic diversity.

MCAT BIOLOGY AND BIOCHEMISTRY: STRATEGY AND PRACTICE

APPENDIX A

Timed Section Scoring Scale

Table 1 Raw Score to Scaled Score Conversion for Science Sections

These scores are rough estimates based on released scales the AAMC has provided. The raw-to-scaled conversion is based on data from past AAMC exams.

Raw Score (Number of Questions Correct)	Scaled Score	Percentile*
58-59	132	100
56-57	131	99
54-55	130	97
51-53	129	93
47-50	128	87
43-46	127	77
39-42	126	67
36-38	125	54
33-35	124	44
30-32	123	32
27-29	122	21
23-26	121	14
18 - 22	120	7
16 - 17	119	3
0 - 15	118	1

* Percentile rank is given in this table as an example of how percentile correlates with scaled score, taken from recent actual MCAT exams. This is for illustration purposes only and does not represent performance of test-takers from the material in this exam.

APPENDIX B

Self-Study Outline

Biology

_____
_____
_____
_____

1. Proteins

_____
_____
_____
_____

A. Structure

_____
_____
_____

Primary CL: _____

_____
_____
_____

Secondary CL: _____

_____
_____
_____
_____

Tertiary CL: _____

_____
_____
_____

Quaternary CL: _____

_____
_____
_____
_____

B. Protein Function

_____
_____
_____
_____

Immune System CL: _____

_____
_____
_____
_____

Motor CL: _____

_____
_____
_____
_____

C. Enzymes

_____
_____
_____
_____

As Catalysts CL: _____

_____
_____
_____
_____

Cofactors CL: _____

_____
_____
_____
_____

Coenzymes CL: _____

_____
_____
_____
_____

Classification CL: _____

_____
_____
_____
_____

a) Substrate interactions

_____
_____
_____
_____

Active Site CL: _____

_____
_____
_____
_____

Induced Fit CL: _____

_____
_____
_____
_____

Vitamins CL: _____

_____
_____
_____
_____

b) Effects on Enzyme Activity

_____
_____
_____
_____

pH CL: _____

_____
_____
_____
_____

Temperature CL: _____

_____
_____
_____
_____

D. Enzyme Control

_____
_____
_____
_____

a) Kinetics

Michaelis-Menten CL: _____

_____
_____
_____
_____

Cooperativity CL: _____

_____
_____
_____
_____

Feedback CL: _____

_____
_____
_____
_____

    b)   Inhibition

_____
_____
_____
_____

Competitive CL: _____

_____
_____
_____
_____

Non-competitive CL: _____

_____
_____
_____
_____

    c)   Regulation

_____
_____
_____
_____

Allosteric enzymes CL: _____

_____
_____
_____
_____

Zymogens CL: _____

_____

_____

_____

Covalently-modified enzymes CL: _____

_____

_____

_____

2. Molecular Genetics

_____

_____

_____

A. Nucleic Acids

_____

_____

_____

Structure CL: _____

_____

_____

_____

Nucleotides CL: _____

_____

_____

_____

Nucleosides CL: _____

_____

_____

_____

Purines CL: _____

_____

_____

_____

APPENDIX C

Self-Study Glossary

Acquired immunity

The portion of the immune system that encounters foreign substances (antigens) and learns the best way to attack each antigen and begin to develop a memory for that antigen.

ACTH (adrenocorticotropic hormone)

A polypeptide hormone formed in the pituitary gland that regulates the activity of the cortex of the adrenal glands, where the glucocorticoid hormones—cortisol and corticosterone are released.

Actin

A thin protein that forms (together with myosin) the contractile filaments of muscle cells, and is also involved in motion in other types of cells.

Action potential

A temporary alteration of the transmembrane voltage (membrane potential) across an excitable membrane in a cell (such as a neuron or myocyte) generated by the movement of ions through of voltage-gated ion channels embedded in the membrane.

Active site

The portion of an enzyme that is directly involved in binding substrate(s).

Active transport

The movement of a substance against its concentration gradient (from low to high concentration).

Adaptive radiation

Process in which organisms diversify rapidly into many new forms, particularly when environmental change makes new resources available.

ADH (antidiuretic hormone)

A peptide hormone released by the posterior pituitary gland after being made in the hypothalamus. It acts to increase water reabsorption in the kidney.

Adipocytes

Cells that primarily compose adipose tissue, specialized in storing energy as fat. Also known as lipocytes and fat cells.

Agonist Any chemical that binds to a receptor and activates the receptor to produce a biological response.

Albumin A protein made by the liver. Its main function is to regulate the osmotic pressure of blood.

Aldosterone A steroid hormone produced by the cortex of the adrenal gland. It regulates the balance of water and electrolytes in the body, by increasing sodium reabsorption in the kidney.

Allosteric effect Interactions between spatially distinct sites; i.e.: a conformational change induced by the binding of a molecule to one site in a protein that alters other sites of the same protein.

Amphipathic Any molecule containing both polar (water-soluble) and nonpolar (not water-soluble) portions in its structure.

Anabolic pathway ATP-consuming.

Anaphase The stage of mitosis when chromosomes are split and the sister chromatids move to opposite poles of the cell.

Antagonist Any receptor ligand or drug that blocks or dampens agonist-mediated responses rather than provoking a biological response itself.

Anterior pituitary A portion of the pituitary (the master gland) that secretes hormones that influence growth, sexual development, skin pigmentation, thyroid function, and adrenocortical function.

Artery A thick walled vessel that (usually) carries blood high in oxygen content away from the heart to the body.

ATP A nucleoside triphosphate used in cells as a coenzyme, often called the "currency" of intracellular energy transfer. Metabolic processes that use ATP as an energy source convert it back into its precursors.

Autonomic nervous system The portion of the CNS that controls involuntary actions, such as the beating of your heart and the widening or narrowing of blood vessels.

Autotrophs
An organism that produces complex organic compounds from simple substances present in its surroundings, generally using energy from light or inorganic chemical reactions.

AV node
A group of specialized cardiac muscle fibers located at the center of the heart, in the floor of the right atrium, between the atria and ventricles. The AV Node takes the signal from the Sinoatrial (SA) Node, and then sends the electrical impulses from the atria to the ventricles.

Bacilli
The genus of Gram-positive, rod-shaped bacteria

Barr body
An inactive X chromosome in female autosomal cells

Beta cells
A cell in the pancreas whose function is to store and release insulin.

Binary fission
Prokaryotic fission, a form of asexual reproduction and cell division used by all prokaryotes, and some organelles within eukaryotic organisms (e.g., mitochondria).

Blood flow pathway
Superior/Inferior vena cavae→Right Atrium→Right Ventricle→Pulmonary Artery→Lungs→Pulmonary veins→Left atrium→Left ventricle→Aorta →Body

Bohr effect
The change in hemoglobin-oxygen affinity due to a change in pH. The presence of higher levels of CO_2 in the capillaries of metabolic active tissue promotes the release of O_2 from hemoglobin.

Bowman's capsule
A thin-walled, saclike structure which surrounds the glomerulus. It serves as a filter to remove organic wastes, excess inorganic salts, and water.

Calcitonin
A peptide hormone secreted by the cells of the thyroid. It helps regulate calcium levels in your body and is involved in the process of bone building.

cAMP
A ubiquitous cyclic nucleotide (adenosine cyclic monophosphate) produced from ATP. It is a regulatory agent that acts as the second messenger for many hormones and transmitter as a signal amplifier or in blood coagulation.

Carbohydrates

A carbohydrate is a large biological molecule, or macromolecule, consisting of carbon (C), hydrogen (H), and oxygen (O) atoms, usually with a hydrogen:oxygen atom ratio of 2:1, with the empirical formula $C_m(H_2O)_n$.

Cardiac muscle

Involuntary, striated muscle that is found in the walls and tissues of the heart. This muscle is self-contracting and autonomically regulated.

Catabolic pathway

ATP-generating.

Catecholamines

An organic compound that has a catechol and a side-chain amine. The main types of catecholamines are dopamine, norepinephrine, and epinephrine.

Cell life cycle

The series of events that take place in a cell leading to its division and replication that produces two daughter cells. In prokaryotes, the cell cycle occurs via binary fission. In eukaryotes, the cell cycle can be divided in three periods: interphase, the mitotic (M) phase, and cytokinesis.

Central nervous system

The part of the nervous system consisting of the brain and spinal cord.

Chief cells

The cells in the stomach that release pepsinogen and gastric lipase.

Cholesterol

A lipid molecule that is synthesized by animal cells as an essential structural component of cell membranes. It is needed to maintain both membrane structural integrity and fluidity.

Chromosomal mutation

Any mutation that causes changes in the structure or number of chromosomes in a cell.

Chymotrypsin

A protease enzyme that cleaves on the C-terminal phenylalanine, tryptophan, and tyrosine on peptide chains.

Coagulation

Also known as clotting, it is the process by which blood changes from a liquid to a gel. The purpose is to cause the cessation of blood loss from a damaged vessel, followed by repair.

Cocci

Any bacterium that has a spherical, ovoid, or generally round shape.

Cochlea
The auditory portion of the inner ear. It is a spiral-shaped cavity in the bony labyrinth that is filled with fluid. It facilitates the transmission of pressure and sound.

Codominance
The case where both alleles are expressed. For example: blood type AB

Coenzyme
A nonprotein organic molecule that combines with an apoenzyme to form the functioning holoenzyme; it aids in enzyme-catalyzed reactions, often by acting as an electron carrier (donor or acceptor).

Compact bone
Contains the yellow bone marrow and contains adipose tissue for fat cell storage.

Competitive inhibition
The enzyme can either bind substrate (ES-complex) or inhibitor (EI-complex); a competitive inhibitor diminishes the rate of catalysis by reducing the proportion of enzyme molecules bound to a substrate; this effect can be overcome by a sufficiently high concentration of substrate.

Conjugation (bacterial)
The transfer of genetic material between bacterial cells by direct cell-to-cell contact or by a bridge-like connection between two cell membranes.

Convergent evolution
The process where two species independently evolve similar structures.

Cortisol
A steroid hormone produced by the adrenal cortex that is released in response to stress and a low level of blood glucose. It functions to increase blood sugar through gluconeogenesis.

Crossing over
The exchange of genetic material between homologous chromosomes that results in recombinant chromosomes.

Cytoskeleton
Intercellular proteins that help a cell with shape, support, and movement. Cytoskeleton has three main structural components: microfilaments, intermediate filaments, and microtubules.

Dendrites
A short branched extension of a nerve cell, along which impulses received from other cells at synapses are transmitted to the cell body.

MCAT BIOLOGY AND BIOCHEMISTRY: STRATEGY AND PRACTICE

Desmosomes

A type of junctional complex, randomly arranged on the lateral sides of plasma membranes. They allow epithelial cells to resist shearing forces and are found in simple and stratified squamous epithelium.

Diastole

The portion of the cardiac cycle when the heart refills with blood following contraction. Ventricular diastole is when the ventricles are filling and relaxing, while atrial diastole when the atria are relaxing.

Diffusion

The passive net movement of material from an area of high concentration to an area with lower concentration.

Divergent evolution

The accumulation of differences between groups which can lead to the formation of new species.

DNA helicase

An enzyme that moves directionally along a nucleic acid phosphodiester backbone, separating two annealed nucleic acid strands (i.e., DNA, RNA).

DNA ligase

An enzyme, that facilitates the joining of DNA strands together by catalyzing the formation of a phosphodiester bond.

DNA polymerase

An enzyme that creates DNA molecules by assembling nucleotides. These enzymes are essential to DNA replication and usually work in pairs to create two identical DNA strands from one original DNA molecule.

Ectoderm

One of the three primary germ cell layers in the very early embryo. The ectoderm differentiates to form the nervous system, tooth enamel and the epidermis.

Endocrine glands

Any gland that secretes its products or hormones directly into the blood rather than through a duct.

Endoderm

One of the three primary germ cell layers in the very early embryo. The endoderm subsequently forms the epithelial lining of multiple systems (e.g. the GI tract, respiratory system, excretory system).

Endoplasmic reticulum

A network of tubules and flattened sacs that serve a variety of functions in the cell. The rough endoplasmic reticulum manufactures membranes and secretory proteins while smooth ER performs carbohydrate and lipid synthesis while also acting as a transitional area for vesicles that transport ER products to various destinations.

Endospores

A dormant, tough, and non-reproductive structure produced by certain bacteria. It allows the bacterium to produce a dormant and highly resistant cell to preserve the cell's genetic material in times of extreme stress.

Enzyme

A biomolecule, usually a protein, that acts as a catalyst for biological reactions.

Erythrocyte (RBC)

An anucleated cell that contains hemoglobin in order to transport oxygen throughout the body.

Estrogen

A steroid hormone important to the maintenance of female secondary sex characteristics.

Euchromatin

A loosely packed form of DNA. Euchromatin is prevalent in cells that are active in the transcription of many of their genes.

Eukaryote

Any organism whose cells contain a nucleus and other organelles enclosed within membranes.

Exocrine glands

Any gland that secretes its product by way of a duct to some environment external to the gland itself.

Exocytosis

The process in which an intracellular vesicle moves to the plasma membrane and subsequent fusion of the vesicular membrane and plasma membrane ensues. The goal is to transport molecules outside of the cell.

Exons

Any nucleotide sequence encoded by a gene that remains present within the final mature RNA product of that gene after introns have been removed by RNA splicing.

Extracellular matrix (ECM)

A collection of extracellular molecules secreted by cells that provides structural and biochemical support to the surrounding cells.

Facilitated diffusion

The process of spontaneous passive transport of molecules or ions across a biological membrane via specific transmembrane integral proteins.

FAD

Flavin Adenine Dinucleotide, a coenzyme formed by the condensation of riboflavin phosphate and adenylic acid; performs an important function in electron transport and as a prosthetic group for some enzymes.

Fatty acids Hydrocarbon chains terminating in a carboxylic acid.

Flagella Small, hair-like structures that act primarily as organelles of locomotion in the cells of many living organisms.

Fluid mosaic model The description of the cell membrane that states that each phospholipid molecule has a head that is attracted to water (hydrophilic) and a tail that repels water (hydrophobic). Both layers of the plasma membrane have the hydrophilic heads pointing toward the outside; the hydrophobic tails form the inside of the bilayer.

Frame shift mutation (insertion or deletion) Any genetic mutation caused by insertions or deletions, of a number of nucleotides in a DNA sequence that is not divisible by three.

Fungi Any member of a large group of eukaryotic organisms that includes microorganisms such as yeasts and molds. Fungal cells have cell walls that contain chitin, yet also have membrane bound organelles similar to eukaryotes.

Gap junctions A specialized intercellular connection that directly connects the cytoplasm of two cells, which allows various molecules, ions and electrical impulses to directly pass through a regulated gate between cells.

Gene mutation Any permanent alteration in the DNA sequence that makes up a gene, such that the sequence differs from what is found in most people. Mutations range in size; they can affect anywhere from a single DNA building block (base pair) to a large segment of a chromosome that includes multiple genes.

Globular proteins Long polymers that maintain and add strength to cellular and matrix structure; includes enzymes, hormones, membrane pumps/channels, membrane receptors, transport, and osmotic regulators

Glucagon A peptide hormone, produced by alpha cells of the pancreas, that raises the concentration of glucose in the bloodstream. Its effect is opposite that of insulin.

Glucocorticoids A hormone that predominantly affects the metabolism of carbohydrates and, to a lesser extent, fats and proteins.

Gluconeogenesis The process of self-synthesized glucose by some organisms which are not able to directly obtain hexose as a primary source of energy. It starts with pyruvate originating from glycolysis or lactate and alanine originating in muscles.

Glycogen A highly branched D-glucose polymer found in animals stored in an energy rich macro-molecule.

Glycosidic bond A type of covalent bond that links sugar units together in a polysaccharide.

Golgi apparatus A series of flattened, stacked pouches called cisternae. The Golgi apparatus is responsible for transporting, modifying, and packaging proteins and lipids into vesicles for delivery to targeted destinations.

Gram-negative bacteria A class of bacteria that do not retain the crystal violet stain used in the Gram staining method of bacterial differentiation. The thin peptidoglycan layer of their cell wall is sandwiched between an inner cell membrane and a bacterial outer membrane.

Gram-positive bacteria A class of bacteria that do retain the crystal violet stain used in the Gram staining method of bacterial differentiation, due a thicker peptidoglycan layer in their cell wall outside the cell membrane.

Haversian canals Small tunnels burrowed by osteoclasts through compact bone. They contain blood vessels, connective tissues, nerve fibers and lymphatic vessels.

Hemoglobin The oxygen carrying pigment of the erythrocytes, formed by the developing erythrocyte in bone marrow. It is a complex protein composed of four heme groups and four globin polypeptide chains.

Heterochromatin A tightly packed form of DNA. Heterochromatin is most abundant in cells that are less active or not active.

Heterotrophs An organism that consumes other organisms because they are unable to produce organic substances from inorganic ones. They must rely on an organic source of carbon that has originated as part of another living organism.

Hexose Name for a 6 membered sugar.

MCAT BIOLOGY AND BIOCHEMISTRY: STRATEGY AND PRACTICE

His bundle	The bundle of conduction fibers, which originates from the A-V node and descends into the ventricles, before the conduction system splits into bundle branches on the ventricles.
Hormone	A signaling molecules produced by glands in organisms that are transported by the circulatory system to target distant organs to regulate physiology and behavior.
Hypertonic	Tonicity is a measure of the effective osmotic pressure gradient (as defined by the water potential of the two solutions) of two solutions separated by a semipermeable membrane. Hypertonic refers to an area of greater solute concentration.
Hypotonic	Tonicity is a measure of the effective osmotic pressure gradient (as defined by the water potential of the two solutions) of two solutions separated by a semipermeable membrane. Hypotonic refers to an area of lesser solute concentration.
Incomplete dominance	An intermediate stage between two alleles. For example: red and white allele = pink flower
Innate immunity	The portion of the immune system that recognizes and responds to pathogens in a generic way, but, unlike the adaptive immune system, it does not confer long-lasting or protective immunity to the host. This includes the skin, lysozymes, and cytokines among others.
Insulin	A peptide hormone produced by beta cells in the pancreas. It regulates the metabolism of carbohydrates and fats by promoting the absorption of glucose by the cells.
Integral/intrinsic proteins	Proteins firmly embedded within the phospholipid bilayer of the cell membrane.
Introns	Noncoding sections of an RNA transcript, or the DNA encoding it, that are spliced out before the RNA molecule is translated into a protein.
Inversion	The process when a chromosome breaks in two places and the resulting piece of DNA is reversed and re-inserted into the chromosome. Inversions that involve the centromere are called pericentric inversions; those that do not involve the centromere are called paracentric inversions.

MCAT BIOLOGY AND BIOCHEMISTRY: STRATEGY AND PRACTICE

Iris

A thin, circular structure in the eye, responsible for controlling the diameter and size of the pupil and thus the amount of light reaching the retina.

Irreversible inhibitor

Tightly bound to the target enzyme (either covalently or non-covalently). Therefore, dissociates very slowly.

Isotonic

Tonicity is a measure of the effective osmotic pressure gradient (as defined by the water potential of the two solutions) of two solutions separated by a semipermeable membrane. Isotonic solution refers to when both areas have the same solute concentration.

Lagging strand

The strand that is synthesized apparently in the 3' to 5' direction, by ligating short fragments synthesized individually in the 5' to 3' direction.

Larynx

A tube-shaped organ in the neck that contains the vocal cords and allows the passages of air into the lungs.

Law of independent assortment

Genes located on different chromosome are sorted independently of each other, while the closer the genes are on the chromosome, the more likely they will remain together.

Law of segregation

The theory that alleles segregate independently of each other when forming gametes, i.e. a gamete is equally as likely to possess any allele.

Leading strand

The strand that is made in the 5' to 3' direction by continuous polymerization at the 3' growing tip.

Leukocyte (WBC)

The cells of the immune system that are involved in protecting the body against both infectious disease and foreign invaders.

Lipase

An enzyme that the body uses to break down fats in food so they can be absorbed in the intestines. Lipase is primarily produced in the pancreas but is also in the mouth and stomach.

Lipids

Includes fatty acids: triglycerols, phospholipids, glycolipids, steroids, and terpenes.

MCAT BIOLOGY AND BIOCHEMISTRY: STRATEGY AND PRACTICE

Lipoproteins
Proteins that transport lipids in the blood since lipids are insoluble; contain a lipid core surrounded by phospholipids and apoproteins

Loop of Henle
A long, U-shaped portion of the tubule that functions to aid in the recovery of water and sodium chloride from the urine. This allows production of urine that is far more concentrated than blood, limiting the amount of water needed as intake for survival.

Lymphatic system
A network of tissues and organs that serve to carry lymph fluid. It aids in the filtration of body fluid as well as maintenance of the immune system.

Lysogenic cycle
One of two methods of viral reproduction characterized by integration of the bacteriophage nucleic acid into the host bacterium's genome or formation of a circular replicon in the bacterium's cytoplasm.

Lysosomes
A membrane-enclosed organelle that contains an array of enzymes capable of breaking down all types of biological polymers—proteins, nucleic acids, carbohydrates, and lipids.

Lysozyme
A glycosidase enzyme which cleaves the polysaccharide component of cell walls in certain bacteria.

Lytic cycle
One of the two cycles of viral reproduction. The lytic cycle results in the destruction of the infected cell and its membrane.

Meiosis
A specialized type of cell division which reduces the chromosome number by half. This process occurs in all sexually reproducing eukaryotes.

Menstrual cycle
The cycle of hormonal changes that occurs in the uterus and ovary as an essential part of making sexual reproduction possible. Its timing is governed by cycles of several hormones.

Mesoderm
One of the three primary germ cell layers. It differentiates to give rise to a number of tissues and structures including bone, cartilage, muscle, connective tissue (including that of the dermis), vasculature, reproductive, excretory and urogenital systems.

Metaphase
A stage of mitosis in the eukaryotic cell cycle in which condensed and highly coiled chromosomes, carrying genetic information, align in the equator of the cell before being separated into each of the two daughter cells.

Microfilaments
Comprised of actin, these are the thinnest filaments of the cytoskeleton, a structure found in the cytoplasm of eukaryotic cells.

Microtubules
Filamentous intracellular structures that are responsible for various kinds of movements in all eukaryotic cells. Microtubules are involved in nucleic and cell division, organization of intracellular structure, and intracellular transport, as well as ciliary and flagellar motility.

Mineralcorticoids
A group of steroid hormones characterized by their influence on salt and water balances. The primary mineralocorticoid is aldosterone.

Minerals (K^+, Na^+)
Dissolved inorganic ions inside and outside of the cell. They establish the electrochemical gradient across cell membranes.

Missense mutation
A mutation where the change of a single base pair causes the substitution of a different amino acid in the resulting protein. This amino acid substitution may have no effect, or it may render the protein nonfunctional.

Mitochondria
A membrane-bound organelle found in the cytoplasm of almost all eukaryotic cells, the primary function of which is to generate large quantities of energy in the form of adenosine triphosphate (ATP).

Mitosis
The cell process by which chromosomes in a cell nucleus are separated into two identical sets of chromosomes, each in its own nucleus.

Motor unit
A motor neuron and the skeletal muscle fibers innervated by that motor neuron's axonal terminals. Groups of motor units work together to coordinate the contractions of a single muscle.

Myoglobin
An iron-containing porphyrin-globin complex found in muscle; serves as a reservoir for oxygen and gives some muscles their red or pink color; the oxygen binding site allows the attachment of a distal and proximal histidine molecule.

Myosin

A thick protein that forms (together with actin) the contractile filaments of muscle cells, and is also involved in motion in other types of cells.

NAD

Nicotinamide Adenine Dinucleotide, a coenzyme participating in many enzymatic reactions; made up of adenine, nicotinamide, and two molecules each of d-ribose and phosphoric acid; it functions as an electron acceptor in many of the oxidation reactions of respiration.

Negative feedback

The diminution or counteraction of an effect by its own influence on the process giving rise to it, as when a high level of insulin in the blood may inhibit further secretion of insulin.

Neuron

An electrically excitable cell that processes and transmits information through electrical and chemical signals.

Neurotransmitter

Endogenous chemicals that transmit signals across a synapse from one neuron to another neuron.

Noncompetitive inhibition

Inhibitor and substrate can bind simultaneously to an enzyme, forming an ESI-complex; a noncompetitive inhibitor acts by decreasing the turnover number; this can't be overcome by increased concentration of substrate and V_{max} is decreased.

Nonsense mutation

A point mutation in DNA that results in a premature stop codon in the transcribed mRNA, and thus creates a shortened, incomplete, and usually nonfunctional protein product.

Nuclear envelope

A double membrane that surrounds the nucleus and that contains multiple pores. The pores regulate the passage of macromolecules like proteins and RNA, but permit free passage of water, ions, ATP and other small molecules.

Nucleolus

A non-membrane bound structure composed of proteins and nucleic acids found within the nucleus. Ribosomal RNA (rRNA) is transcribed and assembled within this structure.

Nucleoside

A purine or pyrimidine base bound to a sugar.

Nucleotide

A purine or pyrimidine base bound to a sugar and a phosphate ester; the basic single unit of nucleic acid composed of a phosphate, a 5-C sugar (either deoxy / ribose)-group, and a purine or pyrimidine attached to it.

Nucleus

The dense, round organelle present in eukaryotic cells, surrounded by a double membrane, containing the genetic material (DNA).

Okazaki fragments

Short, DNA fragments that are formed on the lagging template strand during DNA replication. They are complementary to the lagging template strand, together forming short double-stranded DNA sections.

Osteoblasts

The cells that make bone. They do so by using calcium and other ions to produce a matrix that then becomes mineralized.

Osteoclasts

The large, multinucleated cell responsible for the dissolution and absorption of bone.

Ovulation

The process by which a mature egg is released from the ovary, pushed down the fallopian tube, and is available to be fertilized. Approximately every month an egg will mature within an ovary.

Ovum

An egg cell. The female reproductive cell (gamete) in oogamous organisms.

Oxytocin

A hormone produced by the hypothalamus and stored and secreted by the posterior pituitary gland. Oxytocin acts primarily as a neuromodulator in the brain and during childbirth (as a regulator of uterine contractions).

Pancreatic amylase

An enzyme used to hydrolyze dietary starch into disaccharides and trisaccharides.

Paracrine system

A form of cell-cell communication in which a cell produces a signal to induce changes in nearby cells, altering the behavior or differentiation of those cells.

Pentose

Name for a 5-membered sugar.

Peptide hormones

Hormones built of amino acid precursors that typically have short acting, fast effects.

Peripheral nervous system   The part of the nervous system that consists of the nerves and ganglia outside of the brain and spinal cord.

Peripheral/extrinsic proteins   Proteins loosely attached by ionic bonds or calcium bridges to the electrically charged phosphoryl surface of the bilayer. They can also attach to intrinsic proteins.

Peristalsis   A series of wave-like muscle contractions that moves food to different processing stations in the digestive tract. The process of peristalsis begins in the esophagus when a bolus of food is swallowed.

Peroxisomes   Small, membrane-enclosed organelles that contain enzymes involved in metabolic reactions, including several aspects of energy metabolism.

Phagocytosis   The process by which certain living cells called phagocytes ingest or engulf other cells or particles.

Pharynx   A cone-shaped passageway leading from the oral and nasal cavities in the head to the esophagus and larynx. The pharynx serves both respiratory and digestive functions.

Phosphorylation   A reaction in which phosphate is added to a compound.

Pinocytosis   Any process by which liquid droplets are ingested by living cells. Pinocytosis is one type of endocytosis.

Plasma   The liquid component of blood that normally holds the blood cells in whole blood in suspension.

Platelet   Colorless blood cells that play an important role in blood clotting. Platelets stop blood loss by clumping and forming plugs in blood vessel holes.

Point mutation   A type of mutation that causes the replacement of a single base nucleotide with another nucleotide of the genetic material, DNA or RNA. Can result in a missense, nonsense, or silent mutation.

Polymerase chain reaction   A method used to amplify a specific DNA sequence in vitro by repeated cycles of synthesis using specific primers and DNA polymerase.

MCAT BIOLOGY AND BIOCHEMISTRY: STRATEGY AND PRACTICE

Posterior pituitary

The rear lobe of the pituitary. Unlike the anterior lobe it does not produce hormones but it does release ADH and oxytocin into the circulation.

Post-transcriptional processing

A process by which primary RNA is converted into mature RNA (e.g. the conversion of precursor messenger RNA into mature messenger RNA (mRNA), which includes splicing and occurs prior to protein synthesis).

Primary structure

The sequence of amino acids in a protein.

Primase

A specialized RNA polymerase joins the prepriming complex in a multisubunit assembly called primosome.

Primer

A short RNA nucleic chain required to recognize the origin in DNA replication and to allow binding of the 1st nucleotide during DNA polymerase. The primer is again excised at a later stage of replication.

Prokaryote

A single-celled organism that lacks a membrane-bound nucleus, mitochondria, or any other membrane-bound organelles.

Prolactin

A hormone produced primarily in pregnant women. Its function is to promote lactation (breast milk production).

Prophase

The first phase of mitosis, during which the complex of DNA and proteins contained in the nucleus, known as chromatin, condenses.

Prosthetic group

The tightly bound, nonprotein portion of an enzyme but essential for its function; they differ from coenzymes in that they are more firmly attached to the enzyme protein; e.g.: the heme group present in cytochromes.

Proteins

Consist of a chain of amino acids linked together by peptide bonds (know your amino acids!)

Proton gradient

The energy bucket brigade - the voltage gradient across the mitochondrial wall, drives electrons along with hydrogen ions to the oxygen to generate water.

PTH (parathyroid hormone)

A polypeptide hormone that acts to increase the concentration of calcium in the blood. It is the antagonist to calcitonin (a hormone produced by the thyroid gland).

Purine
A type of double CN-ring base. Adenine pairs with thymine. Guanine pairs with cytosine.

Purkinje fibers
Specialized cardiomyocytes that are able to conduct cardiac action potentials more efficiently. They allow the heart's conduction system to create synchronized contractions of the ventricles.

Pyrimidine
A type of single CN-ring base. Cytosine pairs with guanine. Thymine pairs with adenine; in DNA only. Uracil: In place of thymine (found in RNA only) that pairs with Adenine.

Pyruvate
The end-product of glycolysis; the reduction reaction of pyruvate can yield lactate, ethanol and CO_2 as observed in fermentation processes or acetyl-CoA, water and CO_2 as in the case of aerobic respiration.

Reading frame
The codon sequence that is determined by the reading nucleotides in groups of three from some specific start codon, read consecutively in one direction; the grammar of DNA.

Replication fork
The point at which the two strands of DNA are separated to allow replication of each strand moving from the 3' to the 5' end of the parental sense (coding, upper or + strand).

Repressor
A nucleic acid binding protein that inhibits the expression of one or more genes by binding to the operator or associated silencers. A DNA-binding repressor blocks the attachment of RNA polymerase to the promoter, thus preventing transcription.

Retina
A light-sensitive layer of tissue, lining the inner surface of the eye. The optics of the eye create an image of the visual world on the retina.

Retrovirus
A virus that is composed not of DNA but of RNA. Retroviruses have an enzyme, called reverse transcriptase, that gives them the unique property of transcribing their RNA into DNA after entering a cell.

Reversible inhibitor
Characterized by a rapid dissociation of the enzyme-inhibitor complex. These feedback loops are necessary to control the product concentration; i.e. halt production when sufficient product material is available.

Rho-factor   Protein factor of prokaryota required to recognize certain transcription termination signals.

R-plasmid   A bacterial plasmid that codes for antibiotic resistance.

rRNA   Ribosomal ribonucleic acid (rRNA), the RNA component of the ribosome. rRNA is essential for protein synthesis in all living organisms.

SA node   Also known as the pacemaker of the heart. It controls heart rate by generating electrical impulses. It is located in the right atrium of the heart, at the center of the heart and near the entrance of the superior vena cava.

Secondary structure   Alpha-helix or beta-pleated sheet (can be parallel or anti-parallel); supported by hydrogen bonding.

Semicircular canals   A part of the inner ear, these act as the body's balance organs, detecting acceleration in the three perpendicular planes. Their hair cells detect movements of the fluid in the canals caused by angular acceleration about an axis perpendicular to the plane of the canal. The canals are connected to the auditory nerve.

Semiconservative replication The established model of DNA replication in which each double-stranded molecule is composed of on parental strand and one newly polymerized strand.

Sensory receptors   A sensory nerve ending that responds to a stimulus in the internal or external environment of an organism.

Sigma subunit   Enables RNA-pol to recognize promoter sites.

Smooth muscle   Involuntary, non-striated muscle responsible for the contractility of hollow organs, such as blood vessels, the gastrointestinal tract, the bladder, or the uterus.

Somatic nervous system   The part of the peripheral nervous system associated with the voluntary control of body movements via skeletal muscles. It consists of afferent (incoming signal) and efferent (outgoing signals) nerves.

Species

Two organisms that can reproduce and create fertile offspring

Sperm

The male reproductive cell (gamete).

Spirilla

The family of gram-negative, spiral-shaped bacteria.

Spirochetes

Gram-negative, motile, spiral bacteria that are unique in their possession of endocellular flagella.

Splicing

The reaction that removes introns and joins together exons in eukaryotic RNA.

Spongy bone

Contains red bone marrow and is the site of blood cell production.

Start codon (AUG)

The first codon of a messenger RNA transcript translated by a ribosome. The start codon always codes for methionine in eukaryotes and a modified methionine in prokaryotes.

Steroid hormones

Any hormone that are derived from cholesterol. They can enter the nucleus of a cell and alter gene expression.

Stop codons (UAA, UAG, UGA)

A nucleotide triplet within messenger RNA that signals a termination of translation.

Substrate

The molecule undergoing reaction with an enzyme.

Synapse

The structure that permits a neuron to pass an electrical or chemical signal to another cell (neural or not).

Systole

The phase of the cardiac cycle when the heart muscle contracts and pumps blood from the chambers into the arteries.

Telomeres

A region of repetitive nucleotide sequences at each end of a chromatid, which protects the end of the chromosome from deterioration or from fusion with neighboring chromosomes.

MCAT BIOLOGY AND BIOCHEMISTRY: STRATEGY AND PRACTICE

Telophase   The final stage of cell division where the sister chromatids reach opposite poles. The small nuclear vesicles in the cell begin to re-form around the group of chromosomes at each end.

Template   A molecular sequence that shapes the structure or sequence of another molecule; e.g. the nucleotide sequence of DNA acts as a template to control the nucleotide sequence of RNA during transcription.

Testosterone   A steroid hormone secreted primarily by the testicles of males and the ovaries of females, although small amounts are also secreted by the adrenal glands. It is the principal male sex hormone and an anabolic steroid.

Thyroxine (T3, T4)   The principal hormone secreted by the thyroid gland. It is inactive (T4) and most of it is converted to an active form called triiodothyronine (T3). T3 is primarily responsible for regulation of metabolism.

T-lymphocytes   A type of lymphocyte that plays a central role in cell-mediated immunity. They play a role in the adaptive immune system.

Transcription   The first step in protein production. During this process a portion of the double-stranded DNA template gives rise to a single-stranded RNA molecule. This occurs in the nucleus.

Transcription bubble   During elongation of the RNA transcript, duplex DNA is unwound at the forward end of RNA polymerase and rewound at its rear end.

Transduction (bacterial)   The process by which DNA is transferred from one bacterium to another by a virus or foreign body.

Transformation (bacterial)   The genetic alteration of a cell resulting from the incorporation of exogenous genetic material after direct uptake from its surroundings through the cell membrane.

Translation   The synthesis of proteins directed by a mRNA template. The information contained in the nucleotide sequence of the mRNA is read as three letter codons. This occurs at the ribosomes.

Translocation   A genetic abnormality caused by rearrangement of parts between nonhomologous chromosomes.

Transposons

A small piece of DNA that inserts itself into another place in the genome.

Triacylglycerol

A glycerol backbone esterified to 3 fatty acids. They store metabolic energy, and provide thermal insulation.

tRNA

Transfer ribonucleic acid, a type of RNA molecule that helps decode the messenger RNA (mRNA) sequence into a protein. tRNAs function at specific sites in the ribosome during translation. They carry an amino acid on one end and an anti-codon on the other end.

Trypsin

A protease enzyme that cleaves peptide chains mainly at the carboxyl side of the amino acids lysine or arginine.

TSH (thyroid stimulating hormone)

A tropic hormone released by the anterior pituitary. It serves to cause the thyroid gland to make T3 and T4.

T-tubule

A deep groove in the sarcolemma, which is the plasma membrane of skeletal muscle and cardiac muscle cells. These invaginations allow depolarization of the membrane to quickly penetrate to the interior of the cell.

Vein

A thin walled vessel of the circulatory system that typically carries oxygen-depleted blood toward the heart.

Virus

A small infectious agent, usually consisting of DNA or RNA surrounded by a protein coat, that replicates only inside the living cells of other organisms.

Z-line

The borders that separate and link sarcomeres within a skeletal muscle.

Remove this page from the book and use the grid below to record your answers. Then check your work and carefully review each question. Don't ignore the ones you got right! Review every single question!

TIMED SECTION 1 - ANSWER SHEET

Key		20		40	
1		21		41	
2		22		42	
3		23		43	
4		24		44	
5		25		45	
6		26		46	
7		27		47	
8		28		48	
9		29		49	
10		30		50	
11		31		51	
12		32		52	
13		33		53	
14		34		54	
15		35		55	
16		36		56	
17		37		57	
18		38		58	
19		39		59	

Remove this page from the book and use the grid below to record your answers. Then check your work and carefully review each question. Don't ignore the ones you got right! Review every single question!

TIMED SECTION 2 - ANSWER SHEET

Key		20		40	
1		21		41	
2		22		42	
3		23		43	
4		24		44	
5		25		45	
6		26		46	
7		27		47	
8		28		48	
9		29		49	
10		30		50	
11		31		51	
12		32		52	
13		33		53	
14		34		54	
15		35		55	
16		36		56	
17		37		57	
18		38		58	
19		39		59	

MCAT BIOLOGY AND BIOCHEMISTRY: STRATEGY AND PRACTICE

Remove this page from the book and use the grid below to record your answers. Then check your work and carefully review each question. Don't ignore the ones you got right! Review every single question!

TIMED SECTION 3 - ANSWER SHEET

Key		20		40	
1		21		41	
2		22		42	
3		23		43	
4		24		44	
5		25		45	
6		26		46	
7		27		47	
8		28		48	
9		29		49	
10		30		50	
11		31		51	
12		32		52	
13		33		53	
14		34		54	
15		35		55	
16		36		56	
17		37		57	
18		38		58	
19		39		59	

Remove this page from the book and use the grid below to record your answers. Then check your work and carefully review each question. Don't ignore the ones you got right! Review every single question!

TIMED SECTION 4 - ANSWER SHEET

Key		20		40	
1		21		41	
2		22		42	
3		23		43	
4		24		44	
5		25		45	
6		26		46	
7		27		47	
8		28		48	
9		29		49	
10		30		50	
11		31		51	
12		32		52	
13		33		53	
14		34		54	
15		35		55	
16		36		56	
17		37		57	
18		38		58	
19		39		59	

THIS PAGE LEFT

INTENTIONALLY BLANK

THIS PAGE LEFT

INTENTIONALLY BLANK

THIS PAGE LEFT

INTENTIONALLY BLANK

THIS PAGE LEFT

INTENTIONALLY BLANK

THIS PAGE LEFT

INTENTIONALLY BLANK

THIS PAGE LEFT

INTENTIONALLY BLANK

This Page Left Intentionally Blank.

Pyrimidines CL: _____

_____

_____

_____

_____

Watson-Crick Model CL: _____

_____

_____

_____

_____

Base-Pair Specificity CL: _____

_____

_____

_____

_____

Transmission of genetic information CL: _____

_____

_____

_____

_____

Denaturation, Reannealing, Hybridization CL: _____

_____

_____

_____

_____

B. DNA Replication and Repair

_____

_____

_____

_____

Semi-Conservative CL: _____

_____

_____

_____

Enzymes CL: _____

_____

_____

_____

_____

Replication Origin CL: _____

_____

_____

_____

_____

Replicating the ends of DNA CL: _____

_____

_____

_____

Repair during replication CL: _____

_____

_____

_____

_____

Mutation Repair CL: _____

_____

_____

_____

_____

    C. Genetic Code

_____

_____

_____

_____

      a) Triplets CL: _____

_____

_____

_____

_____

Codon CL: _____

_____

_____

_____

_____

Anticodon CL: _____

_____

_____

_____

_____

Degeneracy CL: _____

_____

_____

_____

_____

Wobble Pairing CL: _____

_____

_____

_____

Missense CL: _____

_____

_____

_____

_____

Nonsense CL: _____

_____

_____

_____

_____

Initiation CL: _____

_____

_____

_____

_____

Termination CL: _____

_____

_____

_____

_____

b) Transcription

_____

_____

_____

_____

tRNA CL: _____

_____

_____

_____

_____

mRNA CL: _____

_____
_____
_____
_____

rRNA CL: _____

_____
_____
_____
_____

snRNPs CL: _____

_____
_____
_____
_____

snRNAs CL: _____

_____
_____
_____
_____

Introns CL: _____

_____
_____
_____
_____

Exons CL: _____

_____
_____
_____
_____

c) Translation CL: _____

_____
_____
_____
_____

mRNA CL: _____

_____
_____
_____
_____

tRNA CL: _____

_____

_____

_____

_____

rRNA CL: _____

_____

_____

_____

_____

Ribosome initiation factors CL: _____

_____

_____

_____

_____

Termination co-factors CL: _____

_____

_____

_____

_____

Post-translational processing CL: _____

_____

_____

_____

_____

D. Chromosomes

_____

_____

_____

Repetitive DNA CL: _____

_____

_____

_____

_____

Supercoiling CL: _____

_____

_____

_____

_____

Heterochromatin CL: _____

_____

_____

_____

_____

Euchromatin CL: _____

_____

_____

_____

_____

Telomeres CL: _____

_____

_____

_____

_____

Centromeres CL: _____

_____

_____

_____

_____

E. Gene Expression

_____

_____

_____

_____

a) Prokaryotes CL: _____

_____

_____

_____

_____

Operons CL: _____

_____

_____

_____

_____

Jacob-Monod Model CL: _____

_____

_____

_____

_____

Repression CL: _____

_____

_____

_____

_____

Positive Control CL: _____

_____

_____

_____

_____

   b)   Eukaryotes

_____

_____

_____

_____

Transcriptional regulation CL: _____

_____

_____

_____

_____

DNA binding proteins CL: _____

_____

_____

_____

_____

Transcription factors CL: _____

_____

_____

_____

_____

Gene amplification, duplication CL: _____

_____

_____

_____

_____

Post-transcriptional control CL: _____

_____

_____

_____

_____

Introns CL: _____

_____
_____
_____
_____

Exons CL: _____

_____
_____
_____
_____

Cancer CL: _____

_____
_____
_____
_____

Methyl regulation of chromatic structure CL: _____

_____
_____
_____
_____

Non-coding RNAs CL: _____

_____
_____
_____
_____

    F.   Biotechnology

_____
_____
_____
_____

Cloning CL: _____

_____
_____
_____
_____

Restriction Enzymes CL: _____

_____
_____
_____
_____

cDNA CL: _____

_____
_____
_____
_____

Hybridization CL: _____

_____
_____
_____
_____

PCR CL: _____

_____
_____
_____
_____

Blotting CL: _____

_____
_____
_____
_____

Electrophoresis CL: _____

_____
_____
_____
_____

    a)   Stem Cells CL: _____

_____
_____
_____
_____

Applications CL: _____

_____
_____
_____
_____

Ethics CL: _____

_____
_____
_____
_____

3. Classical Genetics

_____
_____
_____
_____

A. Mendelian Genetics

_____
_____
_____
_____

Phenotype CL: _____

_____
_____
_____
_____

Genotype CL: _____

_____
_____
_____
_____

Gene CL: _____

_____
_____
_____
_____

Locus CL: _____

_____
_____
_____
_____

Allele CL: _____

_____
_____
_____
_____

Zygosity CL: _____

_____
_____
_____
_____

Wild-type CL: _____

_____

_____

_____

Recessive CL: _____

_____

_____

_____

Dominant CL: _____

_____

_____

_____

Co-dominant CL: _____

_____

_____

_____

Incomplete Dominance CL: _____

_____

_____

_____

Leakage CL: _____

_____

_____

_____

Penetrance CL: _____

_____

_____

_____

Expressivity CL: _____

_____

_____

_____

Hybridization CL: _____

_____
_____
_____
_____

Gene Pool CL: _____

_____
_____
_____
_____

    B. Meiosis and Variability CL: _____

_____
_____
_____
_____

Differences with Mitosis CL: _____

_____
_____
_____
_____

    a) Gene Segregation CL: _____

_____
_____
_____
_____

Independent Assortment CL: _____

_____
_____
_____
_____

Linkage CL: _____

_____
_____
_____
_____

Recombination CL: _____

_____
_____
_____
_____

Sex-Linkage CL: _____

_____

_____

_____

_____

Y Chromosome CL: _____

_____

_____

_____

_____

Sex Determination CL: _____

_____

_____

_____

_____

Extranuclear Inheritance CL: _____

_____

_____

_____

_____

    b)   Mutation CL: _____

_____

_____

_____

_____

Types CL: _____

_____

_____

_____

_____

Effects CL: _____

_____

_____

_____

_____

Errors of Metabolism CL: _____

_____

_____

_____

_____

Mutagens CL: _____

_____
_____
_____
_____

Carcinogens CL: _____

_____
_____
_____
_____

Genetic Drift CL: _____

_____
_____
_____
_____

Crossing-over CL: _____

_____
_____
_____
_____

C. Analysis CL: _____

_____
_____
_____
_____

Hardy-Weinberg CL: _____

_____
_____
_____
_____

Test Cross CL: _____

_____
_____
_____
_____

Crossover Frequency CL: _____

_____
_____
_____
_____

Biometry CL: _____

_____
_____
_____
_____

D. Evolution

_____
_____
_____
_____

Natural Selection CL: _____

_____
_____
_____

Fitness CL: _____

_____
_____
_____
_____

Differential Reproduction CL: _____

_____
_____
_____
_____

Group Selection CL: _____

_____
_____
_____

Speciation CL: _____

_____
_____
_____
_____

Polymorphism CL: _____

_____
_____
_____

Adaptation CL: _____

_____

_____

_____

_____

Inbreeding CL: _____

_____

_____

_____

_____

Outbreeding CL: _____

_____

_____

_____

_____

Bottlenecks CL: _____

_____

_____

_____

_____

Time as gradual random changes in genome CL: _____

_____

_____

_____

_____

4. Metabolism

_____

_____

_____

_____

    A. Glycolysis CL: _____

_____

_____

_____

_____

Aerobic CL: _____

_____

_____

_____

_____

Substrates and Products CL: _____

_____

_____

_____

_____

Anaerobic Fermentation CL: _____

_____

_____

_____

_____

Net Results CL: _____

_____

_____

_____

_____

B. Krebs Cycle

_____

_____

_____

_____

Reactions CL: _____

_____

_____

_____

_____

Substrates CL: _____

_____

_____

_____

_____

Products CL: _____

_____

_____

_____

_____

Regulation CL: _____

_____

_____

_____

_____

C. Metabolism of Fat and Protein

_____
_____
_____
_____
_____

Fat Digestion CL: _____

_____
_____
_____
_____

Fat Transport CL: _____

_____
_____
_____
_____

Fatty Acid Oxidation CL: _____

_____
_____
_____
_____

Saturated Fats CL: _____

_____
_____
_____
_____

Unsaturated Fats CL: _____

_____
_____
_____
_____

Protein Metabolism CL: _____

_____
_____
_____
_____

Anabolism CL: _____

_____
_____
_____
_____

Synthesis of Lipids CL: _____

_____

_____

_____

_____

Synthesis of Polysaccharides CL: _____

_____

_____

_____

_____

D. Oxidative Phosphorylation

_____

_____

_____

_____

a) Electron Transport Chain CL: _____

_____

_____

_____

_____

Substrates CL: _____

_____

_____

_____

_____

Products CL: _____

_____

_____

_____

_____

Function CL: _____

_____

_____

_____

_____

NADH CL: _____

_____

_____

_____

_____

NADPH CL: _____

_____
_____
_____
_____

Flavoproteins CL: _____

_____
_____
_____
_____

Cytochromes CL: _____

_____
_____
_____
_____

ATP Synthase CL: _____

_____
_____
_____
_____

Chemiosmosis CL: _____

_____
_____
_____
_____

Net Results CL: _____

_____
_____
_____
_____

Regulation CL: _____

_____
_____
_____
_____

5. Cell Biology

_____
_____
_____
_____

A. Plasma Membrane

_____
_____
_____
_____

Composition CL: _____

_____
_____
_____
_____

Receptors CL: _____

_____
_____
_____
_____

    a)   Solute transport CL: _____

_____
_____
_____
_____

Osmosis CL: _____

_____
_____
_____
_____

Passive CL: _____

_____
_____
_____
_____

Active CL: _____

_____
_____
_____
_____

Na/K Pump CL: _____

_____
_____
_____
_____

Ion Channels CL: _____

_____

_____

_____

_____

Membrane Potential CL: _____

_____

_____

_____

_____

Exocytosis CL: _____

_____

_____

_____

_____

Endocytosis CL: _____

_____

_____

_____

_____

Gap Junctions CL: _____

_____

_____

_____

_____

Tight Junctions CL: _____

_____

_____

_____

_____

Desmosomes CL: _____

_____

_____

_____

_____

B. Membrane-Bound Organelles CL: _____

_____

_____

_____

_____

Nucleus CL: _____

_____
_____
_____
_____

Nucleolus CL: _____

_____
_____
_____
_____

Nuclear Envelope and Pores CL: _____

_____
_____
_____
_____

    a)   Mitochondria CL: _____

_____
_____
_____
_____

Function CL: _____

_____
_____
_____
_____

Membranes CL: _____

_____
_____
_____
_____

Replication CL: _____

_____
_____
_____
_____

Lysosomes CL: _____

_____
_____
_____
_____

Rough vs. Smooth ER CL: ____

_____
_____
_____
_____

ER Double Membrane CL: ____

_____
_____
_____
_____

ER Biosynthesis CL: ____

_____
_____
_____
_____

Golgi Complex CL: ____

_____
_____
_____
_____

Peroxisomes CL: ____

_____
_____
_____
_____

C. Cytoskeleton

_____
_____
_____
_____

Microfilaments CL: ____

_____
_____
_____

Microtubules CL: ____

_____
_____
_____
_____

Intermediate Filaments CL: _____

_____

_____

_____

_____

Cilia CL: _____

_____

_____

_____

_____

Flagella CL: _____

_____

_____

_____

_____

Centrioles CL: _____

_____

_____

_____

_____

Microtubule Organizing Centers CL: _____

_____

_____

_____

_____

6. Microbiology

_____

_____

_____

A. Cell Theory CL: _____

_____

_____

_____

B. Classification and Structure CL: _____

_____

_____

_____

_____

History CL: _____

_____
_____
_____
_____

Development CL: _____

_____
_____
_____
_____

Impact CL: _____

_____
_____
_____
_____

C. Prokaryotes

_____
_____
_____
_____

Archaea CL: _____

_____
_____
_____
_____

Bacilli CL: _____

_____
_____
_____
_____

Spirilli CL: _____

_____
_____
_____
_____

Cocci CL: _____

_____
_____
_____
_____

Lack of Eukaryotic Features CL: _____

_____

_____

_____

_____

Cell Wall CL: _____

_____

_____

_____

_____

Flagella CL: _____

_____

_____

_____

_____

Fission CL: _____

_____

_____

_____

_____

Exponential Growth CL: _____

_____

_____

_____

_____

Quick Adaptation CL: _____

_____

_____

_____

_____

Antibiotic Resistance CL: _____

_____

_____

_____

_____

Aerobic CL: _____

_____

_____

_____

_____

Anaerobic CL: _____

_____

_____

_____

_____

Parasitic CL: _____

_____

_____

_____

_____

Symbiotic CL: _____

_____

_____

_____

_____

Chemotaxis CL: _____

_____

_____

_____

_____

Plasmids CL: _____

_____

_____

_____

_____

Transformation CL: _____

_____

_____

_____

_____

Conjugation CL: _____

_____

_____

_____

_____

Transposons CL: _____

_____

_____

_____

_____

D. Viruses CL: _____

_____

_____

_____

_____

Structure CL: _____

_____

_____

_____

_____

Size CL: _____

_____

_____

_____

_____

Organelles CL: _____

_____

_____

_____

_____

Bacteriophages CL: _____

_____

_____

_____

_____

DNA vs. RNA CL: _____

_____

_____

_____

_____

Life Cycle CL: _____

_____

_____

_____

_____

Transduction CL: _____

_____

_____

_____

_____

Retroviruses CL: _____

_____
_____
_____
_____

Prions CL: _____

_____
_____
_____
_____

Viroids CL: _____

_____
_____
_____
_____

7. **Cell Division, Cell Development, Reproduction, Embryology**

_____
_____
_____
_____

    A. Mitosis

_____
_____
_____
_____

Phases CL: _____

_____
_____
_____
_____

Structures CL: _____

_____
_____
_____
_____

Growth Arrest CL: _____

_____
_____
_____
_____

Control and Loss of Control CL: _____

_____

_____

_____

_____

B. Reproduction

_____

_____

_____

_____

Gametogenesis CL: _____

_____

_____

_____

_____

Meiosis CL: _____

_____

_____

_____

_____

Ovum CL: _____

_____

_____

_____

_____

Sperm CL: _____

_____

_____

_____

_____

Gamete Formation CL: _____

_____

_____

_____

_____

Gamete Morphology CL: _____

_____

_____

_____

_____

Gamete Contribution to Zygote CL: _____

_____

_____

_____

_____

Sequence: Fertilization to Birth CL: _____

_____

_____

_____

_____

C. Embryogenesis

_____

_____

_____

_____

a) Stages CL: _____

_____

_____

_____

_____

Fertilization CL: _____

_____

_____

_____

_____

Cleavage CL: _____

_____

_____

_____

_____

Blastula CL: _____

_____

_____

_____

_____

Gastrula CL: _____

_____

_____

_____

_____

Cell Movements CL: _____

_____

_____

_____

_____

Neurulation CL: _____

_____

_____

_____

_____

Endoderm CL: _____

_____

_____

_____

_____

Mesoderm CL: _____

_____

_____

_____

_____

Ectoderm CL: _____

_____

_____

_____

_____

Neural Crest CL: _____

_____

_____

_____

_____

Environmental Effects CL: _____

_____

_____

_____

_____

D. Cell Development

_____

_____

_____

_____

Specialization CL: _____

_____

_____

_____

_____

Determination CL: _____

_____

_____

_____

_____

Differentiation CL: _____

_____

_____

_____

_____

Tissue Types CL: _____

_____

_____

_____

_____

Cell communication CL: _____

_____

_____

_____

_____

Cell Migration CL: _____

_____

_____

_____

_____

Stem Cells CL: _____

_____

_____

_____

_____

Gene Regulation CL: _____

_____

_____

_____

_____

Apoptosis CL: ____

_____

_____

_____

_____

Regeneration CL: ____

_____

_____

_____

_____

Senescence CL: ____

_____

_____

_____

_____

Aging CL: ____

_____

_____

_____

_____

8. Nervous and Endocrine Systems

_____

_____

_____

_____

A. Nerve Cell

_____

_____

_____

_____

Structures CL: ____

_____

_____

_____

_____

Soma CL: ____

_____

_____

_____

_____

Dendrites CL: _____

_____
_____
_____
_____

Axon CL: _____

_____
_____
_____
_____

Myelin CL: _____

_____
_____
_____
_____

Nodes of Ranvier CL: _____

_____
_____
_____
_____

Synapse CL: _____

_____
_____
_____
_____

Neurotransmitters CL: _____

_____
_____
_____
_____

Resting Potential CL: _____

_____
_____
_____
_____

Action Potential CL: _____

_____
_____
_____
_____

Excitatory CL: _____

_____
_____
_____
_____

Inhibitory Fibers CL: _____

_____
_____
_____
_____

Summation CL: _____

_____
_____
_____
_____

Firing Frequency CL: _____

_____
_____
_____
_____

Glia CL: _____

_____
_____
_____
_____

Neuroglia CL: _____

_____
_____
_____
_____

B. Nervous System

_____
_____
_____

Organization CL: _____

_____
_____
_____
_____

Efferent CL: _____

_____
_____
_____
_____

Afferent CL: _____

_____
_____
_____
_____

Sympathetic CL: _____

_____
_____
_____
_____

Parasympathetic CL: _____

_____
_____
_____
_____

Reflex Arc CL: _____

_____
_____
_____
_____

Spinal Cord CL: _____

_____
_____
_____
_____

Supraspinal Circuits CL: _____

_____
_____
_____
_____

Endocrine System Integration CL: _____

_____
_____
_____
_____

C. Endocrine System

_____

_____

_____

_____

Major Glands CL: _____

_____

_____

_____

Major Hormones CL: _____

_____

_____

_____

_____

Mechanism of Hormone Action CL: _____

_____

_____

_____

_____

Transport of Hormones and Second Messengers CL: _____

_____

_____

_____

_____

9. Physiology

_____

_____

_____

_____

A. Respiratory System

_____

_____

_____

_____

Function CL: _____

_____

_____

_____

Thermoregulation CL: _____

_____
_____
_____
_____

pH control CL: _____

_____
_____
_____
_____

    B. Circulatory System

_____
_____
_____
_____

Heart Chambers CL: _____

_____
_____
_____
_____

Systolic Pressure CL: _____

_____
_____
_____
_____

Diastolic Pressure CL: _____

_____
_____
_____
_____

Pulmonary circulation CL: _____

_____
_____
_____
_____

System Circulations CL: _____

_____
_____
_____
_____

Arteries CL: _____

_____
_____
_____
_____

Veins CL: _____

_____
_____
_____
_____

Capillaries CL: _____

_____
_____
_____
_____

Blood Composition CL: _____

_____
_____
_____
_____

Plasma CL: _____

_____
_____
_____
_____

Cells CL: _____

_____
_____
_____
_____

Chemicals CL: _____

_____
_____
_____

Clotting CL: _____

_____
_____
_____
_____

Gas Transport CL: _____

_____
_____
_____
_____

    a)   Lymphatic System

_____
_____
_____
_____

Structures CL: _____

_____
_____
_____
_____

Function CL: _____

_____
_____
_____
_____

    C. Immune System

_____
_____
_____
_____

Innate CL: _____

_____
_____
_____
_____

Macrophages CL: _____

_____
_____
_____
_____

Phagocytes CL: _____

_____
_____
_____
_____

Adaptive CL: _____

_____
_____
_____
_____

T cells CL: _____

_____
_____
_____
_____

B cells CL: _____

_____
_____
_____
_____

Bone Marrow CL: _____

_____
_____
_____
_____

Spleen CL: _____

_____
_____
_____
_____

Thymus CL: _____

_____
_____
_____
_____

Lymph Nodes CL: _____

_____
_____
_____
_____

Antigens CL: _____

_____
_____
_____
_____

Antibodies CL: _____

_____
_____
_____
_____

Ag Presentation CL: _____

_____
_____
_____
_____

Ag-Ab Recognition CL: _____

_____
_____
_____
_____

Structure of Ab CL: _____

_____
_____
_____
_____

Autoimmune Diseases CL: _____

_____
_____
_____
_____

Major Histocompatibility Complex CL: _____

_____
_____
_____
_____

    D. Digestive System

_____
_____
_____
_____

Ingestion CL: _____

_____
_____
_____
_____

Peristalsis CL: _____

_____

_____

_____

_____

Stomach CL: _____

_____

_____

_____

_____

Liver CL: _____

_____

_____

_____

_____

Gall Bladder CL: _____

_____

_____

_____

_____

Pancreas CL: _____

_____

_____

_____

_____

Small Intestine CL: _____

_____

_____

_____

_____

Large Intestine CL: _____

_____

_____

_____

_____

    a)   Control CL: _____

_____

_____

_____

_____

Muscular Control CL: _____

_____
_____
_____
_____

Endocrine Control CL: _____

_____
_____
_____
_____

Nervous Control CL: _____

_____
_____
_____
_____

    E. Excretory System

_____
_____
_____
_____

BP regulation CL: _____

_____
_____
_____
_____

Osmoregulation CL: _____

_____
_____
_____
_____

Acid balance CL: _____

_____
_____
_____
_____

Nitrogenous waste CL: _____

_____
_____
_____
_____

Cortex CL: ____

_____
_____
_____
_____

Medulla CL: ____

_____
_____
_____
_____

Glomerulus CL: ____

_____
_____
_____
_____

Bowman's Capsule CL: ____

_____
_____
_____
_____

Tubules CL: ____

_____
_____
_____
_____

Loop of Henle CL: ____

_____
_____
_____
_____

Collecting Duct CL: ____

_____
_____
_____
_____

Filtration CL: ____

_____
_____
_____
_____

Counter-current multiplier CL: ____

_____

_____

_____

_____

Secretion CL: ____

_____

_____

_____

_____

Reabsorption CL: ____

_____

_____

_____

_____

Concentration CL: ____

_____

_____

_____

_____

Ureter CL: ____

_____

_____

_____

_____

Bladder CL: ____

_____

_____

_____

_____

Urethra CL: ____

_____

_____

_____

_____

F. Reproductive System

_____

_____

_____

_____

Gonads CL: _____

_____

_____

_____

_____

Genitals CL: _____

_____

_____

_____

_____

Sexual Development CL: _____

_____

_____

_____

_____

Menstrual Cycle CL: _____

_____

_____

_____

_____

Pregnancy CL: _____

_____

_____

_____

_____

Lactation CL: _____

_____

_____

_____

_____

G. Muscle System

_____

_____

_____

Thermoregulation CL: _____

_____

_____

_____

_____

Shivering CL: _____

_____

_____

_____

_____

Smooth CL: _____

_____

_____

_____

_____

Striated CL: _____

_____

_____

_____

_____

Cardiac CL: _____

_____

_____

_____

_____

T-tubule CL: _____

_____

_____

_____

_____

Contractile Apparatus CL: _____

_____

_____

_____

_____

Sarcoplasmic Reticulum CL: _____

_____

_____

_____

_____

Cardiac Muscle Regulation CL: _____

_____

_____

_____

_____

Oxygen Debt CL: _____

_____
_____
_____
_____

Motor Neurons CL: _____

_____
_____
_____
_____

Neuromuscular Junction CL: _____

_____
_____
_____
_____

Motor End Plates CL: _____

_____
_____
_____
_____

Sympathetic CL: _____

_____
_____
_____
_____

Parasympathetic CL: _____

_____
_____
_____
_____

Voluntary CL: _____

_____
_____
_____
_____

Involuntary CL: _____

_____
_____
_____
_____

Sarcomeres CL: _____

_____

_____

_____

_____

Troponin CL: _____

_____

_____

_____

Tropomyosin CL: _____

_____

_____

_____

H. Skeletal System

_____

_____

_____

_____

Support CL: _____

_____

_____

_____

_____

Protection CL: _____

_____

_____

_____

_____

Calcium Storage CL: _____

_____

_____

_____

_____

Bone Types CL: _____

_____

_____

_____

_____

Joint Types CL: _____

_____
_____
_____
_____

Composition of Bone Matrix and Cells CL: _____

_____
_____
_____
_____

Cartilage CL: _____

_____
_____
_____
_____

Ligaments CL: _____

_____
_____
_____
_____

Tendons CL: _____

_____
_____
_____
_____

I. Skin System CL: _____

_____
_____
_____

a) Structure CL: _____

_____
_____
_____
_____

Impermeability to Water CL: _____

_____
_____
_____
_____

b) Function CL: _____

_____
_____
_____
_____

Homeostasis CL: _____

_____
_____
_____
_____

Osmoregulation CL: _____

_____
_____
_____
_____

Thermoregulation CL: _____

_____
_____
_____
_____

Hormonal Control CL: _____

_____
_____
_____
_____

Biochemistry

_____
_____
_____
_____

1. Proteins

_____
_____
_____
_____

A. Amino Acids CL: _____

_____
_____
_____
_____

Configuration CL: _____

_____

_____

_____

_____

Side Chains CL: _____

_____

_____

_____

_____

Acidic CL: _____

_____

_____

_____

_____

Basic CL: _____

_____

_____

_____

_____

Hydrophobic CL: _____

_____

_____

_____

_____

Hydrophilic CL: _____

_____

_____

_____

_____

B. Structure

_____

_____

_____

Protein Structure CL: _____

_____

_____

_____

Stability and Denaturing CL: _____

_____

_____

_____

_____

Hydrophobic interactions CL: _____

_____

_____

_____

_____

Solvation CL: _____

_____

_____

_____

_____

Entropy CL: _____

_____

_____

_____

_____

C. Enzymes

_____

_____

_____

_____

a) Interactions

_____

_____

_____

_____

Active site CL: _____

_____

_____

_____

_____

Allosteric site CL: _____

_____

_____

_____

_____

D. Enzyme Control

_____
_____
_____
_____

   a) Kinetics

_____
_____
_____
_____

Michaelis-Menten CL: _____

_____
_____
_____
_____

Cooperativity CL: _____

_____
_____
_____
_____

Zymogens CL: _____

_____
_____
_____
_____

2. **Molecular Genetics**

_____
_____
_____
_____

  A. Nucleic Acids

_____
_____
_____
_____

Structure CL: _____

_____
_____
_____
_____

Nucleotides CL: _____

_____
_____
_____
_____

Nucleosides CL: _____

_____
_____
_____
_____

Denaturation CL: _____

_____
_____
_____
_____

Reannealing CL: _____

_____
_____
_____
_____

Hybridization CL: _____

_____
_____
_____
_____

3. Metabolism

_____
_____
_____
_____

A. Bioenergetics

_____
_____
_____
_____

a) Thermodynamics/Bioenergetics

_____
_____
_____
_____

ΔG CL: _____

_____
_____
_____
_____

Keq CL: _____

_____
_____
_____
_____

Concentrations CL: _____

_____
_____
_____
_____

Spontaneity CL: _____

_____
_____
_____
_____

Phosphoryl Groups CL: _____

_____
_____
_____
_____

ATP Hydrolysis CL: _____

_____
_____
_____
_____

Group Transfers CL: _____

_____
_____
_____
_____

Redox Half-Reactions CL: _____

_____
_____
_____
_____

Soluble Electron Carriers CL: _____

_____
_____
_____
_____

Flavoproteins CL: _____

_____
_____
_____
_____

    B. Carbohydrates

_____
_____
_____
_____

Hydrolysis of Glycosides CL: _____

_____
_____
_____
_____

Monomers CL: _____

_____
_____
_____
_____

Polymers CL: _____

_____
_____
_____
_____

    C. Glycolysis and Gluconeogenesis

_____
_____
_____
_____

Aerobic: Substrates and Products CL: _____

_____
_____
_____
_____

Anaerobic: Fermentation CL: _____

_____

_____

_____

_____

Net Results CL: _____

_____

_____

_____

_____

Gluconeogenesis CL: _____

_____

_____

_____

_____

Pentose Phosphate Pathway CL: _____

_____

_____

_____

_____

    D. Regulation of Pathways

_____

_____

_____

_____

Regulation of Glycolysis and Gluconeogenesis CL: _____

_____

_____

_____

_____

Glycogen Regulation CL: _____

_____

_____

_____

_____

Metabolic Regulation CL: _____

_____

_____

_____

_____

E. Krebs Cycle

_____
_____
_____
_____

Acetyl CoA Production CL: _____

_____
_____
_____

Regulation CL: _____

_____
_____
_____

F. Metabolism of Fat and Protein

_____
_____
_____

a) Fats

_____
_____
_____
_____

Digestion CL: _____

_____
_____
_____
_____

Transport CL: _____

_____
_____
_____
_____

b) Fatty Acids CL: _____

_____
_____
_____
_____

Oxidation CL: ____

_____

_____

_____

_____

Saturated Fats CL: ____

_____

_____

_____

_____

Unsaturated Fats CL: ____

_____

_____

_____

_____

Ketone Bodies CL: ____

_____

_____

_____

_____

G. Oxidative Phosphorylation

_____

_____

_____

_____

a) Electron Transport Chain CL: ____

_____

_____

_____

_____

Substrates CL: ____

_____

_____

_____

_____

Products CL: ____

_____

_____

_____

_____

Function CL: _____

_____
_____
_____
_____

Flavoproteins CL: _____

_____
_____
_____

Cytochromes CL: _____

_____
_____
_____
_____

ATP Synthase CL: _____

_____
_____
_____
_____

Chemiosmosis CL: _____

_____
_____
_____
_____

    b)   Mitochondria CL: _____

_____
_____
_____
_____

Apoptosis CL: _____

_____
_____
_____
_____

Oxidative Stress CL: _____

_____
_____
_____
_____

H. Hormonal Regulation

_____

_____

_____

_____

Tissue Specific Metabolism CL: _____

_____

_____

_____

_____

Obesity CL: _____

_____

_____

_____

_____

4. Cell Biology

_____

_____

_____

_____

A. Plasma Membrane

_____

_____

_____

_____

Composition CL: _____

_____

_____

_____

_____

Receptors CL: _____

_____

_____

_____

_____

a) Solute transport

_____

_____

_____

_____

Osmosis CL: _____

_____
_____
_____
_____

Na/K Pump CL: _____

_____
_____
_____
_____

Solute Channels CL: _____

_____
_____
_____
_____

Membrane Potential CL: _____

_____
_____
_____
_____

Exocytosis CL: _____

_____
_____
_____
_____

Endocytosis CL: _____

_____
_____
_____
_____

5. Nervous and Endocrine Systems

_____
_____
_____
_____

A. Nerve Cell

_____
_____
_____
_____

Resting Potential CL: ____

_____

_____

_____

_____

Action Potential CL: ____

_____

_____

_____

_____

    B. Endocrine System

_____

_____

_____

_____

Transport of Hormones and Second Messengers CL: ____

_____

_____

_____

_____

6. Physiology

_____

_____

_____

    A. Respiratory System:

_____

_____

_____

_____

pH control CL: ____

_____

_____

_____

_____

Breathing regulation CL: ____

_____

_____

_____

_____

B. Circulatory System

_____
_____
_____
_____

Gas Transport CL: _____

_____
_____
_____
_____

Oxygen CL: _____

_____
_____
_____
_____

Carbon Dioxide CL: _____

_____
_____
_____
_____

Hemoglobin CL: _____

_____
_____
_____
_____

Hematocrit CL: _____

_____
_____
_____
_____

C. Excretory System

_____
_____
_____
_____

Homeostasis CL: _____

_____
_____
_____
_____

Filtration CL: _____

_____

_____

_____

_____

Counter-current multiplier CL: _____

_____

_____

_____

_____

Secretion CL: _____

_____

_____

_____

_____

Reabsorption CL: _____

_____

_____

_____

_____

Concentration CL: _____

_____

_____

_____

_____

    D. Reproductive System

_____

_____

_____

_____

Menstrual Cycle CL: _____

_____

_____

_____

_____

    E. Muscle System

_____

_____

_____

_____

T-tubule CL: _____

_____
_____
_____
_____

Sarcoplasmic Reticulum CL: _____

_____
_____
_____
_____

Contractile Velocity CL: _____

_____
_____
_____
_____

Cardiac Muscle Regulation CL: _____

_____
_____
_____
_____

Oxygen Debt CL: _____

_____
_____
_____
_____

   a)   Control

_____
_____
_____

Motor Neurons CL: _____

_____
_____
_____

Neuromuscular Junction CL: _____

_____
_____
_____

Motor End Plates CL: _____

_____

_____

_____

_____

Sympathetic CL: _____

_____

_____

_____

_____

Parasympathetic CL: _____

_____

_____

_____

_____

Voluntary CL: _____

_____

_____

_____

_____

Involuntary CL: _____

_____

_____

_____

_____

Sarcomeres CL: _____

_____

_____

_____

_____

Troponin CL: _____

_____

_____

_____

_____

Tropomyosin CL: _____

_____

_____

_____

_____

F. Skeletal System

_____
_____
_____
_____

Function CL: _____

_____
_____
_____
_____

Bone Types CL: _____

_____
_____
_____
_____

Joint Types CL: _____

_____
_____
_____
_____

Composition of Bone Matrix and Cells CL: _____

_____
_____
_____
_____

Cartilage CL: _____

_____
_____
_____
_____

Ligaments CL: _____

_____
_____
_____
_____

Tendons CL: _____

_____
_____
_____
_____

Endocrine Regulation CL: _____

_____

_____

_____

    G. Skin System

_____

_____

_____

        a) Structure

_____

_____

_____

Layers CL: _____

_____

_____

_____

Cell Types CL: _____

_____

_____

_____

Impermeability to Water CL: _____

_____

_____

_____

        b) Function

_____

_____

_____

Homeostasis CL: _____

_____

_____

_____

Osmoregulation CL: _____

_____
_____
_____
_____

Thermoregulation CL: _____

_____
_____
_____
_____

Physical Protection CL: _____

_____
_____
_____
_____

Hormonal Control CL: _____

_____
_____
_____
_____

Organic Chemistry

_____
_____
_____
_____

1. Proteins

_____
_____
_____
_____

    A. Amino Acids

_____
_____
_____
_____

Stereo Configuration CL: _____

_____
_____
_____
_____

Dipolar ions CL: _____

_____
_____
_____
_____

Acidic side chains CL: _____

_____
_____
_____
_____

Basic side chains CL: _____

_____
_____
_____
_____

Hydrophobic side chains CL: _____

_____
_____
_____
_____

Hydrophilic side chains CL: _____

_____
_____
_____
_____

B. Structure

_____
_____
_____
_____

Protein Stability CL: _____

_____
_____
_____
_____

Folding CL: _____

_____
_____
_____
_____

Denaturing CL: _____

_____
_____
_____
_____

Hydrophobic interactions CL: _____

_____
_____
_____
_____

Separation Techniques CL: _____

_____
_____
_____
_____

Isoelectric Point CL: _____

_____
_____
_____
_____

Electrophoresis CL: _____

_____
_____
_____
_____

2.   Metabolism

_____
_____
_____
_____

A.   Carbohydrates

_____
_____
_____
_____

Classification CL: _____

_____
_____
_____
_____

Configuration CL: _____

_____

_____

_____

_____

Isomerism CL: _____

_____

_____

_____

_____

Hydrolysis of Glycosides CL: _____

_____

_____

_____

_____

Glycoside links CL: _____

_____

_____

_____

_____

Mutarotation CL: _____

_____

_____

_____

_____

3.   **Cell Biology**

_____

_____

_____

_____

A. Plasma Membrane

_____

_____

_____

_____

Phospholipids CL: _____

_____

_____

_____

_____

Permeability CL: _____

_____
_____
_____
_____

Steroids CL: _____

_____
_____
_____
_____

Proteins CL: _____

_____
_____
_____
_____

4.   Nervous and Endocrine Systems

_____
_____
_____
_____

A. Lipid Structure CL: _____

_____
_____
_____
_____

Steroids CL: _____

_____
_____
_____
_____

Terpenes CL: _____

_____
_____
_____
_____

Terpenoids CL: _____

_____
_____
_____
_____

Free Online MCAT Diagnostic

Want to see how you would do on the MCAT and understand where you need to focus your prep?

TAKE OUR FREE MCAT DIAGNOSTIC EXAM.

Timed simulations of all 4 sections of the MCAT, including behavioral sciences

Comprehensive reporting on your performance

This exam is provided free of charge to students who purchased our book.

To access your free exam, visit:
http://nextsteptestprep.com/mcat-2015-diagnostic-practice-test/